THE OFFICIAL MANCHESTER UNITED PLAYERS' A-Z

THE OFFICIAL MANCHESTER UNITED PLAYERS' A–Z

Iain McCartney

SIMON & SCHUSTER

London · New York · Sydney · Toronto · New Delhi

A CBS COMPANY

First published in Great Britain by Simon & Schuster UK Ltd, 2013
A CBS COMPANY

1 3 5 7 9 10 8 6 4 2

Simon & Schuster UK Ltd
1st Floor
222 Gray's Inn Road
London WC1X 8HB

www.simonandschuster.co.uk

Simon & Schuster Australia,
Sydney

Simon & Schuster India,
New Delhi

A CIP catalogue record for this book is available
from the British Library

ISBN: 978-1-47112-846-2

Typeset in the UK by M Rules
Printed in the UK by CPI Group (UK) Ltd, Croydon, CR0 4YY

HOW TO USE THIS BOOK

For each player, the following information is provided:

Full name – all known names are given, with the name by which the player is most familiarly known, if different, given in quote marks.

Country – this refers to the country for which the player was either eligible or the national team for which he played. In the case of a player such as Nemanja Vidić, who was born in Yugoslavia but has played for Serbia, it is the latter country that is given. Ireland/Northern Ireland/Republic of Ireland are all used according to the situation that applied at the time of the player's career.

Dates of birth and death – are provided where known.

Debut – this refers to a player's first appearance in an official Newton Heath or Manchester United fixture.

Position – obviously some players, such as John O'Shea, have turned out in many roles during their United career. Where possible, positions as they were known at the time are given.

Appearances/goals scored – these relate only to official fixtures, i.e. games played in the FA Cup, Football/Premier League, League Cup, Charity/Community Shield, Test Matches, European Cup/Champions League, UEFA Cup/Europa League, European Cup-Winners' Cup, plus the Super Cup, Inter-Continental Cup, Club World Cup and Club World Championship.

Seasons – these cover only the seasons in which a player made at least one first-team appearance for United.

Clubs – these include all teams a player played for once they turned professional, and so exclude junior clubs (even if some of them are mentioned in the biographical text). If a player was loaned to another club, and immediately after that loan spell signed for them on a permanent basis, the prior loan spell is not mentioned.

Biographies – are provided for all those players who made ten or more appearances for the club. In a few instances, where a player either went on to have a notable career elsewhere, or where there was another significant reason for including more information, those players who made fewer than ten appearances for United also given a brief biography.

All statistics provided are up to, and including, the 2013/14 FA Charity Shield, while players in/out are up to the close of the 2013 summer transfer deadline.

A

ALPHONSO 'ALF' AINSWORTH

Country: England
Born: 31 Jul 1913 **Died:** 25 Apr 1975
Debut: 3 Mar 1934 v Bury
Position: Inside-forward
Appearances: 2 **Goals scored:** 0
Seasons: 1933/34
Clubs: Manchester United, New Brighton, Congleton

JOHN AITKEN

Country: Scotland
Born: 1870 **Died:** Unknown
Debut: 7 Sep 1895 v Crewe Alexandra
Position: Inside-forward
Appearances: 2 **Goals scored:** 1
Seasons: 1895/96
Clubs: 5th KRV, Newton Heath

GEORGE ALBINSON

Country: England
Born: 14 Feb 1897 **Died:** Apr 1975
Debut: 12 Jan 1921 v Liverpool
Position: Defender
Appearances: 1 **Goals scored:** 0
Seasons: 1920/21
Clubs: Manchester United, Manchester City, Crewe Alexandra

ARTHUR RICHARD ALBISTON

Country: Scotland
Born: 14 Jul 1957
Debut: 9 Oct 1974 v Manchester City
Position: Full-back
Appearances: 467 (18) **Goals scored:** 7
Seasons: 1974/75 – 1987/88
Clubs: Manchester United, West Bromwich Albion, Dundee, Chesterfield, Chester City, Molde (loan), Ayr United

Arthur Albiston represented Edinburgh and Scotland Schools before signing for United in July 1972. Two years later, aged 17, having already experienced a first-team outing in Tony Dunne's testimonial match in October 1973, he was making the first of his 485 appearances, against Manchester City in a League Cup tie, kicking off a career that spanned 14 years. His league debut followed six days later against Portsmouth, but it wasn't until Stewart Houston broke his leg that the young Scot was thrust into the limelight, discarding his inexperience to turn in a commendable display in the 1977 FA Cup final against Liverpool, a game United won 2-1.

He was seldom to put a foot wrong during a career that spanned the reign of four managers, and each one knew that they could depend on the dark, curly-headed full-back, who always displayed a very high level of consistency in defence, while ably supporting his attackers with his forward runs. On 13 February 1988, however, he was to pull on the red No. 3 jersey for the last time, against Chelsea at Stamford Bridge for what was his 379th league match (including 15 as substitute). He also became the first United player to win three FA Cup winners' medals, winning the cup in 1977, 1983 and 1985. In August 1988, he joined West Bromwich Albion on a free transfer.

JOHN THOMAS 'JACK' ALLAN

Country: England
Born: 16 Jan 1883 **Died:** Unknown
Debut: 3 Sep 1904 v Port Vale
Position: Forward
Appearances: 36 **Goals scored:** 22
Seasons: 1904/05 – 1906/07
Clubs: Bishop Auckland, Manchester United, Bishop Auckland

Sixteen goals in 27 outings in 1904/05 was a favourable return for the South Shields-born player, and his five goals in three games the following season helped to ensure a place in the First Division for 1906/07. But he was to find himself omitted from the starting line-up as 1906/07 got underway, leaving him so disappointed that he decided to hang up his boots.

ARTHUR REGINALD 'REG' ALLEN

Country: England
Born: 3 May 1919 **Died:** Apr 1976
Debut: 19 Aug 1950 v Fulham
Position: Goalkeeper
Appearances: 80 **Goals scored:** 0
Seasons: 1950/51 – 1952/53
Clubs: Queens Park Rangers, Manchester United, Altrincham

Reg Allen was signed from Queens Park Rangers in the summer of 1950 for a fee of £11,000, a record for a goalkeeper at that time, as Matt Busby sought a replacement for Jack Crompton. A reliable custodian and all-round sportsman, he could only have dreamed about such a move during his time as a commando during the Second World War, as he was captured in North Africa while on a dangerous mission and was confined to a prisoner-of-war camp for three years.

On his release, he soon recovered from his ordeal and, after joining United, having played alongside Matt Busby while in the army, the 31-year-old found himself on the verge of the England side, but had to be content with Football League and FA XI honours. He was, however, to play a major part in United's 1951/52 Championship-winning side, but the following season he suffered a hand injury which kept him out of the side. Shortly after regaining his place, an illness which required prolonged treatment sidelined him for the remainder of the campaign and indeed was to curtail his career altogether, as the directors, after much consideration, decided to terminate his contract. He was later to team up with former teammate Charlie Mitten at Altrincham.

ARTHUR ALLMAN

Country: England
Born: 24 Dec 1890 **Died:** 22 Dec 1956
Debut: 13 Feb 1915 v Sheffield Wednesday
Position: Full-back
Appearances: 12 **Goals scored:** 0
Seasons: 1914/15
Clubs: Shrewsbury Town, Wolverhampton Wanderers, Swansea Town, Manchester United, Millwall Athletic

A full-back who cost United £150 when signed from Swansea in May 1914, but he was to find his career in Manchester disrupted due to the First World War and left for Millwall at the end of the hostilities.

ALFRED AMBLER

Country: England
Born: 1 Jul 1879 **Died:** Unknown
Debut: 2 Sep 1899 v Gainsborough Trinity
Position: Defender
Appearances: 10 **Goals scored:** 1
Seasons: 1899/1900 – 1900/01
Clubs: Hyde United, Newton Heath, Colne, Stockport County, Exeter City, Colne

Manchester-born Ambler failed to make much of an impression with the Heathens, following his arrival in August 1899, managing only ten appearances before dropping into non-league football.

BENJAMIN PAUL AMOS

Country: England
Born: 10 Apr 1990
Debut: 23 Sep 2008 v Middlesbrough
Position: Goalkeeper
Appearances: 7 **Goals scored:** 0
Seasons: 2008/09 – present
Clubs: Manchester United, Peterborough United (loan), Molde (loan), Oldham Athletic (loan), Hull City (loan)

The Macclesfield-born goalkeeper has had various loan periods, but has also managed to win England Under-21 honours.

GEORGE WALTER ANDERSON

Country: England
Born: Jan 1893 **Died:** 1959
Debut: 9 Sep 1911 v Everton
Position: Forward
Appearances: 86 **Goals scored:** 39
Seasons: 1911/12 – 1914/15
Clubs: Salford United, Bury, Manchester United

Thirty-nine goals in 86 appearances is an impressive record, but unfortunately it has been overshadowed, as George Anderson's name is more associated with the accusation of fixing United's game against Burnley in December 1917. Signed from Bury in September 1911 for a fee of £50, he was to make only one appearance prior to November 1912, but in 1913/14 he was the club's leading scorer.

Although making a handful of wartime appearances for United during 1915/16, he made his way to Belfast in February 1916 to play for Belfast United without permission, and it was only the involvement of the Football League that made him return to Old Trafford where he resumed his United career. In March 1918, despite maintaining his innocence, George Anderson was found guilty of 'conspiring with certain persons unknown to defraud other persons unknown who had made bets on the results of various matches', with United's fixture against Burnley on 29 December 1917 one of those games.

He was subsequently banned from Old Trafford, with reports in the *News of the World* of 24 March 1918 adding fuel to the fire and, following a court appearance, he was jailed for eight months.

JOHN ANDERSON

Country: England
Born: 11 Oct 1921 **Died:** 8 Aug 2006
Debut: 20 Dec 1947 v Middlesbrough
Position: Defender
Appearances: 40 **Goals scored:** 2

Seasons: 1947/48 – 1948/49
Clubs: Plymouth Argyle, Manchester United, Nottingham Forest, Peterborough United

A former captain of Salford Boys and the Lancashire Schools side, Johnny Anderson honed his footballing skills with the Adelphi Lads' Club and Brindle Heath before joining United as an amateur as a 16-year-old, turning professional a year later in November 1938. Winning junior honours as a left-back, his footballing career, like that of many others, was put on hold due to the Second World War. But, upon his demob from the navy, he returned to Old Trafford and was soon converted into a half-back, winning a Central League medal in his first post-war season.

On 20 December 1947, he was on his way to Newcastle with the reserve team, when he received a telegram telling him to return to Manchester as he was required for first-team duty against Middlesbrough. His impressive display saw him keep his place in the side for the remainder of the season, and he also scored the last goal in the 4-2 victory over Blackpool in the FA Cup final at Wembley, one of only two he was to score for the club.

During season 1948/49, he was in and out of the first team, and as he struggled to maintain a regular place, he decided to leave United in October 1949, joining Nottingham Forest for a fee of £9,000. In 1952, he joined Peterborough United, becoming their trainer-coach upon retiring in 1954.

LUIS DE ABREU OLIVEIRA ANDERSON

Country: Brazil
Born: 13 Apr 1988
Debut: 1 Sep 2007 v Sunderland
Position: Midfield
Appearances: 124 (48) **Goals scored:** 9
Seasons: 2007/08 – present
Clubs: Gremio, FC Porto, Manchester United

Following his £13 million transfer from Porto in the summer of 2007, much was expected from the talented Brazilian, who had sprung to prominence in his homeland as a 17-year-old, scoring a notable goal to clinch the Second Division title for his Gremio side. Prior to his move to Old Trafford, reports suggested that Anderson might be the 'new Ronaldinho', which was never really his style as a player and also put undue pressure on the youngster. However, the United support were given glimpses of what the future might hold in crunch games against the likes of Arsenal and Liverpool when he came out on top of midfield battles with Cesc Fabregas and Steven Gerrard.

After a new four-and-a-half-year deal in October 2010, injuries blighted his career in Manchester, preventing him from getting the vital match time so that he can establish himself as a regular first-team player, with knee and hamstring problems forcing him to miss a large portion of the 2011/12 season. For a long time, he also struggled to score, taking 76 games to break his United duck. In 2012/13, he once again showed that there was plenty of Brazilian flare beneath that red No. 8 shirt, as he increasingly became a fans' favourite. Despite more injury problems, he picked up a third Premier League winners' medal at the end of the campaign.

TREVOR ANDERSON

Country: Northern Ireland
Born: 3 Mar 1951
Debut: 31 Mar 1973 v Southampton
Position: Forward
Appearances: 13 (6) **Goals scored:** 2
Seasons: 1972/73 – 1973/74
Clubs: Portadown, Manchester United, Swindon Town, Peterborough United, Linfield

Trevor Anderson was signed for £20,000 by Frank O'Farrell, with hopes that the Belfast-born player would be a 'new George Best'. He never quite made it, and was sold for £25,000 in November 1974.

VIVIAN ALEXANDER 'VIV' ANDERSON

Country: England
Born: 29 Aug 1956
Debut: 15 Aug 1987 v Southampton
Position: Full-back
Appearances: 64 (5) **Goals scored:** 4

Seasons: 1987/88 – 1990/91
Clubs: Nottingham Forest, Arsenal, Manchester United, Sheffield Wednesday, Barnsley

As a teenager, Viv Anderson spent some of his school holidays with United, but for one reason or another, the gangling youngster from Nottingham was never offered a contract. Back on home soil, he soon found himself involved with Forest's youth team, doing enough to secure an apprenticeship in November 1972. His first-team debut followed soon afterwards and he went on to become an integral part of a successful Forest side, winning League Championship, European Cup and League Cup winners' medals, as well as becoming the first black player to be capped by England in 1978.

As his career at the City Ground began to stutter a little, Arsenal stepped in and signed him for £250,000 in July 1984, but 150 appearances and another League Cup winners' medal later, he was on the move again, a telephone call from his England captain Bryan Robson prompting a move to United, where he became Alex Ferguson's first signing in 1987. His £250,000 fee was later decided by a tribunal, much to the Gunners' annoyance.

Sadly, there was to be a lack of silverware during his time at Old Trafford, in comparison with that of his two previous clubs, and niggling injuries began to hamper his first-team involvement with United. With his position coming under constant threat and first-team football no longer guaranteed, he was given a free transfer and in January 1991 he moved to Sheffield Wednesday, helping them to promotion and two cup finals. Later, he became player-manager at Barnsley in June 1993, before joining Bryan Robson as assistant manager at Middlesbrough in May 1994 for a seven-year spell.

WILLIAM JOHN 'WILLIE' ANDERSON

Country: England
Born: 24 Jan 1947
Debut: 28 Dec 1963 v Burnley
Position: Forward
Appearances: 10 (2) **Goals scored:** 0
Seasons: 1963/64 – 1966/67
Clubs: Manchester United, Aston Villa, Cardiff City, Portland Timbers

Liverpool-born Willie Anderson caught United's attention while playing with Prescott and Lancashire Schools and signed for the club on leaving school. Making steady progress through the junior ranks, winning an FA Youth Cup medal in 1964, he made his league debut as a 16-year-old against Burnley at Old Trafford in December 1963, with his cup debut coming the following week at Southampton.

At the start of season 1965/66, which was to turn out as his best for the club, he made history by becoming the first-ever substitute under Football League and FA ruling, coming on in place of former youth-team colleague George Best against Liverpool. He had, however, the rather daunting task of competing against Best and another former youth-team player, John Aston, for a first-team place. So, due to the lack of opportunities, when the possibility of joining Aston Villa arose in January 1967, he decided to move to the Midlands with a cheque of £20,000 changing hands. Despite moving to a Third Division club, he was to enjoy considerable success, helping them to a League Cup final and promotion to Division Two.

MICHAEL ANTHONY APPLETON

Country: England
Born: 4 Dec 1975
Debut: 23 Oct 1996 v Swindon Town
Position: Midfield
Appearances: 1 (1) **Goals scored:** 0
Seasons: 1996/97
Clubs: Manchester United, Lincoln City (loan), Grimsby Town (loan), Preston North End, West Bromwich Albion

THOMAS ARTHUR 'TOMMY' ARKESDEN

Country: England
Born: Jul 1878 **Died:** 25 Jun 1921
Debut: 14 Feb 1903 v Blackpool
Position: Forward
Appearances: 79 **Goals scored:** 33
Seasons: 1902/03 – 1905/06
Clubs: Burton Wanderers, Derby County, Burton United, Manchester United, Gainsborough Trinity

A member of Derby County's losing FA Cup final side of 1899, Tommy Arkesden joined Manchester United in February 1903 from Burton United for a fee of £150. Making his debut at centre-forward at Blackpool, he managed two goals from his nine league appearances in that initial season, but in the two seasons that followed, playing mainly at inside-left, he played a considerable part in United's push for promotion from Division Two.

Having finished third in his first two seasons, promotion was finally achieved in 1905/06, but unfortunately for Arkesden, he was to play in only seven of the 38 fixtures, all but one in the opening two months of the campaign. In the summer of 1907, he left United, moving to Gainsborough Trinity for what was his final season in league football.

JOSEPH EMMANUEL ASTLEY

Country: England
Born: Apr 1889 **Died:** Oct 1967
Debut: 17 Mar 1926
Position: Defender
Appearances: 2 **Goals scored:** 0
Seasons: 1925/26 – 1926/27
Clubs: Cradley Heath, Manchester United, Notts County

JOHN ASTON JNR

Country: England
Born: 28 Jun 1947
Debut: 12 Apr 1965 v Leicester City
Position: Forward
Appearances: 166 (21) **Goals scored:** 27
Seasons: 1964/65 – 1971/72
Clubs: Manchester United, Luton Town, Mansfield Town, Blackburn Rovers

Although he played more than 180 games for United over a seven-year period, John Aston will always be best remembered for his performance in the 1968 European Cup final at Wembley, when he upstaged his more illustrious companions, tantalising the Benfica defence throughout the 120 minutes.

He followed in his father's footsteps to Old Trafford, joining United as a 15-year-old, after representing Manchester and Lancashire Schoolboys. Two years later, he made a big impression in the youth team, playing at wing-half and also outside-left. It was in the latter position that he was to develop and, after making steady progress in the Central League side, he made his league debut against Leicester City at Old Trafford in April 1965, making the outside-left berth his own during the 1966/67 campaign when he helped United to the First Division crown. A European Cup winners' medal followed 12 months later, and if you have to be remembered largely for your performance in the final of this prestige competition, few would care.

At Maine Road on 17 August 1968, in what was only the third game of the season, he suffered a broken leg and it was an injury from which he never recaptured his best form in the red shirt of United, although he did regain a place in the first XI starting line-up towards the end of the season, but it was in the rather unfamiliar No. 9 shirt. England Under-23 international honours also came his way, but at the end of season 1971/72, he was to find himself on the transfer list and moved to Luton Town for a fee of £30,000.

JOHN ASTON SNR

Country: England
Born: 3 Sep 1921 **Died:** 31 Jul 2003
Debut: 18 Sep 1946 v Chelsea
Position: Defender
Appearances: 284 **Goals scored:** 30
Seasons: 1946/47 – 1953/54
Clubs: Manchester United

It was in the summer of 1938 when John Aston joined United as a junior, becoming one of the inaugural members of the newly formed MUJACs (the Manchester United Junior Athletic Club). With the domestic football programme in disarray due to the outbreak of the Second World War, it was in the North Regional League that the Clayton-born youngster made his United debut, appearing at outside-left against Rochdale at Spotland on the opening day of 1940/41, marking the occasion with a goal in United's 3-1 win.

Due to military duty, he didn't feature for United for five years, but once league football returned to normality in season 1946/47, he did not become a regular in Matt Busby's First Division side until late December, and then it was at left-back and not in the forward line as before.

In season 1947/48, he was the only player with a 100 per cent appearance record, as United finished runners-up in the league, while also lifting the FA Cup in a pulsating 4-2 final victory against Blackpool at Wembley in a game still considered as one of the best beneath the old twin towers. On 26 September 1948 he won the first of his 17 England caps against Denmark in Copenhagen, but it was an injury to team-mate Jack Rowley in December 1950 which inadvertently brought an end to John Aston's international career, as Matt Busby switched him from full-back to centre-forward and he adapted so well, scoring twice in that initial outing, that he remained as leader of the attack for the remainder of the season, scoring 14 goals in 22 games.

Winning a League Championship medal in 1951/52, he missed only two games the following season before illness threatened his career and, despite scoring thrice in the final four games of that campaign, he was forced to retire having contracted tuberculosis.

He was awarded a testimonial in April 1956, when United played an All-Star XI, and he returned to the club in 1958 following the Munich Air Disaster, taking on a coaching role and later becoming chief scout. His association with the club finally came to an end in 1972, following the sacking of Frank O'Farrell.

B

GARY RICHARD BAILEY

Country: England
Born: 9 Aug 1958
Debut: 18 Nov 1978 v Ipswich Town
Position: Goalkeeper
Appearances: 375 **Goals scored:** 0
Seasons: 1978/79 – 1986/87
Clubs: Manchester United, Kaizer Chiefs

Although born in Ipswich, where his father Roy was goalkeeper with the local club, winning First, Second and Third Division Championship medals, Gary Bailey spent much of his formative years in South Africa after the family emigrated there in 1964.

Learning the necessary goalkeeping skills from his father, he began his playing career with Witts University, where he came to the attention of former United player Eddie Lewis, who secured the tall, blond-headed youngster a trial at Old Trafford, Bailey paying his own airfare such was his determination to succeed as a professional footballer.

His father's coaching stood him in good stead and, following a promising trial period, he was offered a professional contract in January 1978, learning his trade in the Central League before lady luck played her part. With the then United manager Dave Sexton looking for a new goalkeeper to replace current No. 1 Paddy Roche, he cast his eyes on Coventry City's Scottish international Jim Blyth, but with a contract on the table ready to be signed, Blyth's medical showed that he had a suspect back and the proposed £440,000 deal, which would have made him the world's most expensive 'keeper, fell through.

With Roche injured, it was therefore down to Bailey to fill the gap and, ironically, it was against his father's old team Ipswich Town that he played the first of his 375 games for United, keeping a clean sheet in the 2-0 win. There was no looking back, as his was the first name pencilled into the United team sheet for the majority of the next seven seasons. Only a few games were missed through injury up until February 1986, while he also picked up FA Cup winners' medals in

1983 and 1985, and a runners-up medal in 1979, along with a League Cup runners-up medal in 1983.

Such were his performances, he was elevated to the England Under-21 side a mere four months after his league debut, going on to win a total of 14 caps at this level, stepping up to the full international side against the Republic of Ireland in 1985. But it was while on international duty that his career was dealt a severe blow, injuring his knee during an England training session in 1987, from which he failed to fully recover, forcing him to retire at the age of only 29 with his best years still seemingly ahead of him. He returned to South Africa and joined Kaizer Chiefs for a couple of years before retiring from the game in December 1989, turning his attention to coaching and media work.

DAIVD BAIN

Country: Scotland
Born: 5 Aug 1900 **Died:** Unknown
Debut: 14 Oct 1922 v Port Vale
Position: Forward
Appearances: 23 **Goals scored:** 9
Seasons: 1922/23 – 1923/24
Clubs: Rutherglen Glencairn, Manchester United, Everton, Bristol City, Halifax Town, Rochdale

Signed from Rutherglen Glencairn on professional forms in May 1922, David Bain was no stranger to his new Old Trafford surroundings, having previously had trials with the club on a couple of occasions, but returning home unsigned and disappointed. United manager John Chapman, however, saw something that others had missed and felt that the Scottish junior international would make a good addition to the squad and was hastily recruited.

His first-team opportunities, however, were to be limited during his initial season; following his league debut at inside-right, he was not to reappear in the first team until 11 April the following year. Unable to claim a regular place, he became desperate to be involved at this level of football and eagerly accepted a move to Everton, who paid a fee of £1,000 for his signature, with the player receiving a signing-on fee of £10 and wages of £6 per week plus an extra £1 if in the first team.

JAMES BAIN

Country: Scotland
Born: 1878 **Died:** Unknown
Debut: 16 Sep 1899 v Loughborough Town
Position: Forward
Appearances: 2 **Goals scored:** 0
Seasons: 1899/1900
Clubs: Dundee, Newton Heath

JAMES 'JIMMY' BAIN

Country: Scotland
Born: 6 Feb 1902 **Died:** 22 Dec 1969
Debut: 7 Feb 1925 v Leyton Orient
Position: Defender
Appearances: 4 **Goals scored:** 0
Seasons: 1924/1925 – 1927/28
Clubs: Rutherglen Glencairn, Glasgow Strathclyde, Manchester United, Manchester Central, Brentford

WILLIAM 'BILL' BAINBRIDGE

Country: England
Born: 9 Mar 1922
Debut: 9 Jan 1946 v Accrington Stanley
Position: Forward
Appearances: 1 **Goals scored:** 0
Seasons: 1945/46
Clubs: Ashington, Manchester United, Bury, Tranmere Rovers

HENRY C. 'HARRY' BAIRD

Country: Northern Ireland
Born: 17 Aug 1913 **Died:** 22 May 1973
Debut: 23 Jan 1937 v Sheffield Wednesday
Position: Forward
Appearances: 53 **Goals scored:** 18
Seasons: 1936/37 – 1937/38
Clubs: Bangor, Dunmurry, Linfield, Manchester United, Huddersfield Town, Ipswich Town

Born in Belfast, Harry Baird's early playing days were spent with Bangor and Dunmurry, before joining Linfield, where he was to make something of a name for himself. His ability was noted by many and a move by Manchester United officials to secure his signature was quickly turned down, but, determined to sign the Irishman, the club returned with an improved offer of £3,500 in January 1937 which was accepted.

Baird made his United debut at inside-left in the 1-0 defeat at Sheffield Wednesday soon after signing and in his 14 outings in that first season he scored three goals while flitting between the two inside-forward positions. Those goals could do little to keep United in the top flight of the English league. The following season, 1937/38, saw Baird, having now settled in Manchester, finish second top goalscorer with 13 goals from 35 outings, as United reclaimed their place in the First Division as runners-up. It came as something of a shock and disappointment to many that Harry Baird did not feature in the opening fixtures of 1938/39 and they were even more taken aback when he was subsequently transferred to Huddersfield Town, with the new season only a matter of weeks old.

THOMAS 'TOMMY' BALDWIN

Country: England
Born: 10 Jun 1945
Debut: 18 Jan 1975 v Sunderland
Position: Midfield
Appearances: 2 **Goals scored:** 0
Seasons: 1974/75
Clubs: Arsenal, Chelsea, Millwall, Manchester United, Gravesend & Northfleet, Seattle Sounders, Gravesend & Northfleet, Brentford

JOHN THOMAS 'JACK' BALL

Country: England
Born: 13 Sep 1907 **Died:** 6 Feb 1976
Debut: 11 Sep 1929 v Leicester City
Position: Forward
Appearances: 50 **Goals scored:** 18
Seasons: 1929/30 & 1933/34–1934/35
Clubs: Southport, Darwen, Chorley, Manchester United, Sheffield Wednesday, Manchester United, Huddersfield Town, Luton Town

Jack Ball is one of a select handful of players who enjoyed two separate spells with Manchester United. The Southport-born player joining the Old Trafford payroll from Chorley on 8 May 1928 and again in December 1933 as part of an exchange deal that took Neil Dewar to Sheffield Wednesday, the club he had joined from United in July 1930. Having turned professional in August 1925, he spent two years at Haig Avenue plying his trade for Southport in the Football League North before the club's need to raise some cash saw him move to Darwen in September 1927, and then Chorley in January 1928. In May of that same year, United took him from the Lancashire Combination to the First Division, but two years later, he was on the move again, joining Sheffield Wednesday for a fee of £1,300.

At Hillsborough, he became a firm favourite with the Wednesday supporters, scoring 17 goals in his first 14 outings, surpassing this in both of the following campaigns with 23 and 35, including 11 penalties in the former, a league record that was to stand for some 40 years, but it was not enough to guarantee him a long-term future with the Yorkshire club. A change of manager saw his new boss show an interest in United's Neil Dewar and a deal was arranged, with the man known as 'last minute Ball', due to his ability to snatch late strikes, returning to Old Trafford in December 1933.

If United had hoped that he would remain among the goals, then they were somewhat disappointed, as he was to manage only five in 18 outings during the remainder of 1933/34 as the Reds fought to avoid relegation to the third tier. But you certainly could not keep him out of the history books, as when he joined Huddersfield Town in September 1934 and then Luton Town a month later, he had the distinction of playing in the First, Second and Third Divisions within a six-week period.

JOHN 'JOHNNY' BALL

Country: England
Born: 13 Mar 1925
Debut: 10 Apr 1948 v Everton
Position: Defender
Appearances: 23 **Goals scored:** 0
Seasons: 1947/48 – 1949/50
Clubs: Wigan Athletic, Manchester United, Bolton Wanderers

Having played a few times for Gravesend during the Second World War years, it was as a Lancashire Combination player with Wigan Athletic that Manchester United signed Johnny Ball for a few hundred pounds in March 1948. After only a handful of Central League outings, Ball made his debut in the second fixture of season 1948/49 as a right-back replacement for Johnny Aston, a former colleague in Royal Navy representative fixtures, but it was one of only two outings to be made in the first 30 fixtures of that season.

As Johnny Carey's understudy, games were indeed going to be few and far between, and it was only through the versatile Carey being switched to a forward role later in the season and another injury to Aston, that he managed a few more outings at first-team level. The following campaign, it was once again in the latter stages of the season that he managed a reasonable run in the side and when United showed an interest in Bolton's Harry McShane, the consistent reserve-team player was used as a make-weight to secure the deal.

WILLIAM HENRY 'BILLY' BALL

Country: England
Born: Jun 1876 **Died:** Feb 1929
Debut: 8 Nov 1902 v Lincoln City
Position: Defender
Appearances: 4 **Goals scored:** 0
Seasons: 1902/03
Clubs: Blackburn Rovers, Everton, Notts County, Blackburn Rovers, Manchester United

THOMAS 'TOMMY' BAMFORD

Country: Wales
Born: 2 Sep 1905 **Died:** 12 Dec 1967
Debut: 20 Oct 1934 v Newcastle United
Position: Forward
Appearances: 109 **Goals scored:** 57
Seasons: 1934/35 – 1937/38
Clubs: Wrexham, Manchester United, Swansea Town

Welshman Tommy Bamford was a prolific goalscorer with his first league club, Wrexham, scoring 175 in 204 appearances (still a club record, as were his 44 goals in season 1933/34). On 15 October 1934 the Welsh international found himself running out onto the Old Trafford pitch, but as a member of a Wrexham side invited to Manchester to play a fixture arranged in aid of the Cresford Colliery Disaster. Both sides were made up of mainly reserve-team players, but Wrexham included the player whose goalscoring ability was beginning to attract the attention of numerous clubs, and one wonders if United were attempting to get ahead of the pack with the match being an ideal opportunity to have a look at the player at close quarters and also have a chat with the Wrexham directors as to his availability.

Although he failed to score in the match, his performance still impressed and two days later he was back at Old Trafford to join United. Scoring the only goal of the game on his debut against Newcastle United, it was not until the Second Division title-winning season of 1935/36 that he found his feet in Manchester, scoring six times in the first seven matches, going on to finish top scorer with 21 in his 42 outings.

Dropping back into the Second Division at the end of 1936/37, his 14 goals in 23 appearances helped United back into the top flight in 1937/38 but, troubled by injuries and unsure of his place in the side, he returned to his native Wales in June 1938, joining Swansea. He is one of only ten men in United's history to have scored more than 50 goals at better than one every other game.

JOHN 'JACK' BANKS

Country: England
Born: 14 Jun 1871 **Died:** Jan 1947
Debut: 7 Sep 1901 v Gainsborough Trinity
Position: Defender
Appearances: 44 **Goals scored:** 1
Seasons: 1901/02 – 1902/03
Clubs: West Bromwich Albion, Newton Heath, Plymouth Argyle, Leyton, Exeter City

Hailing from the Midlands, John Banks could be found playing with Oldbury Town as a 15-year-old, before joining West Bromwich Albion in 1894. At the Hawthorns, he became something of a utility player and captained the Albion in the 1895 FA Cup final at outside-left, a game they lost 1-0 against local rivals Aston Villa. He moved to

Newton Heath in the summer of 1901, the club's last season under that particular name, making his debut at centre-half on the opening day of season 1901/02, but it was at left-half that he put in his best games for the Heathens and United. His United career, however, was brief and in May 1903 he was transferred to Plymouth Argyle, then in the Southern League.

JAMES 'JIMMY' BANNISTER

Country: England
Born: 20 Sep 1880 **Died:** Unknown
Debut: 1 Jan 1907 v Aston Villa
Position: Forward
Appearances: 61 **Goals scored:** 8
Seasons: 1906/07 – 1909/10
Clubs: Leyland, Chorley, Manchester City, Manchester United, Preston North End, Burslem Port Vale

Jimmy Bannister joined Manchester City in September 1902, making an immediate impact, with 13 goals in his 21 outings during that initial season. With such a promising start to his senior career, the future certainly looked bright, but he was to make a mere 13 league appearances in the light-blue shirt over the next two seasons. His return of six goals from those games showed, however, that his time in the reserves did little to dampen his scoring ability.

Following events during an end-of-season clash with Aston Villa in 1904/05, the Football Association, already paying close attention to City, carried out an investigation into their financial dealings and found that they had been making illegal payments to their players and suspended their manager Tom Maley for life and 17 players, Bannister among them, were suspended until January 1907.

United manager Ernest Mangnall wasted little time in contacting Bannister and four of his banned team-mates, securing their signatures at the end of their suspension. Season 1907/08 saw him secure a place in the first XI, missing only two games, as United strode to their first-ever First Division Championship, but 12 months later, he was again little more than a bit-part player, missing out on the FA Cup success against Bristol City at Crystal Palace. In October 1909 he decided that his career now lay away from Old Trafford and he joined Preston North End.

JOHN 'JACK' BARBER

Country: England
Born: 8 Jan 1901 **Died:** 30 Mar 1961
Debut: 6 Jan 1923 v Hull City
Position: Forward
Appearances: 4 **Goals scored:** 2
Seasons: 1922/23 – 1923/24
Clubs: Clayton, Manchester United, Southport, Halifax, Rochdale, Stockport County

PHILIP ANTHONY 'PHIL' BARDSLEY

Country: Scotland
Born: 28 Jun 1985
Debut: 3 Dec 2003 v West Bromwich Albion
Position: Defender
Appearances: 10 (8) **Goals scored:** 0
Seasons: 2003/04 – 2007/08
Clubs: Manchester United, Royal Antwerp (loan), Burnley (loan), Rangers (loan), Aston Villa (loan), Sheffield United (loan), Sunderland

Having joined United at the age of eight, Phil Bardsley made his debut in the League Cup ten years later. He struggled to gain a regular place in the side and was often loaned out. After making 15 appearances in 2005/06, he was sold to Sunderland in January 2008.

CYRIL BARLOW

Country: England
Born: 22 Jan 1889 **Died:** Unknown
Debut: 7 Feb 1920 v Sunderland
Position: Defender
Appearances: 30 **Goals scored:** 0
Seasons: 1919/20 – 1921/22
Clubs: Northern Nomads, Manchester United, New Cross

A Newton Heath-born full-back, who played his early football for his local church side, he joined United from the esteemed amateur side Northern Nomads in July 1914, signing professional forms with United after the First World War, following active service in France. He made his initial United appearances during the war years, but it was not until after the hostilities, on 7 February 1920, that he was to make his Football League debut against Sunderland at Old Trafford.

The following season, after missing the opening two fixtures, he enjoyed an 11-match run in the side, occupying both full-back positions, but he lost his place to Charlie Moore and went on to make only nine further appearances that season. In October 1922, it was reported that Barlow had left United to join Lancashire Combination side New Cross, but rather surprisingly, the name Barlow appears in United reserve-team line-ups on three occasions after this, with a look through the United programmes of the period showing that he had also scored one goal. It is thought, however, that he was only back at Old Trafford to cover for injuries.

MICHAEL BARNES

Country: England
Born: 24 Jun 1988
Debut: 25 Oct 2006 v Crewe Alexandra
Position: Forward
Appearances: (1) **Goals scored:** 0
Seasons: 2006/07
Clubs: Manchester United, Chesterfield (loan), Shrewsbury Town (loan)

PETER SIMON BARNES

Country: England
Born: 10 Jun 1957
Debut: 31 Aug 1985 v Nottingham Forest
Position: Winger
Appearances: 24 (1) **Goals scored:** 4
Seasons: 1985/86 – 1986/87
Clubs: Manchester City, West Bromwich Albion, Leeds United, Real Betis (loan), Melbourne J.U.S.T., Manchester United (loan), Manchester City, Coventry City, Manchester United, Bolton Wanderers (loan), Port Vale (loan), Hull City, Drogheda United, SC Farense, Bolton Wanderers, Sunderland, Bury, Tampa Bay Rowdies, Northwich Victoria, Wrexham, Radcliffe Borough, Mossley, Cliftonville

To detail the complete career of Peter Barnes, which spanned some 20 years, would fill a considerable space as he is associated with 21 clubs. Many were short-term loan deals, but the son of the former Manchester City half-back notched up considerable mileage as he plied his trade around the world. The former Manchester and District schoolboy player joined his father's former club in July 1972, making his league debut as a 17-year-old and enjoyed seven years at Maine Road before moving to West Bromwich Albion. Following spells around the world, the former PFA Young Player of the Year, who represented England at Youth, 'B', Under-21 and full international level, joined United on loan in May 1984, but failed to make a first-team appearance during his five months in Manchester.

Spending the remainder of season 1984/85 with Coventry City, he returned to United in the summer of 1985 in a £50,000 deal, scoring on his debut against Nottingham Forest as Ron Atkinson's side stormed to the top of the First Division with a run of ten straight wins. His appearances, however, were to be limited and after mid-November, his name was included on the teamsheet on only one other occasion. In January 1987, he rejoined City for £30,000, but by October, he was on the move again, continuing his nomadic career with numerous clubs at home and abroad before hanging up his boots in November 1992.

FRANCIS 'FRANK' BARRETT

Country: Scotland
Born: 2 Aug 1872 **Died:** Aug 1907
Debut: 26 Sep 1896 v Newcastle United
Position: Goalkeeper
Appearances: 136 **Goals scored:** 0
Seasons: 1896/97 – 1899/1900
Clubs: Dundee, Newton Heath, New Brighton Tower, Arbroath, Manchester City, Dundee, Aberdeen

Despite winning four of their opening five fixtures at the start of the 1896/97 season, Newton Heath introduced a new goalkeeper for the home match against Newcastle United on 26 September, with Joe Ridgway being replaced by Frank Barrett, the first of a long line of first-class custodians who would serve the club over countless decades.

A Scottish international, he had been signed by Newton Heath at the start of the season from Dundee. Despite his confidence between the posts, he was a rather sensitive individual and when criticism was directed towards him, he took it rather badly and on more than one occasion he returned to Dundee with the Newton Heath officials hot on his trail in an effort to entice him back to Manchester.

During his spell with Newton Heath, he missed only four league games out of a possible 122, quite a record, keeping four clean sheets in a row on more than one occasion – one reason for the Heathens' management being keen to maintain his services. Somewhat unorthodox at times, a report from season 1897/98 covering the home match against Arsenal included the news that 'tricks by the home goalkeeper were suddenly put to a stop, when White nearly scored'. There was no mention, however, as to what Barrett was up to. At the end of season 1899/1900 he signed for New Brighton Tower.

FRANK BARSON

Country: England
Born: 10 Apr 1891 **Died:** 13 Sep 1968
Debut: 9 Sep 1922 v Wolverhampton Wanderers
Position: Half-back
Appearances: 152 **Goals scored:** 4
Seasons: 1922/23 – 1927/28
Clubs: Barnsley, Aston Villa, Manchester United, Watford, Hartlepools United

To imagine how some of the post-war players would have coped in today's game does not bear thinking about. Individuals such as Frank Barson, whose name even today creates a picture of a giant of a man with a strong physical presence and someone who took no prisoners in the course of the 90 minutes, would have found it very difficult to adjust as the merest of challenges today can bring a shrill blast from the referee's whistle.

Six foot tall and weighing over 12 stone, Barson was a typical centre-half and his muscular build, from his work as a blacksmith, was enough to strike fear in the hearts of most opponents. Sheffield-born, he signed for Barnsley in August 1911 from Cammell Laird, and it wasn't too long before his reputation was forged when he served a two-month suspension for an incident in a friendly against Birmingham. He also once had to be smuggled out of Goodison Park following an FA Cup tie. Even with his own team, things rarely ran smoothly and following a disagreement involving travelling expenses, he joined Aston Villa for a fee of £2,700 in October 1919, helping them to FA Cup success and picking up an England cap that season.

Despite the move to the Midlands, Barson continued to live in Sheffield, much to the annoyance of the Villa directors. He was always prepared to stand his corner and was rumoured to have pulled a gun on the club's manager (something that was not entirely far-fetched considering some of his associates). On one occasion, along with fellow Yorkshire resident goalkeeper Sam Hardy, they found themselves stranded some seven miles from Old Trafford after missing a rail connection and had to walk to the ground, arriving just in time to face United. Despite such unconventional pre-match preparation, he inspired his side to a 3–1 victory.

Due to his determination to remain in Sheffield, where he had a business, he missed the opening-day fixture of 1920/21 at Bolton and was suspended for 14 days, but this did little to prevent him from becoming captain of the club, celebrating the occasion with a headed goal against Sheffield United from all of 30 yards.

Another argument with a Villa director brought a further suspension and a transfer request. Despite being offered terms to re-sign for season 1922/23, he stuck to his guns and although Villa wanted £6,000 for his signature, they accepted £1,000 less from United, whose permission for the player to remain in Sheffield went some way to sway the deal. Barson was determined to enjoy further success, but neither silverware nor more England caps were to materialise – the latter mainly due to the stiff-collared selectors of the Football Association taking something of a dislike to the centre-half's style of play.

At Old Trafford, where he also captained the side, he added strength to the defence, but continued to walk the thin line between fair and foul. In one stand-out incident, during the 1926 FA Cup semi-final, he knocked out his opposite number Sam Cowan and, despite not being sent off, he was still suspended by the FA for two months.

Due to his style of play, Barson was never going to complete a full season's fixtures for one reason or another, but with United he was never sent off and his presence in the side was enough during season 1924/25 to help them out of the Second Division. In the summer of

1928, at the age of 37, he was given a free transfer by United and finally left his Sheffield home, joining Watford, where he continued to court controversy, having to endure a six-month suspension for yet another indiscretion. Off the field, he was a completely different character, shunning the limelight and enduring the ownership of a pub for only a matter of hours, a far cry from his on-field approach to the game.

FABIEN ALAIN BARTHEZ

Country: France
Born: 28 Jun 1971
Debut: 13 Aug 2000 v Chelsea
Position: Goalkeeper
Appearances: 139 **Goals scored:** 0
Seasons: 2000/01 – 2002/03
Clubs: Toulouse, Marseille, AS Monaco, Manchester United, Marseille (loan), Nantes

A French Championship and Champions League winner with Marseille and a World Cup and European champion with France, Fabien Barthez crossed the channel to Manchester in 2000 to replace Peter Schmeichel (after Mark Bosnich had failed to establish himself in that position the season before) in a £7.8 million deal from Monaco, where he had also enjoyed Ligue 1 success.

The extrovert goalkeeper often produced the unexpected, but he was also an excellent custodian, who made a major contribution to United's title-winning campaigns of 2000/01 and 2002/03 with numerous match-winning saves. But in the latter season, he came under fire following defeat by Real Madrid in the Champions League and was never selected again, returning to France in October 2003, rejoining Marseille when released from his contract.

ARTHUR BEADSWORTH

Country: England
Born: Sep 1876 **Died:** 9 Oct 1917
Debut: 25 Oct 1902 v Arsenal
Position: Forward

Appearances: 12 **Goals scored:** 2
Seasons: 1902/03
Clubs: Hinckley Town, Leicester Fosse, Preston North End, Manchester United, Swindon Town

Arthur Beadsworth enjoyed only one season with United, and had the distinction of scoring on his league debut against Woolwich Arsenal and on his FA Cup debut against Oswaldtwistle Rovers, his only goals for the club. He left in the summer of 1903 to join Swindon Town.

ROBERT HUGHES BEALE

Country: England
Born: 8 Jan 1884 **Died:** 5 Oct 1950
Debut: 2 Sep 1912 v Arsenal
Position: Goalkeeper
Appearances: 112 **Goals scored:** 0
Seasons: 1912/13 – 1914/15
Clubs: Maidstone United, Brighton & Hove Albion, Norwich City, Manchester United, Arsenal (WWI), Gillingham, Manchester United

Goalkeeper Robert Beale was signed from Norwich City for a fee of £275 in May 1912, making his debut at the start of the following campaign. At Old Trafford, he was to enjoy an excellent first season, playing in all but one of the First Division fixtures, keeping 14 clean sheets in his 37 outings, with his performances earning him selection for the Football League side to face their Scottish counterparts. The following season he played for the North against England in an international trial match but failed to impress the selectors.

The First World War more or less brought an end to his playing career, although he did play for both Gillingham and Arsenal during the hostilities and also in the odd reserve-team fixture for United during season 1920/21, before hanging up his boots at the end of that season and taking up a post in the family furniture-selling business.

PETER ANDREW BEARDSLEY

Country: England
Born: 18 Jan 1961

Debut: 6 Oct 1982 v AFC Bournemouth
Position: Forward
Appearances: 1 **Goals scored:** 0
Seasons: 1982/83
Clubs: Carlisle United, Vancouver White Caps, Manchester United, Vancouver White Caps, Newcastle United, Liverpool, Everton, Newcastle United, Bolton Wanderers, Manchester City (loan), Fulham, Hartlepool United, Melbourne Knights

Although he made only one appearance for United, and even that lasted for just 45 minutes of a Milk Cup tie against Bournemouth in October 1982, few would enjoy such a memorable career after leaving Old Trafford. Born in Newcastle, he began his career with the famous Wallsend Boys Club (where the Manchester United connection is strengthened by the likes of Steve Bruce and Michael Carrick and also recent goalkeeping coach Eric Steele).

A trial at Newcastle United came to nothing, so he made the journey along Hadrian's Wall to join Carlisle United in August 1979, making over 130 appearances for the Cumbrians and it was while on his second loan spell with Vancouver Whitecaps that he caught the eye of United manager Ron Atkinson, who paid out around £250,000 for the 21-year-old.

Re-crossing the Atlantic to Manchester, he showed up well in training, but after the one outing he was allowed to go back to Vancouver for a similar fee, despite numerous people, Jimmy Murphy among them, noting the player's natural ability. If Atkinson failed to see Beardsley's potential, Newcastle United, having realised their earlier mistake, certainly didn't and paid the £150,000 that the Canadians wanted for his signature, a figure that was to turn out to be something of a bargain.

RUSSELL PETER BEARDSMORE

Country: England
Born: 28 Sep 1968
Debut: 24 Sep 1988 v West Ham United
Position: Midfield
Appearances: 39 (34) **Goals scored:** 4
Seasons: 1988/89 – 1991/92
Clubs: Manchester United, Blackburn Rovers (loan), AFC Bournemouth

One of a number of youngsters introduced into the United side in the late 1980s, he had been discovered by former player Harry McShane as a Wigan schoolboy, joining the club in April 1984 and making his debut in the league four years later. Despite his slender physique, he was a combative individual who enjoyed three seasons as a member of the first-team squad, gaining England Under-21 honours along the way. A regular first-team spot was just beyond his reach and, in May 1993, following a loan spell at Blackburn, he was given a free transfer and joined Bournemouth.

TIAGO MANUEL DIAS CORREIA 'BÉBÉ'

Country: Portugal
Born: 12 Jul 1990
Debut: 22 Sep 2010 v Scunthorpe United
Position: Forward
Appearances: 3 (4) **Goals scored:** 2
Seasons: 2010/11
Clubs: Estrela da Amadora Club, Vitória de Guimarães, Manchester United, Beşiktaş (loan), Rio Ave (loan), FC Paços de Ferreira

R. BECKETT

Country: England
Born: Unknown **Died:** Unknown
Debut: 30 Oct 1886 v Fleetwood Rangers
Position: Goalkeeper
Appearances: 1 **Goals scored:** 0
Seasons: 1886/87
Clubs: Newton Heath

DAVID ROBERT JOSEPH BECKHAM

Country: England
Born: 2 May 1975
Debut: 23 Sep 1992 v Brighton & Hove Albion
Position: Midfield
Appearances: 356 (38) **Goals scored:** 85
Seasons: 1992/93 – 2002/03
Clubs: Manchester United, Preston North End (loan), Real Madrid, LA Galaxy, AC Milan (loan), Paris Saint-Germain

One of the famed 'Class of '92', David Beckham joined United as a schoolboy and went on to become not simply a footballer of some renown, but a global icon, who retained that status even when his career began to draw to a close. Practice went on to make perfection, but it took a loan move to Preston North End in 1994/95, following his United debut in September 1992 and that Youth Cup success earlier that same year, before he managed to grasp the footballing ladder to the top.

With Alex Ferguson having sold Andrei Kanchelskis, his predecessor on the right flank, during the summer of 1995, he established himself in the side during the next season, helping United to the Double. His star shone even brighter following a goal of individual brilliance, when he scored from just inside his own half against Wimbledon in the first match of the following campaign. With Spice Girl Victoria Adams as his girlfriend and later wife, he quickly became one of the most high-profile players in the team, and he soon edged onto the international stage.

His crossing and expertise from a dead ball became his trademark for both club and country, but he was to suffer a backlash following a sending off playing for England in the 1998 World Cup finals. Determined to answer his critics, he had what many viewed as his finest season during the next campaign. His equalising goal against Spurs in the final league game of 1998/99 edged United to the first leg of the Treble, while his two corners in extra time in the Champions League final led to the goals that fulfilled the dream.

The celebrity lifestyle that came with being one half of 'Posh 'n' Becks' could have distracted him from his day job, but he always worked hard at his game, and in November 2000 he became England captain – a brilliant free-kick at Old Trafford against Greece ensuring qualification for the 2002 World Cup finals. He would eventually win 115 caps for his country, a record for an outfielder.

After winning his sixth Premier League title with United, he was sold to Real Madrid for £25 million in 2003 not long after a boot kicked by his manager had accidentally cut him above his eyebrow. He fitted in well with the *galacticos* of Spain, before eventually moving on to LA Galaxy in 2007, from where he had a couple of loan spells at Milan. During one of them, he made an emotional return to Old Trafford in a Champions League game in March 2010. When his spell in the US ended, he returned briefly to Europe to play for Paris St Germain at the end of the 2012/13 season, donating his salary to charity, before retiring from the game.

JOHN HARRY 'CLEM' BEDDOW

Country: England
Born: Oct 1885 **Died:** Unknown
Debut: 25 Feb 1905 v Barnsley
Position: Forward
Appearances: 34 **Goals scored:** 15
Seasons: 1904/05 – 1906/07
Clubs: Trent Rovers, Burton United, Manchester United, Burnley

Less than a season with Burton United in the Second Division was enough to convince Manchester United that 'Clem' Beddow was worth dipping into the transfer funds for, and he was duly signed in February 1905, going straight into the first team at outside-right at Barnsley. The following season saw United win a place in the First Division and, although he began the campaign as first-choice outside-right, he found himself moved to centre-forward, where nine goals in 13 outings kept their promotion hopes high. He then picked up a knee injury and, with promotion achieved, made only three starts in the top flight, subsequently joining Burnley in July 1907.

WILLIAM 'BILLY' BEHAN

Country: Ireland
Born: 3 Aug 1911 **Died:** 12 Nov 1991
Debut: 3 Mar 1934 v Bury
Position: Goalkeeper
Appearances: 1 **Goals scored:** 0
Seasons: 1933/34
Clubs: Shelbourne, Manchester United, Shelbourne, Shamrock Rovers

Although he played just once, Behan would later spend more than 50 years working as a scout in Ireland, discovering many stars, from Johnny Carey to Liam Whelan to Kevin Moran.

ALEXANDER 'ALEX' BELL

Country: Scotland
Born: 1882 **Died:** 30 Nov 1934
Debut: 24 Jan 1903 v Glossop

Position: Half-back
Appearances: 309 **Goals scored:** 10
Seasons: 1902/03 – 1912/13
Clubs: Ayr Spring Vale, Ayr Westerlea, Ayr Parkhouse, Manchester United, Blackburn Rovers

A 3-1 victory at Glossop on 24 January 1903 marked the debut of an outstanding individual, who went on to make over 300 appearances for the club and feature in one of the most memorable half-back lines in not only United's history but that of the Football League. His name was Alexander Bell.

Born in Cape Town, South Africa of Scottish parents, Bell's family soon returned to their native land and upon leaving school, his early days as an amateur footballer saw him involved with various Ayr teams before the 20-year-old joined United in January 1903, on the recommendation of former Newton Heath player Willie Donaldson, for a fee of £700.

He made only a handful of appearances the following season, but in the fourth match of the 1904/05 campaign, he stepped into the left-half berth for the first time, the position in which he was to make his name, and never looked back, a skilful performer despite his more defensive attributes. In December 1906, Dick Duckworth, who had made only fleeting appearances in a variety of positions, was given the right-half slot on a regular basis to complete the axis of the United side of that time, as the duo linked up with centre-half Charlie Roberts, the third member of the legendary half-back line.

Bell was the quiet man of the trio, becoming known as 'The South African Scotsman', a key member of a team that was to win two league titles, the FA Cup and two FA Charity Shields. Rather surprisingly he was to win only one Scottish international cap, against Northern Ireland in 1912, something that was perhaps due to his football being played south of the border. By the end of season 1912/13, he had run up a total of 278 league and 28 FA Cup appearances for United, but having been refused a second benefit match by United, he asked for a move and in July was transferred to Blackburn Rovers for £1,000.

In 1925, he became Manchester City's trainer, a position he held until his untimely death in November 1934, and he was the City trainer when they met and defeated United in the 1926 FA Cup semi-final at Bramall Lane, inspiring his charges by showing them his own FA Cup winners' medal, which he proudly wore on a gold chain.

DAVID BELLION

Country: France
Born: 27 Nov 1982
Debut: 27 Aug 2003 v Wolverhampton Wanderers
Position: Forward
Appearances: 15 (25) **Goals scored:** 8
Seasons: 2003/04 – 2004/05
Clubs: Cannes, Sunderland, Manchester United, West Ham United (loan), Nice (loan), Nice, Bordeaux, Nice (loan)

A talented and pacy French youngster, he never managed to fully establish himself on the vast Old Trafford stage. He was signed for £2 million from Sunderland in July 2003, and there were brief flashes of his ability during his spell with United but he was soon allowed to leave, at first on loan to West Ham and then Nice, a move that became permanent in June 2006.

SAMUEL RAYMOND 'RAY' BENNION

Country: Wales
Born: 1 Sep 1896 **Died:** 12 Mar 1968
Debut: 27 Aug 1921 v Everton
Position: Half-back
Appearances: 301 **Goals scored:** 3
Seasons: 1921/22 – 1931/32
Clubs: Ragtimes, Crichton's Athletic, Manchester United, Burnley

Originally joining United on a month's trial in April 1920, Ray Bennion was quickly snapped up by the club's management before anyone else became aware of his ability. Born in Gwersyllt, an area of Wrexham, Bennion played his early football for his school old boys' side, paying threepence a week to cover expenses. He began to look for a better class of football and he obtained a trial with Crichton's Athletic, a Chester side who were members of the Cheshire County League. Playing at right-half, he duly impressed and was signed on a professional contract, helping them to the Cheshire County Challenge Cup in his second and last season with the club.

He didn't make his United debut until a 5-0 defeat at Everton in August 1921, but undeterred by that initial setback and the relegation that followed at the end of the campaign, he eventually became an almost permanent fixture in the United first team for the next decade, winning his first Welsh international cap against Scotland in 1926. At the end of season 1931/32, he turned down United's new contract offer and signed for near neighbours Burnley where he enjoyed a couple of years as a player before being appointed coach and then trainer, retiring in February 1964 due to ill health.

GEOFFREY 'GEOFF' BENT

Country: England
Born: 27 Sep 1932 **Died:** 6 Feb 1958
Debut: 11 Dec 1954 v Burnley
Position: Full-back
Appearances: 12 **Goals scored:** 0
Seasons: 1954/55 – 1957/58
Clubs: Manchester United

Geoff Bent could have walked into any club side in the country had he chosen to leave Manchester United, but he stayed faithful to his roots and ultimately was to pay for it with his life. He was a local lad, born in Salford, and attended St John's Junior School, where he won a scholarship for Tootal Grammar. A member of the Boys Brigade, he was a keen sportsman and, although his father was an enthusiastic rugby man, it was football and swimming that the youngster enjoyed most. Strangely, it was in the latter of his two leisure activities that he was awarded his first medal, after rescuing a youngster from drowning in the Salford Canal.

During his early footballing days he occupied the old inside-left position, later moving back to left-half and such were his performances at schoolboy level, he not only represented Salford Boys in the England Schools Trophy of 1947, but captained the side. His performances caught the eye of numerous clubs, but it was his mother who played a major part in the 15-year-old signing for United, as she did not want her only child moving away from home, telling him to sign for a local club.

At Old Trafford, Geoff made his final positional switch, to left-back, and progressed through the junior ranks while also serving his apprenticeship as a junior, alongside Duncan Edwards. A regular place in the Central League side was soon claimed, but his progress was now halted, as the man holding down the first-team left-back spot was England international Roger Byrne. Geoff, however, was more than content to bide his time, and on 11 December 1954 he finally made his first-team debut at Turf Moor, Burnley, a game that United won 4-2.

Despite the lack of opportunities, he remained loyal to United and by February 1958 he had accumulated only a dozen first-team appearances, supplementing his meagre first-team wages with summer employment as a joiner. An injury to Roger Byrne prior to the trip to Belgrade put the United captain's starting place in some doubt, so Geoff made the fateful trip in his role as stand-in, having not long recovered himself from a second broken leg, and it was a journey that was to cost him his life at Munich.

DIMITAR IVANOV BERBATOV

Country: Bulgaria
Born: 30 Jan 1981
Debut: 13 Sep 2008 v Liverpool
Position: Forward
Appearances: 108 (41) **Goals scored:** 57
Seasons: 2008/09 – 2011/12
Clubs: CSKA Sofia, Bayer Leverkusen, Tottenham Hotspur, Manchester United, Fulham

Born into a footballing family, Dimitar Berbatov's father played for Pirin and CSKA Sofia, while his grandfather was also a player of some repute for Blagoevgrad. As a youngster, he was part of the youth set-up at both Blagoevgrad and Pirin, and in 1998 continued to follow in his father's footsteps when he signed for CSKA, but he took a while to settle and at one point was on the verge of throwing in the towel altogether.

Thankfully, his mother persuaded him to persevere and in his second season he made a steady improvement, playing his part in CSKA's Bulgarian Cup success and also winning his first international cap. In January 2001, he was on the move to Bayer Leverkusen, but again took time to settle before helping them to the German title, which led to an appearance at Old Trafford in the Champions League semi-finals in 2002 when the Germans won on away goals.

After 50 goals in 83 outings over two seasons, the name of Berbatov was at the centre of transfer speculation in the summer of 2006, and a fee of £10.9 million took him to Tottenham Hotspur. He won a Carling Cup winners' medal in 2008, but the start of the following season brought rumours that he was unsettled and on transfer deadline day, with the minutes slowly ticking away, he was snatched from under the nose of Manchester City at Manchester airport and whisked away to Old Trafford where he signed a four-year deal, with Tottenham receiving a fee of £30.75 million, a record signing for United.

In his first season in Manchester he won a Premier League medal, but had the disappointment of missing a penalty kick in the FA Cup semi-final shoot-out against Everton at Wembley. May 2010 saw him call time on his international career, having won 78 full caps, scoring 48 goals.

His best season in a red shirt was 2010/11, when he helped United to a record 19th title, during which he claimed the Golden Boot with 20 goals, including two hat-tricks (against Liverpool and Birmingham City), and five against Blackburn Rovers. However, he was omitted from the Champions League final line-up at the end of the season, which some believed heralded the beginning of the end for the Bulgarian. Following the 2011/12 campaign, he was sold to Fulham for an undisclosed fee, linking up with his former manager at Tottenham, Martin Jol.

HENNING STILLE BERG

Country: Norway
Born: 1 Sep 1969
Debut: 13 Aug 1997 v Southampton
Position: Defender
Appearances: 81 (22) **Goals scored:** 3
Seasons: 1997/98 – 2000/01
Clubs: Vålerenga, Lillestrøm, Blackburn Rovers, Manchester United, Blackburn Rovers (loan), Blackburn Rovers, Rangers

Wanted by United in the late 1980s, he was unable to obtain a work permit, but having enjoyed a successful title-winning spell at Blackburn, Alex Ferguson finally got his man for a fee of £5 million in August 1997. The Norwegian international was a strong, reliable defender who would go on to win 100 caps for his country, and could have achieved much more than two Premier League medals had it not been for injuries and, at times, the form of others. It was perhaps typical of his time at

United that he missed both cup finals in the Treble-winning season through injury.

Out of favour, he returned to Blackburn on loan, and was happy to make the move permanent, with United receiving a £1.75 million fee. He finished his career at Rangers, and later had managerial spells back in Norway, as well as briefly at Blackburn Rovers during 2012/13.

JOHN JAMES 'JOHNNY' BERRY

Country: England
Born: 1 Jun 1926 **Died:** 16 Sep 1994
Debut: 1 Sep 1951 v Bolton Wanderers
Position: Winger
Appearances: 276 **Goals scored:** 45
Seasons: 1951/52 – 1957/58
Clubs: Birmingham City, Manchester United

If a player became a thorn in his Manchester United's side, Matt Busby had one way of preventing it happening too often and that was by signing him. Such was the case of Johnny Berry. The Aldershot-born winger displayed his initial promise playing for his school side, St Joseph's, Aldershot Boys and the local YMCA, and upon leaving school went to work as a cinema projectionist. But it was while doing his National Service with the Royal Artillery that he came to the attention of Birmingham City, joining the St Andrew's club as an amateur in 1944.

In the Midlands, the diminutive outside-right broke into the Birmingham City first team during 1947/48, but it was not until season 1949/50 that he commanded a regular place, and his displays against United in both the First Division and the FA Cup made up Matt Busby's mind that he wanted Berry in his line-up. It took the United manager 18 months from his initial approach until he finally got his man, having to pay £25,000 to obtain his signature in August 1951.

After making his United debut at Bolton, he scored the first of his 45 goals a fortnight later in the first Manchester 'derby' of the season at Maine Road and went on to become one of the most consistent wingers of the period, claiming a First Division title medal in his first season. Such were his displays that he was soon in the England international set-up, winning his first cap on the 1953 tour of America, having previously been capped at 'B' level. Unfortunately for him, England were blessed with numerous wing men at this particular time, so he was to gain only a further three caps.

With United, the 'old man' of the team was an integral part of Busby's progressive line-up, providing countless scoring opportunities for his young team-mates, as they stormed to the title in 1955/56 and again the following season, reaching the FA Cup final in 1957 and taking Europe by storm in 1956/57 and 1957/58. But it was Europe that was to curtail Berry's footballing career, with the tragedy at Munich leaving the United No.7 in a coma for the best part of two months, with a fractured skull, broken jaw, broken elbow, broken pelvis and a broken leg.

Upon returning to Manchester, he continued his stay in hospital and only found out what had happened while reading a newspaper and noticing the United line-up was minus many of his friends. Such were his injuries, he had no option but to hang up his boots, taking up a job with Massey Ferguson in Trafford Park, before eventually returning to Aldershot to open a sports shop.

WILLIAM ALEXANDER 'BILL' BERRY

Country: England
Born: Jul 1884 **Died:** 1 Mar 1943
Debut: 17 Nov 1906 v Sheffield Wednesday
Position: Forward
Appearances: 14 **Goals scored:** 1
Seasons: 1906/07 – 1908/09
Clubs: Sunderland, Tottenham Hotspur, Manchester United, Stockport County

Having signed for Sunderland in September 1902, a year later he was on the move south to join Tottenham Hotspur, then in the Southern League, where he spent three years before signing for United in November 1906. His first two appearances in a United shirt saw him fill the outside-right spot, but in his nine outings for season 1906/07 he could also be found at inside-right and centre-forward, without scoring. The next season he was omitted from the first-team line-up until March, managing only three games in those final two months of the title-winning season. February 1909 saw him placed on the transfer list, and within a matter of days he was on his way to Stockport County.

GEORGE BEST

Country: Northern Ireland
Born: 22 May 1946 **Died:** 25 Nov 2005
Debut: 14 Sep 1963 v West Bromwich Albion
Position: Forward
Appearances: 470 **Goals scored:** 179
Seasons: 1963/64 – 1973/74
Clubs: Manchester United, Dunstable Town, Stockport County, Cork Celtic, LA Aztecs, Fulham, LA Aztecs, Fort Lauderdale Strikers, Motherwell, Hibernian, San Jose Earthquakes, See Bea, Hong Kong Rangers, Bournemouth, Brisbane Lions

On the evening of 25 November 2005, George Best once again drew the crowds to Old Trafford, but on that particular evening the ground was in darkness and the gates firmly locked. The artistry of the Irishman was now a mere memory to those supporters who had placed bunches of flowers along the railings facing the statue of Sir Matt Busby in memory of the Belfast Boy who had died that day at the age of 59.

What can one write about Best that has not been penned hundreds, or thousands, of times before? Every adjective available to the writer has been used over and over again to describe a goal, a magical piece of individualistic skill or some moment of over-indulgence.

Born on the Cregagh Estate in Belfast, his early steps to fame, fortune and notoriety came at the local Boys' Club. In one particular outing, the slimly built youngster teased and tormented the opposition defence of the Irish Boys XI – so much so that his manager, Bob McFarlane, was convinced that his jewel in the crown would receive the call-up into the Northern Irish schoolboy side. It was, surprisingly, a call-up that never came, as the selectors felt that he was too small to be considered for the representative side. But word spread around the Belfast shipyards about the talented footballer from the Cregagh, with tales of his performances quickly reaching the ears of Bob Bishop, Manchester United's Northern Ireland scout.

Wanting to see the prodigious talent for himself, Bishop arranged a match between Best's side and his own Boyland Youth team and his efforts were well rewarded, as Best, although only 15, was up against 17-year-olds, but he proved to Bishop that the stories that he had heard were indeed true, with three goals emphasising the point. Bishop quickly contacted Matt Busby, telling him that he had discovered a youngster with exceptional talents and that every effort should be made to secure his signature. Busby heeded the words of his scout and brought him over as an apprentice at Old Trafford.

Manchester, however, was a daunting place for a youngster not used to being away from the familiar environs of Belfast and, along with his travelling companion Eric McMordie, he was back home within two days. The phone lines between Manchester and Belfast crackled furiously as attempts were made to persuade the youngster to return. Fortunately, they did so, but if it had not been for Dick Best spending time with his son in order to change his mind, who knows what would have become of George Best? Meanwhile, McMordie, who had been earmarked for Manchester United since the age of 13, was simply allowed to walk away.

At the Cliff training ground and behind the Stretford End at Old Trafford, the Belfast boy began to gain a host of admirers among the United staff and as he progressed through the junior and youth sides, others around the country were also soon to sit up and take notice. On 14 September 1963, with injuries forcing his hand, Matt Busby gave the 17-year-old his league debut against West Bromwich Albion at Old Trafford, and a look through the archives reveals the following report:

'United were weakened on Saturday by the absence of Law and Moir, and had to bring in Stiles at inside-right and G.Best, a 17-year-old for his first League match ... Young Best came in for some stern treatment by that splendid back Williams and twice sought refuge for short spells on the opposite wing, where he faced Crawford. Best's football was occasionally of high quality, but he also showed his immaturity and it says much for his spirit that he twice returned to the right wing to take on Williams again, who seemed intent on showing a disapproving crowd that there is no sentiment in football.'

The report also recalls that it was Best who began the move that led to United's goal in the 65th minute. The legend was born! It was some three months before he got his second chance in the team, but by the end of the season he was a regular in the side, and had helped the club to FA Youth Cup victory. He followed it up by being a part of the 1964/65 title-winning team, missing just one game out of the 61 the Reds played that season.

From then until the 1970s, he tormented defences at home and abroad, creating goals and newspaper headlines on a more or less match-by-match basis. It was not just on the domestic front that Best gave stunning performances, as foreign sides also came in for much torment, and it was on a foreign field that he perhaps created his superstar personality with a dazzling display as United destroyed Benfica 5-1 in Lisbon on 9 March 1966, in the second leg of a European Cup quarter-final tie. His injury in the first leg of the semi-final against Partizan Belgrade was perhaps the principal reason behind United's failure to reach the final of the competition that same year, with arguably one of the best teams in the club's history.

Best and United recovered, regaining the title in 1967, with amends being made in May 1968, when he scored one of the four goals which destroyed Benfica at Wembley, a stadium he had visited as a skinny youngster, when he was not given a second glance by anyone sitting near him high up in the Wembley stand as he watched United defeat Leicester City in the 1963 FA Cup final. Five years and three days later, however, the 100,000 crowd couldn't take their eyes off him as he glided past defender and goalkeeper to score on that warm evening under the glare of the stadium's floodlights as United at last lifted the European Cup.

In 1968, he was also FWA Footballer of the Year and European Footballer of the Year, but beneath the match-winning ability there was a self-destruct button, which began to become more obvious as the years went by, as he became the most famous footballer in the country. Referees were hit by mud, had the ball knocked out of their hands, suspensions were handed out, games were missed, women came and went as the world of George Best began to spiral downwards. Despite this, he was United's leading scorer in the league for five successive seasons from 1967/68 to 1971/72.

To many, though, his weaknesses are simply forgotten about, as they prefer to recall the moments of genius, such as the frequently repeated goals against Chelsea in the League Cup at Old Trafford in 1970, Sheffield United in the league at Old Trafford in 1971, or the six against Northampton in the FA Cup again in 1970. By the early 1970s, frustrated that the team wasn't being strengthened, he began to miss training sessions, and his problems grew worse. With the appointment of Tommy Docherty as United's manager at the end of 1972, there was always going to be a clash of personalities and January 1974 saw the final parting of the ways.

From then on, he was as likely to make front-page headlines as back-page ones, with appearances for over a dozen different clubs, including something of an Indian summer at Fulham. After he retired, his health eventually began to deteriorate, and he died while still relatively young.

To have seen George Best in his heyday was to see a genius at work. Many would argue that he was indeed the best player of all time, with both Pelé and Maradona, no mean players themselves, openly admitting that George Best was indeed The Best.

PAUL ANTHONY BIELBY

Country: England
Born: 24 Nov 1956
Debut: 13 Mar 1974 v Manchester City
Position: Midfield
Appearances: 2 (2) **Goals scored:** 0
Seasons: 1972/73 – 1975/76
Clubs: Manchester United, Hartlepool (loan), Hartlepool, Huddersfield Town

BRIAN BIRCH

Country: England
Born: 18 Nov 1931 **Died:** Unknown
Debut: 27 Aug 1949 v West Bromwich Albion
Position: Forward
Appearances: 15 **Goals scored:** 5
Seasons: 1949/50 – 1951/52
Clubs: Manchester United, Wolverhampton Wanderers, Lincoln City, Boston United, Barrow, Exeter City, Oldham Athletic, Rochdale

Brian Birch joined Manchester United as an amateur from Salford football in May 1946, having represented the local schoolboy side. Signing professional forms two years later, he made his first-team debut on the tour of Ireland against a Bohemians Select, coming on as substitute for Frank Clempson, with his league debut coming a matter of weeks later in the opening fixture of season 1949/50 at Derby County when aged only 17. Although on the small side at 5'6", he was a clever ball player and, given the opportunity, he could have developed into an exceptional player. However, a first-team place at Old Trafford was beyond him and he was transferred to Wolverhampton Wanderers in March 1952 for £10,000.

HERBERT BIRCHENOUGH

Country: England
Born: 21 Sep 1874 **Died:** 28 Feb 1942
Debut: 25 Oct 1902 v Arsenal
Position: Goalkeeper
Appearances: 30 **Goals scored:** 0
Seasons: 1902/03
Clubs: Haslington, Crewe Hornets, Nantwich, Sandbach St Mary's, Audley, Burslem Port Vale, Glossop, Manchester United, Crewe Alexandra

Goalkeeper Herbert Birchenough was a 'one-season wonder' after joining United from Glossop in October 1902. Having won Football League honours with Port Vale, he was a more than capable keeper and replaced Jimmy Whitehouse in the United goal. But despite enjoying a reasonable inaugural season between the sticks, he surprisingly left Manchester and returned to his native Crewe.

CLIFFORD 'CLIFF' BIRKETT

Country: England
Born: 17 Sep 1933 **Died:** 11 Jan 1997
Debut: 2 Dec 1950 v Newcastle United
Position: Forward
Appearances: 13 **Goals scored:** 2
Seasons: 1950/51 – 1955/56
Clubs: Manchester United, Southport

As an England Schoolboy international Cliff Birkett won a record eight caps before signing for United in August 1949, quickly making progress through the junior and reserve sides before making his debut against Newcastle United in December 1950 as a replacement for Tommy Bogan. At 17 years and 80 days, he was one of the youngest players ever to take the field under Busby. Seven days later at Huddersfield, he scored United's winner in their 3-2 victory. Although a little on the small side, he was quick off the mark, possessed a strong shot and was an excellent crosser of the ball. But, following his initial breakthrough, he soon found himself back in the reserves and behind Harry McShane and Johnny Berry in the pecking order. So, in the summer of 1956, he left United for Southport, moving into the non-league ranks a year later.

GARRY BIRTLES

Country: England
Born: 27 Jul 1956
Debut: 22 Oct 1980 v Stoke City
Position: Forward
Appearances: 63 (1) **Goals scored:** 12
Seasons: 1980/81 – 1981/82
Clubs: Nottingham Forest, Manchester United, Nottingham Forest, Notts County, Grimsby Town

With Nottingham Forest, Garry Birtles began season 1980/81 with an impressive nine goals in 14 outings, which went a long way to persuading Dave Sexton to pay out £1.25 million to bring him to Old Trafford that October. His shooting boots, however, were left on the banks of the River Trent, as it took the big-money signing 30 games before he found the net for United. The bearded frontman was treated with more patience than most by the Old Trafford crowd and when he finally broke his duck against Swansea City with a notable 25-yard drive, there were celebrations both on and off the pitch. Birtles was a hard-working, unselfish individual, but his lack of goals did little to help his United career and it was no real surprise when Ron Atkinson sold him to back to Forest for a mere £275,000 in September 1982.

GEORGE BISSETT

Country: Scotland
Born: 25 Jan 1897 **Died:** 1946
Debut: 15 Nov 1919 v Burnley
Position: Forward
Appearances: 42 **Goals scored:** 10
Seasons: 1919/20 – 1921/22
Clubs: Glencraig Thistle, Third Lanark, Manchester United, Wolverhampton Wanderers, Pontypridd, Southend United

A native of Cowdenbeath, George Bissett's early football was played in the junior ranks with Glencraig Thistle and prior to the First World War he had been on the books of Third Lanark. With the hostilities having taken their toll, Bissett took some time to regain his fitness and settle into ordinary life again, but made his debut against Burnley in a 3-0 defeat. He consolidated his place in the team in the latter half of 1919/20, and managed another extended run late in the following campaign, but joined Wolverhampton Wanderers at the end of November 1921 after struggling to hold down a place in the team.

ARTHUR RICHARD 'DICK' BLACK

Country: Scotland
Born: 18 Feb 1907 **Died:** Unknown
Debut: 23 Apr 1932 v Bradford City
Position: Forward
Appearances: 8 **Goals scored:** 3
Seasons: 1931/32 – 1933/34
Clubs: Stenhousemuir, Blantyre Victoria, Greenock Morton, Manchester United, St Mirren

CLAYTON GRAHAM BLACKMORE

Country: Wales
Born: 23 Sep 1964
Debut: 16 May 1984 v Nottingham Forest
Position: Defender/Midfield
Appearances: 201 (44) **Goals scored:** 26
Seasons: 1983/84 – 1992/93
Clubs: Manchester United, Middlesbrough, Bristol City (loan), Barnsley, Notts County, Leigh RMI, Bangor City, Portmadog, Neath Athletic

Clayton Blackmore was one of those players that every manager loves, a 'play anywhere' man who always gave 100 per cent. A Welsh international at every level, winning 39 caps, he pulled on every United shirt from No.2 to 14, excluding the unused No.13, something no other player could claim, but it was this versatility that was to prevent him from making one position his own, though he was perhaps most often used as a full-back.

Having made his debut in the last game of the 1983/84 season, it wasn't until 1988/89 that he became a regular starter, with his best season coming in 1990/91. He also possessed a powerful shot, which gave him a regular quota of goals. During his time at United, he picked up winners' medals in the Premier League, FA Cup and European Cup-Winners' Cup. His appearances in that title-winning campaign of 1992/93 were limited and in the close season he moved to Middlesbrough on a free transfer.

PETER BLACKMORE

Country: England
Born: Jul 1879 **Died:** Unknown
Debut: 21 Oct 1899 v New Brighton Tower
Position: Forward
Appearances: 2 **Goals scored:** 0
Seasons: 1899/1900
Clubs: Newton Heath

THOMAS 'TOMMY' BLACKSTOCK

Country: Scotland
Born: 1882 **Died:** 8 Apr 1907
Debut: 3 Oct 1903 v Arsenal
Position: Full-back
Appearances: 38 **Goals scored:** 0
Seasons: 1903/04 – 1906/07
Clubs: Dunniker Rovers, Blue Bell, Raith Athletic, Leith Athletic, Cowdenbeath, Manchester United

Tommy Blackstock joined United from Cowdenbeath in the summer of 1903, but was an irregular starter. In 1905/06 he played 21 times, but was again on the fringes of things the following campaign. While playing for United in a Lancashire Combination fixture at Clayton against St Helens Reserves, he collapsed after heading the ball out for a throw-in after only ten minutes' play. Attempts by the trainer to revive him failed, and he was quickly carried from the pitch. Further attempts were made to revive him in the confines of the dressing room, but they were to no avail. The inquest into his untimely death returned the verdict of 'natural causes' and when his body was taken to the station for its final journey back to his native Kirkcaldy, his team-mates followed the coffin and a large gathering of supporters were also present to pay their final respects.

LAURENT ROBERT BLANC

Country: France
Born: 19 Nov 1965
Debut: 8 Sep 2001 v Everton

Position: Centre-back
Appearances: 71 (4) **Goals scored:** 4
Seasons: 2001/02 – 2002/03
Clubs: Montpellier, Napoli, Nimes, St Etienne, Auxerre, Barcelona, Marseille, Internazionale, Manchester United

A cultured, experienced French defender, Blanc was perhaps surprisingly signed in the twilight of his career from Inter Milan on a free transfer in September 2001, Sir Alex's previous attempts to recruit him having failing to lure him to Manchester. A World Cup and European Championship winner with France, he came as a short-term replacement for Jaap Stam, and played his part as United lifted the 2002/03 Premier League title. He retired afterwards, and has now developed into a successful manager, having had spells with Bordeaux and France before taking charge at PSG in the summer of 2013.

JOHN 'JACKIE' BLANCHFLOWER

Country: Northern Ireland
Born: 7 Mar 1933 **Died:** 2 Sep 1998
Debut: 24 Nov 1951 v Liverpool
Position: Half-back
Appearances: 117 **Goals scored:** 27
Seasons: 1951/52 – 1957/58
Clubs: Manchester United

Jackie Blanchflower was undaunted by the shadows cast by his elder brother Danny, with the career of the Belfast-born, Irish schoolboy international beginning with Pitt Street Mission side before progressing to the Boyland Youth team. Spotted by Manchester United scout Bob Harpur, Blanchflower followed his elder brother's footsteps across the Irish Sea, joining United as an amateur in May 1949. (Jackie's brother Danny was a professional with Aston Villa and was later to captain the famous Tottenham Hotspur double-winning side of 1961.)

For a while there was some doubt among the United management and coaching staff whether the tall, well-built inside-forward would make the grade. Busby, well aware that talent was certainly contained within the Blanchflower framework, decided on a last-gasp attempt to determine whether or not to prolong the young Irishman's stay in

Manchester. Moving him back to the half-back line, where his lack of pace was not so much of a problem, produced a few impressive reserve-team performances and his future at United was secured.

An injury to Don Gibson provided him with his first-team debut at Liverpool on 24 November 1951, alongside another young debutant, Roger Byrne. International recognition for Blanchflower was also not too far away, and despite having made only 23 appearances with United, he was selected for his first Northern Ireland cap on 31 March 1954, against Wales, playing alongside his brother Danny.

Competition for places was fierce, but during 1956/57 an injury to Mark Jones presented Matt Busby with a dilemma in defence. Somewhat surprisingly, he turned to Blanchflower to take over the centre-half position. Having already been crowned champions, there was the added incentive to become the first team in the 20th century to win the double if success against Villa at Wembley could be achieved. But a shoulder charge by Peter McParland on Ray Wood in the sixth minute left the United keeper with a broken jaw and Jackie Blanchflower took over between the posts. Despite countless fine saves, he could not prevent Villa scoring twice. Taylor scored a late consolation goal for United, with the Wembley defeat earning the stand-in keeper not simply a runners-up medal, but also fame in the trivia question: 'Who is the only outfield player to wear a cap in a Wembley cup final?'

Jackie's performances in the heart of the Manchester United defence kept Mark Jones out of the side when he was fit again, and he began season 1957/58 as United's first-choice centre-half. An injury in late November allowed Jones back into the side and it was only as a reserve that Blanchflower made the ill-fated journey to Belgrade the following February.

The Munich Air Disaster saw him receive serious injuries to his right arm and leg, along with a shattered pelvis. Having fought for his United career in his early days at Old Trafford, he was now put in the unwanted position of having to do so again. This time, the odds were even more stacked against him. It was a battle that he was never realistically going to win and he was forced to retire from the game. Life had dealt Jackie Blanchflower a cruel blow and it took many years for him to fully recover from the effects of the disaster.

HORACE ELFORD BLEW

Country: Wales
Born: Jan 1878 **Died:** 1 Feb 1957
Debut: 13 Apr 1906 v Chelsea
Position: Full-back
Appearances: 1 **Goals scored:** 0
Seasons: 1905/06
Clubs: Grove Park School, Wrexham Old Boys, Rhostyllen, Wrexham, Druids, Bury, Manchester United, Manchester City

LARS JESPER BLOMQVIST

Country: Sweden
Born: 5 Feb 1974
Debut: 9 Sep 1998 v Charlton Athletic
Position: Left-wing
Appearances: 29 (9) **Goals scored:** 1
Seasons: 1998/99
Clubs: Umea, IFK Gothenburg, AC Milan, Parma, Manchester United, Everton, Charlton Athletic, Djurgarden, Enkoping, Hammarby, Peresbaya 1927

The Swedish international gave Alex Ferguson's United a torrid time in Gothenburg during a Champions League tie in November 1994, with his name written into the manager's notebook on his return home. But first Blomqvist moved from Sweden to Italy in 1996. However, after three seasons in Serie A, Ferguson made his move, bringing him to Manchester for £4.4 million in the summer of 1998.

However, although brought into the squad to provide back-up and competition to Ryan Giggs on the left flank, he was still able to lay claim to a Premiership and a Champions League medal in his first season, with many believing his best was still to come. Sadly, the opportunity was not to arise, as a knee injury during a friendly in Hong Kong during the summer of 1999 effectively brought an end to his United career, as he never played another game for the club, joining Everton in November 2001.

SAMUEL PRINCE BLOTT

Country: England
Born: 1 Jan 1886 **Died:** 1 Jan 1969
Debut: 1 Sep 1909 v Bradford City
Position: Forward
Appearances: 19 **Goals scored:** 2
Seasons: 1909/10 – 1912/13
Clubs: Southend United, Bradford Park Avenue, Southend United, Manchester United, Plymouth Argyle, Newport County,

A Southern League Second Division title winner with Southend United in season 1906/07, Sam Blott joined United in May 1909 following spells with Bradford Park Avenue in 1907/08 and a second spell with Southend the following season. Although he made his United debut at inside-right on the opening day of season 1909/10, he proved to be something of an adaptable individual, filling in at outside-right and both wing-half positions during that first season. His appearances, however, were to be few and far between, and after the war he was transfer listed in May 1919, joining Plymouth Argyle the following month, for a fee of £150.

THOMAS 'TOMMY' BOGAN

Country: Scotland
Born: 18 May 1920 **Died:** 23 Sep 1993
Debut: 8 Oct 1949
Position: Outside-right
Appearances: 33 Goals scored: 7
Seasons: 1948/49 – 1950/51
Clubs: Strathclyde, Blantyre Celtic, Renfrew Juniors, Hibernian, Celtic, Preston North End, Manchester United, Aberdeen, Southampton, Blackburn Rovers, Macclesfield Town

Playing junior football in his native Scotland, Tommy Bogan attracted the attention of many clubs, but was to join Hibernian in September 1943 and in the following two seasons, scored 42 goals in 66 appearances, earning him a place in the Scotland side for the match against England in April 1945. What should have been a memorable day for the Uddington-born player, turned into a nightmare within 45 seconds of the kick-off when he collided with

England goalkeeper Frank Swift and he was carried off, taking no further part in the game.

Joining Celtic in January 1946, he moved south to Preston two years later, before Matt Busby paid £3,500 to take him to Old Trafford in August 1949, where he was to prove a useful addition to the side due to his experience and his forceful style of play combined with the ability to play in any of the forward positions. In a period when Matt Busby was building towards a Championship-winning side, Bogan soon found his outside-right berth under threat and, having made only 33 appearances, he was again on the move, returning to Scotland and joining Aberdeen in March 1951 along with Tommy Lowrie.

JAMES ERNEST 'ERNIE' BOND

Country: England
Born: 4 May 1929
Debut: 18 Aug 1951 v West Bromwich Albion
Position: Outside-left
Appearances: 21 **Goals scored:** 4
Seasons: 1950/51 – 1952/53
Clubs: Preston North End, Leyland Motors, Manchester United, Carlisle United, Queen of the South, Cowdenbeath

Ernie Bond was signed in November 1950 from Leyland Motors, following an 18-month spell as an amateur with his local club, Preston North End. A rather small, slightly built individual, he made his debut in the opening match of season 1951/52 and retained his place for the following five fixtures, going on to win a title medal in that first season. In the following campaign, he was to have only one first-team outing before being transferred to Carlisle United for a fee of £5,000.

ROBERT POLLOCK 'BOB' BONTHRON

Country: Scotland
Born: 1880 **Died:** Unknown
Debut: 5 Sep 1903 v Bristol City
Position: Right-back
Appearances: 134 **Goals scored:** 3
Seasons: 1903/04 – 1906/07

Clubs: Raith Athletic, Raith Rovers, Dundee, Manchester United, Sunderland, Northampton Town, Birmingham, Airdrieonians, Leith Athletic

Bob Bonthron was one of five Scots to make his debut against Bristol City on the opening day of season 1903/04. He was a well-built full-back who gave numerous wingers a difficult time and, during his first two seasons at Clayton, he missed only three games and made a telling contribution during the promotion-winning season of 1905/06. Not a player usually associated with making headlines, his tough tackling, however, certainly brought him to the fore, following the 5-1 victory over Bradford City on 10 February 1906.

The Bradford crowd were unhappy with their favourites having been defeated so comprehensively by United, and at the end of the match a large crowd assembled outside the changing rooms to vent their disapproval. Bonthron, having given the home forwards a hard and unrewarding afternoon, was singled out by the mob for special attention and at one point was physically struck by one spectator, who was immediately arrested by the police.

The walk from the dressing rooms to the waiting transport was no short distance and by the time the United players got to the safety of the vehicles, they had been hit by stones and mud. The United full-back received much more of the mud than his team-mates and was in a sorry-looking state by the time he managed to get into a waiting cab. At the end of season 1906/07, despite having played in 28 of the 38 league fixtures, he decided to leave United and, after considering a number of options, chose to sign for Sunderland.

WILLIAM BOOTH

Country: England
Born: Oct 1880 **Died:** Unknown
Debut: 26 Dec 1900 v Blackpool
Position: Forward
Appearances: 2 **Goals scored:** 0
Seasons: 1900/01
Clubs: Edge Lane, Newton Heath

MARK JOHN BOSNICH

Country: Australia
Born: 13 Jan 1972
Debut: 30 Apr 1990 v Wimbledon
Position: Goalkeeper
Appearances: 38 **Goals scored:** 0
Seasons: 1989/90 – 1990/91 & 1999/2000 – 2000/01
Clubs: Sydney Croatia, Manchester United, Sydney Croatia, Aston Villa, Manchester United, Chelsea, Central Coast Mariners, Sydney Olympic

Originally signed as a non-contract player, he made his debut in April 1990, but he failed to gain a work permit and had to return to his native Australia. Marriage to an English girl allowed him to return, but it was to Aston Villa, where he stayed for seven years before eventually rejoining United in July 1999 as Peter Schmeichel's replacement. His second spell, however, was also brief and although he helped United to the Premier League title and the World Club Championship, he was shown the door in January 2001.

HENRY BOYD

Country: Scotland
Born: 6 May 1868 **Died:** Jul 1935
Debut: 20 Jan 1897 v Blackpool
Position: Forward
Appearances: 62 **Goals scored:** 35
Seasons: 1896/97 – 1898/99
Clubs: Sunderland Albion, Burnley, West Bromwich Albion, Royal Arsenal, Newton Heath, Falkirk

A prominent scorer with Arsenal, netting 32 in 40 league games, Boyd moved north on 18 January 1897 to join Newton Heath for a fee of £45. He made his Heathens debut at centre-forward against Blackpool in an FA Cup replay, scoring the opening goal in a 2–1 win, while a few days later he marked his league debut with a goal in the 6–0 thrashing of Loughborough Town. His goals, four in the remaining nine games, along with his persistent and unselfish play, took the club into the end-of-season Test Matches as Second Division runners-up to Notts County.

Despite failing to gain promotion, Boyd continued to score with much regularity, setting himself a standard that saw him become the first Newton Heath player to score more than 20 goals in one season, with 22 from 30 league games in 1897/98. But no sooner had the new season got under way, than he was suspended for seven days after missing training. Upon being told of the club's decision, he immediately disappeared. He eventually returned, continuing to find the back of the net; however, in mid-March, he was suspended again, for further indiscretions, placed on the transfer list and subsequently never played for the club again.

WILLIAM GILLESPIE 'BILLY' BOYD

Country: Scotland
Born: 27 Nov 1905 **Died:** 14 Dec 1967
Debut: 9 Feb 1935 v Swansea Town
Position: Forward
Appearances: 6 **Goals scored:** 4
Seasons: 1934/35
Clubs: Regent Star, Royal Albert, Larkhill Thistle, Clyde, Sheffield United, Manchester United, Workington, Luton Town, Southampton, Weymouth

THOMAS WILKINSON 'TOMMY' BOYLE

Country: England
Born: 21 Jan 1897 **Died:** Unknown
Debut: 30 Mar 1929 v Derby County
Position: Forward
Appearances: 17 **Goals scored:** 6
Seasons: 1928/29 – 1929/30
Clubs: Sheffield United, Northampton Town, Manchester United, Macclesfield Town, Northampton Town

When he signed for Sheffield United in October 1921, Tommy Boyle was following in his father's footsteps, as Boyle senior had played for the Blades, where he enjoyed FA Cup success in 1899 and 1902. Boyle went on to play over 130 games for the club, scoring 41 goals and was part of the Sheffield United side who won the FA Cup in 1925. Manager Herbert Bamlett splashed out £2,000 to bring Boyle across the Pennines from Sheffield United in March 1929, but following his debut, the former FA Cup winner was not to be seen in first-team action again until the following October. In the summer of 1930 he left Old Trafford and joined Macclesfield, but before kicking a ball in earnest, he moved to Northampton Town a matter of weeks later.

LEONARD 'LEN' BRADBURY

Country: England
Born: Jul 1914 **Died:** 2007
Debut: 28 Jan 1939 v Chelsea
Position: Forward
Appearances: 2 **Goals scored:** 1
Seasons: 1938/39
Clubs: Manchester University, Northwich Victoria, Manchester United, Northwich Victoria, Corinthians, Birmingham University, Moor Green, Corinthians, Manchester University, Manchester United, Old Wittonians

WARREN BRADLEY

Country: England
Born: 20 Jun 1933 **Died:** 6 Jun 2007
Debut: 15 Nov 1958 v Bolton Wanderers
Position: Outside-right
Appearances: 67 **Goals scored:** 21
Seasons: 1957/58 – 1961/62
Clubs: Durham City, Bolton Wanderers, Bishop Auckland, Manchester United, Bury, Northwich Victoria, Macclesfield Town, Bangor City, Macclesfield Town

Warren Bradley arrived at Old Trafford along with two Bishop Auckland team-mates, Bob Hardisty and Derek Lewin, happy to help United in their hour of need following the Munich disaster, hoping perhaps to get a couple of first-team outings, but really expecting to be little more than back-up in the Central League side, but things were to go much better than that.

Although he made the move to Manchester from the north-east, Bradley was actually born in Hyde and had represented Cheshire Schools and the Cheshire County side before furthering his education at Durham University. As an amateur, he played at junior level for Durham City and Bolton Wanderers, before joining Bishop Auckland, where he won amateur England international honours and also two FA Amateur Cup winners' medals.

Upon his move to Manchester, he took up a teaching job in Stretford, but on 10 November 1958, he decided to prolong his stay at Old Trafford, turning professional and making his first-team debut five days later against his previous club, Bolton Wanderers. Despite being only 5'5", he lacked nothing in skill and determination and in his first five league outings, he scored three times, finishing his first season with a dozen goals in 24 games, while also becoming the first player to represent England at both amateur and professional level in the same season, making a goalscoring debut in a 2-2 draw against Italy.

He played an integral part in the rebuilding of the club following Munich, making a further 29 league appearances in his second season, but his stay at Old Trafford was never going to be a long-term one and was to feature in only another 11 first-team games over the next two seasons and on 1 March 1962 he joined Bury, where he spent two seasons before drifting into local non-league football while continuing to pursue his teaching career. He was to return to Old Trafford in later years as one of the founder members of the United Former Players' Association of which he was to become chairman.

ROBERT 'ROBBIE' BRADY

Country: Republic of Ireland
Born: 14 January 1992
Debut: 26 Sep 2012 v Newcastle United
Position: Midfield
Appearances: 0 (1) **Goals scored:** 0
Seasons: 2012/13
Clubs: Manchester United, Hull City (loan), Hull City

HAROLD BRATT

Country: England
Born: 8 Oct 1939
Debut: 2 Nov 1960 v Bradford City
Position: Defender
Appearances: 1 **Goals scored:** 0
Seasons: 1960/61
Clubs: Manchester United, Doncaster Rovers

ALAN BERNARD BRAZIL

Country: Scotland
Born: 15 Jun 1959
Debut: 25 Aug 1984 v Watford
Position: Forward
Appearances: 24 (17) **Goals scored:** 12
Seasons: 1984/85 – 1985/86
Clubs: Ipswich Town, Detroit Express (loan), Tottenham Hotspur, Manchester United, Coventry City, Queens Park Rangers, Witham Town, Chelmsford City, Southend Manor, Bury Town, Stambridge, Chelmsford City, Wivenhoe Town, Wollongong City, FC Baden

Despite playing for Celtic Boys Club in his native Glasgow, Alan Brazil signed for Ipswich Town as an apprentice in August 1975. Following his debut against United in 1977/78, he went on to score 80 goals from his 209 appearances, earning him a £450,000 move to Tottenham Hotspur in March 1983, at a time when it was widely expected that he would actually join Manchester United. His move to United eventually came just over a year later, when, following the £625,000 signing, United manager Ron Atkinson declared that Brazil was 'the player he wanted more than any other, after Bryan Robson'. Such a declaration put undue pressure on the player and he struggled to discover the form of his Portman Road days.

He was often to find himself on the substitutes' bench and only made 17 league starts in his first season. His confidence was also not helped by some of the Old Trafford support, which did not warm to him. During the opening months of the following season, he managed to make the starting line-up only once and it was obvious that his days as a United player were numbered. In January 1986, Coventry City rescued him in a deal which saw Terry Gibson and a cheque for £65,000 go to United. Later in his life, Brazil became a very successful broadcaster on talkSPORT.

DEREK MICHAEL BRAZIL

Country: Republic of Ireland
Born: 14 Dec 1968
Debut: 10 May 1989 v Everton
Position: Defender

Appearances: 0 (2) **Goals scored:** 0
Seasons: 1988/89 – 1989/90
Clubs: Manchester United, Oldham Athletic (loan), Swansea City (loan), Cardiff City, Newport County, Inter Cardiff, Haverfordwest County

JOHN NORMAN 'JACK' BREEDON

Country: England
Born: 29 Dec 1907 **Died:** 12 Dec 1967
Debut: 31 Aug 1935 v Plymouth Argyle
Position: Goalkeeper
Appearances: 35 **Goals scored:** 0
Seasons: 1935/36 – 1938/39
Clubs: Barnsley, Sheffield Wednesday, Manchester United, Burnley

Unfortunately for Jack Breedon, appearances during the Second World War mean very little. Had they been so, his record would have stretched to over 200 games for the club, as he was United's first-choice keeper between 1939 and 1944, clocking up some 164 appearances. He crossed the Pennines to join United from Sheffield Wednesday in the summer of 1935, with a transfer fee of £350 changing hands, making his debut in the opening match of 1935/36. He conceded three goals and immediately found himself dropped, with Jack Hall taking over between the posts for most of that season. He was to make only a handful of appearances until season 1938/39, when he enjoyed his best run in the side, taking over from Tommy Breen. After the war he lost his place again, this time to Jack Crompton and joined Burnley in October 1945.

THOMAS 'TOMMY' BREEN

Country: Ireland/Northern Ireland
Born: 27 Apr 1917 **Died:** 1 Mar 1988
Debut: 28 Nov 1936 v Leeds United
Position: Goalkeeper
Appearances: 71 **Goals scored:** 0
Seasons: 1936/37 – 1938/39
Clubs: Drogheda, Belfast Celtic, Manchester United, Belfast Celtic, Linfield, Shamrock Rovers, Newry Town, Glentoran

Joining United in November 1936 from Belfast Celtic, the Northern Ireland international, although making 71 appearances for the club, has the unwanted distinction of scoring the only own-goal on record direct from a throw-in, throwing the ball into his own net during a 2-2 draw in a fourth round FA Cup tie against Barnsley in January 1938, though he did help United to promotion that season as well. During the Second World War, he returned to Ireland and assisted numerous clubs, but towards the end of 1946, with his contract still held by United and having been made available for transfer at a fee of £1,000 (£1,500 less than what United had paid for him ten years previously), there was much speculation that he was about to return to Manchester, but Breen was content to remain where he was.

SEAMUS ANTHONY 'SHAY' BRENNAN

Country: Republic of Ireland
Born: 6 May 1937 **Died:** 9 Jun 2000
Debut: 19 Feb 1958 v Sheffield Wednesday
Position: Full-back
Appearances: 358 (1) **Goals scored:** 6
Seasons: 1957/58 – 1969/70
Clubs: Manchester United, Waterford United

Brought up in Wythenshawe, South Manchester, Shay Brennan played as an inside-forward for the St John's Old Boys' team in the South Manchester and Wythenshawe League. An eye-catching performance for a League Representative XI against the Manchester Catholic League caught the attention of both United and City scouts, and it was the representatives from the Maine Road club who were first to appear on the Brennan doorstep, but despite the offer of a place on the Manchester City ground staff, the United-supporting youngster decided against signing, in the hope that a similar offer would come from United. A couple of days later, much to his relief, it did.

Signing for Manchester United in April 1955, Brennan progressed through the junior levels of the club in the illustrious company of Duncan Edwards, Eddie Colman, Bobby Charlton and Wilf McGuinness, playing centre-forward in the team that won the FA Youth Cup in season 1954/55. At the time of the Munich Air Disaster, he was still a long way short of the senior side and during the afternoon prior to that memorable Sheffield Wednesday Cup tie afterwards, he played table tennis with friends, completely unaware of Jimmy Murphy's plans to include him in the United starting line-up. Start he did, scoring twice in the famous 3-0 victory.

In 1962, he was named in England's pool of 40 for the 1962 World Cup, following two appearances for an FA XI. However, he failed to make the final squad, but three years later, he became the first player to be capped by the Republic of Ireland under the parentage ruling. By the late 1960s, Brennan's United first-team league appearances were becoming fewer, with only 16 in the title-winning season of 1966/67 and 13 in 1967/68. The European Cup run of that latter season saw him make only three appearances, which fortunately for him included the semi-finals and final.

Following that European Cup win, his career was on a downward slope, with only 13 starts made during 1968/69 and eight the following year. At the end of 1969/70, he was given a free transfer by the club and, upon Matt Busby's suggestion, became player-manager of League of Ireland side Waterford. During season 1970/71, he was awarded a life pension by Manchester United for his loyal years of service and in August 1986, his former club played a Shamrock Rovers XI in a specially arranged testimonial match for him. A place in either of the full-back positions in the United All-Time Great XI would unfortunately pass Shay Brennan by, but you would be hard pushed to find a more popular player at Manchester United during his time there.

FRANK BERNARD BRETT

Country: England
Born: 10 Mar 1899 **Died:** 21 Jul 1988
Debut: 27 Aug 1921 v Everton
Position: Full-back
Appearances: 10 **Goals scored:** 0
Seasons: 1921/22
Clubs: Aston Villa, Manchester United, Aston Villa, Northampton Town, Brighton & Hove Albion, Tunbridge Wells Rangers, Hove FC

Frank Brett joined Redditch as a professional in 1920, having been on Aston Villa's books as an amateur. United, noticing his ability in the local Birmingham League, agreed a fee of £300 to take him to Old Trafford, but as soon as Villa heard about the proposed transfer, they declared that he was still, in effect, their player, even though they had allowed him to join Redditch without a whisper. United ignored Villa's claims, but soon found themselves in front of the Football Association on a charge of registering a player before they had obtained the agreement of his former club and were duly fined ten guineas. Beginning season 1921/22 as United's first choice right-back, he was to play only ten games that relegation season before returning to the Midlands in August 1922 and rather surprisingly rejoining Aston Villa.

WILLIAM RONALD 'RONNIE' BRIGGS

Country: Northern Ireland
Born: 29 Mar 1943 **Died:** 28 Aug 2008
Debut: 21 Jan 1961 v Leicester City
Position: Goalkeeper
Appearances: 11 **Goals scored:** 0
Seasons: 1960/61 – 1961/62
Clubs: Manchester United, Swansea Town, Bristol Rovers

Born in Belfast, Ronnie Briggs graduated through the Boyland Youth side in the city, before joining Manchester United, signing professional forms in March 1960. He made his debut as a 17-year-old against Leicester City, a 6-0 defeat, but due to injuries Matt Busby was forced to keep the youngster in the side for the FA Cup tie at Sheffield Wednesday. A spirited performance saw United earn a creditable draw, with hopes of success in the replay at Old Trafford, but unfortunately for Briggs in particular, the 65,243 crowd squeezed into Old Trafford witnessed a humiliating 90 minutes, with Wednesday running out 7-2 winners.

For many young goalkeepers, losing 14 goals in your initial three first-team games would have been soul-destroying, but Briggs returned to first-team duty with United, almost a year after his Sheffield Wednesday nightmare. His reappearance saw him concede only ten goals in his eight games, but following the 3-2 defeat by Arsenal on 16 April 1962, Briggs returned to the reserve team, never to appear in the first XI again. He was, however, to remain at Old Trafford until May 1964, when, with United well covered in the goalkeeping department, he joined Swansea Town.

WILLIAM HENRY BROOKS

Country: England
Born: Jul 1873 **Died:** Unknown
Debut: 22 Oct 1898 v Loughborough Town
Position: Forward
Appearances: 3 **Goals scored:** 3
Seasons: 1898/99
Clubs: Stalybridge Rovers, Newton Heath, Stalybridge Rovers, Newton Heath, Stalybridge Rovers

ALBERT HENRY BROOME

Country: England
Born: 30 May 1900 **Died:** Dec 1989
Debut: 28 Apr 1923 v Barnsley
Position: Forward
Appearances: 1 **Goals scored:** 0
Seasons: 1922/23
Clubs: Northern Nomads, Oldham Athletic, Manchester United, Oldham Athletic, Welshpool, Stockport County, Mossley

HERBERT C. BROOMFIELD

Country: England
Born: 11 Dec 1878 **Died:** Unknown
Debut: 21 Mar 1908 v Arsenal
Position: Goalkeeper
Appearances: 9 **Goals scored:** 0
Seasons: 1907/08
Clubs: Norwich Wednesday, Northwich Victoria, Bolton Wanderers, Manchester City, Manchester United

JAMES BROWN

Country: Scotland
Born: Unknown **Died:** Unknown
Debut: 3 Sep 1892 v Blackburn Rovers
Position: Full-back

Appearances: 7 **Goals scored:** 0
Seasons: 1892/93
Clubs: Dundee Our Boys, Newton Heath, Dundee

JAMES BROWN

Country: Scotland/USA
Born: 31 Dec 1908 **Died:** 9 Nov 1994
Debut: 17 Sep 1932 v Grimsby Town
Position: Winger
Appearances: 41 **Goals scored:** 17
Seasons: 1932/33 – 1933/34
Clubs: Loans Athletic Juniors, Plainfield, Bayonne Rovers, Newark Skeeters, New York Giants, Brooklyn Wanderers, Manchester United, Brentford, Tottenham Hotspur, Guildford City, Clydebank

In 1927, at the age of 18, James Brown decided to leave not just Kilmarnock but Scotland, and emigrated to America to work as a blacksmith's striker. He joined the New Jersey-based Bayonne Rovers, and his performances were of a standard that did not go unnoticed, even representing America in the 1930 World Cup. Two years later, he decided to return home and news of his impending arrival soon spread swiftly among the football world. In Manchester, United boss Scott Duncan was well aware of Brown's decision and made discreet enquiries as to his route and time of expected arrival.

Duncan then set off for Northern Ireland in what was indeed an undercover mission of extreme secrecy, akin to something from a spy novel. Arriving in Londonderry, with Brown's liner, the SS *Caledonia*, still on the high seas, Duncan managed to make radio contact with the ship, and contacted him to make sure no rival club could secure his signature first. When the liner docked, Scott Duncan was waiting as Brown walked down the gangplank and the signing was agreed. Although scoring on his debut, he was mainly employed in the reserves and eventually moved to Brentford in the summer of 1934, having helped keep the Reds out of the Third Division.

JAMES BROWN

Country: Scotland
Born: 1907 **Died:** Unknown
Debut: 31 Aug 1935 v Plymouth Argyle
Position: Half-back
Appearances: 110 **Goals scored:** 1
Seasons: 1935/36 – 1938/39
Clubs: East Fife, Burnley, Manchester United, Bradford City

To prise James Brown away from their Lancashire neighbours Burnley, United had to pay £1,000, but his sterling displays, as captain throughout 1935/36, soon indicated that it had been money well spent, as he led the side to promotion. Fifty-nine appearances over the following two seasons added to this opinion, even if they involved relegation and promotion again, but only three in the first month of season 1938/39 signalled that his days at Old Trafford were numbered and in February 1939, he moved to Bradford City.

ROBERT BERESFORD 'BERRY' BROWN

Country: England
Born: 6 Sep 1927 **Died:** Jul 2001
Debut: 31 Jan 1948 v Sheffield United
Position: Goalkeeper
Appearances: 4 **Goals scored:** 0
Seasons: 1946/47 – 1948/49
Clubs: Manchester United, Doncaster Rovers, Hartlepools United

WESLEY 'WES' BROWN

Country: England
Born: 13 Oct 1979
Debut: 4 May 1998 v Leeds United
Position: Defender
Appearances: 313 (49) **Goals scored:** 5
Seasons: 1997/98 – 2010/11
Clubs: Manchester United, Sunderland

A superbly talented defender who could perform equally well either at full-back or in the middle of the back four, but despite helping United to five league titles, one FA Cup, one League Cup and the Champions League, as well as winning 23 England caps, his career was often blighted by injuries.

Longsight born, he was spotted as a 12-year-old by former United winger Harry McShane and he made his United debut seven years later and went on to receive his England call-up in quick time, after only a meagre 12 league starts. His most successful season came in 2007/08, when he took his chance in the absence of the injured Gary Neville to make the right-back slot his own. Along with Patrice Evra, Rio Ferdinand, Nemanja Vidić and goalkeeper Edwin van der Sar, he formed part of a solid defensive unit that rarely missed a game. That season, United conceded just 22 goals in the league and he was part of the team that secured United's third European champions title at the Luzhniki Stadium. If it had not been for injuries, Wes Brown could have achieved much more for both club and country, but with his opportunities becoming fewer with United, he joined Sunderland in July 2011 for an undisclosed fee.

WILLIAM 'RIMMER' BROWN

Country: England
Born: Unknown **Died:** Unknown
Debut: 1 Sep 1896 v Gainsborough Trinity
Position: Forward
Appearances: 7 **Goals scored:** 2
Seasons: 1896/97
Clubs: Stalybridge Rovers, Chester, Newton Heath, Stockport County

STEVE ROGER BRUCE

Country: England
Born: 31 Dec 1960
Debut: 19 Dec 1987 v Portsmouth
Position: Centre-back
Appearances: 411 (3) **Goals scored:** 51
Seasons: 1987/88 – 1995/96
Clubs: Gillingham, Norwich City, Manchester United, Birmingham City, Sheffield United

Steve Bruce shared his birthday with Sir Alex Ferguson, and was born in Corbridge, just outside Newcastle, growing up a fan of the Magpies. A product of the Wallsend Boys Club, like Peter Beardsley, he was deemed by many scouts to be too small. He was about to take up a job at the Swan Hunter shipyards, his dream of professional football seemingly gone, when he was spotted by Gillingham while playing in a tournament at Charterhouse School. After six years at the Kent club, he joined Norwich City in 1984.

By the time he became an £825,000 signing for United in December 1987, Steve Bruce was a no-nonsense central defender, and would soon form a perfect partnership with Gary Pallister, as United recaptured the trophy-winning days of old. An England Youth international with Gillingham and an England B cap with Norwich, he was unfortunate never to get a full international call-up, despite his success with United, winning three league medals, two FA Cups, one League Cup and one European Cup-Winners' Cup.

He was denied a goal in the final of the latter competition in 1991, when Mark Hughes finished off his goalbound effort. It was a season that saw him score an astonishing 19 goals in all competitions, including 11 penalties, a total that is considered a record for a defender. Along with Brian McClair, he was even joint top-scorer in the league, with 13. But if it is goals that one is thinking about, then Bruce will always be remembered for his two last-gasp headers against Sheffield Wednesday that did so much in nudging United to that initial 1992/93 title. By then, he was often captaining the side, when Bryan Robson did not play, and the pair both raised the Premier League trophy in 1993

By 1996, at the age of 35, his appearances were numbered and he decided to move on, joining Birmingham City on a free transfer before finishing his career at Sheffield United as a player-manager. Since then, he has managed numerous clubs, with his longest spell at Birmingham City between 2001 and 2007. He took charge of Hull City in the summer of 2012, and at the end of the season he had earned promotion to the Premier League.

WILLIAM 'BILLY' BRYANT

Country: England
Born: 26 Nov 1913 **Died:** 25 Dec 1975
Debut: 3 Nov 1934 v Blackpool

Position: Outside-right
Appearances: 157 **Goals scored:** 42
Seasons: 1934/35 – 1938/39
Clubs: Wolverhampton Wanderers, Wrexham, Manchester United, Bradford City, Altrincham, Stalybridge Celtic

Billy Bryant was a north-easterner who left the Racecourse Ground, Wrexham for Old Trafford in October 1934 for £1,000, making his debut at outside-right at Blackpool on 3 November, scoring in the 2-1 win. Over the course of the following five seasons, during which he won a Second Division Championship medal in 1935/36, he turned in countless commendable displays, his accuracy creating numerous scoring opportunities for his fellow forwards.

The Second World War brought an end to his career in the Football League, but he continued playing during the hostilities for United, adding a further 172 appearances and 49 goals to his total of 160 appearances and 44 goals during peace-time football.

WILLIAM BRYANT

Country: England
Born: 1874 **Died:** 25 Oct 1918
Debut: 1 Sep 1896 v Gainsborough Trinity
Position: Forward
Appearances: 127 **Goals scored:** 33
Seasons: 1896/97 – 1899/1900
Clubs: Chesterfield, Rotherham Town, Newton Heath, Blackburn Rovers

William Bryant moved to Newton Heath in April 1896 after Rotherham Town went out of existence, playing consistently over the course of his first three seasons, missing only four games during that time. Like his namesake from a few decades later, he was not simply content with dribbling down the wing and crossing the ball, he enjoyed cutting inside in the search for scoring opportunities of his own, scoring 33 goals in his 127 games (including two hat-tricks in the 1898/99 season), winning Football League honours in November 1897. In his last season with the Heathens, his appearances were somewhat limited and in April 1900 he joined Blackburn Rovers for a fee of £50.

GEORGE BUCHAN

Country: Scotland
Born: 2 May 1950
Debut: 15 Sep 1973 v West Ham United
Position: Right-wing
Appearances: 0 (4) **Goals scored:** 0
Seasons: 1973/74
Clubs: Aberdeen, Manchester United, Bury, Mossley

MARTIN McLEAN BUCHAN

Country: Scotland
Born: 6 Mar 1949
Debut: 4 Mar 1972 v Tottenham Hotspur
Position: Centre-back
Appearances: 456 **Goals scored:** 4
Seasons: 1971/72 – 1982/83
Clubs: Aberdeen, Manchester United, Oldham Athletic

A token fee of £250 took Martin Buchan from Banks O' Dee to Aberdeen in 1966 and by 1970 he was leading the Dons to a 3-1 Scottish Cup success over Celtic, becoming the youngest player ever to achieve such an honour. A year later, in 1971, he was voted Scottish Player of the Year, while also winning the first of his 34 full Scotland caps against Portugal.

United at this point were a team in severe need of rebuilding and manager Frank O'Farrell cast his eyes northwards and signed the Aberdeen captain on 29 February 1972 for a then club record of £125,000. It was to prove money well spent, as Buchan quickly settled at Old Trafford, becoming an integral part of the team and over the next 11 years, he was to make the No.6 shirt his own, although all his appearances during his initial two months at the club were made with the No.4 on his back.

He was soon regarded as United's most influential player, with his cool, no-nonsense approach to the game along with his on-the-field leadership and, upon his appointment as manager, Tommy Docherty, having given Buchan his first full Scotland cap in 1972, had no hesitation in appointing him team captain. The classy defender was to guide United to both the Second Division Championship in 1975 and the FA Cup in 1977, becoming the first player to captain a side to the latter and also the Scottish equivalent. He rarely scored, but when he did they were often spectacular long-range efforts.

He was a model professional, but was not afraid to speak up to anyone in authority if he thought that they were wrong; he also expected his team-mates to show a similar dedication to the game as he did, something that was clearly displayed during a First Division encounter against Coventry City when he unceremoniously slapped team-mate Gordon Hill across the head for some slack defending. On another occasion, he refused to hand over his passport to club officials prior to a pre-season tour, telling them that he was quite capable of looking after it himself.

An injury during season 1980/81 put him out of action for 12 games and the following season he again missed games because of a similar problem. Season 1982/83 saw him start only three games, spread between the opening four months of the season and because he now felt that he could not reach the high standards that he set himself, he decided to leave United, joining Oldham on a free transfer. In 1985, he had a brief spell as manager of Burnley.

HERBERT EDWARD WILLIAM 'TED' BUCKLE

Country: England
Born: 28 Oct 1924 **Died:** 14 Jun 1990
Debut: 4 Jan 1947 v Charlton Athletic
Position: Outside-forward
Appearances: 24 **Goals scored:** 7
Seasons: 1946/47 – 1949/50
Clubs: Manchester United, Everton, Exeter City, Prestatyn, Dolgellau

While serving in the Royal Navy, Ted Buckle played junior football in the Warrington area, where he came to the attention of United. He was originally signed as an amateur in October 1945, playing a handful of reserve-team games before signing professional forms a month later, making his debut at Leeds and scoring once in the 3-3 draw. In the return fixture seven days later at Old Trafford he scored two in a 6-1 win.

His ability to play in any of the forward positions made him an ideal addition to the squad, but with so many excellent players at the club at this time, his opportunities were few and far between and in November 1949 he joined Everton for a fee of £6,500, making his debut against United, less than 18 hours after joining the Goodison Park side.

FRANKLIN CHARLES 'FRANK' BUCKLEY

Country: England
Born: 9 Nov 1882 **Died:** 22 Dec 1964
Debut: 29 Sep 1906 v Derby County
Position: Defender
Appearances: 3 **Goals scored:** 0
Seasons: 1906/07
Clubs: Aston Villa, Brighton & Hove Albion, Manchester United, Manchester City, Aston Villa, Manchester City, Birmingham, Derby County, Bradford City

Although he played only three games for United, after the First World War (he was wounded in the Battle of the Somme) Major Frank Buckley went on to spend 36 years as a football manager, including 17 years in charge of Wolverhampton Wanderers, where he became one of the first managers to instigate a proper youth policy before the Second World War, and reached the 1939 FA Cup final. After the war, he also spent five years in charge of Leeds United.

JAMES 'JIMMY' BULLOCK

Country: England
Born: 25 Mar 1902 **Died:** 9 Mar 1977
Debut: 20 Sep 1930 v Sheffield Wednesday
Position: Forward
Appearances: 10 **Goals scored:** 3
Seasons: 1930/31
Clubs: Gorton, Crewe Alexandra, Manchester City, Crewe Alexandra, Southampton, Chesterfield, Manchester United, Dundalk, Llanelli, Hyde United

United paid £1,250 in the hope that Gorton-born Jimmy Bullock's goals could help them consolidate their position in the First Division in 1930/31, having scored 31 in 35 games with Chesterfield. A difficult task, as they had lost all six of their opening fixtures, conceding 29 goals in the process, including 19 in three successive games. Bullock's arrival did little to improve things, with United failing to score in his first two outings, sending the new arrival into the reserve side.

He soon found himself back in the first team, scoring three against Leicester, but it was not enough to ensure a regular place and a handful of games later he was back in the reserves. Surprisingly United called on his services on just another two occasions as they struggled to maintain their First Division status, the lack of goals a telling factor, and in the 1931 close season was transfer listed at £1,000. There was no interest, so he crossed the Irish Sea and joined Dundalk.

WILLIAM BUNCE

Country: England
Born: Apr 1877 **Died:** Unknown
Debut: 4 Oct 1902 v Chesterfield
Position: Full-back
Appearances: 2 **Goals scored:** 0
Seasons: 1902/03
Clubs: Rochdale Athletic, Stockport County, Manchester United

HERBERT BURGESS

Country: England
Born: 1 Jan 1883 **Died:** Jul 1954
Debut: 1 Jan 1907 v Aston Villa
Position: Left-back
Appearances: 54 **Goals scored:** 0
Seasons: 1906/07 – 1909/10
Clubs: Gorton St Francis, Openshaw United, Edge Lane, Moss Side, Glossop, Manchester City, Manchester United

Herbert Burgess was one of the select band of players who have represented both Manchester United and Manchester City. With the latter, he was to win an FA Cup medal in 1904 along with England and Football League caps, but with the club suspected of financial irregularities, they were hauled before the Football Association and 17 players, including Herbert Burgess, were fined and suspended until January 1907.

Ernest Mangnall, the United manager, stepped in and signed him and he went straight into the United side against Aston Villa on New Year's Day 1907, adding stability to the defence and playing his part in the club's first Football League success the following season. United were to triumph again in 1909, lifting the FA Cup for the first time, but Herbert Burgess was not a member of the triumphant XI as he was injured in the third game of that 1908/09 season. Although he reappeared some seven games later at Sunderland on 31 October, he lasted only seven minutes before once again being forced to leave the field.

It was Christmas Day 1909 before Burgess reappeared in the United first team, but this was to be his final outing for the club, the knee injury forcing him into early retirement. At the start of his post-football days, he became a publican, but the smell of the liniment and the dubbin proved too strong and he returned to the game, moving overseas to come out of retirement with Kristiania of Denmark, before taking over the manager's job at MTK Budapest. He later moved to Italy in the 1920s, enjoying spells with Padova (twice), Milan and Roma, before returning to Britain in October 1934.

RONALD STEWART 'RONNIE' BURKE

Country: England
Born: 13 Aug 1921 **Died:** Dec 2003
Debut: 26 Oct 1946 v Sunderland
Position: Forward
Appearances: 35 **Goals scored:** 23
Seasons: 1946/47 – 1948/49
Clubs: Manchester United, Huddersfield Town, Rotherham United, Exeter City, Tunbridge Wells United, Biggleswade Town

While playing in an RAF match in Italy, Ronnie Burke caught the eye of Jimmy Murphy and, at the end of the war, despite interest from numerous other clubs, Murphy persuaded Burke to join United, signing first as an amateur in May 1946 and then as a professional three months later. Opportunities during his first season at the club were few and far between, though he made his debut in a 3-0 home defeat against Sunderland, but he did not appear again until January. He scored twice in a 5-1 win over Charlton Athletic, going on to play in 11 of the final 14 games of the season, scoring seven times.

He could perhaps consider himself unfortunate to be at Old Trafford at the same time as Jack Rowley, as there was no way that he could replace such a prolific individual. It was certainly frustrating for the consistent, whole-hearted player and with only 21 appearances over the next couple of seasons, interest from Huddersfield Town, along with the guarantee of first-team football, saw him agree to move to Yorkshire in the summer of 1949, with a fee of £16,000 changing hands.

THOMAS 'TOM' BURKE

Country: Wales
Born: 1862 **Died:** 1914
Debut: 30 Oct 1886 v Fleetwood Rangers
Position: Half-back
Appearances: 1 **Goals scored:** 0
Seasons: 1886/87
Clubs: Wrexham Grosvenor, Wrexham Feb, Wrexham Olympic, Liverpool Cambrians, Newton Heath, Wrexham Victoria

FRANCIS S. BURNS

Country: Scotland
Born: 17 Oct 1948
Debut: 2 Sep 1967 v West Ham United
Position: Left-back
Appearances: 143 (13) **Goals scored:** 7
Seasons: 1965/66 – 1971/72
Clubs: Manchester United, Southampton, Preston North End, Shamrock Rovers

Francis Burns had represented Lanarkshire Schools and captained Scotland Schoolboys on three occasions before joining Manchester United as an amateur upon leaving school in June 1964, signing as a professional the following year. A place on the Australian tour of 1967 saw him make his first-team bow and, having switched from half-back to full-back, he did not have long to wait for his opportunity in the league side, as an injury to Shay Brennan in only the third game of season 1967/68, saw him make his debut at West Ham. He remained first-choice left-back, both in the league and in Europe, but with the second leg of the European Cup semi-final against Real Madrid on the horizon, manager Matt Busby dealt the youngster a killer blow.

Although he had played his part in the first-leg victory against Madrid at Old Trafford, Busby left him out of the return, playing the more experienced Shay Brennan at right-back and switching Tony Dunne back to the left side. This pairing remained for the final, leaving Francis Burns a very disappointed spectator on the sidelines. Injuries caused him to miss most of 1968/69, but he bounced back to win Scottish international honours. Three cartilage operations in 18 months didn't help his United career, and season 1970/71 and 1971/72 saw his opportunities limited to 37 league appearances over the two campaigns. In the summer of 1972, Southampton made an offer of £50,000 for him, which United accepted, and he was soon on his way to the south coast before spending eight years at Preston, where he was Bobby Charlton's first signing.

NICHOLAS 'NICKY' BUTT

Country: England
Born: 21 Jan 1975
Debut: 21 Nov 1992 v Oldham Athletic
Position: Midfield
Appearances: 307 (80) **Goals scored:** 26
Seasons: 1992/93 – 2003/04
Clubs: Manchester United, Newcastle United, Birmingham City (loan), South China

Gorton-born midfielder Nicky Butt caught the eye as a youngster with his aggressive play and eye for goal in the United junior sides. He came to prominence at Boundary Park in Oldham, where he played alongside Paul Scholes and the Neville brothers, and unsurprisingly the club did exceptionally well. He was given a trial at United at 13, and signed apprentice forms in July 1991. He was a key part of the famed 'Class of '92', winning the FA Youth Cup that year, playing in a group that also included Beckham, Giggs, the Nevilles and Scholes.

Fellow youth teamer Robbie Savage described him as a 'hardcore Manc' and it was little surprise when he made his first-team debut in November 1992 against Oldham Athletic, coming on as substitute to replace Paul Ince, the man whose place he was eventually to take on a more regular basis in 1995. With Roy Keane he formed a fearsome partnership in the centre of midfield, helping a new-look side to the Double in 1996. He went on to win a total of six Premiership and three FA Cup medals, plus one for the Champions League. He was part of the Treble-winning side of 1999, though he was rested for the FA Cup final that year, as both Keane and Scholes were suspended for the Champions League final that followed. He achieved a glowing list of honours that also included 39 full England caps, briefly becoming one of the most influential players in the national side.

With a number of talented midfield players at Old Trafford, he was to find his opportunities limited and in January 2004, he handed in a transfer request, eventually moving to Newcastle United for a fee of £2.5 million in July. He went on to become captain of the Magpies, and after he retired (following a brief spell in China) he returned to United to develop a coaching career.

ALEXANDER BŰTTNER

Country: Netherlands
Born: 11 Feb 1989
Debut: 15 Sep 2012 v Wigan
Position: Left-back
Appearances: 12 (1) **Goals scored:** 2
Seasons: 2012/13 – present
Clubs: Ajax, Vitesse Arnhem, Manchester United

It was something of a dream first-team debut for Alexander Bűttner in the red of United, making the second and scoring the third goal in the 4-0 defeat of Wigan Athletic on 15 September 2012. The Dutchman from Doetinchem, who had begun his career with the famed Ajax youth set-up, became another of Sir Alex Ferguson's 'out of the blue' transfer deals, when he penned a five-year deal with United on 21 August following his £3.9 million transfer from Vitesse Arnhem.

There had been interest in the Dutch Under-20 and Under-21 international from a number of clubs, including Fulham, Queens Park Rangers, Hanover and Werder Bremen, with Southampton also on the verge of signing him until the move collapsed. He had a promising debut season, used largely as back-up to Patrice Evra.

DAVID BYRNE

Country: Ireland
Born: 28 Apr 1905 **Died:** May 1990
Debut: 21 Oct 1933 v Bury
Position: Forward
Appearances: 4 **Goals scored:** 3
Seasons: 1933/34
Clubs: St Brendan's, Shamrock Rovers, Bradford City, Shelbourne, Sheffield United, Shamrock Rovers, Manchester United, Coleraine, Larne, Shamrock Rovers

ROGER WILLIAM BYRNE

Country: England
Born: 8 Feb 1929 **Died:** 6 Feb 1958
Debut: 24 Nov 1951 v Liverpool
Position: Defender
Appearances: 280 **Goals scored:** 20
Seasons: 1951/52 – 1957/58
Clubs: Manchester United

One vital ingredient of being a captain is having the respect of those around you and that was certainly something that Roger Byrne had as the leader of Matt Busby's mid-1950s side, making him an ideal successor to Johnny Carey. Gorton-born, the talent he required to make the breakthrough to Football League level was not as obvious as that of many other youngsters and certainly not to the members of the selection committee at his RAF station where he was doing his national service, as he was passed over even for their football team, having to make do with a place in the rugby side.

He was 20 years old before he was signed by United in March 1949, playing in various positions in the junior sides before making his first-team debut at Liverpool, as did Jackie Blanchflower, on 24 November 1951, replacing Billy Redman at left-back. 'No one did better than Byrne,' penned the *Guardian* correspondent, who went on to praise his kicking and positional work, while also writing that he 'in at least one instance showed the coolness of Carey himself'.

Matt Busby must have thought likewise, as the young defender held down his place on the left side of the defence for the following 18 games, before he was to suffer something of a cultural change. With United pushing for the First Division title, Busby was struggling to find the right outside-left and turned to Byrne to fill the No.11 shirt and he became an instant success, scoring seven goals in the final half dozen games of the season as United claimed their first post-war Championship.

But it was as a defender that Byrne envisaged his place in the United set-up and he was disappointed to start season 1952/53 at outside-left, playing seven of the opening nine fixtures in that position. A look at the United statistics for the 1952/53 season will show that the name of Byrne was missing for two games at the start of October, but this was not due to injury or loss of form. So strongly did he feel about being asked to play, in his opinion, out of position, that he asked for a transfer, hence his omission from the United line-up. Few would have challenged Busby's authority, but Byrne had no qualms about doing so and the manager eventually stood down and reinstated his unhappy player to his preferred left-back position.

He was an intelligent defender who read the game extremely well, and his speed was a match for any winger, which also gave him the opportunities to become one of the first of the overlapping full-backs. As a captain, he was firm but fair, with a maturity that was required to guide his younger team-mates along the road to success. By 1954, England manager Walter Winterbottom had introduced him to the international set-up, giving him his first cap against Scotland in April of that year, the first in a run of 33 consecutive games for his country, a record which still stands today.

From his debut until February 1958, the name of Byrne was virtually an ever-present in Matt Busby's team selections, missing no more than an odd game through injury and international selection, but he did almost suffer a prolonged spell on the sidelines, with Matt Busby, no more than a few yards away, oblivious to the fact. One morning while having breakfast in his Kings Road home, Busby and his wife Jean heard a loud crash from outside their house. Looking out to see what had caused the noise, Jean Busby discovered a car had demolished their garden wall, with the United captain sitting at the wheel. Thankfully the United captain was unhurt, the wall, like most opponents, coming out second best.

Roger Byrne guided his young charges to the First Division Championship in 1956 and 1957, but was denied FA Cup success at Wembley in 1957 due to an injury to goalkeeper Ray Wood, which saw United play for some time with ten men against a strong Aston Villa side. He also led them on their European crusade, losing out to the masterly Real Madrid in 1957, but determined to conquer the continent the following year, building on their superiority at home and lessons learned in the previous campaign. Sadly, it all came to a grinding halt on the runway at Munich in February 1958 when Roger perished along with seven of his team-mates. The 28-year-old United captain was never to hear the news that awaited him back in Manchester, that he was to become a father for the first time.

JAMES CAIRNS

Country: Unknown
Born: Unknown **Died:** Unknown
Debut: 15 Apr 1895 v Bury
Position: Full-back
Appearances: 1 **Goals scored:** 0
Seasons: 1894/95
Clubs: Ardwick, Newton Heath

JAMES 'JIM' CAIRNS

Country: Scotland
Born: Unknown **Died:** Unknown
Debut: 8 Oct 1898 v Burslem Port Vale
Position: Inside-right
Appearances: 1 **Goals scored:** 0
Seasons: 1898/99
Clubs: Stevenson Thistle, Glossop North End, Lincoln City, Newton Heath, Berry's Association

FRAIZER LEE CAMPBELL

Country: England
Born: 13 Sep 1987
Debut: 19 Aug 2007 v Manchester City
Position: Forward
Appearances: 1 (3) **Goals scored:** 0
Seasons: 2007/08 – 2008/09
Clubs: Manchester United, Royal Antwerp (loan), Hull City (loan), Tottenham Hotspur (loan), Sunderland, Cardiff City

Having come through the ranks at Old Trafford, the Huddersfield-born striker was unable to establish himself in the United first team, though he did come on as a substitute in the 2008 Community Shield. Soon after, he moved to Spurs on a season-long loan as part of the deal that brought Dimitar Berbatov to United. A year later he was sold to Sunderland for £3.5 million. He moved to Cardiff City in January 2013, helping them to promotion to the Premier League.

WILLIAM CECIL CAMPBELL

Country: Scotland
Born: 25 Oct 1865 **Died:** Unknown
Debut: 25 Nov 1893 v Sheffield United
Position: Forward
Appearances: 5 **Goals scored:** 1
Seasons: 1893/94
Clubs: Royal Arsenal, Preston North End, Middlesbrough, Darwen, Blackburn Rovers, Newton Heath, Notts County, Newark, Everton

ERIC DANIEL PIERRE CANTONA

Country: France
Born: 24 May 1966
Debut: 6 Dec 1992 v Manchester City
Position: Forward
Appearances: 184 (1) **Goals scored:** 82
Seasons: 1992/93 – 1996/97
Clubs: Auxerre, Martigues (loan), Marseille, Bordeaux (loan), Montpellier (loan), Nimes, Leeds United, Manchester United

Few footballers can have made as much of an impact on a club as Eric Cantona did with Manchester United. Certainly, no individual's name rings out from the terraces and stands on a regular basis more than that of the enigmatic Frenchman.

His career began in the lower regions of French football with his local side SO Caillolais before joining Auxerre in 1981, but it was not long before controversy arose. After joining Marseille in 1988, he was suspended for three months following a dangerous tackle in a game against Nantes and the following year he was banned from international matches for comments made on television in relation to the national coach and soon afterwards kicked the ball into the crowd and tore off his shirt after being substituted during a friendly. On loan at Montpellier, having failed to settle in Marseille, he caused a near rebellion after throwing his boots at a team-mate, but helped them win the French Cup, returning to Marseille where he won a French League medal.

Having joined Nimes, a ball-throwing incident at a referee saw him banned for a month in December 1991, but at the disciplinary hearing it was increased to two months after he called the committee 'idiots'. He announced his retirement from the game soon afterwards.

Liverpool were made aware of his availability, while a week's trial with Sheffield Wednesday came to nothing, so Leeds United manager Howard Wilkinson eventually decided Cantona was worth the £900,000 gamble. In England he gained a new lease of life and was pivotal in the Elland Road side's First Division Championship success in 1991/92, but it was an enquiry from Leeds regarding the availability of Denis Irwin that saw Cantona arrive at Old Trafford for a bargain fee of £1.2 million in November 1992. Many fans would argue it was the best piece of business Alex Ferguson ever did. It is strange to contemplate that the deal might never had gone ahead if Dion Dublin hadn't been badly injured and that the club were also reported to be considering a move for David Hirst of Sheffield Wednesday.

As the weeks and months rolled on, the goals and genius shone through, everyone was happy with his contribution to the cause and if he could play a part in any trophy success, well and good. But Cantona was to give us more. Much more. The crowd warmed to him. His team-mates accepted him and his manager gave him the stage he craved, allowing him a free hand, while at the same time putting an arm around his shoulders when it was required. Cantona responded in kind. He now had a sense of belonging.

In that first season, United won the title by ten points, Cantona becoming the first player to lift consecutive titles with different clubs. Twelve months later the trophy was retained, with the FA Cup added for good measure, but still the Frenchman, with his upturned collar, walked on the wild side. Fined for spitting at a fan on his return to Elland Road, successive sendings-off against Swindon and Arsenal brought a five-game ban in 1994. Worse was to follow in January 1995, when he attacked a supporter in the crowd at Crystal Palace following yet another sending-off.

United immediately suspended him for the remaining four months of the season, but the FA increased this to eight months, plus a £20,000 fine. A two-week prison sentence was commuted to 120 hours' community service. Considering quitting the game, he returned to Paris and it was only the persuasive powers of Alex Ferguson that got him to return to Manchester. It was a suspension that arguably cost United the Championship, but the following season the Reds regained the title, with Cantona scoring the only goal in the FA Cup final victory over Liverpool. Despite his indiscretions, he was also voted the Football Writers' Footballer of the Year.

Named as captain for 1996/97, Cantona announced his retirement at the end of the season, bringing to a close the memorable and incident-filled career of one of the biggest names in the history of the club and the hero of the modern-day United supporters.

NOEL CANTWELL

Country: Republic of Ireland
Born: 28 Feb 1932 **Died:** 8 Sep 2005
Debut: 26 Nov 1960 v Cardiff City
Position: Full-back
Appearances: 146 **Goals scored:** 8
Seasons: 1960/61 – 1966/67
Clubs: Western Rovers, Cork Athletic, West Ham United, Manchester United

Noel Cantwell left the Republic of Ireland as a 20-year-old in 1952, joining West Ham United. A year later, he was winning the first of his 36 Republic of Ireland international caps, against Luxembourg. Season 1957/58 saw the Hammers lift the Second Division title and Cantwell's performances soon caught the attention of Matt Busby, who was still in the process of team-building following the Munich disaster, with the United manager paying £29,500 to prise him away from London's East End in November 1960.

He was quick to settle in the north of England and his arrival helped to strengthen the United defence. Following his United debut in a friendly against Bayern Munich on 21 November, he took over the left-back position for the trip to Cardiff five days later, his presence doing little to prevent a 3-0 defeat at the hands of the Welshmen. Results, however, quickly improved, with Cantwell becoming a rock in the sometimes frail defence.

After missing a few games through injury in early 1961/62, he returned to the side, but rather surprisingly at centre-forward, although the international footballer and cricketer soon showed his versatility by notching a couple of goals. He was appointed captain in 1962/63 and, despite the continuing poor form in the league, United strode towards Wembley and the FA Cup final, with Cantwell lifting the trophy following the 3-1 victory over Leicester City.

In January 1964, however, he lost his place in the starting line-up to Tony Dunne, and from then until April 1965, he was to make only four First Division appearances, with two of those coming at centre-forward, scoring once. Season 1965/66 added a further 23 league starts to his list of appearances, but by the start of the following season, it became obvious that his days at Old Trafford were numbered and so he decided to hang up his boots early in season 1967/68. He relinquished his position as chairman of the PFA and took up the post of manager with Coventry City.

JOHN PHILLIPS 'JACK' CAPE

Country: England
Born: 16 Nov 1911 **Died:** 6 Jun 1994
Debut: 27 Jan 1934 v Brentford
Position: Forward
Appearances: 60 **Goals scored:** 18
Seasons: 1933/34 – 1936/37
Clubs: Penrith, Carlisle United, Newcastle United, Manchester United, Queens Park Rangers, Scarborough, Carlisle United

Having played at non-league level with Penrith, 17-year-old Jack Cape signed for his home-town club Carlisle United in May 1929, but after a mere 15 appearances, he was transferred to Newcastle United for a fee of £1,750. In his four years on Tyneside, he scored 20 goals in 53 outings, three of those coming at Old Trafford against United in September 1930, eventually prompting Scott Duncan to pay out £2,000 to secure his services in January 1934. Although coming into the side at outside-right, he made an immediate impact, scoring thrice in his first three outings.

As season 1933/34 progressed, United were struggling for their Second Division survival and, in order to avoid relegation to the Third, they had to win at Millwall on the final day of the season. Having scored a vital goal in a 1-1 draw at Bradford City a few weeks earlier, Cape more than repaid his transfer fee by scoring the all-important first goal at the Den, with United winning 2-0 to avoid the drop. In the Second

Division title-winning season of 1935/36, his appearances were limited and he left to join Queens Park Rangers.

ALFRED 'FREDDIE' CAPPER

Country: England
Born: Jul 1891 **Died:** 31 Oct 1955
Debut: 23 Mar 1912 v Liverpool
Position: Forward
Appearances: 1 **Goals scored:** 0
Seasons: 1911/12
Clubs: Northwich Victoria, Manchester United, Witton Albion, Sheffield Wednesday, Brentford

JOHN JOSEPH 'JOHNNY' CAREY

Country: Ireland
Born: 23 Feb 1919 **Died:** 22 Aug 1995
Debut: 25 Sep 1937 v Southampton
Position: Full-back
Appearances: 344 **Goals scored:** 17
Seasons: 1937/38 – 1952/53
Clubs: Home Farm, St James' Gate, Manchester United

It was perhaps only through a bout of ignorance on his behalf that Johnny Carey ever became a professional footballer. As a youngster at school, he had only played a few games of football 'here and there', as he was more involved in the Gaelic code of the game, as the Association game was considered 'foreign' and schoolboys were not allowed to participate in it. One night, the 16-year-old Carey decided to go dancing, but was unaware that it was an 'English' dance that he was attending. As the rules of the Gaelic Football Association forbade any involvement with the country considered as 'the enemy', he was suspended and had to switch his leisure activities to association football.

His early involvement in the 'new' game was spent with Home Farm, later moving to St James' Gate, and in what was only his sixth game at this level, Johnny Carey was brought to the attention of United and a fee of £200 took the novice to Manchester. Signed as an inside-left, he quickly settled in his new surroundings and progressed from the

'A' team to the Central League side, competing with Stan Pearson for a place in the line-up, before being moved to the right-hand side of the centre-forward, allowing his friend to play on the left.

Carey made his Manchester United first-team debut, on 25 September 1937 against Southampton at Old Trafford, in a Second Division fixture. 'We lost two-one,' said the debutant, 'and the next game was lost too and I went back into the reserves for further polishing.' The United coaching staff must have used a considerable amount of elbow grease as he was soon given his first international cap before returning to the first-team picture, against Nottingham Forest on 28 December, scoring in the 3-2 win. He was to remain a regular in the side for much of the remainder of the season.

The early days of season 1938/39 saw him up against Stan Pearson for the inside-left spot, but Carey won out. By now, he was not only a United regular, but also a regular on the international front. It is interesting to note that he also played seven times for (Northern) Ireland, as well as captaining the Rest of Europe side against Great Britain in 1947. Although exempt from being called up, due to his nationality, Carey felt that it was his duty to serve in the army during the Second World War.

Upon his return to United at the end of the war, he was promptly made captain by new manager Matt Busby and switched to right-back. United finished the first post-war campaign as runners-up to Liverpool. A similar position was achieved at the end of 1947/48 and 1948/49, losing out to Arsenal and Portsmouth respectively, but the former of those two seasons did produce silverware in the shape of the FA Cup. Victories against Aston Villa (a dramatic end-to-end match that finished 6-4 in United's favour), Liverpool, Charlton, Preston and Derby took his side to Wembley, where they faced Lancashire rivals Blackpool in the final. In a match as equally dramatic as the third-round tie at Villa Park, United turned on the style and thrilled a packed stadium, winning 4-2 in a final still talked about today.

Named as the Football Writers' Association Footballer of the Year in 1949, versatile is a word which could have easily have been created just for Carey, as whenever an injury caused Matt Busby a selection problem, it was to his captain that he turned, with the Dubliner slipping quietly and effectively into whatever position he was asked to fill. No season, however, could match 1939/40, when United played in the War League (Western Division). Starting off at inside-right, he worked his way through every outfield position except outside-left during his 19 appearances. He was able to claim a 'full house' during 1942/43, when he played outside-left against Blackburn Rovers on 3 October.

It was, however, during 1952/53 that Johnny Carey was to make his most surprising appearance of all, in goal. United had travelled to Sunderland on 18 February 1953, with Jack Crompton scheduled to play his first league game for two months, following a fractured jaw. A couple of hours prior to kick-off, Crompton complained of feeling unwell, suffering from a touch of flu. Without any hesitation, Carey immediately offered to play in goal, helping United to a point in a 2-2 draw.

That season was also the last in Carey's career as a professional footballer, and he played his last game for the club against Rangers in the Coronation Cup tie at Hampden Park (a fitting arena for any individual to bow out on), with the Scottish press naming him 'man of the match'. Needless to say, he was offered a managerial post, joining Blackburn Rovers, a club he was to take back to the First Division in 1958. Without a doubt, there is no other way to describe Johnny Carey other than as a true Manchester United legend.

JAMES CARMAN

Country: England
Born: 1876 **Died:** Unknown
Debut: 25 Dec 1897 v Manchester City
Position: Forward
Appearances: 3 **Goals scored:** 1
Seasons: 1897/98
Clubs: Darwen, Oldham County, Newton Heath

JOSEPH FRANCIS 'JOE' CAROLAN

Country: Republic of Ireland
Born: 8 Sep 1937
Debut: 22 Nov 1958 v Luton Town
Position: Full-back
Appearances: 71 **Goals scored:** 0
Seasons: 1958/59 – 1960/61
Clubs: Home Farm, Manchester United, Brighton & Hove Albion, Tonbridge, Canterbury City

Joe Carolan was a Dubliner who attracted United's attention while playing for Home Farm. Following a successful trial, he was offered a contract and was soon progressing through the ranks, finding himself thrust into the first team in the season after the Munich disaster, making his debut as a replacement for Ian Greaves at left-back. He was quick to adjust to First Division football and missed only one game during the rest of the season, as a rejuvenated United surprised everyone by finishing runners-up in the First Division.

Early in season 1959/60 he won international recognition with the Republic of Ireland, after having made only 41 appearances with United, and his future looked more than promising. But within a month of season 1960/61 kicking off, Joe Carolan's Manchester United first-team career was at an end. Following a 4-0 defeat at Goodison Park, he was omitted from the team and three weeks later, following the signing of Noel Cantwell, he was sold to Brighton & Hove Albion for a fee of £8,000.

MICHAEL CARRICK

Country: England
Born: 28 Jul 1981
Debut: 23 Aug 2006 v Charlton Athletic
Position: Midfield
Appearances: 276 (44) **Goals scored:** 21
Seasons: 2006/07 – present
Clubs: West Ham United, Swindon Town (loan), Birmingham City (loan), Tottenham Hotspur, Manchester United

A product of the West Ham United Youth Academy, Michael Carrick moved across London to join Tottenham Hotspur for a £2.75 million fee in 2004, where he continued to progress, so much so that his performances for the White Hart Lane side persuaded Sir Alex Ferguson to pay an initial £14 million fee for his services two years later when he replaced Roy Keane in the centre of midfield.

Although not immediately accepted by all the Old Trafford support, who were used to the very different style of the Irishman, he simply stuck to the task at hand and soon matured into a superb holding and influential midfield playmaker, the fulcrum of the majority of United attacks, helping the side to back-to-back league titles in 2006/07 and 2007/08. He was also to the cap the latter season with a Champions League medal, scoring one of the penalties that would defeat Chelsea in the Moscow shoot-out. A third successive title followed in 2008/09.

Injuries to team-mates have occasionally seen the former Wallsend boy move into the back four to take up unfamiliar defensive duties, which he has done with ease. He has continued to flourish at Old Trafford, becoming an important cog in the United machine, winning further Premiership medals in 2010/11 and 2012/13, with his performances in the latter seeing him finally receive the acclaim he deserved from the United support, while also lifting the Players' Player of the Year award.

Despite becoming one of the first names on Sir Alex's teamsheet, his appearances at international level have been limited since his debut in 2001, winning only 29 caps in all that time, often losing out to Steven Gerrard or Frank Lampard.

ROY ERIC CARROLL

Country: Northern Ireland
Born: 30 Sep 1977
Debut: 26 Aug 2001 v Aston Villa
Position: Goalkeeper
Appearances: 68 (4) **Goals scored:** 0
Seasons: 2001/02 – 2004/05
Clubs: Hull City, Wigan Athletic, Manchester United, West Ham United, Rangers, Derby County, Odense Boldklub, OFI Crete, Olympiacos

A native of County Fermanagh, Roy Carroll began his career in local leagues before crossing the Irish Sea in November 1994 to begin his professional career with Hull City. Three years later, having made his debut for Northern Ireland, a fee of £35,000 took him to Wigan Athletic, where he was named the Division Two goalkeeper of the year in 1999/2000, his performances also earning him a £2.5 million move to Old Trafford as back-up for Fabien Barthez.

Carroll, however, found himself called into first-team action quicker than he expected, as an injury to Barthez with the 2001/02 season only weeks old saw the Irishman make his debut against Aston Villa, away, on 26 August. Despite winning a Premier League medal in 2002/03 and an FA Cup winner's medal 12 months later, he was never to become United's undisputed first-choice keeper. He will perhaps be best remembered for the 'goal that never was' against Tottenham Hotspur at Old Trafford in 2004/05, when he allowed a high looping ball from Mendes on the halfway line to drop from his hands and bounce over the line. He clawed the ball away but, despite being clearly over the line, neither the referee nor his linesman could confirm this and play was allowed to continue. He was released at the end of the season, and moved to West Ham United.

ADAM CARSON

Country: Scotland
Born: Unknown **Died:** Unknown
Debut: 3 Sep 1892 v Blackburn Rovers
Position: Forward
Appearances: 13 **Goals scored:** 3
Seasons: 1892/93
Clubs: Glasgow Thistle, Newton Heath, Ardwick, Liverpool

A product of Glasgow Thistle, Adam Carson had caught the eye of numerous clubs with a notable performance in a Scottish League versus the Scottish Alliance fixture, when he was considered to be 'the best forward' on show. He put pen to paper for Newton Heath in June 1892, receiving a £20 signing-on fee and the weekly sum of £3 during the season and £2 in the summer. The latter payment never came into effect, however, as he failed to complete one season with the club, moving to neighbours Ardwick (later to become Manchester City), in March 1893, having made only 13 appearances for the Heathens.

HERBERT REDVERS 'BERT' CARTMAN

Country: England
Born: 28 Feb 1900 **Died:** 5 Apr 1955
Debut: 16 Dec 1922 v Stockport County
Position: Forward
Appearances: 3 **Goals scored:** 0
Seasons: 1922/23
Clubs: Waterloo Temperance, Bolton Wanderers, Manchester United, Tranmere Rovers, Brighton & Hove Albion, Stockport County, Chorley

WALTER CARTWRIGHT

Country: England
Born: Jan 1871 **Died:** Unknown
Debut: 7 Sep 1895 v Crewe Alexandra
Position: Half-back
Appearances: 257 **Goals scored:** 8
Seasons: 1895/96 – 1904/05
Clubs: Nantwich, Heywood Central, Crewe Alexandra, Newton Heath/Manchester United

One of the most versatile individuals ever to play for either Newton Heath or Manchester United was Walter Cartwright, who joined the Heathens from Crewe Alexandra in July 1895. He arrived at Bank Street as a left-half, making his debut against his former club Crewe on the opening day of season 1895/96 and, although it was mainly in this position he made his 250-odd appearances, he filled at least another eight, including a stint as goalkeeper on two separate occasions.

As a thank you from the club for his ten years' service, he was awarded a benefit match, but through no fault of his own, it came at a time when the club was in receivership and what might have been a bumper payday was to earn the player around £1.30, which was spent at the local public house before his journey home. He retired from the game in the summer of 1905.

ARTHUR CASHMORE

Country: England
Born: 30 Oct 1893 **Died:** 1969
Debut: 13 Sep 1913 v Bolton Wanderers
Position: Forward
Appearances: 3 **Goals scored:** 0
Seasons: 1913/14
Clubs: Stourbridge, Manchester United, Oldham Athletic, Darlaston, Cardiff City, Notts County, Darlaston, Nuneaton, Shrewsbury Town

CHRISTOPHER MARTIN 'CHRIS' CASPER

Country: England
Born: 28 Apr 1975
Debut: 5 Oct 1994 v Port Vale
Position: Defender
Appearances: 4 (3) **Goals scored:** 0
Seasons: 1993/94 – 1996/97
Clubs: Manchester United, Bournemouth (loan), Swindon Town (loan), Reading (loan), Reading

Part of the fabled Class of '92 Youth Cup-winning side, Burnley-born defender Chris Casper had joined the club aged 13. He won England Under-21 honours, but moved to Reading for a fee of £300,000 after the arrival of Jaap Stam blocked his way to the first team. Soon after, he suffered a career-ending injury. He briefly managed Bury.

JOSEPH 'JOE' CASSIDY

Country: Scotland
Born: 30 Jul 1872 **Died:** Unknown
Debut: 31 Mar 1893 v Stoke City
Position: Forward
Appearances: 174 **Goals scored:** 100
Seasons: 1892/93 – 1899/1900
Clubs: Motherwell Athletic, Blythe, Newton Heath, Celtic, Newton Heath, Manchester City, Middlesbrough, Workington

Joe Cassidy originally joined Newton Heath on loan from Blythe towards the end of 1892/93, but he returned to his native Scotland during the close season, winning numerous honours with Celtic before returning to Manchester in March 1895, due to some disharmony in the Celtic dressing room. His return produced a noticeable improvement to the team, and he went on to become club captain, scoring a further 99 goals in 168 appearances, with six hat-tricks among them. In four of the next five campaigns, he was the club's top scorer, but at the end of season 1899/1900, despite this and his undoubted popularity with the supporters, the Newton Heath directors were forced to sell him due to the financial difficulties surrounding the club, and he was subsequently sold to neighbours City for the sum of £250.

LAWRENCE 'LAURIE' CASSIDY

Country: England
Born: 10 Mar 1923 **Died:** Unknown
Debut: 10 Apr 1948 v Everton
Position: Forward
Appearances: 4 **Goals scored:** 0
Seasons: 1947/48 – 1951/52
Clubs: Manchester United, Oldham Athletic

LUKE HARRY CHADWICK

Country: England
Born: 18 Nov 1980
Debut: 13 Oct 1999 v Aston Villa
Position: Winger
Appearances: 18 (21) **Goals scored:** 2
Seasons: 1999/2000 – 2002/03
Clubs: Manchester United, Royal Antwerp (loan), Reading (loan), Burnley (loan), West Ham United, Stoke City (loan), Stoke City, Norwich City (loan), Norwich City, Milton Keynes Dons (loan), Milton Keynes Dons

The Cambridge-born youngster came through the United youth system and was a gifted winger with natural ability and a notable burst of speed that earned him England Under-21 honours. He enjoyed a loan spell at Royal Antwerp, helping them to the Belgian Second Division title, before returning to United, where he was to win a Premiership medal in 2000/01. Injury ruined a possible first-class career and following numerous loan spells, he joined West Ham on a free transfer in 2004. He has had his most consistent spell in league football at his current club, MK Dons.

WILLIAM STEWART CHALMERS

Country: Scotland
Born: 5 Mar 1907 **Died:** Unknown
Debut: 1 Oct 1932 v Preston North End
Position: Inside-forward
Appearances: 35 **Goals scored:** 1

Seasons: 1932/33 – 1933/34
Clubs: Queen's Park, Heart of Midlothian, Manchester United, Dunfermline Athletic

A typical Scottish inside-forward, Chalmers was small in stature and big in heart; he possessed exceptional ball control and great distribution skills. Born in the Mount Florida district of Glasgow, Chalmers not unexpectedly joined Queen's Park, whose Hampden headquarters were within easy walking distance of his home. After gaining a full international cap while still an amateur, he joined Hearts in the summer of 1929, spending three years in Edinburgh before moving to Manchester on 26 September 1932 for a fee of £2,500.

A qualified chartered accountant, he sometimes found it difficult to get the necessary time off work required for games and he failed to make the same impression south of the border as he had done in Scotland, losing his place to Ernie Hine. With limited opportunities, he decided that he had had enough of life in Manchester and returned to Scotland to join Dunfermline Athletic in September 1934.

WILLIAM 'BILLY' CHAPMAN

Country: England
Born: 21 Sep 1902 **Died:** 2 Dec 1967
Debut: 18 Sep 1926 v Burnley
Position: Outside-right
Appearances: 26 **Goals scored:** 0
Seasons: 1926/27 – 1927/28
Clubs: Sheffield Wednesday, Manchester United, Watford

Billy Chapman joined Sheffield Wednesday in May 1924, but was to make only four league appearances at Hillsborough before being signed by United in May 1926 for a fee of £250. He was to find first-team opportunities limited, enjoying only 26 outings over two seasons before moving south to join Watford in the summer of 1928.

ROBERT 'BOBBY' CHARLTON

Country: England
Born: 11 Oct 1937
Debut: 6 Oct 1956 v Charlton Athletic
Position: Midfield/Forward
Appearances: 756 (2) **Goals scored:** 249
Seasons: 1956/57 – 1972/73
Clubs: Manchester United, Preston North End, Waterford

Bobby Charlton is a name synonymous around the world with that of Manchester United, despite having hung up his boots more than four decades ago. Born into a footballing family, with both uncles and brother involved in the game, he left his Ashington home upon leaving school in 1953, having won England schoolboy honours. He moved to Manchester to join United, signing professional forms two years later, springing into prominence with three United Youth Cup-winning teams before making his debut against Charlton Athletic in October 1956, scoring twice in the 4-2 win. It was the beginning of a playing career that would take him to all corners of the world, lifting countless personal and team honours with both United and England.

Despite not commanding a regular place, he made enough appearances to claim a Championship medal and ended that first season with an appearance in the FA Cup final, finishing on the losing side against Aston Villa. Still not a regular the following season, he was, however, on that fateful trip to Belgrade, but escaped the carnage at Munich, returning to the fray a few weeks later, before winning his first full England cap in April 1958, scoring against Scotland at Hampden.

He kicked off the first post-Munich season with a hat-trick against Chelsea, scoring nine in the first seven games, finishing the campaign with 29, maintaining an excellent scoring rate throughout the 1960s, playing mainly at outside-left, having moved wide from inside-forward, as United won the league twice and the FA Cup once. Sandwiched in between the two league titles in 1965 and 1967, he was named as Footballer of the Year and European Footballer of the Year in 1966, a year that saw him share in England's World Cup triumph.

As the decade approached its end, Charlton was now captain of his beloved United, playing a more central role, but there was still one trophy that eluded him and his manager Matt Busby; however, with a 4-3 aggregate win over Real Madrid in the 1968 European Cup semi-final, United were 90 minutes from lifting the sought-after trophy. Those 90 minutes were to stretch to 120, but on an emotional May night at Wembley, having scored United's first and fourth goals, he was to lift the European Cup high above his head after United had defeated Benfica 4-1.

The following year he was awarded the OBE for his services to football, and won his 100th cap against Northern Ireland at Wembley in April 1970, marking the occasion with his 48th England goal. Earning his 106th cap during the 1970 Mexico World Cup, he decided to call time on his international career following England's quarter-final defeat by West Germany.

Awarded a testimonial by United in September 1972, during a season that also saw him set a club record of 606 league appearances, he had amassed an overall total of 758 appearances, scoring a record 249 goals by the time he announced his retirement, bowing out against Verona in an Anglo-Italian Cup tie on 2 May 1973. The record of appearances remained unbroken until 2008, when Ryan Giggs brushed it aside.

Upon leaving United, he managed and came out of retirement to play for Preston North End, finally hanging up his boots following three games with Waterford in the Republic of Ireland. A spell as director and caretaker manager of Wigan Athletic in the early 1980s preceded his return to Old Trafford as a director. Awarded a knighthood in 1994, having added a CBE to his earlier OBE, Bobby Charlton is today still a familiar face at Old Trafford and beyond, one of the most respected individuals in not simply British, but world football.

JAMES GRANT CHESTER

Country: England
Born: 23 Jan 1989
Debut: 20 Jan 2009 v Derby County
Position: Centre-back
Appearances: 0 (1) **Goals scored:** 0
Seasons: 2008/09
Clubs: Manchester United, Peterborough United (loan), Plymouth Argyle (loan), Carlisle United (loan), Hull City

REGINALD ARTHUR 'REG' CHESTER

Country: England
Born: 21 Nov 1904 **Died:** 24 Apr 1977

Debut: 31 Aug 1935 v Plymouth Argyle
Position: Forward
Appearances: 13 **Goals scored:** 1
Seasons: 1935/36
Clubs: Aston Villa, Manchester United, Huddersfield Town, Darlington

The Derbyshire-born forward played for just one season for United, scoring his only goal in his second game, a 3-0 win over Charlton Athletic.

ARTHUR CHESTERS

Country: England
Born: 14 Feb 1910 **Died:** 23 Mar 1963
Debut: 28 Dec 1929 v Newcastle United
Position: Goalkeeper
Appearances: 9 **Goals scored:** 0
Seasons: 1929/30 – 1931/32
Clubs: Manchester United, Exeter City

ALLENBY C. CHILTON

Country: England
Born: 16 Sep 1918 **Died:** 15 Jun 1996
Debut: 5 Jan 1946 v Accrington Stanley
Position: Centre-back
Appearances: 391 **Goals scored:** 3
Seasons: 1945/46 – 1954/55
Clubs: Liverpool, Manchester United, Grimsby Town

Allenby Chilton was with Liverpool as an amateur during the opening months of season 1938/39, having joined the Merseysiders from Seaham Colliery, but without having featured at first-team level he was allowed to leave Anfield and make the short journey along the East Lancs Road to Manchester, joining United in November 1938. It was not, however, until September of the following year that he made his United debut, playing in what was to be the last First Division fixture prior to the Second World War at Charlton in a game played the day before war was declared and that was subsequently expunged from the record books.

His playing days almost came to something of a premature end during the Normandy D-Day landings as he was wounded twice, but he made a complete recovery and was able to resume his Manchester United career when football got back to normality in August 1946. Chilton was a typical rugged, old-fashioned centre-half, who enjoyed the physical side of the game and, having trained as a boxer at one time, certainly knew how to handle himself, missing only 13 league games over the next eight seasons, taking over as captain upon Johnny Carey's retirement.

Despite winning an FA Cup medal in 1948 and a First Division Championship medal in 1952, he won only two England caps, his rugged, uncompromising style perhaps not appealing to the selectors. Up until February 1955, he had played a record 175 consecutive league and cup ties for United, a run that only came to an end as Chilton himself felt that he was playing a little below his normal form and that a rest might help. Into his No.5 shirt came Mark Jones, and a month later Chilton was packing his bags and leaving Old Trafford for Grimsby Town on a free transfer, taking up the role of player-manager.

JOHN PHILIP 'PHIL' CHISNALL

Country: England
Born: 27 Oct 1942
Debut: 2 Dec 1961 v Everton
Position: Inside-forward
Appearances: 47 **Goals scored:** 10
Seasons: 1961/62 – 1963/64
Clubs: Manchester United, Liverpool, Southend United, Stockport County

Former Stretford and Lancashire Schools and England schoolboy international Phil Chisnall joined United as a 15-year-old amateur straight from school, progressing through the ranks and making his first-team debut in December 1961 against Everton at Goodison Park, scoring his first goal eight games later in a 2-0 win over Manchester City at Maine Road. A run of 16 games at the start of season 1963/64 earned him a place in the England Under-23 side, but with Graham Moore joining the club, he was to make only a further four appearances for United before moving to Liverpool in April 1964 for £25,000.

THOMAS 'TOM' CHORLTON

Country: England
Born: 1882 **Died:** 1952
Debut: 11 Oct 1913 v Burnley
Position: Full-back
Appearances: 4 **Goals scored:** 0
Seasons: 1913/14
Clubs: Stockport County, Accrington Stanley, Liverpool, Manchester United, Stalybridge Celtic

DAVID CHRISTIE

Country: Scotland
Born: 1885 **Died:** Unknown
Debut: 7 Sep 1908 v Bury
Position: Inside-left
Appearances: 2 **Goals scored:** 0
Seasons: 1908/09
Clubs: Hurlford, Manchester United

JOHN CHRISTIE

Country: England
Born: 1883 **Died:** Unknown
Debut: 28 Feb 1903 v Doncaster Rovers
Position: Full-back
Appearances: 1 **Goals scored:** 0
Seasons: 1902/03
Clubs: Sale Homefield, Manchester United, Manchester City, Bradford Park Avenue

JOSEPH 'JOE' CLARK

Country: Scotland
Born: 1874 **Died:** Unknown
Debut: 30 Sep 1899 v Sheffield Wednesday
Position: Forward
Appearances: 9 **Goals scored:** 0
Seasons: 1899/1900
Clubs: Dundee, Newton Heath, Dunfermline Athletic, East Fife

JONATHAN 'JON' CLARK

Country: Wales
Born: 12 Nov 1958
Debut: 10 Nov 1976 v Sunderland
Position: Midfield
Appearances: 0 (1) **Goals scored:** 0
Seasons: 1976/77
Clubs: Manchester United, Derby County, Preston North End, Bury, Carlisle United

JOHN CLARKIN

Country: Scotland
Born: 1872 **Died:** Unknown
Debut: 13 Jan 1894 v Sheffield Wednesday
Position: Forward
Appearances: 74 **Goals scored:** 23
Seasons: 1893/94 – 1895/96
Clubs: Neilston, Glasgow Thistle, Newton Heath, Blackpool

Born in Neilston, Renfrewshire, John Clarkin began his career with his home-town club before joining Glasgow Thistle in July 1893, moving to Manchester in January 1894. He was a consistent performer, even following Newton Heath's relegation to the Second Division, missing only one game and scoring 11 goals from the outside-right position. The following season, 1895/96, continued on a similar vein, with seven goals from 26 outings and it came as something of a surprise when he was allowed to leave in the close season to join Blackpool, a club who were just beginning their career in the Football League.

GORDON CLAYTON

Country: England
Born: 3 Nov 1936 **Died:** 29 Sep 1991
Debut: 16 Mar 1957 v Wolverhampton Wanderers
Position: Goalkeeper
Appearances: 2 **Goals scored:** 0
Seasons: 1956/57
Clubs: Manchester United, Tranmere Rovers

HARRY CLEAVER

Country: England
Born: 1880 **Died:** Unknown
Debut: 4 Apr 1903 v Burnley
Position: Forward
Appearances: 1 **Goals scored:** 0
Seasons: 1902/03
Clubs: Desborough Town, Manchester United

MICHAEL JAMIE CLEGG

Country: England
Born: 3 Jul 1977
Debut: 23 Nov 1996 v Middlesbrough
Position: Defender
Appearances: 15 (9) **Goals scored:** 0
Seasons: 1996/97 – 2001/02
Clubs: Manchester United, Ipswich Town (loan), Wigan Athletic (loan), Oldham Athletic

Manchester-born and one of a number of talented youngsters who broke into the first team, Michael Clegg showed considerable promise, but was unable to stake a claim for a regular place. A quick and confident full-back, his 24 appearances were spread over six seasons, with loan spells at Ipswich and Wigan sandwiched in between. He eventually left United on a free transfer in February 2002, joining Oldham Athletic. He retired in 2004.

JOHN 'ERNEST' CLEMENTS

Country: England
Born: 1867 **Died:** Unknown
Debut: 3 Oct 1891 v Manchester City
Position: Full-back
Appearances: 42 **Goals scored:** 0
Seasons: 1891/92 – 1893/94
Clubs: Notts County, Newton Heath, Rotherham Town, Newcastle United

John Clements, a rough, robust, no-nonsense defender, joined Notts County in October 1888 from Nottingham St Saviours, before moving to Newton Heath in 1890, making his debut against Crewe in the Football Alliance in October of that year. He was a cornerstone of the defence as the club moved from the Alliance to the Football League, but he was to lose his place during the 1893/94 season, when he was suspended for 14 days by the Football Association, along with two team-mates following the match at Derby County on 7 October, when their conduct during the match was considered unacceptable. Although he made fleeting appearances following his suspension, he never managed a run in the team and in August 1894 he joined Rotherham Town.

FRANK CLEMPSON

Country: England
Born: 27 May 1930 **Died:** 24 Dec 1970
Debut: 18 Feb 1950 v Sunderland
Position: Wing-half
Appearances: 15 **Goals scored:** 2
Seasons: 1949/50 – 1952/53
Clubs: Manchester United, Stockport County, Chester, Hyde United

A member of the Adelphi Lads Club, Frank Clempson joined United as an amateur in March 1948, turning professional six months later. In February 1950, an injury to Tommy Bogan gave the 19-year-old his first-team debut at Sunderland, but his opportunities were always going to be few and far between. He had a desire to play first-team football, something that United could not give him, and in February 1953 he joined Stockport County, where he was to play over 260 games, scoring 35 goals.

THOMAS WILLIAM 'TOM' CLEVERLEY

Country: England
Born: 12 August 1989
Debut: 7 Aug 2011 v Manchester City
Position: Midfield
Appearances: 38 (10) **Goals scored:** 4
Seasons: 2011/12 – present
Clubs: Manchester United, Leicester City (loan), Watford (loan), Wigan Athletic (loan)

Some doubt the worth of loan spells, but for Tom Cleverley, they proved to be the launching pad to a first-team spot with both Manchester United and England. Basingstoke-born Cleverley sprang to prominence with loan deals at Leicester, Watford and Wigan, turning in more than creditable performances at all three, and winning the 'Player of the Year' award with Watford.

Appearances on United's pre-season tour of America in July 2010 gave many the impression that he would be challenging for a first-team place, but he was to spend the season at Wigan before returning to Manchester to kick-start his United career at the start of the 2011/12 season. Making his competitive debut against Manchester City in the Community Shield, he made his league debut in the opening match of the season against West Bromwich Albion, but what early promise he displayed was brought to a sudden end with a bad tackle during the match at Bolton. An ankle injury was soon to follow, leaving his season in disarray.

But those black clouds were soon to disperse, as he regained his place in the United starting XI on something of a regular basis, as he did with England after winning his first full England cap against Italy in August 2012. Winning a Premier League medal at the end of season 2012/13, he is looked upon as part of the future at Old Trafford.

HENRY COCKBURN

Country: England
Born: 14 Sep 1921 **Died:** 2 Feb 2004
Debut: 5 Jan 1946 v Accrington Stanley
Position: Left-half
Appearances: 275 **Goals scored:** 4
Seasons: 1946/47 – 1954/55
Clubs: Manchester United, Bury, Peterborough United, Corby

As a youngster, Ashton-under-Lyne-born Henry Cockburn was due to go to Blackpool for a trial, but a bout of influenza prevented him from making his Bloomfield Road appointment. But if the Oldham mill fitter thought his opportunity to become a professional footballer had passed him by, then he was mistaken, as he came under the watchful eye of a United scout while playing for the noted amateur side Goslings and he was taken on as an amateur at United on 29 September 1943, turning professional a year later.

Cockburn had to wait until 31 August 1946 before making his official league debut, in the opening fixture of season 1946/47 against Grimsby Town. Despite measuring 5'6" and weighing in at 10st, he was an extremely clever footballer with a hard, forceful tackle, possessing the ability to distribute the ball with precise accuracy and within a month of his debut, he was somewhat surprisingly selected for England international duty against Northern Ireland at Windsor Park, Belfast, the first of 13 caps.

A member of the 1948 FA Cup-winning side, he was to add a League Championship medal in 1952, but with the emergence of the famed 'Busby Babes' in the early 1950s, Cockburn was one of the players to lose out, as a broken jaw sustained during a friendly at Kilmarnock on 28 October 1953 saw him substituted by a certain Duncan Edwards and from that moment on, his days at Old Trafford were numbered. Although he made a full recovery from his injury, he was to make only another four first-team appearances in a red shirt and as reserve-team football wasn't something that he contemplated, he decided that it was time to move on, joining Bury in October 1954.

ANDREW ALEXANDER 'ANDY' COLE

Country: England
Born: 15 Oct 1971
Debut: 22 Jan 1995 v Blackburn Rovers
Position: Forward
Appearances: 231 (44) **Goals scored:** 121
Seasons: 1994/95 – 2001/02
Clubs: Arsenal, Fulham (loan), Bristol City, Newcastle United, Manchester United, Blackburn Rovers, Fulham, Manchester City, Portsmouth, Birmingham City (loan), Sunderland, Burnley (loan), Nottingham Forest

Scoring the match-winning second goal against Spurs at Old Trafford to secure the Premier League, as the first leg of the 1999 Treble was secured, Andy Cole was one of four first-class strikers at the club in the late 1990s. He formed a deadly partnership with Dwight Yorke that campaign, scoring 53 goals between them, as United brushed all challengers aside.

Having been born in Nottingham, he began his career at Arsenal, but really came to the fore with Newcastle United following a £1.75 million move. Hailed as 'Goal King Cole' on Tyneside, with a record bettered only by Hughie Gallacher, he was perhaps surprisingly allowed to join United in January 1995 for £6 million plus Keith Gillespie in what was then a record transfer.

Taking his scoring boots to Old Trafford, he scored a Premier League record five against a hapless Ipswich Town, who were trounced 9-0, but he failed to nudge United to the Premier League title in that first season and came under some criticism from fans during the following campaign for the occasional missed chance, while a double leg break against Liverpool did little to help. But his free-scoring form soon returned, and after the retirement of Eric Cantona, he went from strength to strength, scoring 71 goals in the next three seasons. He blossomed especially after the arrival of Dwight Yorke, with the pair making a telling contribution in the 1999 Champions League semi-final second leg against Juventus, in which he scored the first and third goals.

The signing of van Nistelrooy added to the competition for places up front and in December 2001, he was sold to Blackburn Rovers for £8 million. He then played for a variety of clubs before eventually retiring in 2008. He also won 15 caps for England, and remains United's fifth highest Premier League goalscorer.

LARNELL JAMES COLE

Country: England
Born: 9 March 1993
Debut: 20 Sep 2011 v Leeds United
Position: Midfield
Appearances: 0 (1)
Seasons: 2011/12 – present
Clubs: Manchester United

Local boy Cole has played just once, as a substitute, for United, but the midfielder has since gone on to join England in the Under-20 World Cup during the summer of 2013.

CLIFFORD 'CLIFF' COLLINSON

Country: England
Born: 3 Mar 1920 **Died:** Sep 1990
Debut: 2 Nov 1946 v Aston Villa
Position: Goalkeeper

Appearances: 7 **Goals scored:** 0
Seasons: 1946/47
Clubs: Manchester United

JAMES 'JIMMY' COLLINSON

Country: England
Born: 1876 **Died:** Unknown
Debut: 16 Nov 1895 v Lincoln City
Position: Forward
Appearances: 71 **Goals scored:** 17
Seasons: 1895/96 – 1900/01
Clubs: Newton Heath

Jimmy Collinson is considered the first local-born player to represent Newton Heath, although conflicting information suggests that he was born further down the road in Prestwich. He signed for the club in August 1895 and made his debut in a 5-5 draw against Lincoln City in November 1895, scoring once, but after a dozen games in the side, he failed to re-emerge until 12 January 1898, reborn as an inside-forward. The transformation to a more attacking role was certainly a success, as he soon developed a nose for goal, scoring five in four games, including two in the final of the Lancashire Senior Cup, won for the first time following a 2-1 victory over Blackburn Rovers in March 1898. He left the club in 1901.

EDWARD 'EDDIE' COLMAN

Country: England
Born: 1 Nov 1936 **Died:** 6 Feb 1958
Debut: 12 Nov 1955 v Bolton Wanderers
Position: Half-back
Appearances: 108 **Goals scored:** 2
Seasons: 1955/56 – 1957/58
Clubs: Manchester United

Back in the 1950s, there were no footballers' homes in the leafy suburbs of south Manchester; indeed, there were no leafy suburbs, with some of United's first-team stars contentedly living in digs. Others, such as Eddie Colman, still lived with their parents, the family home being situated on

Archie Street (later to be used in the credits for television's *Coronation Street*) on the Ordsall Estate, a short walk from his Old Trafford place of employment.

As a schoolboy, he represented Salford Boys and Lancashire Boys at both cricket and football, but it was with the larger, leather ball that he was to come to the fore, catching Matt Busby and Jimmy Murphy's attention while playing for Salford Boys at Old Trafford. Joining United in 1952, he captained the youth team in 1954/55 and made his first-team debut at Bolton in November 1955, 11 days after his 19th birthday, combining life as a professional footballer with his national service at Catterick Army Camp in North Yorkshire. Having broken into the first team, replacing Jeff Whitefoot, he kept his place, missing only one league game during the remainder of the campaign. Indeed, he was to miss only ten First Division fixtures between his debut and Munich.

He was small in stature, but very creative, augmented by his deceiving body swerve that earned him the nickname 'Snake Hips'. Many were later to comment that when Eddie swayed to one side, sections of the crowd would move in unison. Off the field, Eddie Colman loved the popular music of the time and, despite his confident swagger, with his 'teddy boy' look, drainpipe trousers, crepe-soled shoes, and duffle coat, he would seldom admit to being a professional footballer, simply content to be one of the lads.

Along with Duncan Edwards, they were the 'Little and Large' of the United midfield and, had it not been for Munich, the Manchester United pairing would have undoubtedly been a similar duo in the white of England. Sadly, it was something that was never to materialise as, at the age of 21, he was to perish on the slush-covered runway at Munich.

JAMES COLVILLE

Country: Scotland
Born: Unknown **Died:** Unknown
Debut: 12 Nov 1892 v Notts County
Position: Forward
Appearances: 10 **Goals scored:** 1
Seasons: 1892/93
Clubs: Annbank, Newton Heath, Fairfield Athletic, Notts County (trial), Annbank

One of seven players tried at outside-right during 1892/93, the club's first season in the Football League, James Colville's ten appearances failed to secure him the position on a permanent basis. Born in Ayrshire, a footballing hot-bed, Colville was signed from Annbank in October 1892, making his debut the following month against Notts County, scoring his only goal for the club two games later. His stay with the Heathens was brief, and he dropped down into the Manchester Amateur League with Fairfield in the summer of 1893.

JAMES CONNACHAN

Country: Scotland
Born: 29 Aug 1874 **Died:** Unknown
Debut: 5 Nov 1898 v Grimsby Town
Position: Forward
Appearances: 4 **Goals scored:** 0
Seasons: 1898/99
Clubs: Glasgow Perthshire, Duntocher Hibernian, Celtic, Airdrieonians, Newton Heath, Glossop North End, Leicester Fosse, Morton, Renton, Britannia FC, Dumbarton Harp

JOHN PATRICK CONNAUGHTON

Country: England
Born: 23 Sep 1949
Debut: 4 Apr 1972 v Sheffield United
Position: Goalkeeper
Appearances: 3 **Goals scored:** 0
Seasons: 1971/72 – 1972/73
Clubs: Manchester United, Halifax Town (loan), Torquay United (loan), Sheffield United, Port Vale, Altrincham

THOMAS EUGENE 'TOM' CONNELL

Country: Northern Ireland
Born: 25 Nov 1957
Debut: 22 Dec 1978 v Bolton Wanderers
Position: Full-back

Appearances: 2 **Goals scored:** 0
Seasons: 1978/79
Clubs: Newry Town, Coleraine, Manchester United, Glentoran

JOHN MICHAEL CONNELLY

Country: England
Born: 18 Jul 1938 **Died:** 25 Oct 2012
Debut: 22 Aug 1964 v West Bromwich Albion
Position: Winger
Appearances: 112 (1) **Goals scored:** 35
Seasons: 1964/65 – 1966/67
Clubs: Burnley, Manchester United, Blackburn Rovers, Bury

It took John Connelly 43 years to get his hands on a World Cup winners' medal, as, despite being a part of the successful England 1966 squad, only those who played in the final were given the small golden award, but in 2009 FIFA altered the rules and a visit to 10 Downing Street saw the former United winger, who had played in the opening match of the campaign against Uruguay, pick up his medal from Prime Minister Gordon Brown.

Born in St Helens, Connelly was spotted by Burnley scouts as an 18-year-old in 1956, playing for his local side in the Lancashire Combination and was signed on a part-time basis, as his father insisted that he continued with his work as a joiner. Following his debut in March 1957, he went on to score 20 goals in 34 games in Burnley's title-winning season of 1959/60, winning the first of his 20 England caps that same season, while still a part-timer.

Switched from the right to the left-wing, he became unhappy and quickly agreed to join United towards the end of season 1963/64 when Matt Busby clinched a £56,000 deal with the assurance that the No.7 jersey would be his. Having been signed after the transfer deadline, Connelly was unable to play in those final few games, but in his first full season at Old Trafford, he played in all 42 league fixtures, scoring an excellent 15 goals, as United strode towards their first post-Munich Championship success. In total, he played all 60 games that season as Busby fielded one of the most settled sides in United's history.

Early in season 1966/67, a stand-off with Matt Busby regarding his wages was to produce only one winner and he was transferred to Blackburn Rovers for a fee of £40,000.

EDWARD 'TED' CONNOR

Country: England
Born: 1884 **Died:** 1955
Debut: 27 Dec 1909 v Sheffield Wednesday
Position: Forward
Appearances: 15 **Goals scored:** 2
Seasons: 1909/10 – 1910/11
Clubs: Eccles Borough, Walkden Central, Manchester United, Sheffield United, Exeter City, Rochdale, Chesterfield

Ted Connor learned his trade in the Lancashire Combination with Eccles Borough and Walkden Central, before signing for Manchester United in May 1909. He had to wait, however, until 27 December 1909 before making his first-team debut, playing at outside-left against Sheffield Wednesday in a 4–1 defeat. Competing against George Wall for the outside-left spot, his opportunities were always going to be few and far between and he was to make only 15 appearances over the course of two seasons, before joining Sheffield United in the summer of 1911 for a fee of £750. He was later to do scouting work for United, while also being employed on the Old Trafford office staff.

TERENCE JOHN 'TERRY' COOKE

Country: England
Born: 5 Aug 1976
Debut: 16 Sep 1995 v Bolton Wanderers
Position: Midfield
Appearances: 2 (6) **Goals scored:** 1
Seasons: 1995/96 – 1996/97
Clubs: Manchester United, Sunderland (loan), Birmingham City (loan), Wrexham (loan), Manchester City (loan), Manchester City, Wigan Athletic (loan), Sheffield Wednesday (loan), Grimsby Town (loan), Sheffield Wednesday, Colorado Rapids, North Queensland Fury, Gabala

SAMUEL PERCY 'SAM' COOKSON

Country: Wales
Born: 1891 **Died:** Unknown
Debut: 26 Dec 1914 v Liverpool
Position: Half-back
Appearances: 13 **Goals scored:** 0
Seasons: 1914/15
Clubs: Bargoed Town, Manchester United

Thirteen certainly proved to be an unlucky number for Sam Cookson, as this was the total number of appearances he made in the United first team following his transfer from his local club Bargoed Town for a fee of £50 in February 1914. Signing professional terms two months later, he made his debut against Liverpool on Boxing Day 1914 at right-half. Just four seasons after they were champions, United avoided relegation by only one point. A further handful of appearances during the war years was the sum of his United appearances and he was put up for sale in the summer of 1919.

RONALD 'RONNIE' COPE

Country: England
Born: 5 Oct 1934
Debut: 29 Sep 1956 v Arsenal
Position: Centre-back
Appearances: 106 **Goals scored:** 2
Seasons: 1956/57 – 1960/61
Clubs: Manchester United, Luton Town, Northwich Victoria

A former Crewe schoolboy, Ronnie Cope joined the United groundstaff in June 1950, after representing England Schools, turning professional in October the following year. Like many others, he had to be content to be a member of the United Central League side, biding his time, managing the odd first-team game here and there, but was suddenly thrust into the thick of things following the Munich disaster.

In the wake of the events in Germany, he was handed the No.5 shirt and played his part in helping United maintain some form of stability in the league and to reach the FA Cup final. Over the following two seasons, Cope was considered a first-team regular, with season 1959/60 seeing him play in both the centre-half and right-back positions.

In season 1960/61, however, after playing in six of the opening nine fixtures, Bill Foulkes made a permanent switch from full-back to centre-half and Cope suddenly found himself out of the side. He adapted to second-team football, but when Luton Town offered him the opportunity of regular first-team action, he decided that he would end his association with United, with the Hatters paying £10,000 for his services.

STEPHEN JAMES 'STEVE' COPPELL

Country: England
Born: 9 Jul 1955
Debut: 1 Mar 1975 v Cardiff City
Position: Right-midfield
Appearances: 393 (3) **Goals scored:** 70
Seasons: 1974/75 – 1982/83
Clubs: Tranmere Rovers, Manchester United

Snatched from under the noses of Liverpool and Everton, when signed from Tranmere Rovers for £60,000 in February 1975, Steve Coppell was still studying at university when he made his debut for United as a substitute against Cardiff City, winning a Second Division Championship medal at the end of that first season. Nudging Willie Morgan out of the team and making the outside-right spot his own, he gave United a notable front line, with Gordon Hill on the opposite flank, and it was not long before he was adding the first of his 42 full England international honours to the Under-23 cap already won.

An FA Cup runners-up medal in 1976 was followed by a winner's medal 12 months later, with further runners-up awards in the 1979 Cup final and the 1983 Milk Cup final. Converted to more of a midfield role by Dave Sexton, he enjoyed a record unbroken run of 206 consecutive games between January 1977 and November 1981, a month that saw him suffer a knee injury while on international duty and one that would ultimately force him to retire in October 1983.

Although never a particularly prolific goalscorer, he had his best season in 1978/79 when he was on target 12 times. He also set up both of United's late goals in the 1979 FA Cup final, when it appeared they had saved the tie. He was soon back in the game, however, becoming one of the youngest ever managers at just 28 when he took over at

Crystal Palace for the 1984/85 season. It was the start of a long and successful managerial careeer.

JAMES 'JIMMY' COUPAR

Country: Scotland
Born: 1869 **Died:** Jan 1953
Debut: 3 Sep 1892 v Blackburn Rovers
Position: Forward
Appearances: 34 **Goals scored:** 10
Seasons: 1892/93 & 1901/02
Clubs: Dundee Our Boys, Newton Heath, St Johnstone, Rotherham Town, Luton Town, Swindon Town, Linfield, Swindon, Newton Heath

James Coupar was one of a trio of Dundee Our Boys players to be signed by Newton Heath officials in June 1892 ahead of the club's first season in the Football League. Slimly built, but a very effective individual who played in three of the five forward positions during the Heathens' first season of league football, he scored in their first-ever league game, against Blackburn Rovers on 3 September 1892.

An injury received during 1892/93 proved troublesome and he was advised to rest for 12 months. It was later reported that, due to his popularity and the directors' disappointment at losing a player of such prominence, he would be paid the sum of £1/5/- (£1.25p) per week while he recovered. It was therefore something of a shock when the player decided to return north and sign for St Johnstone prior to the commencement of season 1893/94. He returned to Newton Heath in September 1901, playing 11 games and scoring four goals. He also had the distinction of scoring in his first and last games for the club.

PETER DAVID COYNE

Country: England
Born: 13 Nov 1958
Debut: 21 Feb 1976 v Aston Villa
Position: Forward
Appearances: 1 (1) **Goals scored:** 1
Seasons: 1975/76 – 1976/77

Clubs: Manchester United, Ashton United, Crewe Alexandra, Los Angeles Aztecs, Hyde United, Swindon Town, Aldershot (loan), Colne Dynamoes, Glossop North End, Radcliffe Borough

T. CRAIG

Country: Unknown
Born: Unknown **Died:** Unknown
Debut: 18 Jan 1890 v Preston North End
Position: Forward
Appearances: 2 **Goals scored:** 1
Seasons: 1889/90 – 1890/91
Clubs: Newton Heath

CHARLES 'CHARLIE' CRAVEN

Country: England
Born: 2 Dec 1909 **Died:** 30 Mar 1972
Debut: 27 Aug 1938 v Middlesbrough
Position: Inside-left
Appearances: 11 **Goals scored:** 2
Seasons: 1938/39
Clubs: Boston United, Grimsby Town, Manchester United, Birmingham

Born in Boston, Lincolnshire, Charlie Craven did the rounds of his local sides Boston Trinity, Town and United before joining Grimsby Town. With the Mariners, he was on the verge of England honours, but the nearest he got to pulling on the white shirt of his country was being named as reserve against Holland in 1935. His performances with Grimsby also persuaded Manchester United to pay out £6,000 to bring him to Old Trafford after they were promoted to the First Division. He began his United career in a fashion expected of him, scoring twice in the opening three fixtures, but then the goals mysteriously dried up and at the end of the season, he was on the move to Birmingham.

PATRICK TIMOTHY 'PAT' CRERAND

Country: Scotland
Born: 19 Feb 1939
Debut: 23 Feb 1963 v Blackpool
Position: Midfield
Appearances: 397 **Goals scored:** 15
Seasons: 1962/63 – 1970/71
Clubs: Duntocher Hibernian, Celtic, Manchester United

The signing of Pat Crerand was arguably the last piece of the jigsaw, as Busby completed his rebuilding programme following the demise of his team at Munich. Born in the east end of Glasgow, Crerand joined his beloved Celtic from Duntocher Hibernian in August 1957. The old adage of 'practice makes perfect' was particularly true in the case of the young Celtic player, as he was soon developing into one of the best half-backs in Scotland, having made his debut in the green and white hoops in October 1958 in a Scottish League Cup tie against Queen of the South. It was not an uncommon sight at Celtic Park to see Crerand attempting to knock over traffic cones from various distances, often 70 to 80 yards, as he honed his passing skills.

Having won international honours, a half-time flare-up with trainer Sean Fallon, during a game with rivals Rangers, spelled the end of the fiery wing-half's time at Parkhead. Two weeks later, he was trying on the red jersey of Manchester United, with Matt Busby quickly agreeing to pay a sum of £56,000 for the talented player. With Britain under a blanket of snow and ice for weeks on end, Crerand's Manchester United debut came in a friendly against Bolton Wanderers in Cork, on 13 February 1963, with his talent clearly visible despite playing on a mud-covered pitch. His league debut came ten days later at Blackpool.

His Scotland career, having won 16 full caps, came to an end in 1966, following various confrontations with the Scottish selectors, but his country's loss was clearly United's gain, as he added League Championship and European Cup winner's medals, in 1965, 1967 and 1968, to the FA Cup one of 1963. 'When Crerand plays well, United play well' soon became a common saying, something that George Best was to back up when he said, 'Paddy made the team tick, he always gave United the edge when it mattered.'

As the league appearances became fewer at the beginning of the 1970s, more time was taken up coaching the younger players at Old

Trafford and he was eventually appointed reserve-team manager. With the appointment of Tommy Docherty as manager, Pat Crerand was appointed his assistant, but the relationship wasn't a smooth one. He quickly grasped the opportunity to become manager at Northampton Town in January 1976, quitting his £8,500-a-year job with United. Today, Crerand extols the virtues of the present United side through his work with the club's in-house television channel.

JOHN 'JACK' CROMPTON

Country: England
Born: 18 Dec 1921 **Died:** 4 Jul 2013
Debut: 5 Jan 1946 v Accrington Stanley
Position: Goalkeeper
Appearances: 212 **Goals scored:** 0
Seasons: 1945/46 – 1955/56
Clubs: Newton Heath Loco, Goslings, Oldham Athletic (amateur), Manchester City (amateur), Manchester United

A product of the famous Goslings club, Jack Crompton played his first game for United in 1944 while still an amateur, becoming Busby's first-choice keeper after the war and continuing to play, as captain, with the Central League side until the mid-1950s. A strong, reliable goalkeeper, with a noted ability for stopping penalty kicks, he was unfortunate that international honours were to pass him by, despite winning League and FA Cup winner's medals at club level. He left United to become trainer-coach of Luton Town during season 1956/57, the last of the 1948 Cup-winning side to do so, but was to return in the aftermath of Munich to take on the role of trainer. It was a position that he held until the early 1970s when he left for a spell in charge of Barrow, before joining Bobby Charlton at Preston. Prior to season 1974/75 he returned to Old Trafford once again, taking up the position of reserve-team trainer until 1981 when he finally cut his ties with the club after the arrival of Ron Atkinson.

Crompton, the only United player to make appearances on all four of the club's 'official' home grounds – North Road, Bank Street, Maine Road and Old Trafford – was still a regular at United fixtures, in particular the reserves/Under-21s up until his death.

GARTH ANTHONY CROOKS

Country: England
Born: 10 Mar 1958
Debut: 19 Nov 1983 v Watford
Position: Forward
Appearances: 6 (1) **Goals scored:** 2
Seasons: 1983/84
Clubs: Stoke City, Tottenham Hotspur, Manchester United (loan), West Bromwich Albion, Charlton Athletic

Although he played for United only briefly, the centre-forward had a long and successful career, mainly at Stoke City and Spurs. He eventually retired in 1990, having become the chairman of the PFA. Since retiring from the game, he has worked on the BBC as a pundit.

STANLEY 'STAN' CROWTHER

Country: England
Born: 3 Sep 1935
Debut: 19 Feb 1958 v Sheffield Wednesday
Position: Wing-half
Appearances: 20 **Goals scored:** 0
Seasons: 1957/58 – 1958/59
Clubs: Aston Villa, Manchester United, Chelsea, Brighton & Hove Albion, Rugby Town

Stan Crowther has the rare distinction of having played for two different clubs in the FA Cup during the same season, after joining United in the aftermath of the Munich disaster, having already played in the competition with Aston Villa. Signed a couple of hours prior to United's fifth round cup-tie with Sheffield Wednesday, for a fee of £18,000, he was given special permission by the Football Association to play in the competition, and his experience helped Jimmy Murphy's depleted side march proudly to Wembley where they were beaten by Bolton Wanderers, Crowther adding a runners-up medal to the winner's one he had won 12 months previously for Aston Villa against United. Once United recovered, Crowther became surplus to requirements and joined Chelsea for £10,000 in December 1958.

JOHAN JORDI CRUYFF

Country: Netherlands
Born: 9 Feb 1974
Debut: 17 Aug 1996 v Wimbledon
Position: Forward
Appearances: 26 (32) **Goals scored:** 8
Seasons: 1996/97 – 1999/2000
Clubs: Barcelona, Manchester United, Celta Vigo (loan), Alaves, Espanyol, Metalurh Donetsk, Valletta

Jordi Cruff came through the ranks with Barcelona, following the footsteps of his famous father, who was manager of the Spanish giants at the time, before moving to United in 1996 for a fee of £1.4 million after UEFA changed the rules on the number of foreign players each club was allowed to field in European competition. Scoring in two of his first three appearances, things were looking good for the talented youngster, but a knee injury a couple of months later curtailed his appearances and, although he won a Premier league medal in 1997, injuries were to keep him on the sidelines longer than his actual time on the pitch and when his contract expired in June 2000, he was allowed to leave on a free transfer, joining Alaves.

NICHOLAS JAMES 'NICK' CULKIN

Country: England
Born: 6 Jul 1978
Debut: 22 Aug 1999 v Arsenal
Position: Goalkeeper
Appearances: 0 (1) **Goals scored:** 0
Seasons: 1999/2000
Clubs: Manchester United, Hull City (loan), Bristol Rovers (loan), Livingstone (loan), Queens Park Rangers, Radcliffe Borough

Nick Culkin holds the record for the shortest debut (and only United appearance) in Premier League history, having just 80 seconds of action over seven years at the club, after replacing Raimond van der Gouw in stoppage time against Arsenal at Highbury on 22 August 1999.

JOHN CUNNINGHAM

Country: Scotland
Born: 1868 **Died:** Unknown
Debut: 5 Nov 1898 v Grimsby Town
Position: Forward
Appearances: 17 **Goals scored:** 2
Seasons: 1898/99
Clubs: Celtic (trial), Burnley, Glasgow Hibs, Celtic, Partick Thistle, Heart of Midlothian, Rangers, Glasgow Thistle, Preston North End, Sheffield United, Aston Villa, Newton Heath, Wigan County, Barrow

Glasgow-born John Cunningham had covered countless miles while pursuing his playing career prior to joining Newton Heath from Aston Villa in October 1898. For a player who had spent so little time with a number of teams, it was difficult to see him ever enjoying a lengthy spell with a prominent club of that period. True to form, his time in Manchester was brief and during his five-month career with the Heathens, he played in four of the five forward positions during his 17-match spell, scoring two goals. He was made available for transfer in March 1899, following an internal disagreement, subsequently joining Wigan County.

LAWRENCE PAUL 'LAURIE' CUNNINGHAM

Country: England
Born: 8 Mar 1956 **Died:** 15 Jul 1989
Debut: 19 Apr 1983 v Everton
Position: Forward
Appearances: 3 (2) **Goals scored:** 1
Seasons: 1982/83
Clubs: Leyton Orient, West Bromwich Albion, Real Madrid, Manchester United (loan), Sporting Gijon (loan), Marseille, Leicester City, Rayo Vallecano, FC Betis, Charleroi, Wimbledon, Rayo Vallecano

Laurie Cunningham made his name at West Bromwich Albion under Ron Atkinson, and when he was surplus to requirements at Real Madrid (the first British player to be signed by the Spanish giants), his former manager brought him to Old Trafford on loan at the end of the 1982/83 season.

JOSEPH J. 'JOE' CURRY

Country: England
Born: 1887 **Died:** 1 Apr 1936
Debut: 21 Nov 1908 v Bradford City
Position: Defender
Appearances: 14 **Goals scored:** 0
Seasons: 1908/09 – 1910/11
Clubs: Scotswood, Manchester United, Southampton

A Geordie who joined United in February 1908 and, despite his time at Old Trafford spanning FA Cup and First Division Championship-winning seasons, centre-half Joe Curry was unfortunately not included in any medal presentations due to the presence of Charlie Roberts. With opportunities few and far between, he joined Southampton in April 1911.

JOHN CHARLES KEYWORTH CURTIS

Born: 3 Sep 1978
Debut: 14 Oct 1997 v Ipswich Town
Position: Full-back
Appearances: 9 (10) **Goals scored:** 0
Seasons: 1997/98 – 1999/2000
Clubs: Manchester United, Barnsley (loan), Blackburn Rovers, Sheffield United (loan), Leicester City, Portsmouth, Preston North End (loan), Nottingham Forest, Queens Park Rangers, Worcester City, Wrexham, Northampton Town, Gold Coast United

A member of the United FA Youth Cup-winning side of 1995, alongside Phil Neville, many thought that John Curtis would enjoy a long career with the club. However, following his debut in October 1997, he found it almost impossible to dislodge the likes of Gary Neville and Denis Irwin and joined Barnsley on loan, before making the more permanent move to Blackburn Rovers for a fee of £1.2 million in the summer of 2000.

D

FABIO DA SILVA

Country: Brazil
Born: 9 Jul 1990
Debut: 24 Jan 2009 v Tottenham Hotspur
Position: Full-back
Appearances: 36 (17) **Goals scored:** 2
Seasons: 2008/09 – present
Clubs: Fluminense, Manchester United, Queens Park Rangers (loan)

Considered at one point to be the more promising of the da Silva twins, his place in the starting XI for the 2011 Champions League final confirming this, but a combination of injuries and the excellent form of his brother Rafael and Patrice Evra saw his early progress blocked. A year out on loan at Queens Park Rangers was designed to give him more opportunities in the Premier League, but it was a move that was dogged by further injuries and their battle against relegation. As he himself admitted: 'It didn't go the way I wanted.'

RAFAEL PEREIRA DA SILVA

Country: Brazil
Born: 9 Jul 1990
Debut: 17 Aug 2008 v Newcastle United
Position: Full-back
Appearances: 116 (15) **Goals scored:** 5
Seasons: 2008/09 – present
Clubs: Fluminense, Manchester United

While his twin brother's career briefly stalled, season 2012/13 saw Rafael, who had sometimes been guilty of overly enthusiastic defending in the past, progress onto a different level with countless excellent performances, including goals, making him United's most-improved player in the title-winning campaign. Hampered by injuries early in his career, he has overcome those early setbacks and made the right-back position his own. Only Michael Carrick and Patrice Evra made more appearances than he did in 2012/13 as he picked up his third Premier League winner's medal.

Always looking to move forward in support of his forwards, his goals at Anfield and against Queens Park Rangers will be, for many, stand-out points of the 2012/13 season. A slip at international level cost his country dear in the 2012 Olympics, but if he can continue to progress, then he should also become a regular with Brazil as well as Manchester United.

HERBERT DALE

Country: England
Born: Jan 1867 **Died:** Dec 1925
Debut: 25 Oct 1890 v Bootle Reserves
Position: Forward
Appearances: 1 **Goals scored:** 0
Seasons: 1889/90
Clubs: Manchester FA, Newton Heath

JOSEPH 'JOE' DALE

Country: England
Born: 3 Jul 1921 **Died:** 11 Sep 2000
Debut: 27 Sep 1947 v Preston North End
Position: Outside-right
Appearances: 2 **Goals scored:** 2
Seasons: 1947/48
Clubs: Witton Albion, Manchester United, Port Vale, Witton Albion

WILLIAM 'BILLY' DALE

Country: England
Born: 17 Feb 1905 **Died:** 30 May 1987
Debut: 25 Aug 1928 v Leicester City
Position: Full-back
Appearances: 68 **Goals scored:** 0
Seasons: 1928/29 – 1931/32
Clubs: Manchester United, Manchester City, Ipswich Town, Norwich City

Billy Dale began his United career as a triallist in 1925, signing initially on amateur forms, but it was not until 1928 that he made his debut. Never a regular, he remained at the club until 1931, when he moved across town and joined City in a player-plus-cash deal along with Harry Rowley, which brought Bill Ridding and £2,000 to Old Trafford.

EDWARD 'TED' DALTON

Country: England
Born: Apr 1882 **Died:** Unknown
Debut: 25 Mar 1908 v Liverpool
Position: Full-back
Appearances: 1 **Goals scored:** 0
Seasons: 1907/08
Clubs: Pendlebury, Manchester United, Pendlebury

GERARD ANTHONY 'GERRY' DALY

Country: Republic of Ireland
Born: 30 Apr 1954
Debut: 25 Aug 1973 v Arsenal
Position: Midfield
Appearances: 137 (5) **Goals scored:** 32
Seasons: 1973/74 – 1976/77
Clubs: Bohemians, Manchester United, Derby County, New England Tea Men (loan), Coventry City, Leicester City (loan), Birmingham City, Shrewsbury Town, Stoke City, Doncaster Rovers, Telford United

Soon after taking over at Old Trafford, Tommy Docherty launched a scouting programme in Ireland and 19-year-old Gerry Daly was one of those discovered and signed, with Bohemians receiving a fee of £12,000. His initial appearance was in the Anglo-Italian Cup against Bari on 4 April 1973, making his official debut in the league at the start of the following season.

By now a Republic of Ireland international, he found the pace of the game difficult to adjust to, especially in a struggling side, but following a spell in the reserves, he returned to the first team and a regular place. Scoring five goals in the opening four games of 1974/75, he began to make a name for himself as a deadly penalty taker and was an important player in the immediate return to the First Division at the end of that season. The arrival of Jimmy Greenhoff in November 1976 saw him lose his first-team place and he immediately asked for a transfer, eventually joining Derby County for around £180,000 in March 1977.

PETER DAVENPORT

Country: England
Born: 24 Mar 1961
Debut: 15 Mar 1986 v Queens Park Rangers
Position: Forward
Appearances: 83 (23) **Goals scored:** 26
Seasons: 1985/86 – 1988/89
Clubs: Cammell Laird, Nottingham Forest, Manchester United, Middlesbrough, Sunderland, Airdrieonians, St Johnstone, Stockport County, Southport, Macclesfield Town

Merseyside-born Peter Davenport arrived at Old Trafford in March 1986 as a noted goalscorer with Nottingham Forest, something reflected in his £570,000 fee and the fact he was lined up as a replacement for Barcelona-bound Mark Hughes. Only one goal in his first 11 outings that season was perhaps a worry, but he was soon to recapture his scoring form becoming the leading scorer in 1986/87. However, luck was not on his side, as Hughes returned to the fold under Alex Ferguson and, with Brian McClair also joining the club, Davenport was soon on his way to Middlesbrough in November 1988.

WILLIAM R. 'WILL' DAVIDSON

Country: Scotland
Born: Unknown **Died:** Unknown
Debut: 2 Sep 1893 v Burnley
Position: Half-back
Appearances: 44 **Goals scored:** 2
Seasons: 1893/94 – 1894/95
Clubs: Annbank, Newton Heath

One of the many early Scots at Newton Heath, he was first-choice left-half from the start of season 1893/94, until an injury against Crewe on 1 December 1894 ended his career.

ALAN DAVIES

Country: Wales
Born: 5 Dec 1961 **Died:** 4 Feb 1992
Debut: 1 May 1982 v Southampton
Position: Winger
Appearances: 8 (2) **Goals scored:** 1
Seasons: 1981/82 – 1983/84
Clubs: Manchester United, Newcastle United, Charlton Athletic (loan), Carlisle United (loan), Swansea City, Bradford City, Swansea City

In his ten appearances for United, Alan Davies made two of them in the FA Cup, but one was in the final of 1983 and the other in the replay the following week, where he played a part in two of the four goals. Manchester-born of Welsh parents, he made his first appearance of the 1982/83 season only two weeks prior to that final, as United searched for a replacement for the injured Steve Coppell. But a broken ankle and torn ligaments in a pre-season friendly halted his immediate progress and, despite scoring in his comeback against Juventus in the European Cup-Winners' Cup semi-final, his days at the club were numbered and he joined Newcastle United in July 1985. He won 13 caps for Wales. Davies sadly committed suicide early in 1992.

L. DAVIES

Country: Unknown
Born: Unknown **Died:** Unknown
Debut: 30 Oct 1886 v Fleetwood Rangers
Position: Forward
Appearances: 1 **Goals scored:** 0
Seasons: 1886/87
Clubs: Newton Heath

RONALD TUDOR 'RON' DAVIES

Country: Wales
Born: 25 May 1942 **Died:** 24 May 2013
Debut: 30 Nov 1974 v Sunderland
Position: Forward

Appearances: 0 (10) **Goals scored:** 0
Seasons: 1974/75
Clubs: Chester, Luton Town, Norwich City, Southampton, Portsmouth, Manchester United, Arcadia Shepherds, Millwall (loan), LA Aztecs, Dorchester Town, Tulsa Roughnecks, Seattle Sounders

The Welsh international Ron Davies was a man of many clubs, but it was in the latter stages of his career that he made his way to Manchester, joining United as part of the deal that took George Graham to Portsmouth in November 1974. Scoring four goals (all headers) at Old Trafford was undoubtedly one of the highlights of his career, but it came at a time when he was a Southampton player in August 1969. With United he made only ten appearances, every one as a substitute, failing to find the net in any of them. His stay was also brief, leaving four months later to join Arcadia Shepherds of South Africa.

RONALD WYN DAVIES

Country: Wales
Born: 20 Mar 1942
Debut: 23 Sep 1972 v Derby County
Position: Forward
Appearances: 16 (1) **Goals scored:** 4
Seasons: 1972/73
Clubs: Locomotive Llanberis, Caernarfon Town, Wrexham, Bolton Wanderers, Newcastle United, Manchester City, Manchester United, Blackpool, Crystal Palace (loan), Stockport County, Crewe Alexandra, Bangor City

Like his namesake, Wyn Davies was a player with a lengthy CV, and it was late in his career that he joined United, signed by Frank O'Farrell for £25,000 from neighbours City in September 1972, in the hope that his goalscoring ability would help a struggling United. But a change of manager soon afterwards saw Davies out of favour, having scored only four goals in 16 games, and he subsequently joined Blackpool in June 1973.

SIMON ITHEL DAVIES

Country: Wales
Born: 23 Apr 1974
Debut: 21 Sep 1994 v Port Vale
Position: Midfield
Appearances: 10 (10) **Goals scored:** 1
Seasons: 1995/95 – 1996/97
Clubs: Manchester United, Exeter City (loan), Huddersfield Town (loan), Luton Town, Macclesfield Town, Rochdale, Bangor City, Total Network Solutions, Bangor City, Rhyl, Chester City, Airbus UK

Simon Davies was a Welsh international, who despite Youth Cup success in 1992 (when he often captained a side featuring the likes of Beckham, Giggs, Gary Neville and Scholes) could not achieve the senior opportunities he sought and eventually left to join Luton Town for £150,000 in August 1997.

JIMMY ROGER WILLIAM DAVIS

Country: England
Born: 6 Feb 1982 **Died:** 9 Aug 2003
Debut: 5 Nov 2001 v Arsenal
Position: Winger
Appearances: 1 **Goals scored:** 0
Seasons: 2001/02
Clubs: Manchester United, Royal Antwerp (loan), Swindon Town (loan), Watford (loan)

JOHN DAVIS

Country: Unknown
Born: Unknown **Died:** Unknown
Debut: 14 Jan 1893 v Nottingham Forest
Position: Goalkeeper
Appearances: 10 **Goals scored:** 0
Seasons: 1892/93 – 1893/94
Clubs: Hurst, Burslem Port Vale, Newton Heath

JOSEPH 'JOE' DAVIS

Country: Wales
Born: 12 Jul 1864 **Died:** 7 Oct 1943
Debut: 30 Oct 1886 v Fleetwood Rangers
Position: Half-back
Appearances: 2 **Goals scored:** 0
Seasons: 1886/87 – 1889/90
Clubs: Druids, Newton Heath, Wolverhampton Wanderers, Druids

ALEXANDER DOWNIE 'ALEX' DAWSON

Country: Scotland
Born: 21 Feb 1940
Debut: 22 Apr 1957 v Burnley
Position: Forward
Appearances: 93 **Goals scored:** 54
Seasons: 1956/57 – 1961/62
Clubs: Manchester United, Preston North End, Bury, Brighton & Hove Albion, Brentford (loan), Corby Town

Alex Dawson was one of the youngsters thrown in at the deep end amid the turmoil surrounding the aftermath of Munich. Born in Aberdeen, the Dawson family moved south to Hull when he was only 11, due to his father's occupation as a trawlerman (Denis Law's story was eerily similar). His footballing ability quickly helped him settle in at school and during season 1954/55, he was chosen to represent England Schoolboys on six occasions. Such were his performances at this level that many clubs took an interest in the dark-haired youngster. But it was Manchester United who signed him up, moving him from his regular outside-right role to the position where he was to make his name – centre-forward.

He took little time in adapting to his new position and his goals played a major part in the United's FA Youth Cup success in 1956 and 1957. Such was his progress within the junior and reserve ranks that, with the 1957 First Division title wrapped up with three fixtures remaining, Matt Busby decided to give Dawson his first-team debut against Burnley at Old Trafford on 22 April, celebrating with a goal in United's 2-0 win.

Prior to the events in Germany on that cold February afternoon, he made only one more appearance, before being thrust into the limelight, leading the attack and scoring one of the goals in the 3-0 FA Cup fifth-round tie against Sheffield Wednesday on 19 February, 13 days after that fateful Thursday. He was to score again, the only goal of the match, in United's first league fixture following the crash, against Nottingham Forest, but it was in the FA Cup that Dawson continued to show his ability, scoring United's second in the 2-2 sixth-round draw against West Bromwich Albion, then notching a hat-trick in the 5-3 semi-final replay against Fulham at Highbury (one of only two for United since the war at this stage of the tournament).

Unfortunately, he failed to conjure up a goal in the final itself, when United's luck finally ran out. Appearances during 1958/59 were limited through injury, while in January 1961, he was to prove himself as not only as a goalscorer but also a goal stopper, taking over from the injured Harry Gregg against Tottenham Hotspur at Old Trafford – a game United won 2-0.

Despite Dawson finishing second top scorer in season 1960/61 with 20 from 34 outings, Busby signed David Herd from Arsenal, forcing him back into the reserves and, when interest was shown by Preston North End, he decided that perhaps now was the time to move on and an £18,000 fee took him to Deepdale in October 1961.

DAVID DE GEA QUINTANA

Country: Spain
Born: 7 Nov 1990
Debut: 7 Aug 2011 v Manchester City
Position: Goalkeeper
Appearances: 81 **Goals scored:** 0
Seasons: 2011/12 – present
Clubs: Atlético Madrid, Manchester United

Selection as goalkeeper in the PFA Premier League team for 2012/13 was proof enough that David De Gea had indeed weathered the storm and established himself as a more than capable custodian in the hotbed of the top flight in English football. Following in the footsteps of Edwin van der Sar, his introduction into English football was enough to make lesser individuals reconsider their decision to leave their more familiar surroundings. It was certainly a baptism of fire for the young, inexperienced Spaniard, with the media quick to pounce on his every error.

Initially, the £18 million signing had to alternate with Anders Lindegaard for the No.1 position, despite having won the Europa League with his previous club. Press reports speculated that the Spanish Under-21 international would return home, but under the guidance of goalkeeping coach Eric Steele, he stuck to the job in hand and established himself as United's first-choice keeper. He has developed a reputation for pulling off numerous, often unorthodox, vital saves, and played a key role as United clinched the 2012/13 Premiership title.

RITCHIE RIA ALFONS DE LAET

Country: Belgium
Born: 28 Nov 1988
Debut: 24 May 2009 v Hull City
Position: Defender
Appearances: 4 (2) **Goals scored:** 0
Seasons: 2008/09 – 2009/10
Clubs: Royal Antwerp, Stoke City, Wrexham (loan), Manchester United, Sheffield United (loan), Preston North End (loan), Portsmouth (loan), Norwich City (loan), Leicester City

HAROLD DEAN

Country: England
Born: 1910 **Died:** Unknown
Debut: 26 Sep 1931 v Chesterfield
Position: Forward
Appearances: 2 **Goals scored:** 0
Seasons: 1931/32
Clubs: Old Trafford FC, Manchester United, Mossley

JAMES 'JIMMY' DELANEY

Country: Scotland
Born: 3 Sep 1914 **Died:** 26 Sep 1989
Debut: 31 Aug 1946 v Grimsby Town
Position: Outside-right
Appearances: 184 **Goals scored:** 28

Seasons: 1946/47 – 1950/51
Clubs: Celtic, Manchester United, Aberdeen, Falkirk, Derry City, Cork Athletic, Elgin City

League title medals in 1936 and 1938 and a Scottish Cup winner's medal in 1937 endeared Jimmy Delaney to the Celtic support, but a broken arm kept him on the sidelines for over two years, casting some doubt over the Scottish international's future. Insurance cover also became a problem, but it did not stop Matt Busby bringing him south in February 1946, with many being of the opinion that the United manager had wasted £4,000. They were soon proved wrong as, a fortnight after his United debut, he was scoring twice for Scotland, becoming an integral part of United side, helping them to FA Cup success in 1948. His pace on the wing, crossing ability and his experience were vital additions to the Reds' success.

Shortly after the start of season 1950/51, he lost his place in the side and, following a friendly against Aberdeen that September, the Scottish club enquired as to his availability. Busby felt that there was still some mileage in the 36-year-old and wanted the player to stay in Manchester, but Delaney himself considered his opportunities at Old Trafford were now limited and that a move was probably to his advantage. Reluctantly, Busby relented and a £3,500 fee exchanged hands.

MARK JAMES DEMPSEY

Country: England
Born: 14 Jan 1964
Debut: 2 Nov 1983 v Spartak Varna
Position: Midfield
Appearances: 1 (1) **Goals scored:** 0
Seasons: 1983/84 – 1985/86
Clubs: Manchester United, Swindon Town (loan), Sheffield United, Chesterfield (loan), Rotherham United, Macclesfield Town

J. DENMAN

Country: Unknown
Born: Unknown **Died:** Unknown
Debut: 5 Dec 1891 v Blackpool
Position: Full-back

Appearances: 1 **Goals scored:** 0
Seasons: 1891/92
Clubs: South Bank, Newton Heath

WILLIAM 'BILLY' DENNIS

Country: England
Born: 21 Sep 1896 **Died:** Unknown
Debut: 13 Oct 1923 v Oldham Athletic
Position: Full-back
Appearances: 3 **Goals scored:** 0
Seasons: 1923/24
Clubs: Ashton PSA, Stalybridge Celtic, Blackburn Rovers, Stalybridge Celtic, Manchester United, Chesterfield, Wigan Borough, Macclesfield Town, Hurst

NEIL HAMILTON DEWAR

Country: Scotland
Born: 11 Nov 1908 **Died:** Unknown
Debut: 11 Feb 1933 v Preston North End
Position: Forward
Appearances: 36 **Goals scored:** 14
Seasons: 1932/33 – 1933/34
Clubs: Third Lanark, Manchester United, Sheffield Wednesday, Third Lanark

Leaving the Highlands for Glasgow was a wise move for Neil Dewar, who joined Third Lanark in October 1929 and carved out an excellent career during which he won Scottish international honours. His 23 goals in 28 games during 1932/33 made Scott Duncan decide that he wanted Dewar at Old Trafford and he paid £5,000 for his signature in February 1933. At 6ft and 13st, he was an imposing figure, but following a goal on his debut, he suffered a dip in form and, ten months later, United and Neil Dewar (who was known by the nickname 'Silversleeves' due to his habit of wiping his nose on the sleeve of his shirt during games) parted company, with the player crossing the Pennines to join Sheffield Wednesday in exchange for Jack Ball.

MAME BIRAM DIOUF

Country: Senegal
Born: 16 Dec 1987
Debut: 9 Jan 2010 v Birmingham City
Position: Forward
Appearances: 3 (6) **Goals scored:** 1
Seasons: 2009/10 – 2011/12
Clubs: ASC Diaraf, Molde, Manchester United, Molde (loan), Blackburn Rovers (loan), Hanover

ERIC DANIEL DJEMBA-DJEMBA

Country: Cameroon
Born: 4 May 1981
Debut: 10 Aug 2003 v Arsenal
Position: Midfield
Appearances: 27 (12) **Goals scored:** 2
Seasons: 2003/04 – 2004/05
Clubs: Brasseries Du Cameroun, Kadji Sport Academie De Douala, Nantes, Manchester United, Aston Villa, Burnley (loan), Qatar SC, Odense Boldklub, Hapoel Tel Aviv, Bnei Sakhnin

Eric Djemba-Djemba was signed from Nantes in August 2003 with high expectations of the combative midfielder, but his was to be a career mixed with Cameroon international duties and family illness, which meant he spent less time in Manchester than he would have hoped. Despite the occasional highlight, such as an excellent goal against Leeds United, he never quite managed to establish himself in the side. Following little more than a couple of dozen starts, he was allowed to join Villa for £1.35 million, much less than the club had paid for him. Subsequently he had his most successful spell in Denmark with Odense, and now plays his football in Israel.

BOJAN DJORDJIC

Country: Sweden
Born: 6 Feb 1982
Debut: 19 May 2001 v Tottenham Hotspur
Position: Midfield

Appearances: 1 (1) **Goals scored:** 0
Seasons: 2000/01 – 2001/02
Clubs: Brommapojkarna, Manchester United, Sheffield Wednesday (loan), AGF Aarhus (loan), Red Star Belgrade (loan), Rangers, Plymouth Argyle, AIK Athens, Videoton, Blackpool, Royal Antwerp, Brommapojkarna

JOHN PETER DOHERTY

Country: England
Born: 12 Mar 1935 **Died:** 13 Nov 2007
Debut: 6 Dec 1952 v Middlesbrough
Position: Inside-right
Appearances: 26 **Goals scored:** 7
Seasons: 1952/53 – 1957/58
Clubs: Manchester United, Leicester City, Rugby Town, Altrincham

One of the many young players who joined the club after playing for Manchester and Lancashire Schools, Doherty signed professional forms on his 17th birthday, making his debut against Middlesbrough in December 1952, while still a member of the youth team. A knee injury and a further cartilage operation did little to help his career, but in 1955/56, he was a member of the United side that lifted the First Division title, but with the wide array of talent available and the lack of opportunities, he moved to Leicester City in October 1957 for a fee of £6,500. He subsequently became chairman of the club's former players' association.

BERNARD DONAGHY

Country: Ireland
Born: 3 Dec 1882 **Died:** 1 Jul 1916
Debut: 4 Nov 1905 v Lincoln City
Position: Inside-forward
Appearances: 3 **Goals scored:** 0
Seasons: 1905/06
Clubs: Derry Celtic, Glentoran, Derry Celtic, Manchester United, Derry Celtic, Burnley

Ten years after his brief career at Manchester United was over, Bernard Donaghy tragically lost his life on the first day of the Battle of the Somme.

MALACHY MARTIN 'MAL' DONAGHY

Country: Northern Ireland
Born: 13 Sep 1957
Debut: 30 Oct 1988 v Everton
Position: Defender
Appearances: 98 (21) **Goals scored:** 0
Seasons: 1988/89 – 1991/92
Clubs: Cromac Albion, Larne, Luton Town, Manchester United, Luton Town (loan), Chelsea

£650,000 took 31-year-old Mal Donaghy from Luton Town to United in October 1988, initially to line up alongside Steve Bruce in the centre of United's defence. Upon Gary Pallister's arrival during the following summer, he was often played at right-back while also adding some cover in the centre of defence if ever there was an injury. Because of his age, he was only ever going to be something of a stop-gap signing, but his dedication and professionalism won him many admirers. He moved back to Luton Town on loan in December the following year, Les Sealey coming to Old Trafford, before joining Chelsea in August 1992 for £100,000.

IAN RICHARD DONALD

Country: Scotland
Born: 28 Nov 1951
Debut: 7 Oct 1970 v Portsmouth
Position: Full-back
Appearances: 6 **Goals scored:** 0
Seasons: 1970/71 – 1972/73
Clubs: Manchester United, Partick Thistle, Arbroath

ROBERT 'BOB' DONALDSON

Country: Scotland
Born: 27 Aug 1871 **Died:** 28 Apr 1947
Debut: 3 Sep 1892 v Blackburn Rovers
Position: Forward
Appearances: 155 **Goals scored:** 66
Seasons: 1892/93 – 1897/98
Clubs: Aidrieonians, Blackburn Rovers, Newton Heath, Luton Town, Glossop North End, Ashford Town

Bob Donaldson became a Newton Heath player in August 1892 after having previously been with Airdrieonians and Blackburn Rovers. His signing, however, caused some dispute between the two clubs, with the Football Association having to step in and sort the matter out. The stockily built individual, a typical centre-forward of the period who played the game hard, was to score 20 goals in 22 games during that first season, while also scoring the club's first-ever Football League goal in September 1892. He narrowly escaped serious injury during a training session when a hammer, thrown by a team-mate, knocked him unconscious, but he made a full recovery. His Heathens career came to an end in December 1897, when he moved to Luton Town.

DONG FANGZHOU

Country: China
Born: 23 Jan 1985
Debut: 9 May 2007 v Chelsea
Position: Forward
Appearances: 2 (1) **Goals scored:** 0
Seasons: 2006/07 – 2007/08
Clubs: Dalian Saidelong, Dalian Shide, Manchester United, Royal Antwerp (loan), Dalian Shide, Legia Warsaw, Portimonense, Mika, Hunan Billows

DONNELLY

Country: Unknown
Born: Unknown **Died:** Unknown
Debut: 25 Oct 1890 v Bootle Reserves
Position: Forward
Appearances: 1 **Goals scored:** 0
Seasons: 1890/91
Clubs: Newton Heath

ANTHONY 'TONY' DONNELLY

Country: England
Born: Apr 1886 **Died:** Apr 1947
Debut: 15 Mar 1909 v Sunderland
Position: Full-back

Appearances: 37 **Goals scored:** 0
Seasons: 1908/09 – 1912/13
Clubs: Tongue FC, Heywood United, Manchester United, Heywood United, Glentoran, Heywood United, Chester, Southampton, Middleton Borough

Tony Donnelly began as a goalkeeper before turning to full-back, joining United from Heywood in July 1908. He took over the No.2 shirt in December 1910, making 15 appearances as United lifted the First Division title but, unable to retain a place in the team, he returned to Heywood early in season 1912/13.

THOMAS 'TOMMY' DOUGAN

Country: Scotland
Born: 22 Nov 1915 **Died:** Unknown
Debut: 29 Mar 1939 v Everton
Position: Forward
Appearances: 4 **Goals scored:** 0
Seasons: 1938/39 – 1939/40
Clubs: Alloa Athletic, Tunbridge Wells Rangers, Plymouth Argyle, Manchester United, Heart of Midlothian, Kilmarnock, Dunfermline

JOHN DOUGHTY

Country: Wales
Born: Oct 1865 **Died:** Apr 1937
Debut: 30 Oct 1886 v Fleetwood Rangers
Position: Forward
Appearances: 3 **Goals scored:** 3
Seasons: 1886/87 and 1891/92
Clubs: Druids, Newton Heath, Hyde, Fairfield

ROGER DOUGHTY

Country: Wales
Born: Oct 1865 **Died:** 19 Dec 1914
Debut: 18 Jan 1890 v Preston North End
Position: Half-back

Appearances: 8 **Goals scored:** 1
Seasons: 1889/90 – 1891/92 and 1896/97
Clubs: Druids, Newton Heath, Fairfield, West Manchester, Newton Heath

WILLIAM DOUGLAS

Country: Scotland
Born: Unknown **Died:** Unknown
Debut: 3 Feb 1894 v Aston Villa
Position: Goalkeeper
Appearances: 57 **Goals scored:** 0
Seasons: 1893/94 – 1895/96
Clubs: Dundee Our Boys, Ardwick, Newton Heath, Derby County, Blackpool, Warmley, Dundee

Goalkeeper William Douglas was introduced into the Newton Heath line-up as a replacement for local lad Joe Fall in February 1894, having arrived at Clayton from neighbours Ardwick the previous month. Following a 5-2 home defeat against Fairfield in a Manchester Cup tie in 1895/96, Douglas had received the brunt of the criticism, suffering as much from the crowd behind his goal – so much so, that he packed his bags and disappeared back to Dundee. In the furore that followed, he was suspended *sine die*.

JOHN DOW

Country: Scotland
Born: 1873 **Died:** Unknown
Debut: 24 Mar 1894 v Bolton Wanderers
Position: Defender
Appearances: 50 **Goals scored:** 6
Seasons: 1893/94 – 1895/96
Clubs: Dundee, Dundee Our Boys, Dundee, Newton Heath, Fairfield, Glossop North End, Middlesbrough, West Ham United, Luton Town

Another Dundonian, Jack Dow joined the Newton Heath ranks in February 1894, making his debut at right-back, and appearing under the name of 'Woods' for some unknown reason. A versatile individual, who filled numerous positions, his career in Manchester was brief and he played his last game for the club in March 1896, before moving to Fairfield.

ALEXANDER LEEK BROWN 'ALEX' DOWNIE

Country: Scotland
Born: 1876 **Died:** 9 Dec 1953
Debut: 22 Nov 1902 v Leicester City
Position: Half-back
Appearances: 191 **Goals scored:** 14
Seasons: 1902/03 – 1909/10
Clubs: Glasgow Perthshire, Third Lanark, Bristol City, Swindon Town, Manchester United, Oldham Athletic, Crewe Alexandra

Born in Dunoon, Alex Downie was already an experienced player by the time he arrived at United in October 1902. During his time at the club, United won both the League Championship and FA Cup, but unfortunately in the latter competition he failed to play in any of the ties despite playing in 23 of the league fixtures. Indeed, he played in the league fixtures before and after both the quarter-final and semi-final ties, while also playing at right-half against Leicester Fosse the Saturday prior to the Cup final. Unlucky or what! The disappointment of losing out on an FA Cup winner's medal was something that Alex Downie did not really get over, and in October 1909 he joined Oldham Athletic for a fee of £600.

JOHN DENNIS DOWNIE

Country: Scotland
Born: 19 Jul 1925 **Died:** 19 Feb 2013
Debut: 5 Mar 1949 v Charlton Athletic
Position: Forward
Appearances: 116 **Goals scored:** 37
Seasons: 1948/49 – 1952/53
Clubs: Bradford Park Avenue, Manchester United, Luton Town, Hull City, Wisbech, Mansfield Town, Darlington, Hyde United, Mossley, Stalybridge Celtic

John Downie was signed for United in March 1949 as a replacement for Johnny Morris, costing a then record fee of £18,000, a transfer which came about thanks to his performances against United in the epic three-match FA Cup confrontations a few weeks earlier. Following a promising start, winning a Championship medal in 1952, he never completely fulfilled his potential and became unsettled when a request to switch from inside-forward to half-back was turned down and he left the club in August 1953, joining Luton Town for £10,000.

WILLIAM LEVI 'BILLY' DRAYCOTT

Country: England
Born: 15 Feb 1869 **Died:** Unknown
Debut: 1 Sep 1896 v Gainsborough Trinity
Position: Half-back
Appearances: 95 **Goals scored:** 6
Seasons: 1896/97 – 1898/99
Clubs: Burslem Port Vale, Stoke City, Burton Wanderers, Newton Heath, Bedminster, Bristol Rovers, Wellingborough, Luton Town

Billy Draycott was a regular in the Heathens' half-back line during his three seasons at the club. Having scored in only his second appearance, he would soon find opportunities in front of goal becoming rarer, with only one strike in his final two campaigns.

DION DUBLIN

Country: England
Born: 22 Apr 1969
Debut: 15 Aug 1992 v Sheffield United
Position: Forward
Appearances: 6 (11) **Goals scored:** 3
Seasons: 1992/93 – 1993/94
Clubs: Norwich City, Cambridge City, Barnet (loan), Manchester United, Coventry City, Aston Villa, Millwall (loan), Leicester City, Celtic, Norwich City

After scoring on his United debut at Southampton, Dion Dublin was unfortunate to break his leg on his home debut against Crystal Palace, putting him out of the game for five months. Having been signed from Cambridge United in August 1992 for £1 million, by the time he returned from his injury, Alex Ferguson had added Eric Cantona to the squad. Despite scoring regularly for the reserve side, he failed to obtain a spot in the first-team set-up, and left United in September 1994 for £2 million. He went on to have a long and successful career, also winning four England caps in 1998.

RICHARD 'DICK' DUCKWORTH

Country: England
Born: 14 Sep 1882 **Died:** Unknown
Debut: 19 Dec 1903 v Gainsborough Trinity
Position: Half-back
Appearances: 254 **Goals scored:** 11
Seasons: 1903/04 – 1913/14
Clubs: Newton Heath Athletic, Manchester United

Dick Duckworth was one of the few local players to grace the United line-up in those distant pre-First World War days. A solitary appearance during 1903/04 at right-half was followed with eight in the following campaign, six of those in the forward line, scoring six goals, including a hat-trick against Doncaster Rovers. But it wasn't until season 1906/07 that he managed to command a regular first-team place, making his name as a right-half, as part of the formidable Duckworth, Roberts and Bell trio who took United to FA Cup and First Division success between 1908 and 1911, although he was to miss almost half the games in the latter season. Capped in the Commonwealth tour of South Africa in 1910, it was surprising that he never received a full cap. He played his final first-team game for United in November 1913, but remained at Old Trafford until 1919, when he was given a free transfer and decided to hang up his boots.

WILLIAM DUNN

Country: England
Born: Jul 1877 **Died:** Unknown
Debut: 4 Sep 1897 v Lincoln City
Position: Forward
Appearances: 12 **Goals scored:** 0
Seasons: 1896/97 – 1898/99
Clubs: South Bank, Newton Heath

Dunn was a versatile individual from the north-east, whose career was brought to something of a premature end due to a knee injury.

PATRICK ANTHONY JOSEPH 'PAT' DUNNE

Country: Republic of Ireland
Born: 9 Feb 1943
Debut: 8 Sep 1964 v Everton
Position: Goalkeeper
Appearances: 67 **Goals scored:** 0
Seasons: 1964/65 – 1966/67
Clubs: Everton (amateur), Shamrock Rovers, Manchester United, Plymouth Argyle, Shamrock Rovers, Thurles Town, Shelbourne

As a quiet 15-year-old schoolboy international, Pat Dunne was a member of the Dublin-based Stella Maris club and he was seduced across the Irish Sea, along with fellow custodian Ronnie Briggs, to Old Trafford for trials. His travelling companion was signed, but Dunne was forced into using the return portion of his ticket. Three months later, former Manchester United captain Johnny Carey, now manager at Everton, saw enough of the big goalkeeper in a game to offer him a trial at Goodison Park and, after impressing on his second trip across the Irish Sea, Dunne was duly signed.

Sadly, a holiday incident, when he fell on a broken bottle, cost him his career at Everton. He signed for Shamrock Rovers and, after a notable performance in the Irish Cup final, he was snapped up by United for £10,500 in May 1964. Having won a League Championship medal at the end of 1964/65, he was dropped two games into the following season in favour of David Gaskell, who in turn lost his place to the returning Harry Gregg. The arrival of Alex Stepney from Chelsea in September 1966 saw the goalkeeping position more than adequately covered and he moved to Plymouth Argyle, with £5,000 changing hands.

ANTHONY PETER 'TONY' DUNNE

Country: Republic of Ireland
Born: 24 Jul 1941
Debut: 15 Oct 1960 v Burnley
Position: Left-back
Appearances: 534 (1) **Goals scored:** 2
Seasons: 1960/61 – 1972/73
Clubs: Shelbourne, Manchester United, Bolton Wanderers, Detroit Express

In April 1960, £5,000 bought United a player who went on to give 12 years of consistency at the highest level and one who would certainly be a candidate for any All-Time United XI. His name? Tony Dunne. He had plenty of pace, which meant he was invaluable covering for those in the centre, and he could also get forward when required.

A Dubliner who won Republic of Ireland amateur caps, playing in the 1960 Olympic Games, and an FAI Cup winner's medal with Shelbourne that same year, Dunne made his first-team debut a matter of weeks after signing, coming on as a substitute for Shay Brennan in a friendly against Real Madrid. An injury to Noel Cantwell in November 1961 saw him claim a regular place and, except for missing a dozen or so games in the middle of 1962/63, he was an automatic choice until 1973, switching between the two full-back positions with ease, winning FA Cup and First Division Championship medals, as well as being part of the European Cup-winning team. He also won 33 caps for the Republic of Ireland and the Irish Footballer of the Year award. He scored just twice: v West Brom on 4 May 1966 and v Newcastle United on 9 December 1967.

With United struggling during season 1972/73, he continued to give his usual 100 per cent effort and commitment, and it was something of a shock when he was given a free transfer by Tommy Docherty in April 1973, especially when his experience would have been most beneficial. Moving to Bolton Wanderers, Dunne maintained his high standard of play in the Second Division, as the Burnden Park side strode towards the title, while United were relegated. Despite having left Old Trafford, he was awarded a testimonial match, against Manchester City, for his services to the club and a crowd of 17,859 turned up to show their gratitude and earn Dunne around £12,000.

MICHAEL 'MIKE' DUXBURY

Country: England
Born: 1 Sep 1959
Debut: 23 Aug 1980 v Birmingham City
Position: Full-back
Appearances: 345 (33) **Goals scored:** 7
Seasons: 1980/81 – 1989/90
Clubs: Manchester United, Blackburn Rovers, Bradford City, Golden FC

One of those 'cannot do without' utility men, Mike Duxbury was to enjoy a career of over 370 games, spanning 15 years with United. Joining the club as a schoolboy in May 1975, he made his debut five years later, going on to fill numerous positions, while always turning in a commendable performance that was often unappreciated. Quick in the tackle, with good distribution skills, he won the first of his ten England caps in November 1983 at right-back, while winning FA Cup medals in 1983 and 1985.

In 1982/83, he was the only player to appear in each of United's 60 games, a testament to the consistency of the Accrington-born defender. The arrival of Viv Anderson and a knee injury in 1988 saw his appearances restricted and, at the end of 1989/90, having been awarded a testimonial by United, he was given a free transfer for his services and joined Blackburn Rovers.

JAMES ARTHUR 'JIMMY' DYER

Country: England
Born: 24 Aug 1883 **Died:** Unknown
Debut: 14 Oct 1905 v West Bromwich Albion
Position: Forward
Appearances: 1 **Goals scored:** 0
Seasons: 1905/06
Clubs: Wombwell, Barnsley, Doncaster Rovers, Ashton Town, Manchester United, West Ham United

CHRISTOPHER MARK 'CHRIS' EAGLES

Country: England
Born: 19 Nov 1985
Debut: 28 Oct 2003 v Leeds United
Position: Midfield

Appearances: 7 (10) **Goals scored:** 1
Seasons: 2003/04 – 2007/08
Clubs: Manchester United, Watford (loan), Sheffield Wednesday (loan), Watford (loan), NEC Nijmegen (loan), Burnley, Bolton Wanderers

A talented, Hertfordshire-born youngster, Chris Eagles came through Watford's youth system before moving to United as a 14-year-old. After a debut in the League Cup against Leeds in October 2003, he made nine appearances over two seasons, before loan spells with Watford, Sheffield Wednesday and Nijmegen, before returning to United in 2006. A further eight appearances for United followed, including his only goal at Everton as United chased the title, but such was the quality of players at the club at this time, he joined Burnley on a three-year deal in July 2008 for an undisclosed fee.

JOHN EARP

Country: England
Born: 1860 **Died:** Unknown
Debut: 30 Oct 1886 v Fleetwood Rangers
Position: Forward
Appearances: 1 **Goals scored:** 0
Seasons: 1886/87
Clubs: Newton Heath

SYLVAN AUGUSTUS EBANKS-BLAKE

Country: England
Born: 29 Mar 1986
Debut: 27 Oct 2004 v Crewe Alexandra
Position: Forward
Appearances: 1 (1) **Goals scored:** 1
Seasons: 2004/05 – 2005/06
Clubs: Manchester United, Royal Antwerp (loan), Plymouth Argyle, Wolverhampton Wanderers

ADAM JAMES ECKERSLEY

Country: England
Born: 7 Sep 1985
Debut: 26 Oct 2005 v Barnet
Position: Full-back
Appearances: 1 **Goals scored:** 0
Seasons: 2005/06
Clubs: Manchester United, Royal Antwerp (loan), Brondby (loan), Barnsley (loan), Port Vale (loan), Horsens, AGF Aarhus

RICHARD JON ECKERSLEY

Country: England
Born: 12 Mar 1989
Debut: 24 Jan 2009 v Tottenham Hotspur
Position: Defender
Appearances: 0 (4) **Goals scored:** 0
Seasons: 2008/09
Clubs: Manchester United, Burnley, Plymouth Argyle (loan), Bradford City (loan), Bury (loan), Toronto FC (loan)

ALFRED 'ALF' EDGE

Country: England
Born: Oct 1864 **Died:** 11 Apr 1941
Debut: 3 Oct 1891 v Manchester City
Position: Inside-forward
Appearances: 3 **Goals scored:** 3
Seasons: 1891/92
Clubs: Stoke, Newton Heath, Stoke, Northwich Victoria, Ardwick, Macclesfield

HUGH EDMONDS

Country: Scotland
Born: 1884 **Died:** Unknown
Debut: 11 Feb 1911 v Bristol City
Position: Goalkeeper
Appearances: 51 **Goals scored:** 0

Seasons: 1910/11 – 1911/12
Clubs: Hamilton Academical, Belfast Distillery, Linfield, Bolton Wanderers, Manchester United, Glenavon

Born in Chryston, Ayrshire, Hugh Edmonds had made only a handful of appearances with Bolton Wanderers before he was signed by United in February 1911, as successor to Harry Moger. By the end of season 1910/11, he had kept six clean sheets in 13 appearances and was the owner of a League Championship medal. Such were his performances that it began to look as if he would enjoy a reign similar to that of his predecessor, but after playing in 30 of the 38 league fixtures of the following season, he left the club to become player-manager of Irish side Glenavon.

DUNCAN EDWARDS

Country: England
Born: 1 Oct 1936 **Died:** 21 Feb 1958
Debut: 4 April 1953 v Cardiff City
Position: Half-back
Appearances: 177 **Goals scored:** 21
Seasons: 1952/53 – 1957/58
Clubs: Manchester United

Old Trafford has had many heroes, but for many there is one individual who surpasses all others from either before or after his time in a red shirt. That player is Duncan Edwards. The mere mention of his name still brings tears to the eyes of men of a certain age and he is considered the greatest player of his generation, at both club and international level.

Born in the Black Country town of Dudley, he had the physique of a man while still a boy and, much to his mother's concern, could often be found on the local rec enjoying a kick-about with lads many years older. Captain of his school side, he was soon representing England Schoolboys, games that found countless club scouts on the touchline in the hope of securing his signature. Among them was one from United, and Matt Busby was duly informed that this was a youngster that he had to get.

Fortunately, despite living close to Wolves and Aston Villa, there was only one club that Duncan Edwards wanted to join and that was United. But it still took a midnight trip to the West Midlands by Jimmy Murphy and Bert Whalley, on 2 June 1952, to get his signature on paper for

Manchester United. Joining the groundstaff, while also taking on an apprenticeship as a carpenter, something that was soon pushed to the side, he progressed through the junior ranks, often winning Youth Cup ties on his own, switching from his normal wing-half position to that of centre-forward, before he was given his first-team debut against Cardiff City on 4 April 1953, less than a year after signing.

It was not, however, until October 1953, following an injury to Henry Cockburn, that he claimed the No.6 shirt on a permanent basis, forcing the fit-again Cockburn to look elsewhere for first-team football. Two years later, with a First Division Championship medal in his pocket, he became the youngest post-war England international at the age of 18 years and 183 days, making his debut against Scotland at Wembley. He now had the world at his feet.

He was soon to be called up for his national service and could be found representing the army in countless competitions in midweek, while playing for United or his country at the weekend. There were countless talented players in the United side of this time but, not simply due to his physique, he stood out among them all and once established in the side, his place was never threatened, although he did miss the odd game through illness or the occasional knock, and it was a foregone conclusion that he would one day be captain of both his club and country.

This was, however, not to be. Initially surviving the Munich disaster, despite fractures to both legs and ribs and damage to his kidneys – it was 15 days after the crash, on 21 February 1958, that he finally lost his fight for life, amazing doctors and nurses to the end of one battle that he just could not win. Even if he had survived, he would have never played again, such were his injuries. The nation mourned.

Today, he is fondly remembered with a statue in Dudley town centre, two stained glass windows in St Francis' Church, Dudley, while his grave is a place of pilgrimage for United supporters. His like will never be seen again.

PAUL FRANCIS EDWARDS

Country: England
Born: 7 Oct 1947
Debut: 19 Aug 1969 v Everton
Position: Defender
Appearances: 66 (2) **Goals scored:** 1

Seasons: 1969/70 – 1972/73
Clubs: Trainee, Manchester United, Oldham Athletic (loan), Oldham Athletic, Stockport County (loan), Stockport County, Ashton United

Edwards was an Oldham-born defender who won England Under-23 honours and filled both the full-back and centre-half positions, but failed to make either his own. Upon the departure of Wilf McGuinness as manager, he found his opportunities limited and in March 1973, he moved to his hometown club for £15,000.

DAVID ELLIS

Country: Scotland
Born: 2 Mar 1900 **Died:** Unknown
Debut: 25 Aug 1923 v Bristol City
Position: Outside-right
Appearances: 11 **Goals scored:** 0
Seasons: 1923/24
Clubs: Airdrieonians, Maidstone United, Manchester United, St Johnstone, Bradford City, Arthurlie

Signed for United by his former manager at Airdrieonians, John Chapman, for a fee of £1,250 in 1923, David Ellis failed to make much of an impression in his new surroundings, returning to Scotland just over a year later, joining St Johnstone for a cut-price £500. Ellis claimed half the transfer fee, but the claim was dismissed.

FREDRICK CHARLES 'FRED' ERENTZ

Country: Scotland
Born: Mar 1870 **Died:** 6 Apr 1938
Debut: 3 Sep 1892 v Blackburn Rovers
Position: Defender
Appearances: 310 **Goals scored:** 9
Seasons: 1892/93 – 1901/02
Clubs: Dundee Our Boys, Newton Heath

Of the other five Scots who made up the backbone of that initial Football League side on the opening day of season 1892/93, only Fred Erentz enjoyed a prolonged and successful career with the club. Born in

Dundee in 1870, he moved south to take his place in the Newton Heath side as a 22-year-old from Dundee Our Boys, going on to play 310 games over ten seasons before retiring with a knee injury in 1902. He remains eighth in the list of Scottish players to have made the most appearances for United, and having played throughout the entirety of Newton Heath's league history (the club changed its name to Manchester United in 1902), he remained the club's leading appearance-maker until the outbreak of the First World War, when George Wall overtook his record. He also holds the record for the most appearances by a United player in the second tier, with 229.

HENRY BERNT 'HARRY' ERENTZ

Country: Scotland
Born: 17 Sep 1874 **Died:** 19 Jul 1947
Debut: 18 Jan 1898 v Arsenal
Position: Right-back
Appearances: 9 **Goals scored:** 0
Seasons: 1897/98
Clubs: Dundee, Oldham County, Newton Heath, Tottenham Hotspur, Swindon Town

GEORGE EVANS

Country: Unknown
Born: Unknown **Died:** Unknown
Debut: 4 Oct 1890 v Higher Walton
Position: Forward
Appearances: 1 **Goals scored:** 1
Seasons: 1890/91
Clubs: Newton Heath

JONATHAN GRANT 'JONNY' EVANS

Country: Northern Ireland
Born: 2 Jan 1988
Debut: 26 Sep 2007 v Coventry City
Position: Centre-back

Appearances: 140 (16) **Goals scored:** 5
Seasons: 2007/08 – present
Clubs: Manchester United, Royal Antwerp (loan), Sunderland (loan)

From the age of nine, Jonny Evans was playing at the Manchester United Centre of Excellence in Belfast, and eventually his family moved to Manchester so that he could move through the Academy. After playing for United during the summer tour of 2006, he was loaned out twice the following season, first to Royal Antwerp and then to Sunderland. He made his full international debut for Northern Ireland, in a famous 3–2 victory over Spain, before he had worn the red shirt of United in a competitive fixture. Although he then went on to make his United debut, a further six-month loan spell at Sunderland in 2007/08 helped increase his confidence, and the young Irishman returned to Manchester ready to fight for a first-team place.

Some wondered if his footballing future might lie elsewhere, but the transfers of Gerard Pique to Barcelona and Wes Brown to Sunderland, in 2008 and 2011 respectively, created an opening into the first team. So in 2008/09, he was able to earn his first Premier League title, but still had formidable competition for a starting place from Nemanja Vidić and Rio Ferdinand. But a serious injury to Vidić in 2011/12 meant he was soon a regular in the side, and over the course of the past two seasons, he has established himself as one of the most consistent players at the club, turning in some excellent performances.

Even a red card against Manchester City in the 6–1 horror show at Old Trafford during 2011/12 did little to stint his continuing progress. The name of Evans continues to feature regularly on the United team-sheet, despite competition from Chris Smalling and Phil Jones as well as the two senior players, and it looks as though it will remain there for some time to come.

SIDNEY 'SID' EVANS

Country: England
Born: 1893 **Died:** Unknown
Debut: 12 Apr 1924 v Crystal Palace
Position: Forward
Appearances: 6 **Goals scored:** 2
Seasons: 1923/24 – 1924/25
Clubs: Darlaston, Cardiff City, Manchester United, Pontypridd

PATRICE LATYR EVRA

Country: France
Born: 15 May 1981
Debut: 14 Jan 2006 v Manchester City
Position: Left-back
Appearances: 314 (21) **Goals scored:** 7
Seasons: 2005/06 – present
Clubs: Paris Saint-Germain, Marsala, Monza, Nice, AS Monaco, Manchester United

As far as debuts went, Patrice Evra's against Manchester City in January 2006, a matter of days after his £5.5 million transfer from Monaco, was certainly not one to remember fondly, as he was taken off at half-time in United's 3-1 defeat. But it was to be a rare blemish in the Frenchman's Manchester United career, as he progressed to become an important cog in Sir Alex Ferguson's team, which he was to later captain with distinction.

As comfortable in attack as he is in defence, few wingers manage to get the better of the United No.3, who is widely regarded as one of the best in the world in his position. He was given an early taste of trophy-winning success when he came on as a late substitute in the Carling Cup final victory over Wigan a few weeks after joining the club. It was to be the first of many trophies he has since accumulated, including five Premier League titles, and the Champions League in 2008. When a number of media critics began to question his form during the title-winning campaign of 2012/13, he stepped up a gear and played a crucial part in the club's 20th title success, adding a goal threat to his other qualities. He is not only a regular captain, but also the man in charge of the dressing room music.

He has come a long way from his childhood in Senegal, where he was the son of a diplomat. He made his mark at Monaco, playing a part in the club's journey to the Champions League final in 2004, and became a French international, eventually captaining his country in the 2010 World Cup. His career, especially in Manchester, is one that any young player could take as a prime example as to what can be achieved in the game with the proper dedication.

F

JOSEPH WILLIAM 'JOE' FALL

Country: England
Born: 1872 **Died:** Unknown
Debut: 2 Sep 1893 v Burnley
Position: Goalkeeper
Appearances: 27 **Goals scored:** 0
Seasons: 1893/94
Clubs: Middlesbrough Ironopolis, Newton Heath, Small Heath, Altrincham

Manchester-born Joe Fall was signed from Middlesbrough Ironopolis in August 1893. His time between the posts at Clayton lasted only one season and, following relegation to the Second Division for the first time at the end of 1893/94, his contract was not renewed.

ALFRED H. 'FRED' FARMAN

Country: England
Born: Apr 1869 **Died:** Unknown
Debut: 18 Jan 1890 v Preston North End
Position: Forward
Appearances: 61 **Goals scored:** 28
Seasons: 1889/90 – 1894/95
Clubs: Birmingham Excelsior, Aston Villa, Bolton Wanderers, Newton Heath

Alf Farman had the distinction of scoring Newton Heath's first goal at Bank Street, Clayton; in fact, he scored all three in the 3-2 win over Burnley at the start of the 1893/94 season. Although a winger, joining the club from Bolton Wanderers in April 1889, he possessed a powerful shot and could often be found on the scoresheet.

JOHN IGNATIUS 'SONNY' FEEHAN

Country: Republic of Ireland
Born: 17 Sep 1926 **Died:** 11 Mar 1995
Debut: 5 Nov 1949 v Huddersfield Town

Position: Goalkeeper
Appearances: 14 **Goals scored:** 0
Seasons: 1949/50
Clubs: Bohemians, Waterford, Manchester United, Northampton Town, Brentford, Headington United

Sonny Feehan crossed the Irish Sea to join United in November 1948, but with Jack Crompton as first choice, he had to wait a year before making his debut. His opportunities were to be few and far between and with the arrival of Reg Allen in June 1950, he was allowed to leave, joining Northampton Town for £525 two months later.

MAROUANE FELLAINI BAKKIOUI

Country: Belgium
Born: 22 Nov 1987
Debut: –
Position: Midfield/Forward
Seasons: 2013/14 – present
Appearances: – **Goals scored:** –
Clubs: Standard Liege, Everton

The 25-year-old Belgian was signed on deadline day, 2 September 2013, from Everton for an undisclosed fee. After joining Everton in 2008, the Belgian international made 177 appearances for the Goodison Park side, scoring 33 goals. His move to Old Trafford saw him re-united with his former manager David Moyes.

GEORGE FELTON

Country: England
Born: 1859 **Died:** Unknown
Debut: 25 Oct 1890 v Bootle Reserves
Position: Half-back
Appearances: 1 **Goals scored:** 0
Seasons: 1890/91
Clubs: Newton Heath

RIO GAVIN FERDINAND

Country: England
Born: 7 Nov 1978
Debut: 27 Aug 2002 v Zalaegerszeg
Position: Defender
Appearances: 423 (9) **Goals scored:** 8
Seasons: 2002/03 – present
Clubs: West Ham United, AFC Bournemouth (loan), Leeds United, Manchester United

In any discussion about who has been United's greatest centre-back, the name of Rio Ferdinand is sure to crop up. His consistency since his £30 million move from Leeds United in the summer of 2002 has been an outstanding feature in United's quest for silverware.

The Peckham-born star has twice held the tag as the world's most expensive defender, first when he moved from West Ham to Leeds for £18 million, and then with his transfer to United two years later. Already an established England international by the time he moved to Old Trafford, he brought stability to the heart of a United defence that had been missing it somewhat since the departure of Jaap Stam, helping United to the title in his first season at the club.

Thereafter, there was the embarrassment of missing a drugs test, which brought him an eight-month ban, and it wasn't until the arrival of Nemanja Vidić that he had a settled defensive partner. That pairing brought United title success again in 2006/07, and since then the trophies have arrived with great regularity. His great strengths include his pace, his reading of the game and his distribution. For a defender, he concedes remarkably few free kicks, and is rarely booked during the course of a season.

His only weakness has been a back injury, which was to cost him both the United and the England captaincy. But with his career at both club and international level in doubt, he went on to silence the doubters by continuing to perform at a level few can reach. He has also played a huge part in the development of the club's younger players, especially when the Serb was out through injury. Now moving into the twilight of his career, his presence will be sorely missed when he finally decides to hang up his boots, but during the summer of 2013 he signed another 12-month contract to ensure that new manager David Moyes will benefit from his experience in his first season in charge of the club.

ARCHIBALD DANIEL 'DANNY' FERGUSON

Country: Wales
Born: 25 Jan 1903 **Died:** Oct 1971
Debut: 7 Apr 1928 v Burnley
Position: Forward
Appearances: 4 **Goals scored:** 0
Seasons: 1927/28
Clubs: Rhyl Athletic, Manchester United, Reading, Accrington Stanley, Chester, Halifax Town, Stockport County, Macclesfield Town

DARREN FERGUSON

Country: Scotland
Born: 9 Feb 1972
Debut: 26 Feb 1991 v Sheffield United
Position: Midfield
Appearances: 22 (8) **Goals scored:** 0
Seasons: 1990/91 – 1993/94
Clubs: Manchester United, Wolverhampton Wanderers, Sparta Rotterdam, Wrexham, Peterborough United

On a hiding to nothing at the club managed by his father, Darren Ferguson proved that he had the ability to deserve his place in the first team, making his debut at Sheffield United in February 1991. Three knee operations, rather than who his father was, kept him out of first-team action and, followed by a hamstring injury, his appearances were limited, although he notched up enough games to claim a Premier League medal at the end of 1992/93. A £500,000 bid from Wolves was accepted in January 1994 and he duly moved to the Midlands, though he spent most of his career at Wrexham. More recently he has begun to develop a reputation as a manager, having begun his career at Peterborough United.

JOHN JOSEPH FERGUSON

Country: England
Born: 12 Dec 1904 **Died:** 23 Feb 1973
Debut: 29 Aug 1931 v Bradford Park Avenue
Position: Forward

Appearances: 8 **Goals scored:** 1
Seasons: 1931/32
Clubs: Grimsby Town, Workington, Spen Black and White, Wolverhampton Wanderers, Watford, Burton Town, Manchester United, Derry City, Gateshead United

RONALD JOHNSON 'RON' FERRIER

Country: England
Born: 26 Apr 1914 **Died:** 11 Oct 1991
Debut: 4 Sep 1935 v Charlton Athletic
Position: Forward
Appearances: 19 **Goals scored:** 4
Seasons: 1935/36 – 1938/39
Clubs: Grimsby Wanderers, Grimsby Town, Manchester United, Oldham Athletic

Signed from Grimsby Town in May 1935, Ron Ferrier was to feature mainly in the reserve side during his three years at the club, although he did manage seven games during the 1935/36 Second Division title-winning campaign. An undisclosed fee took him to Oldham Athletic in March 1938.

WILLIAM JOHN 'BILL' FIELDING

Country: England
Born: 17 Jun 1915 **Died:** May 2006
Debut: 25 Jan 1947 v Nottingham Forest
Position: Goalkeeper
Appearances: 7 **Goals scored:** 0
Seasons: 1946/47
Clubs: Cardiff City, Bolton Wanderers, Manchester United

JAMES FISHER

Country: Scotland
Born: 1876 **Died:** Unknown
Debut: 20 Oct 1900 v Walsall
Position: Forward

Appearances: 46 **Goals scored:** 3
Seasons: 1900/01 – 1901/02
Clubs: East Stirlingshire, St Bernard's, Aston Villa, King's Park, Newton Heath

Signed from King's Park in October 1900, James Fisher's early outings in the Newton Heath side saw him feature in four different positions, but in the latter half of the season he laid claim to the outside-left spot, where he was to enjoy an unbroken run of 34 games. Following his last appearance in January 1902, he was reported as having returned to his native Scotland.

JOHN FITCHETT

Country: England
Born: Apr 1880 **Died:** Unknown
Debut: 21 Mar 1903 v Leicester City
Position: Full-back
Appearances: 18 **Goals scored:** 1
Seasons: 1902/03 & 1904/05
Clubs: Bolton Wanderers, Southampton, Manchester United, Plymouth Argyle, Manchester United, Fulham, Sale Holmfield, Barrow, Exeter

John Fichett captained Manchester Schools, but it was from Southampton that he joined United in March 1903. Despite scoring on his debut, he left the club within two months, returning south to join Plymouth Argyle. Following a year on the south coast, he was back in Manchester in June 1904, but it was not until January 1905 that he reappeared in the first-team picture. His second spell at the club ended in May 1905 when he again moved south, joining Fulham.

GEORGE ARTHUR FITTON

Country: England
Born: 30 May 1902 **Died:** 10 Sep 1984
Debut: 26 Mar 1932 v Oldham Athletic
Position: Forward
Appearances: 12 **Goals scored:** 2
Seasons: 1931/32 – 1932/33
Clubs: Kidderminster Harriers, West Bromwich Albion, Manchester United, Preston North End, Coventry City, Kidderminster Harriers

After a dozen appearances between the final weeks of 1931/32 and the opening months 1932/33, the former West Bromwich player might have fared better had there not been a change of manager in the summer of 1932, as his career blossomed following his move to Preston North End and later with Coventry.

JOHN HERBERT NORTON FITZPATRICK

Country: Scotland
Born: 18 Aug 1946
Debut: 24 Feb 1965 v Sunderland
Position: Defender/Midfield
Appearances: 141 (6) **Goals scored:** 10
Seasons: 1964/65 – 1972/73
Clubs: Manchester United

Aberdeen-born John Fitzpatrick was a member of 1964 Youth Cup-winning side, alongside George Best, going on to make his United debut in February 1965. It wasn't, however, until 1967/68 that he managed an extended run in the side, although he did have the distinction of being the club's first substitute in league football, replacing Denis Law at Tottenham on 16 October 1965. Often in trouble with officials, he was sent off against AC Milan in the away leg of the 1969 European Cup semi-final and had to be given a police escort to the dressing rooms.

It was in 1970/71 that he had his most regular season in the side, but then a second cartilage operation produced a setback to his hopes of becoming a first-team regular and, after a further five knee operations, he eventually had to call it a day, at the age of only 26.

DAVID FITZSIMMONS

Country: Scotland
Born: 1875 **Died:** Unknown
Debut: 7 Sep 1895 v Crewe Alexandra
Position: Half-back
Appearances: 31 **Goals scored:** 0
Seasons: 1895/96 & 1899/1900
Clubs: Annbank, Newton Heath, Fairfield, Chorley, Wigan County, Newton Heath

David Fitzsimmons had followed the footsteps of his brother Tom to Newton Heath, having also moved south from Annbank, one of three Scots to make their debuts on the opening day of 1895/96. A determined and excellent team player, he missed only four games during that season, playing in both half-back positions. However, once again the financial situation of the club came to the fore, and, with the lack of funds to pay close-season wages, he duly signed for Fairfield, though he returned briefly a few seasons later.

THOMAS 'TOM' FITZSIMMONS

Country: Scotland
Born: 21 Oct 1870 **Died:** Unknown
Debut: 19 Nov 1892 v Aston Villa
Position: Forward
Appearances: 30 **Goals scored:** 6
Seasons: 1892/93 – 1893/94
Clubs: Annbank, Celtic (trial), Newton Heath, Annbank, St Mirren, Annbank, Fairfield, Glossop North End, Fairfield, Oldham County, Chorley, Wigan County, Annbank

Tom Fitzsimmons was a former Celtic triallist who joined Newton Heath from Annbank in November 1892, making an impressive start with five goals in 18 league starts during 1892/93. His form, however, faded somewhat and he subsequently returned home, something he seemed inclined to do as he had four different spells with the Ayrshire junior side.

DARREN BARR FLETCHER

Country: Scotland
Born: 1 Feb 1984
Debut: 12 Mar 2003 v Basel
Position: Midfield
Appearances: 249 (63) **Goals scored:** 24
Seasons: 2002/03 – present
Clubs: Manchester United

Joining United at the age of 11, the Dalkeith-born youngster was soon tipped for greatness and was earmarked to make his first-team debut at

Aston Villa on the final day of season 1999/2000, at the age of 16 years and 74 days, but this was thwarted due to Premier League rules which prevented players on a schoolboy contract from playing at senior level.

An injury in a youth team friendly halted that initial progress, but he fought back and eventually made his first-team debut in March 2003 in 1-1 draw against Basel in the Champions League. In August that same year he was to make his Scotland debut, coming on as substitute against Norway in a friendly at Hampden Park; less than a year later, in May 2004, he was to become the youngest Scotland captain for 118 years, leading the side against Estonia in Tallinn.

At Old Trafford, he was to take a while to win over the United support, but there was to be a notable difference when he was not in the side, and he played his part in the 2004 FA Cup triumph with a sterling performance against Arsenal in the semi-finals. Goals were something of an omission from his career statistics, with his first for United not coming until November 2005, with his header ending Chelsea's 40-match unbeaten run.

Having started his career often playing on the right of midfield, by 2008/09 he had established himself in the centre and was one of the most influential players in the side. A controversial sending-off against Arsenal in the Champions League semi-final of 2009 ruled him out of the final, yet another disappointment in the Scot's rollercoaster career, who had missed out on the previous year's final success. But worse was to follow in March 2011, when what was described by the club as a 'virus' led to severe weight loss and saw him sidelined. The following December it was announced that he was taking an extended break from the game, as he was suffering from ulcerative colitis, a condition that did not see him return to first-team action until August 2012.

He made his first competitive appearance for ten months against Galatasaray at Old Trafford, crowning what was thought as being a comeback with a goal against Queens Park Rangers, but in the early days of 2013, it was announced that he had undergone surgery with the aim to resolve his ulcerative colitis and that he would not play again that season. His unavailability was a big loss to Sir Alex Ferguson's squad.

PETER FLETCHER

Country: England
Born: 2 Dec 1953
Debut: 14 Apr 1973 v Stoke City
Position: Forward
Appearances: 2 (5) **Goals scored:** 0
Seasons: 1972/73 – 1973/74
Clubs: Manchester United, Hull City, Stockport County, Huddersfield Town

ALAN FOGGON

Country: England
Born: 23 Feb 1950
Debut: 21 Aug 1976 v Birmingham City
Position: Forward
Appearances: 0 (3) **Goals scored:** 0
Seasons: 1976/77
Clubs: Newcastle United, Cardiff City, Middlesbrough, Hartford Bi-Centennials, Rochester Lancers, Hartford Bi-Centennials, Manchester United, Sunderland, Southend United, Hartlepool United (loan), Consett

GEORGE FOLEY

Country: England
Born: 1875 **Died:** Unknown
Debut: 17 Mar 1900 v Barnsley
Position: Forward
Appearances: 7 **Goals scored:** 1
Seasons: 1899/1900
Clubs: Ashford FC, Newton Heath

JOSEPH BERTRAM 'JOE' FORD

Country: England
Born: 7 May 1886 **Died:** Unknown
Debut: 31 Mar 1909 v Aston Villa
Position: Forward
Appearances: 5 **Goals scored:** 0

Seasons: 1908/09 – 1909/10
Clubs: Witton Albion, Crewe Alexandra, Manchester United, Nottingham Forest, Goole Town

DIEGO FORLAN CORAZO

Country: Uruguay
Born: 19 May 1979
Debut: 29 Jan 2002 v Bolton Wanderers
Position: Forward
Appearances: 37 (61) **Goals scored:** 17
Seasons: 2001/02 – 2004/05
Clubs: Club Atletico Penarol, Danubio Futbol Club, Club Atletico Independiente, Manchester United, Villarreal, Atlético Madrid, Internazionale, Internacional

Two goals at Anfield in a 2-1 win in December 2002 will always be the defining moments of the Uruguayan international's United career. Signed in January 2002 from Independiente for a £7.5 million fee, he took 23 games before opening his scoring account. Despite this, he was always a firm supporters' favourite for his energy, commitment and enthusiasm, but the majority of his appearances were to be from the bench. So, unable to grasp a regular starting place, he was allowed to leave in August 2004, joining Villarreal for £1.5 million where he reached the semi-finals of the Champions League in 2006. He won the Golden Boot in the 2010 World Cup.

THOMAS 'TOM' FORSTER

Country: England
Born: Apr 1894 **Died:** 6 Feb 1955
Debut: 8 Nov 1919 v Burnley
Position: Full-back
Appearances: 36 **Goals scored:** 0
Seasons: 1919/20 – 1921/22
Clubs: Northwich Victoria, Manchester United, Northwich Victoria

Signed from Northwich Victoria in January 1916, Tom Forster did not make his debut until November 1919, following his return from the forces.

His Old Trafford career, however, was a short one, as he returned to Northwich in the close season of 1922 having made only 36 appearances.

ALEXANDER 'ALEX' FORSYTH

Country: Scotland
Born: 5 Feb 1952
Debut: 6 Jan 1973 v Arsenal
Position: Right-back
Appearances: 116 (3) **Goals scored:** 5
Seasons: 1972/73 – 1977/78
Clubs: Arsenal, Partick Thistle, Manchester United, Rangers, Motherwell, Hamilton Academical, Queen of the South

A Scottish League Cup winner with Partick Thistle, Alex Forsyth caught the eye of manager Tommy Docherty while on Scotland duty and became one of a number of Scots in the Old Trafford dressing room, joining United in January 1973 for a fee of £100,000. He took a few games to settle in, but soon showed his ability as an attacking full-back with a powerful shot. He was regular in the side until 1975/76, but soon regained his place, only to lose out again to Jimmy Nicholl the following season. Seemingly content in the reserves, he remained at United until 1978 when he moved to Rangers.

QUINTON FORTUNE

Country: South Africa
Born: 21 May 1977
Debut: 30 Aug 1999 v Newcastle United
Position: Midfield
Appearances: 88 (38) **Goals scored:** 11
Seasons: 1999/2000 – 2004/05
Clubs: RCD Mallorca, Atlético Madrid, Manchester United, Bolton Wanderers, Brescia, Tubize, Doncaster Rovers

The ever-smiling South African was signed from Atlético Madrid in August 1999 for £1.5 million, but was to find injuries to be his most troublesome opponent. Quick, strong, skilful and versatile, he was an ideal squad player; however, Charity Shield and Intercontinental Cup medals were all he could claim during his six years at the club due to his bad luck with injuries. His most consistent run in the side came during 2003/04 when he made 34 appearances.

BENJAMIN ANTHONY 'BEN' FOSTER

Country: England
Born: 3 Apr 1983
Debut: 15 Mar 2008 v Derby County
Position: Goalkeeper
Appearances: 23 **Goals scored:** 0
Seasons: 2007/08 – 2009/10
Clubs: Stoke City, Bristol City (loan), Tiverton Town (loan), Stafford Rangers (loan), Kidderminster Harriers (loan), Wrexham (loan), Manchester United, Watford (loan), Birmingham City, West Bromwich Albion

A £1 million buy from Stoke City in the summer of 2005, Ben Foster was widely tipped to reign supreme with both United and England, but he was to manage only one United outing in his first three years at the club, due to being loaned to Watford for the first two seasons, helping them to promotion to the Premier League in his first and keeping them up in his second. Hindered upon his return in 2007/08 by knee surgery, he regained his fitness and went on to win the man-of-the-match award in the 2009 League Cup final, as he helped United win the penalty shoot-out against Tottenham. However, he was unable to dislodge Edwin van der Sar as first-choice keeper, and a further thumb injury did little to help his career. So in May 2010, he was allowed to join Birmingham City for a reported £4 million, before signing for West Brom (initially on loan) a year later. Having made his England debut in February 2007, he has since gone on to win six caps.

WILLIAM ANTHONY 'BILL' FOULKES

Country: England
Born: 5 January 1932
Debut: 13 Dec 1952 v Liverpool
Position: Defender
Appearances: 685 (3) **Goals scored:** 9
Seasons: 1952/53 – 1969/70
Clubs: Manchester United

Bill Foulkes was a former miner and a no-nonsense defender who joined the club in March 1950 from Whiston Boys Club. As a young professional, he continued to play on a part-time basis, working down the mine during the day and training at night, continuing to do so following his first-team debut in December 1952. But after breaking into the side on a regular basis in September 1953, he decided to give up his day job and concentrate on his footballing career.

It proved to be a wise move, as apart from three months out of the side in 1956, he remained a first-choice defender, at either full-back or centre-half, until the late 1960s, winning one England cap in 1955, along with Under-23 and Football League honours. At club level, he was to win four League Championship medals, one FA Cup winner's medal and a European Cup winner's medal in 1968.

Surviving the Munich disaster, along with Harry Gregg he was one of only two players to appear in both games either side of the tragedy, and remarkably he played in every game during that campaign – an achievement of not only remarkable physical consistency but of mental resilience. He was appointed captain of the rebuilt side and continued in that role until he felt the pressure was becoming too much for him. In the six seasons from 1959/60 to 1964/65, he missed just six league games.

But his finest hour in the red shirt undoubtedly came on 15 May 1968 in Madrid. United were 3-2 down on the night and fighting to salvage their European Cup semi-final second-leg tie, when he forsook his defensive duties and meandered up field to score a rare goal from a George Best cross. That goal gave United a 4-3 aggregate lead and took them into the final. Then, on an emotional night at Wembley, he played his part in the historic 4-1 win over Benfica.

By then, at 36, age was beginning to tell, even though he always worked incredibly hard on his fitness, and following a 4-1 defeat against Southampton in August 1969, he played the last of his 688 games for the Reds, taking up a coaching role at the club.

THOMAS 'TOMMY' FRAME

Country: Scotland
Born: 5 Sep 1902 **Died:** 17 Jan 1988
Debut: 1 Oct 1932 v Preston North End
Position: Half-back
Appearances: 52 **Goals scored:** 4

Seasons: 1932/33 – 1933/34
Clubs: Burnbank, Cowdenbeath, Manchester United, Southport, Rhyl Athletic, Bridgnorth Town

Centre-half Tommy Frame was signed from Cowdenbeath by Scott Duncan for a fee of £1,000. An ex-miner, he had the physique to make an impression in the heart of the defence and perhaps in his early days at the club, he used the physical side of his game just that little bit too much, as he was sent off in only his fourth game. However, he was to miss only two fixtures during his first season in English football, contributing two goals.

The following season, 1933/34, saw him fill not only the centre-half position but also right-half, inside-right and left-back, as Scott Duncan's side struggled to avoid relegation, a cause dealt a severe blow when Frame suffered a broken leg during the 2-0 win against Blackpool at Old Trafford on 3 March. Although United escaped the drop, the injury effectively brought an end to his United career, but it was the summer of 1936 before he was to leave Manchester, signing for Southport.

EZEKIEL 'DAVID' FRYERS

Country: England
Born: 9 Sep 1992
Debut: 20 Sep 2011 v Leeds United
Position: Defender
Appearances: 2 (4) Goals: 0
Seasons: 2009/10 – 2011/12
Clubs: Manchester United, Standard Liège, Tottenham Hotspur

STANLEY HUGH 'STAN' GALLIMORE

Country: England
Born: 14 Apr 1910 **Died:** Sep 1994
Debut: 11 Oct 1930 v Wrexham
Position: Forward
Appearances: 76 **Goals scored:** 20
Seasons: 1930/31 – 1933/34
Clubs: Witton Albion, Manchester United, Altrincham, Northwich Victoria

Signed from Witton Albion in September 1929, Stan Gallimore enjoyed an extended run in the side between October 1930 and March 1932. Back in the first team in 1932/33, an injury saw him lose his place and he was subsequently given a free transfer. Following a cartilage operation, he was re-signed in February 1934 and scored twice on his comeback, but was one of many players released at the end of that season, the worst in United's history.

CHARLES RICHARD 'DICK' GARDNER

Country: England
Born: 22 Dec 1913
Debut: 28 Dec 1935 v Plymouth Argyle
Position: Forward
Appearances: 18 **Goals scored:** 1
Seasons: 1935/36 – 1936/37
Clubs: Evesham Town, Birmingham, Notts County, Stourbridge, Manchester United, Sheffield United

Gardner failed to establish himself at the club following his move from Stourbridge in May 1935, mainly due to his lack of goals. He scored just once, on his second game, against Barnsley, on New Year's Day 1936, and joined Sheffield United in May 1937.

WILLIAM FRANCES 'BILLY' GARTON

Country: England
Born: 15 Mar 1965
Debut: 26 Sep 1984 v Burnley
Position: Defender/Full-back
Appearances: 47 (4) **Goals scored:** 0
Seasons: 1984/85 – 1988/89
Clubs: Manchester United, Birmingham City (loan), Salford City, Witton Albion, Hyde United

Salford-born Billy Garton was a competent defender whose career suffered through injury and illness, and therefore he never quite fulfilled his early potential. After being diagnosed with chronic fatigue syndrome, he was forced to retire at the age of only 25, although he did go on to manage a couple of seasons in non-league football.

JAMES PATRICK GARVEY

Country: England
Born: Jan 1878 **Died:** Unknown
Debut: 1 Sep 1900 v Glossop North End
Position: Goalkeeper
Appearances: 6 **Goals scored:** 0
Seasons: 1900/01
Clubs: Wigan County, Manchester United, Middleton, Stalybridge Rovers, Southport Central, Bradford City

JOHN DAVID GASKELL

Country: England
Born: 5 Oct 1940
Debut: 24 Oct 1956 v Manchester City
Position: Goalkeeper
Appearances: 119 (1) **Goals scored:** 0
Seasons: 1956/57 – 1966/67
Clubs: Manchester United, Wrexham, Arcadia Shepherds

Although he didn't sign professional forms until 1957, David Gaskell made his United debut at 16 years and 19 days in October 1956, coming on as substitute in the FA Charity Shield match against Manchester City. He remains the youngest player ever to appear for United in an official fixture. He had gone to simply watch the game from the stand, but following an injury to Ray Wood, he was sent for to take over between the posts, with many watching the game unaware that a change had actually taken place. His full debut did not come until 15 months later. His career was hampered by injuries, although he did earn an FA Cup winner's medal in 1963 and, after beginning season 1966/67 as first choice keeper, he was dropped following the signing of Alex Stepney and decided to leave, joining Wrexham in 1969.

RALPH GAUDIE

Country: England
Born: Jan 1876 **Died:** Unknown
Debut: 5 Sep 1903 v Bristol City
Position: Forward
Appearances: 8 **Goals scored:** 0
Seasons: 1903/04
Clubs: South Bank, Sheffield United, Aston Villa, Woolwich Arsenal, Manchester United

COLIN JOHN GIBSON

Country: England
Born: 6 Apr 1960
Debut: 30 Nov 1985 v Watford
Position: Full-back/Midfield
Appearances: 89 (6) **Goals scored:** 9
Seasons: 1985/86 – 1989/90
Clubs: Aston Villa, Manchester United, Port Vale (loan), Leicester City, Blackpool, Walsall

Gibson was one of those individuals whose ability to fill numerous roles prevented him from holding down a regular first-team place. A First Division title winner with his previous club Aston Villa, injury denied him a place in their European Cup triumph the following season, and it was injuries that were to blight his United career following his £275,000 move in November 1985. Capable of playing in either midfield or defence, a lack of first-team outings saw him eventually transferred to Leicester City for £100,000 in December 1990.

DARRON THOMAS DANIEL GIBSON

Country: Republic of Ireland
Born: 25 Oct 1987
Debut: 26 Nov 2005 v Barnet
Position: Midfield
Appearances: 35 (23) **Goals scored:** 10
Seasons: 2005/06 – 2011/12
Clubs: Manchester United, Royal Antwerp (loan), Wolverhampton Wanderers (loan), Everton

A Republic of Ireland international, Darron Gibson enjoyed loan deals at Royal Antwerp and Wolves before making his United debut in November 2005. A talented midfield player with a thundering shot, he was unable to break into the team on a regular basis, because competition for places was so tough. He failed to agree terms for a move to Sunderland in 2011, eventually leaving United to join Everton in January 2012 for an undisclosed fee. At his new club, under manager David Moyes, there were more opportunities for him to display his skills.

THOMAS RICHARD DONALD 'DON' GIBSON

Country: England
Born: 12 May 1929
Debut: 26 Aug 1950 v Bolton Wanderers
Position: Half-back
Appearances: 115 **Goals scored:** 0
Seasons: 1950/51 – 1954/55
Clubs: Manchester United, Sheffield Wednesday, Leyton Orient

Don Gibson broke into the United first team in August 1950, following his demob from the Royal Marines, keeping his place for most of the season. It wasn't until 1954/55 that he enjoyed a similar lengthy run in the side, but competition from the likes of Eddie Colman and Jackie Blanchflower meant he was struggling to get into the side. By then he was married to Matt Busby's daughter and it was thought best if he moved to a different club, joining Sheffield Wednesday for £8,000 in June 1955.

RICHARD SAMUEL GIBSON

Country: England
Born: Feb 1889 **Died:** Unknown
Debut: 27 Aug 1921 v Everton
Position: Winger
Appearances: 12 **Goals scored:** 0
Seasons: 1921/22
Clubs: Sultan FC, Birmingham, Manchester United

A United player for less than a year, Gibson made only a dozen appearances after joining the club from Birmingham in June 1921 for £250.

TERRENCE BRADLEY 'TERRY' GIBSON

Country: England
Born: 23 Dec 1962
Debut: 2 Feb 1986 v West Ham United
Position: Forward
Appearances: 27 **Goals scored:** 1
Seasons: 1985/86 – 1986/87
Clubs: Tottenham Hotspur, GAIS Gothenburg, Coventry City, Manchester United, Wimbledon, Swindon Town, Peterborough United, Barnet

The diminutive former Tottenham and Coventry striker joined United from the latter for a fee of £600,000, which also included Alan Brazil, in January 1986. Appearances were few and far between following his move, although he did get the opportunity to impress new manager Alex Ferguson in a run of eight consecutive games, but his lack of goals saw him released and he joined Wimbledon for £200,000 in August 1987.

JOHN GIDMAN

Country: England
Born: 10 Jan 1954
Debut: 29 Aug 1981 v Coventry City
Position: Full-back
Appearances: 116 (4) **Goals scored:** 4
Seasons: 1981/82 – 1985/86
Clubs: Aston Villa, Everton, Manchester United, Manchester City, Stoke City, Darlington

John Gidman was Ron Atkinson's first signing for the club in August 1981, in a deal which saw Everton receive £50,000 and Mickey Thomas in exchange. An experienced overlapping full-back, he was an almost ever-present during his first season at the club, but missed most of the following two through injury. Regaining his place early in 1984/85, he was a member of the FA Cup-winning side, but an injury the following season once again saw him miss numerous games. Despite finishing the campaign playing in eight of the final nine games, he was given a free transfer and joined Manchester City.

RYAN JOSEPH GIGGS

Country: Wales
Born: 29 Nov 1973
Debut: 2 Mar 1991 v Everton
Position: Midfield/Winger
Appearances: 788 (154) **Goals scored:** 168
Seasons: 1990/91 – present
Clubs: Manchester United

Few who witnessed his initial performances at Old Trafford for Salford and England Schoolboys, under the guise of Ryan Wilson, could ever have imagined that they were watching a youngster who would go on to become the most decorated player in the history of British football, with 34 winner's medals, and one who would make over 1,000 senior appearances at club and international level.

Born in Cardiff, Giggs moved to Manchester at the age of six when his father, rugby star Danny Wilson, changed codes and began to play rugby league for Swinton. The slimly built youngster was a United fan, but initially came to the attention of neighbours City thanks to the coach at Deans FC. But newsagent Harold Wood wrote to Alex Ferguson to tell him to have a look at the youngster, and the new manager moved quickly to bring him into the United fold. It was clear from the outset that the player, who was to take his mother's maiden name of Giggs following his parents' split, was something special.

Tasting senior action against Everton at Old Trafford in March 1991 and scoring his first goal against Manchester City with a deflected shot a few weeks later, he was soon hailed as the 'next George Best', as he ghosted past defenders with ease, adding goals to an ever-increasing repertoire. His career blossomed quickly, and in 1991/92 he was a first-team regular, though he was still occasionally to line up with youth team colleagues, such as Beckham, Neville and Butt, in the pursuit of the FA Youth Cup in 1992. By the time he won that trophy, he had already picked up his first senior cup, helping United to League Cup success against Nottingham Forest.

The Treble-winning season of 1998/99 would bring, for many, what would be their lasting memory of a player who was to go on to defy his critics time and time again, scoring one of the greatest-ever United goals. It came in extra time during the FA Cup semi-final replay at Villa Park against Arsenal. In a match already full of drama, he intercepted an errant pass from Patrick Vieira and went off on a mesmerising run through the Gunners' defence, before blasting his shot into the top of the net and then pulling off his shirt and dashing down the touchline twirling it above his head.

Had it not been for some niggling injuries, especially earlier in his career, his appearance record could have been even more impressive, but in later years he adopted a different training programme to combat this, introducing yoga into his routine, prolonging his playing career beyond that of his contemporaries. At various stages of his career, potential replacements have been signed up, but he kept on seeing them off. Along the way, he picked up numerous honours, including the OBE for his services to the game in 2007. He became United's all-time leading appearance-maker in the 2008 Champions League final, an occasion he marked by winning his second European title.

Towards the end of the 2012/13 season he confirmed that he would play on for another year, taking him past his 40th birthday. In that campaign, he extended his record of having appeared and scored in every Premier League season, and ended up with his 13th title-winning medal. During the summer, after the appointment of David Moyes as the new manager, he took on the role of player/coach. In years to come, many may be tagged as the 'next Ryan Giggs', but while the boy from Cardiff did more than emulate the career and honours of a certain Irishman, no one will ever enjoy such a decorated and lengthy career as that of Ryan Giggs.

MICHAEL JOHN 'JOHNNY' GILES

Country: Republic of Ireland
Born: 6 Nov 1940
Debut: 12 Sep 1959 v Tottenham Hotspur
Position: Forward
Appearances: 115 **Goals scored:** 13
Seasons: 1959/60 – 1963/64
Clubs: Home Farm, Manchester United, Leeds United, West Bromwich Albion, Philadelphia Fury, Shamrock Rovers

A Republic of Ireland Schoolboy international who joined United from Home Farm in July 1956, Johnny Giles made his debut three years later, gaining full international honours that same season. Beginning as an inside-forward, he was moved to the wing with considerable success until suffering a broken leg during 1960/61. He soon recovered, going on to win an FA Cup medal in 1963, but was frustrated at playing on the wing, and insisted to Busby that he should be allowed to play in his favoured position of inside-forward. The two men couldn't resolve the issue, and he was surprisingly allowed to leave the club in August of that year, joining Leeds United for £37,500. While at Leeds, he went on to become one of the key figures in Don Revie's hugely successful side, eventually leaving that club in 1975. He also won 60 caps for the Republic of Ireland.

ANTHONY 'TONY' DEAN GILL

Country: England
Born: 6 Mar 1968
Debut: 3 Jan 1987 v Southampton
Position: Midfield/Full-back
Appearances: 7 (7) **Goals scored:** 2
Seasons: 1986/87 – 1988/89
Clubs: Manchester United, Bath City

Tony Gill was one of the numerous youngsters who broke into the United side in the late 1980s, but two Achilles injuries curtailed his progress and limited his appearances, while a broken leg against Nottingham Forest in March 1989 brought a premature end to his career.

KEITH ROBERT GILLESPIE

Country: Northern Ireland
Born: 18 Feb 1975
Debut: 5 Jan 1993 v Bury
Position: Winger
Appearances: 7 (7) **Goals scored:** 2
Seasons: 1992/93 – 1994/95
Clubs: Manchester United, Newcastle United, Blackburn Rovers, Wigan Athletic, Leicester City, Sheffield United, Charlton Athletic, Bradford City, Glentoran

A highly talented winger, Keith Gillespie scored on his debut against Bury in the 1992/93 FA Cup, following promising displays at youth level, when he was part of the 1992 FA Youth Cup-winning squad. Perhaps unfortunate that he was in competition with the likes of Kanchelskis, Sharpe and Giggs for a first-team place, his opportunities were limited. In January 1995, he was part of the £7 million deal that brought Andy Cole from Newcastle to United, with his value placed at £1 million.

MATTHEW 'MATT' GILLESPIE

Country: Scotland
Born: 24 Dec 1869 **Died:** Unknown
Debut: 28 Nov 1896 v Small Heath
Position: Forward
Appearances: 89 **Goals scored:** 21
Seasons: 1896/97 – 1899/1900
Clubs: Glasgow Thistle, Blackburn Rovers, Leith Athletic, Lincoln City, Newton Heath

A hat-trick in a friendly gave Matt Gillespie the ideal springboard for his United career, although following his debut in November 1896, he was to score only twice in 17 games he played that season. He remained something of a regular over the course of the following two seasons, but following what was to be his best return of five goals in ten games during 1899/1900, he was released by the club.

THOMAS SAVILL 'TOMMY' GIPPS

Country: England
Born: Jan 1888 **Died:** Unknown
Debut: 25 Dec 1912 v Chelsea
Position: Half-back
Appearances: 23 **Goals scored:** 0
Seasons: 1912/13 – 1914/15
Clubs: Walthamstow, Tottenham Hotspur, Barrow, Manchester United

Signed as a 24-year-old from Barrow in the summer of 1912, Tommy Gipps had previously spent three years with Tottenham.

Had it not been for the First World War, this promising player would surely have featured more prominently for United, but as it was, he made only 23 appearances. He was released on a free transfer in May 1920.

DANIEL JOSEPH 'DON' GIVENS

Country: Republic of Ireland
Born: 9 Aug 1949
Debut: 9 Aug 1969 v Crystal Palace
Position: Forward
Appearances: 5 (4) **Goals scored:** 1
Seasons: 1969/70
Clubs: Manchester United, Luton Town, Queens Park Rangers, Birmingham City, Bournemouth, Sheffield United, Neuchatel Xamax

The Republic of Ireland international went on to win 56 caps for his country, but was unable to make a breakthrough at United, eventually spending his best years with QPR, who he helped to the league runners-up position in 1975/76, when United finished third.

GEORGE WILLIE E. GLADWIN

Country: England
Born: 28 Mar 1907 **Died:** Unknown
Debut: 27 Feb 1937 v Chelsea
Position: Midfield
Appearances: 28 **Goals scored:** 1
Seasons: 1936/37 – 1938/39
Clubs: Doncaster Rovers, Manchester United

Joining United from Doncaster Rovers in February 1937 for a fee of £3,000, Gladwin could do little to prevent relegation a couple of months later. Although he started the Second Division campaign the following season, he was soon out of the side and it wasn't until the start of 1938/39 that he again enjoyed a reasonable run in the first team. Injuries received during the Second World War were to bring an end to his playing career.

GILBERT GODSMARK

Country: England
Born: Jan 1877 **Died:** Feb 1901
Debut: 3 Feb 1900 v Sheffield Wednesday
Position: Forward
Appearances: 9 **Goals scored:** 4
Seasons: 1899/1900
Clubs: Ashford, Newton Heath

Godsmark's promising career was cut short when he was called up to serve in the army during the Boer War. While on service, he died of an illness contracted in southern Africa.

ERNEST HOLROYD 'ERNIE' GOLDTHORPE

Country: England
Born: 8 Jun 1898 **Died:** 5 Nov 1929
Debut: 11 Nov 1922 v Leyton Orient
Position: Forward
Appearances: 30 **Goals scored:** 16
Seasons: 1922/23 – 1924/25
Clubs: Bradford City, Leeds United, Bradford City, Manchester United, Rotherham United

Following his second spell with Bradford City, Ernie Goldthorpe joined United on a free transfer in March 1922. Injuries, however, were to mar his career in Manchester, as he made only 30 appearances in three years, before joining Rotherham United in October 1925. When he was fit, he was a prolific goalscorer, leading the charts in 1922/23, and once hitting four against Notts County. He died at the age of 31 from heart failure brought on by double pneumonia and 'severe exertion while playing badminton'.

FREDRICK 'FREDDIE' GOODWIN

Country: England
Born: 28 Jun 1933
Debut: 20 Nov 1954 v Arsenal
Position: Half-back
Appearances: 107 **Goals scored:** 8
Seasons: 1954/55 – 1959/60
Clubs: Manchester United, Leeds United, Scunthorpe United

Freddie Goodwin joined the club as an amateur, making rapid progress through the ranks prior to his debut during 1954/55 after leaving the forces. Goodwin was a Lancashire cricketer, who spent most his early United career as understudy to Eddie Colman, stepping into the void following Munich and playing in the 1958 FA Cup final. Despite playing every game in 1958/59, as rebuilding continued, he was to find himself back in the reserves following the signing of Maurice Setters, and soon left to join Leeds United for £100,000 in March 1960. After retiring as a player, he managed various sides.

WILLIAM 'BILLY' GOODWIN

Country: England
Born: Jan 1892 **Died:** 9 Jul 1951
Debut: 28 Aug 1920 v Bolton Wanderers
Position: Forward
Appearances: 7 **Goals scored:** 1
Seasons: 1920/21 – 1921/22
Clubs: Chesterfield, Blackburn Rovers, Exeter City, Manchester United, Southend United, Dartford

ANDY LEWIS GORAM

Country: Scotland
Born: 13 Apr 1964
Debut: 14 Apr 2001 v Coventry City

Position: Goalkeeper
Appearances: 2 **Goals scored:** 0
Seasons: 2000/01
Clubs: Oldham Athletic, Hibernian, Rangers, Notts County, Sheffield United, Motherwell, Manchester United, Hamilton Academical, Coventry City, Oldham Athletic, Queen of the South, Elgin City

Andy Goram began his career with Oldham, but it was north of the border with Rangers that he made his name, winning countless honours while also making a name for himself as a cricketer. When United faced goalkeeping problems due to injuries to both Fabien Barthez and Raimond van der Gouw, Sir Alex Ferguson called upon the experienced Scottish international to fill the gap in a loan deal from Motherwell in 2001, as United chased the Championship. He was to play in only two games.

JAMES GOTHERIDGE

Country: England
Born: 1863 **Died:** Unknown
Debut: 30 Oct 1886 v Fleetwood Rangers
Position: Forward
Appearances: 1 **Goals scored:** 0
Seasons: 1886/87
Clubs: Newton Heath, West Manchester

JOHN GOURLAY

Country: Scotland
Born: 1879 **Died:** Unknown
Debut: 18 Feb 1899 v Loughborough Town
Position: Defender
Appearances: 1 **Goals scored:** 0
Seasons: 1898/99
Clubs: Annbank, Newton Heath

ALAN EDWIN GOWLING

Country: England
Born: 16 Mar 1949
Debut: 30 Mar 1968 v Stoke City
Position: Forward
Appearances: 77 (10) **Goals scored:** 21
Seasons: 1967/68 – 1971/72
Clubs: Manchester United, Huddersfield Town, Newcastle United, Bolton Wanderers, Preston North End

Signed as a part-time professional while he continued his university studies, Alan Gowling made good progress after switching from midfield to the forward line. A big, strong player, his club performances earned him England Under-23 caps, as captain, but this did not guarantee first-team football and he felt he would be better off elsewhere when the club recruited other forwards, joining Huddersfield Town in June 1972 for £65,000.

ARTHUR GRAHAM

Country: Scotland
Born: 26 Oct 1952
Debut: 20 Aug 1983 v Liverpool
Position: Winger
Appearances: 52 **Goals scored:** 7
Seasons: 1983/84 – 1984/85
Clubs: Aberdeen, Leeds United, Manchester United, Bradford City

Arthur Graham cost Ron Atkinson a fee of over £45,000 when he was bought from Leeds United in 1983 at the age of 30. He had enjoyed a favourable spell with Aberdeen before moving south, but was one of five Scotland players banned for life from playing for their country following an incident in a Copenhagen nightclub. Pleading his innocence, the ban was lifted two years later. Making his United debut in the 1983 Charity Shield match against Liverpool, he was obviously a short-term recruit and the signing of Jesper Olsen curtailed his stay and in June 1985 he joined Bradford City.

DEINIOL WILLIAM THOMAS GRAHAM

Country: Wales
Born: 4 Oct 1969
Debut: 7 Oct 1987 v Hull City
Position: Forward
Appearances: 1 (3) **Goals scored:** 1
Seasons: 1987/88 – 1989/90
Clubs: Manchester United, Barnsley, Preston North End, Carlisle United, Stockport County, Scunthorpe United, Halifax Town, Dagenham & Redbridge

GEORGE GRAHAM

Country: Scotland
Born: 30 Nov 1944
Debut: 6 Jan 1973 v Arsenal
Position: Midfield
Appearances: 44 (2) **Goals scored:** 2
Seasons: 1972/73 – 1974/75
Clubs: Aston Villa, Chelsea, Arsenal, Manchester United, Portsmouth, Crystal Palace, California Surf

Although born in Bargeddie, Lanarkshire, George Graham played all his football south of the border, enjoying a successful career with Chelsea and Arsenal, winning League, FA Cup and League Cup medals, as well as Scottish international honours. He became Tommy Docherty's first signing as Manchester United manager in December 1972, costing £120,000 from Arsenal, having previously played under the United manager at Chelsea. Upon the departure of Bobby Charlton, Graham was made team captain, but as United's form went from bad to worse, his own form suffered and after losing his place in January 1974, he joined Portsmouth in an exchange deal for Ron Davies.

JOHN GRAHAM

Country: England
Born: 1873 **Died:** Unknown
Debut: 11 Nov 1893 v Wolverhampton Wanderers
Position: Forward

Appearances: 4 **Goals scored:** 0
Seasons: 1893/94
Clubs: Blyth, Newton Heath

WILLIAM GRASSAM

Country: Scotland
Born: 20 Nov 1878 **Died:** Unknown
Debut: 3 Oct 1903 v Arsenal
Position: Forward
Appearances: 37 **Goals scored:** 14
Seasons: 1903/04 – 1904/05
Clubs: Redcliffe Thistle, Glasgow Maryhill, Burslem Port Vale, West Ham United, Celtic, Manchester United, Leyton, West Ham United, Brentford

The Scottish junior international was signed from Celtic in May 1903, having previously enjoyed spells south of the border with Port Vale and West Ham. He took a few games to settle, but was to contribute 11 goals in 23 games during 1903/04. He faded from the scene during the following season and left to join Leyton in the summer of 1905.

DAVID GRAY

Country: Scotland
Born: 4 May 1988
Debut: 25 Oct 2006 v Crewe Alexandra
Position: Full-back
Appearances: 1 **Goals scored:** 0
Seasons: 2006/07
Clubs: Manchester United, Preston North End

IAN DENZIL GREAVES

Country: England
Born: 26 May 1932 **Died:** 2 Jan 2009
Debut: 2 Oct 1954 v Wolverhampton Wanderers
Position: Full-back
Appearances: 75 **Goals scored:** 0
Seasons: 1954/55 – 1959/60
Clubs: Manchester United, Lincoln City, Oldham Athletic

Ian Greaves joined United in May 1953 from Cheshire League side Buxton, making his debut in October 1954, but like many others at the club in the 1950s he found his opportunities limited due to the quality of the playing staff. Capable of playing in either full-back position, or in the half-back line, it was in the aftermath of Munich that he gained a regular place, but a knee injury early in 1959/60 saw him sidelined and he was to make only two further appearances, both in the reserves, before joining Lincoln City in December 1960.

ROBERT EDWARD 'EDDIE' GREEN

Country: England
Born: Jan 1912 **Died:** Unknown
Debut: 26 Aug 1933 v Plymouth Argyle
Position: Forward
Appearances: 9 **Goals scored:** 4
Seasons: 1933/34
Clubs: Bournemouth & Boscombe Athletic, Derby County, Manchester United, Stockport County

BRIAN GREENHOFF

Country: England
Born: 28 Apr 1953 **Died:** 22 May 2013
Debut: 8 Sep 1973 v Ipswich Town
Position: Midfield/Defender
Appearances: 268 (3) **Goals scored:** 17
Seasons: 1973/74 – 1978/79
Clubs: Manchester United, Leeds United, Rovaniemen Palloseura, Rochdale

Signed on apprentice forms as a 15-year-old in August 1968, Brian Greenhoff went on to become one of the most versatile players at the club during the 1970s, even managing a stint between the posts at Birmingham City in August 1975, taking over from the injured Alex Stepney. Following his debut in September 1973, he looked to have secured a settled place in the United midfield, but when central defender Jim Holton broke his leg in December the following year, Brian was moved into the back four to partner Martin Buchan.

Having represented England at Under-23 level during 1973/74, he won the first of his 18 full caps in 1975/76, adding an FA Cup winner's medal to his trophy cabinet in 1977, following the disappointment of a Wembley defeat the previous year. The arrival of Gordon McQueen and Ray Wilkins saw both defensive and midfield opportunities become fewer, and when Leeds United made an approach, he decided to leave, with United obtaining a cheque for £350,000 in August 1979.

JAMES 'JIMMY' GREENHOFF

Country: England
Born: 19 Jun 1946
Debut: 20 Nov 1976 v Leicester City
Position: Forward
Appearances: 119 (4) **Goals scored:** 36
Seasons: 1976/77 – 1980/81
Clubs: Leeds United, Birmingham City, Stoke City, Manchester United, Crewe Alexandra, Toronto Blizzard, Port Vale, Rochdale

Jimmy Greenhoff was one of the best post-war English players never to receive a full international cap, although he did gain Under-23 honours with Birmingham City. He must also be the only player to be transferred in the middle of a cup final, leaving Leeds United between the first and second legs of the Inter-Cities Fairs Cup final in 1968. Having moved to Stoke in August 1969, it looked as though he would finish his career there, but with the Potteries club desperate for money, they were forced to sell their prized asset to United for £100,000 in November 1976.

Joining his brother Brian, he went on to win an FA Cup medal in 1977, scoring the winning goal with a deflection off his chest. His goal in the 1979 semi-final took United to Wembley again, but it was a runners-up medal on this occasion. He struck up an instant understanding with Stuart Pearson, and the pair were for a brief period a hugely effective strike force. An injury cost him his first-team place and he eventually left to join Crewe in December 1980.

JONATHAN GREENING

Country: England
Born: 2 Jan 1979
Debut: 28 Oct 1998 v Bury

Position: Midfield
Appearances: 13 (14) **Goals scored:** 0
Seasons: 1998/99 – 2000/01
Clubs: York City, Manchester United, Middlesbrough, West Bromwich Albion, Fulham, Nottingham Forest, Barnsley (loan)

Just over a year after arriving at Old Trafford as a £350,000 signing from York City, Jonathan Greening found himself sitting on the bench for the Champions League final. Making only a handful of first-team appearances, he was unable to grasp the opportunity and was transferred to Middlesbrough for £2 million in August 2001, before moving on to West Brom in 2004.

WILSON GREENWOOD

Country: England
Born: Jul 1871 **Died:** Jan 1943
Debut: 20 Oct 1900 v Walsall
Position: Forward
Appearances: 3 **Goals scored:** 0
Seasons: 1900/01
Clubs: Blue Star, Brierfield, Accrington Stanley, Sheffield United, Rossendale, Nelson, Rochdale Athletic, Warmley, Grimsby Town, Newton Heath

HENRY 'HARRY' GREGG

Country: Northern Ireland
Born: 25 Oct 1932
Debut: 21 Dec 1957 v Leicester City
Position: Goalkeeper
Appearances: 247 **Goals scored:** 0
Seasons: 1957/58 – 1966/67
Clubs: Doncaster Rovers, Manchester United, Stoke City

Forever known as the hero of the Munich air disaster, Harry Gregg was equally as brave as a goalkeeper and was one of the best to represent the club. Signed from Doncaster Rovers for a then world-record fee for a keeper of £23,500 in December 1957, the Northern Ireland international ruled his penalty area with an iron fist, giving the team a renewed confidence as they attempted to conquer both domestically and in Europe.

He was monumental in the team rebuilding following the crash, but could do little to prevent the FA Cup final defeat by Bolton Wanderers three months later. He was, however, voted the best goalkeeper in the 1958 World Cup finals in Sweden. But domestic honours were to pass him by, due to injuries more than anything else, which caused him to miss out on the 1963 FA Cup win and the 1964/65 League Championship. Upon the arrival of Alex Stepney in 1967, he decided that, at 34, he should move on and joined Stoke City. He was appointed an MBE in 1995, and the club gave him a testimonial at Old Trafford in May 2012.

WILLIAM 'BILLY' GRIFFITHS

Country: England
Born: 1877 **Died:** Unknown
Debut: 1 Apr 1899 v Arsenal
Position: Half-back
Appearances: 175 **Goals scored:** 30
Seasons: 1898/99 – 1904/05
Clubs: Berry's Association FC, Newton Heath, Atherton Church House

Signed from local football, Billy Griffiths soon became first-choice centre-half and during the 1903/04 campaign he was joint leading scorer on 11 goals. He lost his place to Charlie Roberts the following season and spent most of his final days at the club in the reserves.

CLIVE LESLIE GRIFFITHS

Country: Wales
Born: 22 Jan 1955
Debut: 27 Oct 1973 v Burnley
Position: Half-back
Appearances: 7 **Goals scored:** 0
Seasons: 1973/74
Clubs: Manchester United, Plymouth Argyle (loan), Tranmere Rovers (loan), Chicago Sting, Tulsa Roughnecks

JOHN GRIFFITHS

Country: England
Born: 15 Sep 1908 **Died:** 1 Jan 1975
Debut: 17 Mar 1934 v Fulham
Position: Full-back
Appearances: 173 **Goals scored:** 1
Seasons: 1933/34 – 1938/39
Clubs: Fenton Boys Brigade, Shirebrook, Wolverhampton Wanderers, Bolton Wanderers, Manchester United, Hyde United

Sidelined by injuries at Bolton, John Griffiths moved to United in March 1934, resurrecting his career to the verge of the England side two years later, as United strode to the Second Division Championship. However, like countless other individuals, his career was brought to a premature end by the Second World War.

AUGUSTINE ASHLEY GRIMES

Country: Republic of Ireland
Born: 2 Aug 1957
Debut: 20 Aug 1977 v Birmingham City
Position: Midfield/Winger
Appearances: 77 (30) **Goals scored:** 11
Seasons: 1977/78 – 1982/83
Clubs: Stella Maris, Bohemians, Manchester United, Coventry City, Luton Town, CA Osasuna, Stoke City

Ashley Grimes had trials with the club as a youngster, but was to cost £35,000 five years later when he was signed from Bohemians in March 1977. The gangly left-sided player was unfortunate that illness and injury curtailed his United appearances and, after losing out on a 1983 FA Cup final place, he joined Coventry City for £200,000 in August 1983.

ANTHONY 'TONY' GRIMSHAW

Country: England
Born: 8 Dec 1957
Debut: 10 Sep 1975 v Brentford
Position: Midfield

Appearances: 0 (2) **Goals scored:** 0
Seasons: 1975/76
Clubs: Manchester United, Mossley

JOHN BARTON 'JACK' GRIMWOOD

Country: England
Born: 25 Oct 1898 **Died:** 26 Dec 1977
Debut: 11 Oct 1919 v Manchester City
Position: Half-back
Appearances: 205 **Goals scored:** 8
Seasons: 1919/20 – 1926/27
Clubs: Marsden Rescue, Marsden PM, South Shields Parkside, Manchester United, Aldershot Town, Blackpool, Altrincham

A half-back who joined United from South Shields in May 1919, Jack Grimwood went on to make a name for himself, following his debut against City the following October. Despite a knee injury, which forced him to miss most of 1925/26, he still made over 200 appearances for the club, being awarded a benefit match in 1925. After sharing the centre-half berth with Frank Barson during 1926/27, he decided to leave United and joined Aldershot Town, moving to Blackpool a matter of weeks later for a fee of £2,750.

JOHN GRUNDY

Country: England
Born: 1873 **Died:** Unknown
Debut: 28 Apr 1900 v Chesterfield
Position: Winger
Appearances: 11 **Goals scored:** 3
Seasons: 1894/95 & 1899/1900 – 1900/01
Clubs: Wigan County, Newton Heath

John Grundy had two separate spells with Newton Heath. A one-match reserve outing in April 1895 failed to secure a contract, but he was re-signed in April 1900 and this time managed 11 first-team outings before being released.

WILLIAM GYVES

Country: England
Born: Jul 1867 **Died:** Unknown
Debut: 25 Oct 1890 v Bootle Reserves
Position: Goalkeeper
Appearances: 1 **Goals scored:** 0
Seasons: 1890/91
Clubs: Newton Heath

JOHN 'JACK' HACKING

Country: England
Born: 22 Dec 1897 **Died:** 31 May 1955
Debut: 17 Mar 1934 v Fulham
Position: Goalkeeper
Appearances: 34 **Goals scored:** 0
Seasons: 1933/34 – 1934/35
Clubs: Blackpool, Fleetwood, Oldham Athletic, Manchester United, Accrington Stanley

Blackburn-born goalkeeper Jack Hacking joined United from Oldham Athletic in March 1934 and played a major part in keeping United out of the Third Division with an inspired performance at Millwall on the final day of the season. Just over a year after joining United, he was offered the player-manager's job at Accrington Stanley, which he accepted.

JOHN 'JACK' HALL

Country: England
Born: Jan 1905 **Died:** Unknown
Debut: 6 Feb 1926 v Burnley
Position: Outside-right

Appearances: 3 **Goals scored:** 0
Seasons: 1925/26 – 1926/27
Clubs: Lincoln City, Accrington Stanley, Manchester United

JOHN 'JACK' HALL

Country: England
Born: 23 Oct 1912 **Died:** Aug 2000
Debut: 30 Sep 1933 v Oldham Athletic
Position: Goalkeeper
Appearances: 73 **Goals scored:** 0
Seasons: 1933/34 – 1935/36
Clubs: Newton Heath Loco, Manchester United, Tottenham Hotspur, Stalybridge Celtic, Runcorn, Stalybridge Celtic

Jack Hall was signed from Newton Heath Loco in September 1932, making his debut the following year. It wasn't until the Second Division Championship-winning season of 1935/36 that he secured a regular first-team place, turning in performances that saw Tottenham Hotspur persuade him to move south rather than play First Division football with United.

PROCTOR HALL

Country: England
Born: Jan 1884 **Died:** Unknown
Debut: 26 Mar 1904 v Grimsby Town
Position: Forward
Appearances: 8 **Goals scored:** 2
Seasons: 1903/04 – 1904/05
Clubs: Oswaldtwistle Rovers, Manchester United, Brighton & Hove Albion, Aston Villa, Bradford City, Luton Town, Chesterfield, Hyde, Newport County

HAROLD JAMES HALSE

Country: England
Born: 1 Jan 1886 **Died:** 25 Mar 1949
Debut: 23 Mar 1908 v Sheffield Wednesday
Position: Forward
Appearances: 125 **Goals scored:** 56

Seasons: 1907/08 – 1911/12
Clubs: Clapton Orient, Southend United, Manchester United, Aston Villa, Chelsea, Charlton Athletic

A Londoner, Harold Halse moved north from Southend United in March 1908, scoring on his debut at centre-forward against Sheffield Wednesday. Four goals in six appearances helped United secure the league title, and the following season saw the slightly built individual drift between the centre- and inside-forward positions, going on to win England and Football League honours.

A member of the 1909 FA Cup-winning and the 1911 First Division Championship-winning sides, he set a so-far unbeatable record by scoring six goals in the 8-4 FA Charity Shield victory over Swindon Town in September 1911, an achievement that has only once been matched in the club's history, by George Best. In the summer of 1912, he joined Aston Villa and in 1915, while with Chelsea, he became the first player to appear in FA Cup finals with three different clubs.

REGINALD LLOYD 'REG' HALTON

Country: England
Born: 11 Jul 1916 **Died:** 17 Mar 1988
Debut: 12 Dec 1936 v Middlesbrough
Position: Forward
Appearances: 4 **Goals scored:** 1
Seasons: 1936/37
Clubs: Stafford Rangers, Buxton, Cheddington Mental Hospital, Manchester United, Notts County, Bury, Chesterfield, Leicester City, Scarborough

MICHAEL 'MICKEY' HAMILL

Country: Ireland
Born: 19 Jan 1889 **Died:** 23 Jul 1943
Debut: 16 Sep 1911 v West Bromwich Albion
Position: Wing-half
Appearances: 60 **Goals scored:** 2
Seasons: 1911/12 – 1914/15
Clubs: Belfast Celtic, Manchester United, Belfast Celtic, Celtic (loan), Manchester City, Fall River Marksmen, Boston SC, New York Giants

Mickey Hamill moved to Old Trafford from Belfast Celtic in January 1911. At one time he was the right-wing partner of Billy Meredith, but was to get into a dispute with the United management over a possible benefit match and subsequently returned to Belfast Celtic in the close season of 1914. In 1920, he returned to Manchester, this time as a City player, a move that saw them having to pay United £1,000.

JOHN JAMES 'JIMMY' HANLON

Country: England
Born: 12 Oct 1917 **Died:** 12 Jan 2002
Debut: 26 Nov 1938 v Huddersfield Town
Position: Forward
Appearances: 69 **Goals scored:** 22
Seasons: 1938/39 – 1948/49
Clubs: Manchester United, Bury, Norwich Victoria

A quick-footed centre-forward, Hanlon's goal contribution, 12 in 27 games, played a major part in earning United mid-table respectability in 1938/39. His career was interrupted by the Second World War and during active service he was captured and spent three years as a prisoner of war. Upon his release, he resumed his career in 1945/46, but due to lack of opportunities, he joined Bury in 1948.

CHARLES HANNAFORD

Country: England
Born: 8 Jan 1896 **Died:** Jul 1970
Debut: 28 Dec 1925 v Leicester City
Position: Forward
Appearances: 12 **Goals scored:** 0
Seasons: 1925/26 – 1926/27
Clubs: Maidstone United, Millwall, Charlton Athletic, Clapton Orient, Manchester United, Clapton Orient

Hannaford was a Londoner who joined United from Clapton Orient in December 1925, but his appearances were to be few and far between and he re-signed for his previous club in September 1928.

JAMES 'JIMMY' HANSON

Country: England
Born: 6 Nov 1904 **Died:** Unknown
Debut: 15 Nov 1924 v Hull City
Position: Forward
Appearances: 147 **Goals scored:** 52
Seasons: 1924/25 – 1929/30
Clubs: Stalybridge Celtic, Manchester United

Jimmy Hanson made a name for himself in local Manchester football before signing for United in May 1924 from Stalybridge Celtic. The former Manchester and England schoolboy star scored a hat-trick in his first United trial and, after signing, scored in each of his first three senior outings, going on to score five in a reserve fixture in 1925/26 and six in a similar fixture the following season. Sadly, 15 minutes into the Christmas Day Old Trafford fixture against Birmingham in 1929, he broke his fibia and was forced to retire from the game.

HAROLD PAYNE HARDMAN

Country: England
Born: 4 Apr 1882 **Died:** 9 Jun 1965
Debut: 19 Sep 1908 v Manchester City
Position: Half-back
Appearances: 4 **Goals scored:** 0
Seasons: 1908/09
Clubs: Blackpool, Everton, Manchester United, Bradford City, Stoke

Although he made only four appearances for United as an amateur, Harold Hardman was to serve the club over a period of 50 years as a director and chairman, holding the latter post for 14 of those years, and helping to rebuild the club after the Munich disaster. An England full and amateur international, he won a gold medal in the 1908 Olympics and also picked up an FA Cup winner's medal with Everton in 1906.

OWEN LEE HARGREAVES

Country: England
Born: 20 Jan 1981
Debut: 19 Aug 2007 v Manchester City

Position: Midfield
Appearances: 26 (13) **Goals scored:** 2
Seasons: 2007/08 – 2010/11
Clubs: Bayern Munich, Manchester United, Manchester City

A £17 million signing from Bayern Munich in July 2007, Owen Hargreaves' United career was dominated by injury. In his first season with the club, the England international picked up Premier and Champions League winner's medals, but from there on, it was downhill due to persistent knee injuries, with one first-team return outing lasting no more than five minutes due to a hamstring injury. When his contract expired in May 2011, it was not renewed and he joined Manchester City on a one-year deal.

FRANCIS EDGAR 'FRANK' HARRIS

Country: England
Born: 1 Dec 1899 **Died:** Dec 1983
Debut: 14 Feb 1920 v Sunderland
Position: Full-back
Appearances: 49 **Goals scored:** 2
Seasons: 1919/20 – 1922/23
Clubs: Manchester United

A local lad from Urmston, Frank Harris marked his United debut against Sunderland at Old Trafford, playing as an amateur, with a goal. However, in his three years with the club, he was to score on only one other occasion in his 49 appearances.

THOMAS 'TOMMY' HARRIS

Country: England
Born: 18 Sep 1905 **Died:** Mar 1985
Debut: 30 Oct 1926 v West Ham United
Position: Forward
Appearances: 4 **Goals scored:** 1
Seasons: 1926/27 – 1927/28
Clubs: Skelmersdale United, Manchester United, Wigan Borough, Rotherham United, Crewe, Chorley

CHARLES 'CHARLIE' HARRISON

Country: England
Born: Unknown **Died:** Unknown
Debut: 18 Jan 1890 v Preston North End
Position: Full-back
Appearances: 1 **Goals scored:** 0
Seasons: 1889/90
Clubs: Newton Heath

WILLIAM EWART 'BILLY' HARRISON

Country: England
Born: 27 Dec 1886 **Died:** Aug 1948
Debut: 23 Oct 1920 v Preston North End
Position: Outside-right
Appearances: 46 **Goals scored:** 5
Seasons: 1920/21 – 1921/22
Clubs: Crewe Alexandra, Wolverhampton Wanderers, Manchester United, Port Vale, Wrexham

Considered one of the best wingers in the country when a member of the 1908 Wolves FA Cup-winning side, Billy Harrison was possibly past his best by the time he joined United in October 1920. Signed as cover for Billy Meredith, he spent two seasons with the club, but following relegation at the end of 1921/22, he was transferred to Port Vale.

ROBERT 'BOBBY' HARROP

Country: England
Born: 25 Aug 1936 **Died:** 8 Nov 2007
Debut: 5 Mar 1958 v West Bromwich Albion
Position: Half-back
Appearances: 11 **Goals scored:** 0
Seasons: 1957/58 – 1959/60
Clubs: Wolverhampton Wanderers, Manchester United, Tranmere Rovers, Margate

Bobby Harrop began as an amateur with Wolves before joining United in 1954, but it was not until after Munich that he got his first-team chance. His opportunities were always going to be limited and he moved to Tranmere along with Gordon Clayton in 1959 for a combined fee of £4,000.

WILLIAM HARTWELL

Country: England
Born: 1880 **Died:** Unknown
Debut: 30 Apr 1904 v Leicester City
Position: Forward
Appearances: 4 **Goals scored:** 0
Seasons: 1903/04 – 1904/05
Clubs: Kettering Town, Manchester United, Northampton Town

GEORGE HASLAM

Country: England
Born: 23 Mar 1898 **Died:** 13 Aug 1980
Debut: 25 Feb 1922 v Birmingham
Position: Full-back
Appearances: 27 **Goals scored:** 0
Seasons: 1921/22 – 1927/28
Clubs: Darwen, Manchester United, Portsmouth

A fee of £750 took George Haslam and his Darwen team-mate John Howarth to Old Trafford in May 1921. He made only 27 appearances, although he did captain the reserve side and he was awarded a benefit, along with Clarence Hilditch and Jack Silcock, against Sunderland in April 1927. Despite his fringe status, it still cost Portsmouth a fee of £2,500 to prise him away from United in November 1927.

ANTHONY 'TONY' HAWKSWORTH

Country: England
Born: 15 Jan 1938
Debut: 27 Oct 1956 v Blackpool
Position: Goalkeeper
Appearances: 1 **Goals scored:** 0
Seasons: 1956/57
Clubs: Manchester United, Bedford Town, Rushden Town

RONALD HAWORTH

Country: England
Born: 10 Mar 1901 **Died:** Oct 1973
Debut: 28 Aug 1926 v Liverpool
Position: Inside-forward
Appearances: 2 **Goals scored:** 0
Seasons: 1926/27
Clubs: Blackburn Rovers, Hull City, Manchester United, Darwen

THOMAS 'TOM' HAY

Country: England
Born: Jul 1858 **Died:** 10 Jan 1940
Debut: 18 Jan 1890 v Preston North End
Position: Goalkeeper
Appearances: 1 **Goals scored:** 0
Seasons: 1889/90
Clubs: Staveley, Bolton Wanderers, Great Lever, Halliwell, Burslem, Newton Heath, Accrington Stanley, Burton Swifts

FRANK HAYDOCK

Country: England
Born: 29 Nov 1940
Debut: 20 Aug 1960 v Blackburn Rovers
Position: Centre-back
Appearances: 6 **Goals scored:** 0
Seasons: 1960/61 – 1962/63
Clubs: Manchester United, Charlton Athletic, Portsmouth, Southend United

VINCENT JAMES 'VINCE' HAYES

Country: England
Born: Apr 1879 **Died:** Unknown
Debut: 25 Feb 1901 v Walsall
Position: Full-back
Appearances: 128 **Goals scored:** 2
Seasons: 1900/01 – 1904/05 & 1908/09 – 1910/11
Clubs: Newton Heath Athletic, Newton Heath, Brentford, Manchester United, Bradford

Rochdale-born Vince Hayes joined Newton Heath from local football, making his debut in 1901, but due to two broken legs, it was not until 1904 that he secured a regular place in the side at full-back, going on to play 40 consecutive games between 1903/04 and 1904/05. He lost his place due to injury and another broken leg in 1905 and moved to Brentford in May 1907. A year later, however, he returned to United and was a member of the 1909 Cup-winning side, while also representing the Football League before joining Bradford in 1910.

JOSEPH H. 'JOE' HAYWOOD

Country: England
Born: Apr 1893 **Died:** Unknown
Debut: 22 Nov 1913 v Sheffield United
Position: Half-back
Appearances: 26 **Goals scored:** 0
Seasons: 1913/14 – 1914/15
Clubs: Hindley Central, Manchester United

Joe Haywood was signed for £50 from Hindley Central in May 1913. Following a promising start, he failed to establish himself in the first team and was transfer listed in 1919 and it is thought he moved to the oval ball game.

DAVID JONATHAN HEALY

Country: Northern Ireland
Born: 5 Aug 1979
Debut: 13 Oct 1999 v Aston Villa
Position: Forward
Appearances: 0 (3) **Goals scored:** 0
Seasons: 1999/2000 – 2000/01
Clubs: Manchester United, Port Vale, Preston North End, Norwich City, Leeds United, Fulham, Sunderland, Ipswich Town

Although David Healy signed for United just before he turned 20, he was unable to break into the first team and signed for Preston North End during the following season. He went on to become his country's all-time leading goalscorer (with 36) and has won more caps than any other outfield player (94).

JOSEPH 'JOE' HEATHCOTE

Country: England
Born: Jan 1878 **Died:** Unknown
Debut: 16 Dec 1899 v Middlesbrough
Position: Inside-forward
Appearances: 8 **Goals scored:** 0
Seasons: 1899/1900 – 1901/02
Clubs: Berry's Association, Newton Heath

GABRIEL IVAN HEINZE

Country: Argentina
Born: 19 Apr 1978
Debut: 11 Sep 2004 v Bolton Wanderers
Position: Defender
Appearances: 75 (8) **Goals scored:** 4
Seasons: 2004/05 – 2006/07
Clubs: Newell's Old Boys, Real Valladolid, Sporting CP, Paris Saint-Germain, Manchester United, Real Madrid, Marseille, Roma, Newell's Old Boys

Signed for £6.9 million from Paris Saint-Germain in June 2004, the Argentinian international went on to become something of a cult hero. Missing the first few weeks of his new career due to international duties, he was soon first-choice left-back, winning the club's Player of the Season award at the end of his first campaign. Cruciate knee damage in September 2005 put him on the sidelines, and another injury following his comeback in April 2006 saw him lose his place to Patrice Evra. A £6 million move to Liverpool was suggested, but a clause in his contract did not allow him to join another Premiership club so, unable to regain his first-team place, he moved to Real Madrid in August 2007 for £8 million.

WILLIAM 'BILL' HENDERSON

Country: Scotland
Born: 1898 **Died:** 1964
Debut: 26 Nov 1921 v Aston Villa
Position: Forward

Appearances: 36 **Goals scored:** 17
Seasons: 1921/22 – 1924/25
Clubs: St Bernards, Airdrieonians, Manchester United, Preston North End, Clapton Orient, Hearts, Morton, Torquay United, Exeter City

United manager John Chapman had obviously kept up to date with the Scottish game, so had no hesitation in paying out £1,750 to take Billy Henderson to Old Trafford from Airdrieonians in November 1921. Taking over the No.9 shirt from Joe Spence, he scored on his debut against Aston Villa, but strangely, after featuring in ten of the next 13 games, he disappeared from view in that relegation-haunted campaign.

The following season, 1922/23, saw only two appearances in early October, with none at all during the following campaign. An injury to Ernie Goldthorpe in the opening fixture of 1924/25 gave Henderson a surprise break and he found himself back in the limelight as the replacement centre-forward. His performances astonished many of the Old Trafford regulars as he scored 14 goals in a run of 22 appearances, with a notable hat-trick against Oldham Athletic on 20 September. Preston North End, noting his return to form, made a move for the big front man in January 1925 and, despite his recent successful run in the United side, Henderson decided to move to Deepdale.

JAMES HENDRY

Country: Scotland
Born: Unknown **Died:** Unknown
Debut: 15 Oct 1892 v Wolverhampton Wanderers
Position: Winger
Appearances: 2 **Goals scored:** 1
Seasons: 1892/93
Clubs: Alloa Athletic, Newton Heath

ARTHUR HENRYS

Country: England
Born: 1870 **Died:** Unknown
Debut: 3 Oct 1891 v Manchester City
Position: Half-back
Appearances: 6 **Goals scored:** 0

Seasons: 1891/92 – 1892/93
Clubs: Newton Heath, Notts Jardines, Newton Heath, Leicester Fosse, Notts County

DAVID GEORGE HERD

Country: Scotland
Born: 15 Apr 1934
Debut: 19 Aug 1961 v West Ham United
Position: Forward
Appearances: 264 (1) **Goals scored:** 145
Seasons: 1961/62 – 1967/68
Clubs: Stockport County, Arsenal, Manchester United, Stoke City, Waterford United

In the lower regions of non-league and amateur football, it is not unusual for father and son to line up alongside each other, but in the world of the professional game, it is certainly something of an unusual occurrence. But on the final day of season 1950/51, Alec Herd (aged 39) and his 17-year-old son David, filled the inside-forward positions for Stockport County in their home fixture against Hartlepools United, with the youngster marking his league debut with a goal.

A fee of £10,000 took him to Arsenal in August 1954 and he soon began scoring freely for the Londoners, finishing top scorer in 1958/59, 1959/60 and 1960/61, before joining United in the summer of 1961 for £35,000. In his first season at United, he was the leading scorer, with 17. With the signing of fellow Scotland international Denis Law, he soon formed a fine partnership up front. In a relegation-threatened season in 1962/63, the pair scored 50 goals between them, with Herd on target twice and Law once in the 3-1 FA Cup victory over Leicester City. Herd played a vital part in the 1964/65 title-winning season, and on 26 November 1966, against Sunderland, he had the distinction of scoring against three different goalkeepers.

In 1966/67 he scored his 100th United league goal, but later that season a broken leg against Leicester City effectively brought an end to his Old Trafford career and in the close season of 1967/68 he joined Stoke City.

JAVIER 'CHICHARITO' HERNANDEZ BALCAZAR

Country: Mexico
Born: 1 Jun 1988
Debut: 8 Aug 2010 v Chelsea
Position: Forward
Appearances: 71 (46) **Goals scored:** 50
Seasons: 2010/11 – present
Clubs: Chivas Guadalajara, Manchester United

Chicharito was another of those 'unknown' signings by Sir Alex Ferguson who went on to etch his name into United folklore, after making the move from Mexican side Chivas in April 2010 for an undisclosed fee – it was a transfer that was a closely guarded secret, with only the player and his father involved in the move. Chief scout Jim Lawlor had provided a good report on him, and the club moved fast to sign him up ahead of the 2010 World Cup, where FIFA analysis stated he was the fastest player in the tournament.

With 29 goals from 79 games with Chivas on his CV, Chicharito – 'the Little Pea' – quickly set about adding to this, scoring a further 20 goals in his debut season for United (the first since Ruud van Nistelrooy to achieve this feat), with his mobility around the penalty area catching defences unaware. Likened to Ole Gunnar Solskjaer in both stature and his ability to come off the bench and score vitally important goals, his performances were rewarded with an extended five-year deal in 2011 and fans voted him the Sir Matt Busby Player of the Year. Although his second season was blighted by niggling injuries, he bounced back in 2012/13 to help United to the title, his second Premier League trophy, and he remains one of United's most prolific scorers in terms of minutes per goal.

THOMAS RUSSELL FERRIE 'TOMMY' HERON

Country: Scotland
Born: 31 Mar 1936
Debut: 5 Apr 1958 v Preston North End
Position: Full-back/Winger
Appearances: 3 **Goals scored:** 0
Seasons: 1957/58 – 1960/61
Clubs: Queen's Park, Kilmarnock, Portadown, Manchester United, York City, Altrincham, Droylsden

HERBERT 'BERT' HEYWOOD

Country: England
Born: Jul 1913
Debut: 6 May 1933 v Swansea Town
Position: Winger
Appearances: 4 **Goals scored:** 2
Seasons: 1932/33 – 1933/34
Clubs: Oldham Athletic (amateur), Northwich Victoria, Manchester United, Tranmere Rovers, Altrincham, Wigan Athletic

DANIEL JOHN 'DANNY' HIGGINBOTHAM

Country: England
Born: 29 Dec 1978
Debut: 10 May 1998 v Barnsley
Position: Defender
Appearances: 4 (3) **Goals scored:** 0
Seasons: 1997/98 – 1999/2000
Clubs: Manchester United, Royal Antwerp (loan), Derby County, Southampton, Stoke City, Sunderland, Stoke City, Nottingham Forest (loan), Ipswich Town (loan), Sheffield United

Although Higginbotham made his debut as a substitute in the last game of the 1997/98 season, he was unable to establish himself in the first team at United and moved to Derby County in the summer of 2000, eventually going on to play almost 200 Premier League games for a variety of clubs.

MARK NICHOLAS HIGGINS

Country: England
Born: 29 Sep 1958
Debut: 9 Jan 1986 v Rochdale
Position: Defender
Appearances: 8 **Goals scored:** 0
Seasons: 1985/86
Clubs: Everton, Manchester United, Bury, Stoke City, Burnley (trial)

WILLIAM ALEXANDER HIGGINS

Country: England
Born: 1870 **Died:** Unknown
Debut: 12 Oct 1901 v Burton United
Position: Midfield
Appearances: 10 **Goals scored:** 0
Seasons: 1901/02
Clubs: Albion Swifts, Birmingham St George's, Grimsby Town, Bristol City, Newcastle United, Middlesbrough, Newton Heath, Manchester United

Higgins played in Newton Heath's final season, having been signed from Middlesbrough in May 1900, and made his debut at centre-forward, but ended up at centre-half. He was not retained by the club following the change of name in 1902.

JAMES HIGSON

Country: England
Born: 1876 **Died:** Unknown
Debut: 1 Mar 1902 v Lincoln City
Position: Inside-forward
Appearances: 5 **Goals scored:** 1
Seasons: 1901/02
Clubs: Manchester Wednesday, Newton Heath

CLARENCE GEORGE 'LAL' HILDITCH

Country: England
Born: 2 June 1894 **Died:** 31 Oct 1977
Debut: 30 Aug 1919 v Derby County
Position: Half-back
Appearances: 322 **Goals scored:** 7
Seasons: 1919/20 – 1931/32
Clubs: Witton Albion, Altrincham, Manchester United

Although he spent 16 seasons with United, Lal Hilditch failed to win a major honour during that time, although he did represent England, in a Victory international, the FA and the Football League. Signed in January 1916 from Altrincham, he was soon switched from the forward line to the half-back line, filling any of the three positions with ease, while going on to be an important member of the team as United flitted between the First and Second Divisions.

Reputed to have never given away a foul, Hilditch was a regular fixture in the side for the first five seasons after the war, but in the promotion campaign of 1924/25 he missed much of the season. Hilditch was called upon to serve United in a new position in October 1926, that of player-manager after John Chapman was suspended, a position he held until April 1927 when Herbert Bamlett took over. He played his last game for the club in January 1932, having amassed a total of 322 appearances, but he remains unique in the club's history for that brief spell as a player-manager.

GORDON ALEX HILL

Country: England
Born: 1 Apr 1954
Debut: 15 Nov 1975 v Aston Villa
Position: Winger
Appearances: 133 (1) **Goals scored:** 51
Seasons: 1975/76 – 1977/78
Clubs: Millwall, Chicago Sting (loan), Manchester United, Derby County, Queens Park Rangers, Montreal Manic, Chicago Sting, Inter-Montreal, FC Twente, HJK Helsinki, Northwich Victoria

Rejected by a number of clubs before signing for Millwall, Gordon Hill was snapped up by Tommy Docherty for £70,000 in November 1975. He soon became a firm favourite with the United supporters, adding goals to his repertoire of tricks, while going on to win both Under-23 and full England international honours.

His two semi-final goals took United to Wembley in 1977, but he was to be substituted for the second consecutive season in the Wembley showpiece. The change of playing style under Dave Sexton, who took over for the start of 1977/78, meant he was expected to defend more than had previously been the case and, following a meeting with the manager, he was transfer listed at £250,000, joining the 'Doc' at Derby County in April 1978. Thereafter he regularly moved between clubs.

CHARLES EMMANUEL 'CHARLIE' HILLAM

Country: England
Born: 6 Oct 1908 **Died:** Apr 1958
Debut: 26 Aug 1933 v Plymouth Argyle
Position: Goalkeeper
Appearances: 8 **Goals scored:** 0
Seasons: 1933/34
Clubs: Clitheroe, Burnley, Manchester United, Leyton Orient, Southend United

ERNEST WILLIAM 'ERNIE' HINE

Country: England
Born: 9 Apr 1901 **Died:** 15 Apr 1974
Debut: 11 Feb 1933 v Preston North End
Position: Inside-forward
Appearances: 53 **Goals scored:** 12
Seasons: 1932/33 – 1934/35
Clubs: Barnsley, Leicester City, Huddersfield Town, Manchester United, Barnsley

Having won six England caps with Leicester City, much was expected from Ernie Hine following his transfer from Huddersfield Town in February 1933. However, he failed to produce anything like his best football in a struggling side, and was to make only 53 appearances, scoring 12 goals, before returning to his native Yorkshire to rejoin his first club Barnsley in December 1934. He went on to score a record 123 league goals at Oakwell.

JAMES A. HODGE

Country: Scotland
Born: 5 Jul 1891 **Died:** 2 Sep 1970
Debut: 17 Apr 1911 v Sheffield Wednesday
Position: Half-back
Appearances: 86 **Goals scored:** 2
Seasons: 1910/11 – 1919/20
Clubs: Stenhousemuir, Manchester United, Millwall Athletic, Norwich City, Southend United

Signed in May 1910 from Stenhousemuir, James Hodge had languished in the reserves until the third last fixture of season 1910/11, before making his debut at right-half. The following season saw him back in the reserves until February before enjoying a ten-match run, appearing in both wing-half positions. His luck took a turn for the better in December 1912, when he finally got a long run in the side, missing only three games during the rest of the season, a run that continued until February 1914.

In 1914/15 he was ousted by his brother, but following the war, he was recalled into action, at outside-right and in the two inside-forward positions. Although in the side, he was unhappy and when the chance of a move to Millwall materialised, he took it, with a fee of £1,500 changing hands.

JOHN HODGE

Country: Scotland
Born: Unknown **Died:** Unknown
Debut: 27 Dec 1913 v Sheffield Wednesday
Position: Full-back
Appearances: 30 **Goals scored:** 0
Seasons: 1913/14 – 1914/15
Clubs: Stenhousemuir, Manchester United

John Hodge joined his brother James at Old Trafford in the summer of 1913, having also been signed from Stenhousemuir.

Like his brother, John made his league debut against Sheffield Wednesday, with his initial appearance coming on 27 December 1913 in the centre-half position, taking over from Arthur Whalley. At the start of season 1914/15, John Hodge took over the right-back berth on a more regular basis, but like many others, was to find his footballing career curtailed by the outbreak of war. He was to subsequently disappear from the scene following his being made available for transfer at the princely sum of £25!

FRANK CHARLES HODGES

Country: England
Born: 26 Jan 1891 **Died:** 5 Jun 1985
Debut: 18 Oct 1919 v Manchester City

Position: Inside-forward
Appearances: 20 **Goals scored:** 4
Seasons: 1919/20 – 1920/21
Clubs: Birmingham, Manchester United, Wigan Borough, Crewe Alexandra

Frank Hodges joined United immediately after the First World War, having played for Birmingham and St Mirren during the hostilities. He had a decent first season, but failed to agree terms for a second campaign and United reclaimed their original £100 outlay when he joined Wigan Borough in June 1921.

LESLIE BROWN 'LES' HOFTON

Country: England
Born: 3 Mar 1888 **Died:** Jan 1971
Debut: 18 Feb 1911 v Newcastle United
Position: Full-back
Appearances: 19 **Goals scored:** 0
Seasons: 1910/11 – 1920/21
Clubs: Worksop Town, Denaby United, Glossop North End, Manchester United, Denaby Main

Signed for £1,000 from Glossop in July 1910, Les Hofton was found to require a knee operation, so United refused to pay the money until he proved his fitness. Prove it he did, but having shown much potential, an injury while playing for the Football League saw him sidelined and put up for sale. Not surprisingly no one was prepared to pay the required £500 and he left the club. Strangely, he reappeared at Old Trafford six years later and, following a trial, he was re-signed and went on to play once in the league and captain the reserves to the Central League title in 1920/21.

GRAEME JAMES HOGG

Country: Scotland
Born: 17 Jun 1964
Debut: 7 Jan 1984 v Bournemouth
Position: Centre-back
Appearances: 108 (2) **Goals scored:** 1

Seasons: 1983/84 – 1987/88
Clubs: Manchester United, West Bromwich Albion (loan), Portsmouth, Heart of Midlothian, Notts County, Brentford

For one United youngster, the campaign of 1983/84 provided mixed memories, as Graeme Hogg had not only made his first-team debut in January, but by April, he had played in both legs of the quarter- and semi-final ties of the European Cup-Winners' Cup, against European giants Barcelona and Juventus, scoring an own goal in the home leg against the latter.

His father had played for the same Aberdeen side as Martin Buchan, and he had trained with the Pittodrie side for a brief period, before signing for United in July 1980. Graduating through the junior ranks, an injury to Gordon McQueen against Liverpool at Anfield during the first league match of 1984 presented him with his first-team debut against Bournemouth in the FA Cup third round, five days later. Ron Atkinson had no qualms about throwing the well-built 19-year-old defender in at the deep end, but it was not to be a headline-making debut for Hogg, as the following day, the only headlines were 'United Crash in Cup Sensation', following Bournemouth's surprising 2-0 victory.

The debutant, however, kept his place in the heart of the defence for the remainder of that season, enjoying the experience, particularly the European interludes. Season 1984/85 saw him start as one of the first-choice central defenders, with his defensive displays winning him Scotland Under-21 caps, but he was to miss several games in mid-season due to injury, while 1985/86 also saw him start as a first choice, but again, injury curtailed his appearances. After making fewer than a dozen league starts during 1986/87, he went on loan and with the arrival of Steve Bruce, he decided to leave the following season, joining Portsmouth for £150,000. He retired in 1998.

RICHARD 'DICK' HOLDEN

Country: England
Born: 12 Jun 1885 **Died:** Unknown
Debut: 24 Apr 1905 v Blackpool
Position: Full-back

Appearances: 117 **Goals scored:** 0
Seasons: 1904/05 – 1912/13
Clubs: Manchester United

Signed as an amateur in May 1904, Dick Holden took over the left-back spot from Tommy Blackstock, going on to win a Championship medal in 1908 and selection for an international trial. A cartilage operation affected his form, thus missing the FA Cup run of 1909, but he recaptured his place and went on to play in the 1910/11 title-winning campaign, earning a benefit match that same season. Despite limited appearances, he remained with the club until 1914 when he quit the game.

EDWARD HOLT

Country: England
Born: 1879 **Died:** Unknown
Debut: 28 Apr 1900 v Chesterfield
Position: Winger
Appearances: 1 **Goals scored:** 1
Seasons: 1899/1900
Clubs: Newton Heath Athletic, Newton Heath

JAMES ALLAN 'JIM' HOLTON

Country: Scotland
Born: 11 Apr 1951 **Died:** 5 Oct 1993
Debut: 20 Jan 1973 v West Ham United
Position: Centre-back
Appearances: 69 **Goals scored:** 5
Seasons: 1972/73 – 1974/75
Clubs: Celtic, West Bromwich Albion, Shrewsbury Town, Manchester United, Miami Toros, Sunderland, Coventry City, Detroit Express, Sheffield Wednesday

He wasn't six foot two; he was an inch shorter, if you must know. Neither did he have 'eyes of blue'; but when his terrace anthem echoed around Old Trafford and other venues in the 1970s, the opposition knew that the hulk-like figure from Lesmahagow, just south of Glasgow, would present them with considerable problems at both ends of the pitch.

Joining United in January 1973 from Shrewsbury for £80,000, where he had been managed by Harry Gregg, he immediately became a cult hero, but the Scottish international's career in Manchester was to be dogged by injury. In the Second Division, Holton's presence was going to play a major part in the plans for an instant return, but a broken leg in the 4-4 draw at Sheffield Wednesday on 7 December 1974 brought a premature ending to the big man's season. In reality, it also brought an end to his United career.

A knee injury prior to a pre-season match against Red Star Belgrade and a second broken leg in a reserve match against Bury set him back further, and with Brian Greenhoff and Colin Waldron in front of him, he went to the United States to play for Miami Toros in the summer of 1976. On his return, he joined Sunderland on a one-month loan deal, before signing a permanent contract on a £40,000 move in October.

THOMAS PERCY 'TOM' HOMER

Country: England
Born: Apr 1886 **Died:** Unknown
Debut: 30 Oct 1909 v Arsenal
Position: Forward
Appearances: 25 **Goals scored:** 14
Seasons: 1909/10 – 1911/12
Clubs: Stourbridge, Kidderminster Harriers, Manchester United

Fourteen goals in 25 outings is an excellent return, but it could not guarantee Tom Homer a regular place in the United line-up, losing out to Jimmy Turnbull and Enoch West. A knee injury ended his career.

WILLIAM 'BILLY' HOOD

Country: Unknown
Born: Unknown **Died:** Unknown
Debut: 1 Oct 1892 v West Bromwich Albion
Position: Forward
Appearances: 38 **Goals scored:** 6
Seasons: 1891/92 – 1893/94
Clubs: Newton Heath

Billy Hood scored twice on his Football Alliance debut, a 10-1 victory over Lincoln City in November 1891, and also found the net in Newton Heath's 10-1 record league victory over Wolves the following season. He was a versatile and hugely popular individual during his three years with the club.

ARTHUR HENRY HOOPER

Country: England
Born: Jan 1889 **Died:** Unknown
Debut: 22 Jan 1910 v Tottenham Hotspur
Position: Forward
Appearances: 7 **Goals scored:** 1
Seasons: 1909/10 – 1913/14
Clubs: Kidderminster Harriers, Manchester United, Crystal Palace

FRED HOPKIN

Country: England
Born: 23 Sep 1895 **Died:** 5 Mar 1970
Debut: 30 Aug 1919 v Derby County
Position: Winger
Appearances: 74 **Goals scored:** 8
Seasons: 1919/20 – 1920/21
Clubs: Darlington, Manchester United, Liverpool, Darlington

Eight goals in 74 appearances was all Fred Hopkin, a speedy winger, could muster during his two seasons with United, but following his transfer to Liverpool in May 1921, he went on to win two successive league titles in 1922 and 1923, making over 300 appearances for the Merseysiders.

JAMES HOPKINS

Country: England
Born: 1876 **Died:** Unknown
Debut: 18 Mar 1899 v New Brighton Tower
Position: Inside-forward
Appearances: 1 **Goals scored:** 0
Seasons: 1898/99
Clubs: Berry's Association, Newton Heath

SAMUEL 'SAM' HOPKINSON

Country: England
Born: 9 Feb 1903 **Died:** 9 May 1958
Debut: 17 Jan 1931 v Newcastle United
Position: Forward
Appearances: 53 **Goals scored:** 12
Seasons: 1930/31 – 1933/34
Clubs: Ashton National, Manchester United, Tranmere Rovers

A former England Schoolboy international, Sam Hopkinson joined United in May 1929 from non-league football, but it was not until January 1931 that he made his debut, his four goals from 17 games failing to keep United in the First Division. He left to join Tranmere in May 1935.

STEWART MACKIE HOUSTON

Country: Scotland
Born: 20 Aug 1949
Debut: 1 Jan 1974 v Queens Park Rangers
Position: Full-back
Appearances: 248 (2) **Goals scored:** 16
Seasons: 1973/74 – 1979/80
Clubs: Chelsea, Brentford, Manchester United, Sheffield United, Colchester United

Stewart Houston was a £35,000 buy from Brentford in December 1973, teaming up again with Tommy Docherty whom he had played under at Chelsea. Going straight into the United team, his defensive and attacking qualities were an excellent addition; he held down the left-back spot and missed only five games before suffering torn ankle ligaments in May 1977, forcing him to miss the FA Cup final two weeks later. Returning to fitness, he was unable to regain his No.3 shirt from Arthur Albiston on a regular basis and joined Sheffield United in July 1980 on a free transfer. He picked up one cap for Scotland, and after he retired he became assistant manager at Arsenal and then had a brief spell in charge of Queens Park Rangers.

TIMOTHY MATTHEW 'TIM' HOWARD

Country: USA
Born: 6 Mar 1979
Debut: 10 Aug 2003 v Arsenal
Position: Goalkeeper
Appearances: 76 (1) **Goals scored:** 0
Seasons: 2003/04 – 2005/06
Clubs: North Jersey Imperials, Metro Stars, Manchester United, Everton

Something of an unknown prior to his £1.3 million move from New Jersey Metro Stars in July 2003, the 6'3" keeper enjoyed a favourable start to his career in England, but made a costly error in the Champions League against Porto, although he was to claim an FA Cup winners' medal at the end of that first campaign. Rotated in his second season with Roy Carroll, he eventually joined Everton on loan following the arrival of Edwin van der Sar, a move that was to become permanent in February 2007 for around £3 million. He has remained a fixture in the Everton line-up ever since, missing just six Premier League games in his first seven seasons at the club.

JOHN THOMAS HOWARTH

Country: England
Born: 1899 **Died:** Unknown
Debut: 2 Jan 1922 v Sheffield Wednesday
Position: Full-back
Appearances: 4 **Goals scored:** 0
Seasons: 1921/22
Clubs: Manchester City, Darwen, Manchester United

E. HOWELLS

Country: Unknown
Born: Unknown **Died:** Unknown
Debut: 30 Oct 1886 v Fleetwood Rangers
Position: Midfield
Appearances: 1 **Goals scored:** 0
Seasons: 1886/87
Clubs: Newton Heath

EDWARD KEARNEY 'TED' HUDSON

Country: England
Born: Jan 1887 **Died:** Jan 1945
Debut: 24 Jan 1914 v Oldham Athletic
Position: Full-back
Appearances: 11 **Goals scored:** 0
Seasons: 1913/14 – 1914/15
Clubs: Walkden Central, Manchester United, Stockport County

A fee of £75 brought Ted Hudson from Walkden Central in January 1912, but he was to make only 11 appearances in just over seven years before moving to Stockport County in August 1919.

LESLIE MARK HUGHES

Country: Wales
Born: 1 Nov 1963
Debut: 26 Oct 1983 v Port Vale
Position: Forward
Appearances: 453 (14) **Goals scored:** 163
Seasons: 1983/84 – 1985/86 & 1988/89 – 1994/95
Clubs: Manchester United, Barcelona, Bayern Munich (loan), Manchester United, Chelsea, Southampton, Everton, Blackburn Rovers

Mark Hughes was a staunch crowd favourite during his two spells with the club. He joined United as a Wrexham schoolboy in March 1978, scoring on his starting debut in November 1983 against Oxford United in the League Cup, and he also scored on his league debut. The following season, he became a regular in the side, topping the scoring charts with 24 in all competitions, ensuring that the more experienced Alan Brazil and Frank Stapleton had more sporadic appearances. He scored two hat-tricks that campaign as well, helping United to fourth place.

Quiet off the field, but a physically combative front man on it, he won an FA Cup winner's medal and the PFA Young Player of the Year award in 1985. He started the 1985/86 season with ten goals in the first 15 games as United raced to the top of the table, undefeated. However, rumours of a possible move away seemed to affect him, and at the end of the season, he was off to Barcelona for £2.5 million, but following a loan spell at Bayern Munich, Alex Ferguson brought him back to United in July 1988 and to further success.

Voted PFA Player of the Year in 1989 and 1991, he won a second FA Cup winner's medal in 1990 and scored both goals in the European Cup-Winners' Cup success the following season, an emphatic response to the Barcelona side that had rejected him. Despite the arrival of Eric Cantona in 1992/93, it was Hughes who was the leading scorer that season, with 15 league goals, as United ended up champions by a ten-point margin. Another Premier League medal followed in 1994 and also a third FA Cup winner's medal, as United earned their first Double. However, it was his last-gasp goal in the semi-final against Oldham, earning United a replay, that ranked as one of his best.

Another Cup final appearance in 1995, a defeat by Everton, was his last for United and he joined Chelsea of a fee of £1.5 million where he became the only player in the 20th century to win the FA Cup four times. He played on until he was 38 before the Welsh international moved into management, initially taking charge of his country. Subsequently, he has managed Blackburn Rovers, Manchester City, Fulham, Queens Park Rangers, and in the summer of 2013 he took over at Stoke City.

AARON HULME

Country: England
Born: Apr 1886 **Died:** Nov 1933
Debut: 25 Apr 1908 v Preston North End
Position: Full-back
Appearances: 4 **Goals scored:** 0
Seasons: 1907/08 – 1908/09
Clubs: Newton Heath Athletic, Colne, Oldham Athletic, Manchester United, Nelson

GEORGE C. HUNTER

Country: England
Born: 1885 **Died:** Feb 1934
Debut: 14 Mar 1914 v Aston Villa
Position: Half-back
Appearances: 23 **Goals scored:** 2
Seasons: 1913/14 – 1914/15
Clubs: Aston Villa, Oldham Athletic, Chelsea, Manchester United

George Hunter was a tough uncompromising individual, who cost £1,300 from Chelsea in March 1914, but it was to prove a waste of money, as he made only 23 appearances before being suspended *sine die* by the United directors in January 1915 for a breach of training regulations.

REGINALD JOHN 'REG' HUNTER

Country: Wales
Born: 25 Oct 1938
Debut: 27 Dec 1958 v Aston Villa
Position: Winger
Appearances: 1 **Goals scored:** 0
Seasons: 1958/59
Clubs: Colwyn Bay, Manchester United, Wrexham, Bangor City

WILLIAM 'BILLY' HUNTER

Country: England
Born: 1888 **Died:** Unknown
Debut: 29 Mar 1913 v Liverpool
Position: Forward
Appearances: 3 **Goals scored:** 2
Seasons: 1912/13
Clubs: Sunderland West End, Liverpool, Sunderland, Lincoln City, Wingate Albion, Airdrieonians, South Shields, Barnsley, Manchester United, Clapton Orient

DANIEL JAMES 'DAN' HURST

Country: England
Born: Oct 1876 **Died:** Unknown
Debut: 6 Sep 1902 v Gainsborough Trinity
Position: Winger
Appearances: 21 **Goals scored:** 4
Seasons: 1902/03
Clubs: Black Diamonds, Blackburn Rovers, Workington, Manchester City, Manchester United

Dan Hurst was a goalscoring winger who joined United from City in 1902, scoring on his home debut against Burton United, but was to spend only one season with the newly named club.

I

RICHARD 'DICK' IDDON

Country: England
Born: 22 Jun 1901 **Died:** 26 Feb 1975
Debut: 29 Aug 1925 v West Ham United
Position: Forward
Appearances: 2 **Goals scored:** 0
Seasons: 1925/26 – 1926/27
Clubs: Tarlton, Preston North End, Leyland, Chorley, Manchester United, Chorley

PAUL EMERSON CARLYLE INCE

Country: England
Born: 21 Oct 1967
Debut: 16 Sep 1989 v Millwall
Position: Midfield
Appearances: 276 (5) **Goals scored:** 29
Seasons: 1989/90 – 1994/95
Clubs: West Ham United, Manchester United, Internazionale, Liverpool, Middlesbrough, Wolverhampton Wanderers, Swindon Town, Macclesfield Town

Paul Ince was criticised by the Upton Park faithful when photographed in a United shirt while still a West Ham player, as he lined up a move to Old Trafford in the summer of 1989. It took a couple of months and £2.4 million to seal the deal, but he soon became an important cog in the team.

Alongside Bryan Robson, the combative midfielder was soon at the heart of the action for United. Ince added bite to the side as well as contributing his fair share of goals as he helped United to FA Cup, League Cup, Premier League and European Cup-Winners' Cup success. He missed just one game in the 1992/93 league season, as United ended 26 years of waiting for a league title, scoring in each of the last three games of the season; he also earned his first England cap that campaign.

The year after, he was more regularly paired with new arrival Roy Keane, and the pair drove United to the Double. By now he was an England regular, and would become the first black player to captain the side. Despite such success, he was not considered indispensable and in the summer of 1995, he was sold to Inter Milan for £7.5 million, a decision that surprised many at the time, but which allowed the emergence of Nicky Butt in the centre of United's midfield, as Ferguson rebuilt his side. When he returned to English football, for many United fans he blotted his copybook by signing for Liverpool. After retiring as a player, he moved into management, eventually becoming the first black British manager in the Premier League at Blackburn Rovers. He is currently manager of Blackpool.

WILLIAM WHITE 'BILL' INGLIS

Country: Scotland
Born: 2 Mar 1894 **Died:** 20 Jan 1968
Debut: 20 Mar 1926 v Everton
Position: Full-back
Appearances: 14 **Goals scored:** 1
Seasons: 1925/26 – 1928/29
Clubs: Inverkeithing United, Kirkcaldy United, Raith Rovers, Sheffield Wednesday, Manchester United, Northampton Town

Following a brief stay with Sheffield Wednesday, Bill Inglis joined United in the summer of 1925, but had to wait until 20 March 1926 before making his debut against Everton in a 0–0 draw. He began the following season as first-choice right-back, but after only six games lost his place and was soon to find himself further down the pecking order following the signing of Charlie Moore. In the reserve XI, he became captain and seemed to be content to play at this level, making his last appearance in the United first team on Boxing Day 1928.

Upon his eventual retirement, he took up the post of trainer at Northampton, returning to United in August 1934 as assistant trainer to Tom Curry. While there he had a very big influence over the playing careers of many future stars, enthusiastically filling the role before retiring in May 1961 after 31 years with the club.

DENIS JOSEPH IRWIN

Country: Republic of Ireland
Born: 31 Oct 1965
Debut: 18 Aug 1990 v Liverpool
Position: Full-back
Appearances: 511 (18) **Goals scored:** 33
Seasons: 1990/91 – 2001/02
Clubs: Leeds United, Oldham Athletic, Manchester United, Wolverhampton Wanderers

Denis Irwin came to Alex Ferguson's attention in United's FA Cup semi-finals against Oldham in 1990 and was duly signed for £625,000 that summer, a fee that was to prove a bargain in the years to come. Initially signed as a right-back, he moved across to the left when Paul Parker joined the following season and would spend most of his career on that side.

He played to the highest level of consistency, as he was seldom, if ever, off form and no matter the occasion, he never looked flustered or under any pressure. His first trophy came when he was a member of the European Cup-Winners' Cup side of 1991, the same year he won his first Republic of Ireland cap, and he went on to add seven Premier League winner's medals, one in the League Cup, two in the FA Cup and one in the Champions League to his overflowing trophy cabinet. He should have added a third FA Cup medal in 1999, but a booking in a league match at Liverpool for kicking the ball away was to cost him his final place. There was, of course, plenty of consolation to be had that year, as United also won the Premier League and Champions League titles.

Although a full-back, he enjoyed making overlapping runs and contributed to the team's success with his quota of goals, some from the penalty spot, as he became only the sixth United player (and the second Irishman, after Tony Dunne, another unsung hero of a full-back) to pass the 500-game milestone. In 2002, at the age of 36, he finally felt that his time at the club had run its course and he left United, having been awarded the captain's armband in his final game. He signed for Wolves for a two-season swansong. Irwin won 56 caps for the Republic of Ireland, appearing in the 1994 World Cup finals.

THOMAS A. 'TOMMY' JACKSON

Country: Northern Ireland
Born: 3 Nov 1946
Position: Midfield
Debut: 16 Aug 1975 v Wolverhampton Wanderers
Appearances: 22 (1) **Goals scored:** 0
Seasons: 1975/76 – 1977/78
Clubs: Glentoran, Everton, Nottingham Forest, Manchester United, Waterford United

A highly experienced individual, Tommy Jackson was something of a stop-gap signing on a free transfer in the summer of 1975 from Nottingham Forest. Most of his United appearances were in the reserve side and he moved to Waterford as player-manager in 1978.

WILLIAM JAMES JACKSON

Country: Wales
Born: 27 Jan 1876 **Died:** 25 Mar 1954
Position: Forward
Debut: 2 Sep 1899 v Gainsborough Trinity
Appearances: 64 **Goals scored:** 14
Seasons: 1899/90 – 1900/01
Clubs: Rhyl, Flint, St Helens Recreation, Newton Heath, Barrow, Burnley, Wigan County, Chester

Jackson was an inside-forward who joined Newton Heath a few months after making his only international appearance for Wales against Ireland at Grosvenor Park. He played for two seasons at Bank Street, scoring his first goal in his ninth game, before moving on to Barrow.

STEVEN ROBERT 'STEVE' JAMES

Country: England
Born: 29 Nov 1949

Position: Centre-back
Debut: 12 Oct 1968 v Liverpool
Appearances: 160 (1) **Goals scored:** 4
Seasons: 1968/69 – 1974/75
Clubs: Manchester United, York City, Kidderminster Harriers

Steve James was an England Youth international who joined United in 1965, making his debut three years later, where it was hoped he would replace Bill Foulkes. It was, however, 1971/72 before he managed an extended run in the side at centre-half, although he often filled in at full-back. The arrival of Martin Buchan and manager Tommy Docherty meant he was then in and out of the side, which was sadly in decline, as United were relegated in 1974. In 1974/75, he helped the club to the Second Division title, but at the end of the season he was given a free transfer and joined York City.

ADNAN JANUZAJ

Country: Belgium
Born: 5 Feb 1995
Position: Winger
Debut: 11 Aug 2013 v Wigan Athletic
Appearances: 0 (1) **Goals scored:** 0
Seasons: 2013/14 – present
Clubs: Manchester United

Snapped up from the junior ranks at Anderlecht, the young Belgian winger impressed after joining United in 2011. After a good pre-season tour, he made his senior debut as a substitute in the Community Shield.

CAESAR AUGUSTUS LLEWELLYN JENKYNS

Country: Wales
Born: 24 Aug 1866 **Died:** 23 Jul 1941
Position: Defender
Debut: 1 Sep 1896 v Gainsborough Trinity
Appearances: 47 **Goals scored:** 6
Seasons: 1896/97 – 1897/98
Clubs: Small Heath St Andrews, Walsall Swifts, Unity Gas, Small Heath, Woolwich Arsenal, Newton Heath, Walsall, Coventry City

A fiery character of the Victorian era, the rugged defender was sent off on several occasions, and once assaulted two spectators after having been dismissed. The Welshman joined Newton Heath from Woolwich Arsenal in May 1896 and was immediately made captain. Guiding them to second place in Division Two in 1896/97, he failed to take them past the Test Matches and 11 games into the following season, he left to join Walsall in November 1897. He won one of his eight Wales caps while with the Heathens, the club's first international since they joined the Football League.

RONALD WILLIAM 'ROY' JOHN

Country: Wales
Born: 29 Jan 1911 **Died:** 12 Jul 1973
Position: Goalkeeper
Debut: 29 Aug 1936 v Wolverhampton Wanderers
Appearances: 15 **Goals scored:** 0
Seasons: 1936/37
Clubs: Swansea Town, Walsall, Stoke City, Preston North End, Sheffield United, Manchester United, Newport County, Swansea Town

The Wales international goalkeeper had already won 12 caps before he joined United, for a fee of £600. Strangely, he began his career as a full-back and half-back, only becoming a keeper when he joined Walsall after impressing in a practice match. After playing the first 15 games of the season, he lost his place to Tommy Breen and was sold at the end of the campaign, when United were relegated.

JEAN RONNY JOHNSEN

Country: Norway
Born: 10 Jun 1969
Position: Defender
Debut: 17 Aug 1996 v Wimbledon
Appearances: 131 (19) **Goals scored:** 9
Seasons: 1996/97 – 2001/02
Clubs: Eik Tønsberg, Lyn Oslo, Lillestrøm, Beşiktaş, Manchester United, Aston Villa, Newcastle United, Vålerenga

A Norwegian international who was signed from Turkish side Beşiktaş for £1.5 million in July 1996, Ronny Johnsen was more than capable of filling a position in either midfield or the back four. With the change in rules that summer, meaning that clubs could field unlimited numbers of foreign players in European competition, there was an influx of overseas talent that season.

Winning a title medal in his first campaign, his cool, calm approach and pace played an important part in the Treble-winning season two years later, when he played in all three of the trophy-clinching games. Unfortunately, a knee injury put him out of action until late the following season, and when he returned against Southampton on 22 April he helped United to another title – it meant that in four consecutive games with United they had won a trophy after each one.

Another Championship medal came his way in 2000/01, but he was sidelined again with another knee problem, which in effect finished his United career, as he failed to gain an extension to his contract and left to join Aston Villa on a free transfer at the end of the 2001/02 season.

EDWARD WILLIAM 'EDDIE' JOHNSON

Country: England
Born: 20 Sep 1984
Position: Forward
Debut: 28 Oct 2003 v Leeds United
Appearances: 0 (1) **Goals scored:** 0
Seasons: 2003/04
Clubs: Manchester United, Royal Antwerp (loan), Coventry City (loan), Crewe Alexandra (loan), Bradford City, Chester City, Austin Aztex, Portland Timbers

SAMUEL C. JOHNSON

Country: England
Born: Jul 1881 **Died:** Unknown
Position: Forward
Debut: 20 Mar 1901 v Leicester City
Appearances: 1 **Goals scored:** 0
Seasons: 1900/01
Clubs: Tongue, Newton Heath, Heywood

WILLIAM GIFFORD 'BILLY' JOHNSTON

Country: Scotland
Born: 16 Jan 1901 **Died:** 23 Nov 1964
Position: Forward
Debut: 15 Oct 1927 v Cardiff City
Appearances: 77 **Goals scored:** 27
Seasons: 1927/28 – 1928/29 & 1931/32
Clubs: Huddersfield Town, Stockport County, Manchester United, Macclesfield Town, Manchester United, Oldham Athletic, Frickley Colliery

Johnston was a former Scotland Schoolboy international who was signed from Stockport County in October 1927 at a cost of £3,000, but following a favourable start to his United career, missing only one game during that initial season and starting the following season in the No.10 shirt, he was allowed to leave and join Macclesfield in June 1929. However, he was there for only two years before returning to Old Trafford, going on to make a further 28 appearances, scoring 11 goals before departing for Oldham Athletic in May 1932.

DAVID FRANK LLWYD JONES

Country: England
Born: 4 Nov 1984
Position: Midfield
Debut: 1 Dec 2004 v Arsenal
Appearances: 3 (1) **Goals scored:** 0
Seasons: 2004/05 – 2006/07
Clubs: Manchester United, Preston North End (loan), NEC Nijmegen (loan), Derby County (loan), Derby County, Wolverhampton Wanderers, Wigan Athletic, Blackburn Rovers (loan), Wigan Athletic

DAVID GWILYM JONES

Country: Wales
Born: 10 Jun 1914 **Died:** 30 May 1988
Position: Half-back
Debut: 11 Dec 1937 v Bradford Park Avenue
Appearances: 1 **Goals scored:** 0
Seasons: 1937/38
Clubs: Wigan Athletic, Manchester United, Swindon Town

ERNEST PETER JONES

Country: England
Born: 30 Nov 1937
Position: Full-back
Debut: 19 Oct 1957 v Portsmouth
Appearances: 1 **Goals scored:** 0
Seasons: 1957/58
Clubs: Manchester United, Wolverhampton Wanderers, Manchester United, Wrexham, Stockport County, Altrincham

MARK JONES

Country: England
Born: 15 Jun 1933 **Died:** 6 Feb 1958
Position: Defender
Debut: 7 Oct 1950 v Sheffield Wednesday
Appearances: 121 **Goals scored:** 1
Seasons: 1950/51 – 1957/58
Clubs: Manchester United

Barnsley-born Mark Jones was a former England Schoolboy international who came to United's attention while playing at Old Trafford, and joined the groundstaff straight from school. He made his debut at just 17 years of age, in place of Allenby Chilton. The more experienced man groomed the teenager for success, but his appearances for the first team were limited over the next few years, as Chilton played every game in the next three seasons. Jones had to wait until February 1955 before taking over from the United stalwart.

The next campaign, it was Jones who didn't miss a game, as Busby's young side raced to the title, winning the league by a massive 11 points. He scored the only goal of his senior career on 17 December that season, in a 2-1 victory over Birmingham City at Old Trafford. The following campaign, United retained the title, but Jones had an eye injury and so missed the FA Cup final when the Reds missed out on becoming the first side in the 20th century to do the Double.

A strong and fearless defender, Jones was powerful in the air, and enjoyed the simple things in life – his pipe, his pigeons and taking his dog for country walks. He had a battle with Jackie Blanchflower for his first-team place and played in the fateful game against Red Star Belgrade on 5 February 1958. Had it not been for the Munich disaster, he would surely have gone on to win full England international honours.

OWEN JOHN JONES

Country: Wales
Born: Jul 1871 **Died:** 23 Sep 1955
Position: Forward
Debut: 3 Sep 1898 v Gainsborough Trinity
Appearances: 2 **Goals scored:** 0
Seasons: 1898/99
Clubs: Bangor City, Crewe Alexandra, Chorley, Newton Heath, Bangor City, Earlestown, Stalybridge Rovers

PHILIP ANTHONY 'PHIL' JONES

Country: England
Born: 21 Feb 1992
Debut: 7 Aug 2011 v Manchester City
Position: Defender/Midfield
Appearances: 55 (11) **Goals scored:** 2
Seasons: 2011/12 – present
Clubs: Blackburn Rovers, Manchester United

Sadly, injuries have been a prominent factor in the brief United career of Phil Jones, a £16.5 million signing from Blackburn Rovers in the summer of 2011. The 19-year-old was thrown in at the deep end, following injuries to both Rio Ferdinand and Nemanja Vidić in the opening match of the 2011/12 season, and was undaunted at being thrust into the spotlight, turning in impressive displays in both a central defensive role and at full-back. A stint in midfield also revealed his versatility and he was soon being talked about in comparison to a certain Duncan Edwards, with him capable of doing a man-marking job, as he showed against Cristiano Ronaldo in United's Champions League tie against Real Madrid.

His performances for United saw him adding full England international honours to his Under-21 caps, as his meteoric progress continued, but injuries were to keep him sidelined for lengthy spells. Although still learning the game, his future in the side is guaranteed and there are many fans who see him as a potential United captain in the years ahead.

RICHIE GLYNN JONES

Country: England
Born: 26 Sep 1986
Position: Midfield
Debut: 26 Oct 2005 v Barnet
Appearances: 3 (2) **Goals scored:** 0
Seasons: 2005/06 – 2007/08
Clubs: Manchester United, Royal Antwerp (loan), Colchester United (loan), Barnsley (loan), Yeovil Town (loan), Hartlepool, Oldham Athletic, Bradford City, Rochdale

THOMAS 'TOM' JONES

Country: Wales
Born: 6 Dec 1899 **Died:** 20 Feb 1978
Position: Full-back
Debut: 8 Nov 1924 v Portsmouth
Appearances: 200 **Goals scored:** 0
Seasons: 1923/24 – 1936/37
Clubs: Acrefair, Druids, Oswestry Town, Manchester United, Scunthorpe & Lindsay United

Signed from non-league football in May 1924, Tom Jones went on to make 200 appearances for United, over the following 13 years, winning four Welsh international caps, but it was not until 1933/34 that he managed to secure a regular place in the team. He often played in defence with Charlie Moore during that time, and the pair hold the record as the two players who appeared the most times for United without scoring, Moore going 328 games without finding the back of the net.

THOMAS JOHN 'TOMMY' JONES

Country: Wales
Born: 6 Dec 1909 **Died:** Unknown
Position: Forward

Debut: 25 Aug 1934 v Bradford City
Appearances: 22 **Goals scored:** 4
Seasons: 1934/35
Clubs: Tranmere Rovers, Sheffield Wednesday, Manchester United, Watford

The former Sheffield Wednesday player moved to Manchester in June 1934, but was to play only 22 games before joining Watford a year later for a fee of £1,500.

JOSEPH 'JOE' JORDAN

Country: Scotland
Born: 15 Dec 1951
Position: Centre-forward
Debut: 28 Jan 1978 v West Bromwich Albioni
Appearances: 125 (1) **Goals scored:** 41
Seasons: 1977/78 – 1980/81
Clubs: Greenock Morton, Leeds United, Manchester United, AC Milan, Hellas Verona, Southampton, Bristol City

From the same Lanarkshire village as Jimmy Delaney, Joe Jordan came to Old Trafford from Leeds United in January 1978 for a record fee of £350,000, having won a League Championship medal and played in two European finals with the Elland Road side.

A physical, old-style centre-forward, the Scottish international, whose goal against Czechoslovakia in 1974 took his country to the World Cup finals, was an excellent header of the ball and soon settled at Old Trafford, developing under Dave Sexton.

Initially, he played alongside Jimmy Greenhoff, with Stuart Pearson being sold on, helping United to the 1979 FA Cup final. He was the leading scorer in 1979/80, when United finished as runners-up to Liverpool. He was the top scorer again the next campaign, which saw the Reds fade away to mid-table, after which Sexton lost his job. At the end of his contract with United, he decided to move to Italy and joined AC Milan for £323,000 in July 1981. Since he retired as a player, he has had a long career as a coach, often working alongside Harry Redknapp.

NIKOLA JOVANOVIC

Country: Yugoslavia
Born: 18 Sep 1952
Position: Defender
Debut: 2 Feb 1980 v Derby County
Appearances: 25 (1) **Goals scored:** 4
Seasons: 1979/80 – 1980/81
Clubs: Red Star Belgrade, Manchester United, Budućnost Podgorica

Nikola Jovanovic was United's first foreign signing, when he moved from Red Star Belgrade in January 1980 for a fee of £300,000.

Although a strong, commanding central defender, he found it hard to adapt to the English game, struggling with back problems, and returned to Yugoslavia in December 1981, having played mainly in the reserve side.

SHINJI KAGAWA

Country: Japan
Born: 17 March 1989
Debut: 20 Aug 2012 v Everton
Position: Midfield
Appearances: 22 (5) **Goals scored:** 6
Seasons: 2012/13 – present
Clubs: Cerezo Osaka, Borussia Dortmund, Manchester United

Signed from Borussia Dortmund in June 2012, for a fee expected to reach around £17 million with add-ons, Shinji Kagawa was United's first-ever Japanese player. Having won back-to-back Bundesliga titles in Germany, where he was also named in the Bundesliga team of the season, he added a Premier League winner's medal in his first year at United, helping his new club to their 20th title. Considered by some ill-informed media critics, who failed to notice how highly he had been rated in Germany, to be little more than a marketing ploy to capture the vast Japanese market, Kagawa proved otherwise. He enjoyed a favourable first season at Old Trafford, which was capped with a superb hat-trick against Norwich City. Capable of playing in a number of different roles, he has set a solid foundation to build a successful career with the club.

ANDREI ANTANASOVICH KANCHELSKIS

Country: USSR/CIS/Russia
Born: 23 Jan 1969
Position: Winger
Debut: 11 May 1991 v Crystal Palace
Appearances: 132 (29) **Goals scored:** 36
Seasons: 1990/91 – 1994/95
Clubs: Dynamo Kiev, Shakhtar Donetsk, Manchester United, Everton, Fiorentina, Rangers, Manchester City (loan), Southampton, Al-Hilal, Saturn Moscow Oblast, Krylia Sovetov

A speedy, devastating winger whose direct style would often terrify defenders, Andrei Kanchelskis joined the club from Shakhtar Donetsk in March 1991. Although born in Kirovograd, Ukraine, on the break-up of the USSR, he chose to play for the CIS and then Russia, rather than his home nation.

He won a League Cup medal in his first full season at the club and followed it up with a Premier League medal 12 months later, though he played a relatively minor role that season. So it was in the Double-winning campaign of 1993/94 that he came to the fore with some superb displays and goals, a season that also saw him sent off for handball in the League Cup final at Wembley. If anything, he improved during the 1994/95 season, when United ended up narrowly missing out on both the league title and the FA Cup, but he will always be remembered by Reds fans for his hat-trick in the 5-0 demolition of Manchester City on 10 November 1994, when he seemed almost unstoppable.

There was plenty of surprise when he moved to Everton in July 1995 for a fee of £5 million, as Alex Ferguson cleared out some of his senior players to create space for the youngsters coming up through the ranks. In his case, it was David Beckham who was to prove the long-term beneficiary.

MICHAEL VINCENT KEANE

Country: England
Born: 11 Jan 1993
Debut: 25 Oct 2011 v Aldershot
Position: Defender
Appearances: 2 (1)
Seasons: 2009/10 – present
Clubs: Manchester United, Leicester City (loan)

Part of the 2011 Youth Cup-winning side, the adaptable defender who was born in Stockport has won England Under-19 honours.

ROY MAURICE KEANE

Country: Republic of Ireland
Born: 10 Aug 1971
Position: Midfield
Debut: 7 Aug 1993 v Arsenal
Appearances: 458 (22) **Goals scored:** 51
Seasons: 1993/94 – 2005/06
Clubs: Cobh Ramblers, Nottingham Forest, Manchester United, Celtic

For many United fans, Roy Keane would be an automatic choice in any All-Time United side, but despite that his was a career awash with controversy in the years following his British record £3.75 million transfer from Nottingham Forest in July 1993, after the side had been relegated. Alex Ferguson had to pay a record fee to sign him, and prevent new challengers Blackburn Rovers from adding him to their squad. His box-to-box play was what United needed, especially as Bryan Robson's best days were coming to an end. Like Robson, he had everything: he could pass, tackle, head the ball and score goals – he was, in short, the complete midfielder.

He helped United to win the Double in his first season, and once Robson and then Paul Ince had left the club, he became the unchallenged master of United's midfield, forming a successful partnership with Nicky Butt that helped the Reds to the double Double in 1995/96. When Cantona retired, Alex Ferguson had no hesitation in naming the Republic of Ireland man as his captain in 1997, and Keane guided United to countless honours in the years that followed.

However, his time as skipper didn't start well, as he was out for a long spell due to cruciate ligament trouble in 1997/98, but when he returned the following season he was back to his very best, inspiring his side to the Treble. His performance in the semi-final of the Champions League, when he drove United on to come back from a 2-0 deficit away at Juventus, despite having picked up a booking that meant he knew he would miss the final, was one of the greatest ever in a red shirt. Somehow, he was overlooked as Footballer of the Year by his fellow players and the football writers, an oversight that was corrected a year later when United retained the Premier League title by an astonishing 18 points.

A crude tackle on Manchester City's Haaland in 2001, which saw him sent off, suspended for five games and fined £150,000, did little to help his reputation, as did a fall-out with Mick McCarthy while on World Cup duty with his country in 2002, but his formidable competitive instincts were never better highlighted than the during the famous eye-balling of Patrick Vieira in the tunnel before kick-off against Arsenal in 2004/05. By then, injuries were beginning to compromise his effectiveness as a player, though never his desire for victory and to play to the highest standards, something he demanded of himself and all those around him.

He left the club in November 2005 and was later to sign for Celtic, before retiring at the end of the season. He has subsequently managed Sunderland and Ipswich Town, and is now working as a forthright pundit for ITV.

WILLIAM DAVID 'WILL' KEANE

Country: England
Born: 11 Jan 1993
Debut: 31 Dec 2011 v Blackburn Rovers
Position: Forward
Appearances: 0 (1)
Seasons: 2011/12 – present
Clubs: Manchester United

Michael Keane's twin brother missed the entire 2012/13 season with a knee ligament injury, but the striker is tipped for a bright future.

JAMES WILLIAM 'JIMMY' KELLY

Country: England
Born: 2 May 1957
Position: Midfield
Debut: 20 Dec 1975 v Wolverhampton Wanderers
Appearances: (0) 1 **Goals scored:** 0
Seasons: 1975/76
Clubs: Manchester United, Chicago Sting, Los Angeles Aztecs, Tulsa Roughnecks, Toronto Blizzard

FRED KENNEDY

Country: England
Born: 23 Oct 1902 **Died:** 14 Nov 1963
Position: Forward
Debut: 6 Oct 1923 v Oldham Athletic
Appearances: 18 **Goals scored:** 4
Seasons: 1923/24 – 1924/25
Clubs: Rossendale United, Manchester United, Everton, Middlesbrough, Reading, Oldham Athletic, Rossendale, Northwich Victoria, Racing Club de Paris, Blackburn Rovers, Racing Club de Paris, Stockport County

Fred Kennedy spent only two years at Old Trafford, joining the club from Rossendale in May 1923. However, during his brief 18-game spell there, Everton must have seen something that the United management didn't and they paid £2,000 to take him to Goodison Park, which in turn became a launch pad to a career that took him as far afield as Racing Club de Paris.

PATRICK ANTHONY 'PADDY' KENNEDY

Country: Republic of Ireland
Born: 9 Oct 1934 **Died:** 18 Mar 2007
Position: Full-back
Debut: 2 Oct 1954 v Wolverhampton Wanderers
Appearances: 1 **Goals scored:** 0
Seasons: 1954/55
Clubs: Johnville, Manchester United, Blackburn Rovers, Southampton, Oldham Athletic

WILLIAM JOHN KENNEDY

Country: Scotland
Born: Unknown **Died:** Unknown
Position: Forward
Debut: 7 Sep 1895 v Crewe Alexandra
Appearances: 33 **Goals scored:** 12
Seasons: 1895/96 – 1896/97
Clubs: Ayr Parkhouse, Newton Heath, Stockport County, Morton

William Kennedy was one of nine Scots in the starting line-up for the opening game of 1895/96, but despite scoring 12 goals (including one on his debut) and playing in all but one of the fixtures that season, he was to feature only once during the opening weeks of the following campaign and signed for Stockport County in December 1896.

HUGH KERR

Country: Scotland
Born: 1882 **Died:** Unknown
Position: Forward
Debut: 9 Mar 1904 v Blackpool
Appearances: 2 **Goals scored:** 0
Seasons: 1903/04
Clubs: Westerlea, Ayr, Manchester United

BRIAN KIDD

Country: England
Born: 29 May 1949
Position: Forward
Debut: 12 Aug 1967 v Tottenham Hotspur
Appearances: 257 (9) **Goals scored:** 70
Seasons: 1967/68 – 1973/74
Clubs: Manchester United, Arsenal, Manchester City, Everton, Bolton Wanderers, Atlanta Chiefs (loan), Fort Lauderdale Strikers

Brian Kidd joined the club as an apprentice in December 1963 and was soon moving through the ranks, earning a place on the 1967 pre-season tour of Australia with some emphatic displays. Having made an impression Down Under, he was in the first team for the start of 1967/68, when he played in the Charity Shield, and was able to take his chance to become a regular in the side once David Herd broke his leg, missing only a handful of games that debut season. He crowned the campaign by scoring the third goal in the European Cup final on his 19th birthday, having also set up George Best to score the second a minute or so earlier.

Despite the positive start, he found himself back in the reserves during 1968/69, but soon regained his form, if not his scoring touch, but the goals did return in 1969/70 when he had his most prolific campaign at United, scoring 20 goals in all competitions. Thereafter, as the European Cup-winning side began to break up or retire, it became increasingly difficult for the Collyhurst-born forward to shine, though he did win a couple of England caps ahead of the 1970 World Cup finals.

Eventually, following United's relegation to the Second Division, he moved to Arsenal for £110,000 in August 1974 and was leading scorer for them in both campaigns, before he returned to Manchester, this time to play at Maine Road. Following a spell in the States, he eventually made his way back to United, initially working with the youth team, becoming a huge influence for the golden generation that emerged from the Class of '92. He was then promoted to assistant manager in 1991, but left to take charge of Blackburn Rovers during the 1998/99 season. There followed other roles, including becoming assistant coach of England during Sven-Göran Eriksson's reign. Most recently, he has been assistant manager at Manchester City, having taken the job at the end of 2009. It created a unique double, in that he had played and been assistant manager at both Manchester clubs.

JOSHUA CHRISTIAN KOJO KING

Country: Norway
Born: 15 Jan 1992
Debut: 23 Sep 2009 v Wolverhampton Wanderers
Position: Forward
Appearances: 0 (1)
Seasons: 2009/10
Clubs: Manchester United, Preston North End (loan), Borussia Mönchengladbach (loan), Hull City (loan), Blackburn Rovers (loan), Blackburn Rovers

JOSEPH 'JOE' KINLOCH

Country: England
Born: Jan 1864 **Died:** Unknown
Position: Forward
Debut: 29 Oct 1892 v Nottingham Forest
Appearances: 1 **Goals scored:** 0
Seasons: 1892/93
Clubs: Newton Heath

ALBERT JOHN KINSEY

Country: England
Born: 19 Sep 1945
Position: Forward
Debut: 9 Jan 1965 v Chester City
Appearances: 1 **Goals scored:** 1
Seasons: 1964/65
Clubs: Manchester United, Wrexham, Crewe Alexandra, Wigan Athletic

JOSÉ PEREIRA KLÉBERSON

Country: Brazil
Born: 19 Jun 1979
Position: Midfield
Debut: 27 Aug 2003 v Wolverhampton Wanderers
Appearances: 24 (6) **Goals scored:** 2
Seasons: 2003/04 – 2004/05
Clubs: Atlético Paranaense, Manchester United, Beşiktaş, Flamengo, Atlético Paranaense (loan), Bahia, Philadelphia Union (loan)

José Kléberson was signed for £5.5 million from Paranaense in August 2003, having won the World Cup with Brazil in 2002, where manager Luiz Felipe Scolari said he had played a crucial role. Because of that, the midfielder promised so much, but although he was tried in numerous midfield positions, never quite managed to settle in England, perhaps hindered by picking up an injury in his second game for the club. Eventually, he joined Beşiktaş in August 2005 for £2.5 million.

FRANK KNOWLES

Country: England
Born: Apr 1891 **Died:** 20 Jan 1951
Position: Half-back
Debut: 30 Mar 1912 v Aston Villa
Appearances: 47 **Goals scored:** 1
Seasons: 1911/12 – 1914/15
Clubs: Stalybridge Celtic, Manchester United, Hyde Park, Oldham Athletic, Sandbach Ramblers, Hartlepools United

Frank Knowles won a Central League medal with United's reserve side in 1911/12 and broke into the first team towards the end of that same season. He was, however, unable to hold down a regular place until 1914/15, but like others, found his United career interrupted by the First World War, moving to Hartlepools in 1919 after guesting for various clubs.

FRANK KOPEL

Country: Scotland
Born: 28 Mar 1949
Position: Full-back
Debut: 9 Sep 1967 v Burnley
Appearances: 10 (2) **Goals scored:** 0
Seasons: 1967/68 – 1968/69
Clubs: Manchester United, Blackburn Rovers, Dundee United, Arbroath

Falkirk-born Frank Kopel joined United upon leaving school and during his early days with the club, he was converted from a half-back to full-back. He was selected as a substitute against Burnley on 9 September 1967, coming on in place of fellow Scot John Fitzpatrick, but had to wait a further few weeks before his full debut, against Nottingham Forest, at the City Ground on 28 October.

With Shay Brennan and Tony Dunne ahead of him, first-team opportunities were few and far between and in March 1969, an enquiry from Blackburn Rovers led to his £25,000 transfer to Ewood Park.

TOMASZ KUSZCZAK

Country: Poland
Born: 20 Mar 1980
Position: Goalkeeper
Debut: 17 Sep 2006 v Arsenal
Appearances: 56 (5) **Goals scored:** 0
Seasons: 2006/07 – 2010/11
Clubs: Hertha BSC, West Bromwich Albion, Manchester United (loan), Manchester United, Watford (loan), Brighton & Hove Albion

Tomasz Kusczczak arrived in August 2006, initially on loan from West Bromwich Albion, but was to cost over £2 million a year later when the deal was made permanent. The Polish international was essentially signed as an understudy to Edwin van der Sar. Saving a penalty on his debut, he proved to be an excellent shot-stopper, but was never able to replace the Dutch star as the first-choice keeper. He won a League Cup medal in 2010, but appearances were few and far between. After van der Sar retired, Sir Alex bought in two new keepers in David De Gea and Anders Lindegaard, so he joined Watford on loan in February 2012 before signing for Brighton four months later.

JOSEPH GERARD LANCASTER

Country: England
Born: 28 Apr 1926
Position: Goalkeeper
Debut: 14 Jan 1950 v Chelsea
Appearances: 4 **Goals scored:** 0
Seasons: 1949/50 – 1950/51
Clubs: Manchester United, Accrington Stanley

THOMAS 'TOMMY' LANG

Country: Scotland
Born: 3 Apr 1906 **Died:** Unknown
Position: Winger
Debut: 11 Apr 1936 v Bradford Park Avenue
Appearances: 13 **Goals scored:** 1
Seasons: 1935/36 – 1936/37
Clubs: Newcastle United, Huddersfield Town, Manchester United, Swansea Town, Queen of the South, Ipswich Town

An FA Cup winner with Newcastle in 1932, Tommy Lang joined United from Huddersfield Town in December 1935 in exchange for Reg Chester. His stay with United was brief, as it had been with Huddersfield, lasting 16 months and spanning 13 games before he joined Swansea Town in April 1937.

LEONARD 'LEN' LANGFORD

Country: England
Born: 30 May 1899 **Died:** 26 Dec 1973
Position: Goalkeeper
Debut: 22 Sep 1934 v Norwich City
Appearances: 15 **Goals scored:** 0
Seasons: 1934/35 – 1935/36
Clubs: Nottingham Forest, Manchester City, Manchester United

Goalkeeper Len Langford, having won an FA Cup runners-up medal with Manchester City, moved to Old Trafford in June 1934, but the majority of his time with the club was spent in the reserves.

HUBERT HENRY 'HARRY' LAPPIN

Country: England
Born: 16 Jan 1879 **Died:** May 1925
Position: Forward
Debut: 27 Apr 1901 v Chesterfield
Appearances: 27 **Goals scored:** 4
Seasons: 1900/01 – 1902/03
Clubs: Oldham Athletic, Newton Heath, Grimsby Town

Manchester-born Harry Lappin joined the club towards their latter days as Newton Heath, signed following a trial in the final match of 1900/01. He enjoyed a favourable first season, but following the change of name, he faded from view and moved to Grimsby Town in August 1903.

HENRIK EDWARD LARSSON

Country: Sweden
Born: 20 Sep 1971
Position: Forward
Debut: 7 Jan 2007 v Aston Villa
Appearances: 10 (3) **Goals scored:** 3
Seasons: 2006/07
Clubs: Högaborg, Helsingborg, Feyenoord, Celtic, Barcelona, Helsingborg, Manchester United (loan)

Having made his international debut in October 1993, Swedish striker Henrik Larsson followed his former Feyenoord manger Wim Jansen to Celtic in 1997, where he became a cult hero, scoring an astonishing 242 goals in 315 matches, and helping them to eight major trophies as well as the UEFA Cup final. Leaving Glasgow, he joined Barcelona, where although not always a regular starter he was able to add two La Liga titles and the Champions League in 2006 to his trophy cabinet. After the 2006 World Cup, he returned to Sweden, expecting to see out his career in his native land, but it came as a major surprise when he was offered the opportunity to join United on a three-month loan in January 2007. Scoring on his debut in the FA Cup against Aston Villa, managed by his former boss Martin O'Neill, his United career was brief, but his presence was certainly enjoyed by the supporters.

DENIS LAW

Country: Scotland
Born: 24 February 1940
Position: Forward
Debut: 18 August 1962 v West Bromwich Albion
Appearances: 398 (6) **Goals scored:** 237
Seasons: 1962/63 – 1972/73
Clubs: Huddersfield Town, Manchester City, Torino, Manchester United, Manchester City

In the 1990s, a Frenchman arrived at Old Trafford in a surprise transfer. The enigmatic talisman was soon to be hailed as 'the King' by countless adoring fans, but for those who had stood on the Old Trafford terraces during the 1960s, he was but a mere pretender to the throne, as there was, and only ever would be, one 'King of Old Trafford'. His name was Denis Law.

If there was ever an unlikely-looking footballer as a youngster, then it was the skinny, bespectacled, little Aberdonian, but despite his physical appearance, Law had an inbuilt talent as a footballer and Archie Beattie, a scout with Huddersfield Town, noted that special something and quickly recommended him to his brother Andy, then manager with the Yorkshire side. Impressing in a trial, Denis was signed on amateur forms in April 1955, earning £5 per week, with half of that going on food and rent.

Twenty months later, on 24 December 1956, he made his Huddersfield debut against Notts County, and soon after Matt Busby tried to sign the youngster for United. By then, the club had sent him to have an operation to correct his squint, and under new manager Bill Shankly he quickly grew in confidence. By the autumn of 1958, he had Scotland international recognition, scoring on his debut, and on 15 March 1960, Manchester City paid a record fee of £55,000 for his signature.

His stay at Maine Road was brief and in the summer of 1961 Torino made City an offer of £100,000 that they could not refuse and he became the first in Britain to be transferred for a six-figure fee. Despite having a decent season there, he struggled to settle, so when United came in with another record offer of £115,000, he was keen to return home.

He scored on his debut against West Bromwich Albion, and thereafter the honours flowed almost as frequently as the goals. He scored the only goal in the 1963 FA Cup semi-final against Southampton, and then added his sixth of the cup run in the final against Leicester. In 1963/64 he was almost unstoppable as United began to challenge once more for the league title, his 46 goals that season remain a club record and his form saw him named as European Footballer of the Year. The next season, United won their first league title since Munich, with Law scoring 28 league goals.

He also gained the club captaincy and a further league title in 1967. Law was all about goals – everything he did was to ensure that he could maximise his return, and he was fearless in pursuit of them, with an instinctive knack of finishing. But it was not all roses, as his fiery Scottish temperament, which could be as quick as his lightning goalscoring reflexes, sometimes had him in trouble with officials, bringing three lengthy suspensions between 1963 and 1967. His daredevil performances also brought injuries, and it was a knee injury that robbed him of an appearance in the 1968 European Cup final.

Law bounced back, but by the beginning of the 1970s, Manchester United were not the team who had taken the previous decade by storm as they were now on a downward slide. Now in his 30s, he still had much to offer, but with the arrival of Tommy Docherty, his days as a Manchester United player were numbered. On 7 April 1973, unbeknown to the 48,593 supporters inside Old Trafford for the match against Norwich City, they were watching his last match in the red of United.

At the end of that season, Docherty gave Law a free transfer, amid much controversy, and he went to Maine Road for the start of the 1973/74 campaign, climaxing in what was to be a dramatic swansong. Returning to Old Trafford to face a relegation-threatened United, with a cheeky backheel he scored the only goal of a game which came to a premature end due to a pitch invasion, and United went down, though results elsewhere rendered Law's goal irrelevant to United's fate.

In February 2002 he unveiled a ten-foot high bronze statue of himself under the Stretford End and six years later, in May 2008, he was immortalised again along with Best and Charlton on the Old Trafford forecourt.

REGINALD OPENSHAW 'REG' LAWSON

Country: England
Born: Nov 1880 **Died:** Unknown
Position: Forward
Debut: 1 Sep 1900 v Glossop
Appearances: 3 **Goals scored:** 0
Seasons: 1900/01 – 1901/02
Clubs: Cheshire College, Newton Heath, Bolton Wanderers, Southport Central

NORBERT 'NOBBY' LAWTON

Country: England
Born: 25 Mar 1940 **Died:** 22 Apr 2006
Position: Half-back

Debut: 9 Apr 1960 v Luton Town
Appearances: 44 **Goals scored:** 6
Seasons: 1959/60 – 1962/63
Clubs: Manchester United, Preston North End, Brighton & Hove Albion, Lincoln City

Like the club itself, born in Newton Heath, Nobby Lawton was a product of Manchester Schools football. He joined the groundstaff, turning professional in April 1958. After a life-threatening bout of pneumonia, he made his debut against Luton two years later, mostly at half-back, but was later to appear as an inside-forward. Dropping out of the first-team picture in 1962/63 after the arrival of Pat Crerand, he joined Preston in March 1963, captaining them in the FA Cup final a year later.

EDWIN LEE

Country: England
Born: Jul 1879 **Died:** Unknown
Position: Forward
Debut: 25 Mar 1899 v Lincoln City
Appearances: 11 **Goals scored:** 5
Seasons: 1898/89 – 1899/1900
Clubs: Hurst Ramblers, Newton Heath

Signed from Hurst Ramblers in May 1898, Edwin Lee scored four goals in his first seven appearances towards the end of season 1898/99 and they were enough to see him retained for the following campaign. But despite a goal in the opening fixture of the new season, and then featuring in the next two games, he did not reappear until the second last game of the season and was then allowed to leave.

KIERAN CHRISTOPHER LEE

Country: England
Born: 22 Jun 1988
Position: Full-back/Midfield
Debut: 25 Oct 2006 v Crewe Alexandra
Appearances: 1 (2) **Goals scored:** 1

Seasons: 2006/07 – 2007/08
Clubs: Manchester United, Queens Park Rangers (loan), Oldham Athletic, Sheffield Wednesday

THOMAS 'TOM' LEIGH

Country: England
Born: Jan 1875 **Died:** Unknown
Position: Forward
Debut: 17 Mar 1900 v Barnsley
Appearances: 46 **Goals scored:** 15
Seasons: 1899/1900 – 1900/01
Clubs: Derby County, Burton Swifts, New Brighton Tower, Newton Heath

Tom Leigh scored on his debut for the Heathens in a 3-0 win at Bank Street, but was unable to add to his tally during the next eight games that campaign. The following season he was an ever-present for the financially troubled club, and ended as the leading scorer with 14 before he moved on.

JAMES 'JIM' LEIGHTON

Country: Scotland
Born: 24 Jul 1958
Position: Goalkeeper
Debut: 27 Aug 1988 v Queens Park Rangers
Appearances: 94 **Goals scored:** 0
Seasons: 1988/89 – 1990/91
Clubs: Aberdeen, Deveronvale (loan), Manchester United, Arsenal (loan), Reading (loan), Dundee, Sheffield United (loan), Hibernian, Aberdeen

Alex Ferguson's first-choice keeper during the glory years at Aberdeen, when he won ten honours, including three SPL titles and the European Cup-Winners' Cup in 1983, Jim Leighton was to follow his old manager to Old Trafford for a record-breaking £450,000 fee in June 1988. The Scottish international was a first-class goalkeeper and shot-stopper, who developed a reputation for reliability and went on to win 91 caps for his country.

However, once at United he did endure the odd slip-up and it was a far from confident display in the 1990 FA Cup final against Crystal

Palace that saw him dropped for the replay, which effectively brought an end to his United career after two seasons where he had barely missed a game. For the manager, it was a hugely tough decision to drop someone he had worked so closely with, but it was an early sign to Reds fans that here was someone who would never be afraid to do what he felt was right for the club. Following numerous loan spells, he joined Dundee in February 1992 for a fee of £200,000.

HENRY 'HARRY' DOXFORD LEONARD

Country: England
Born: Jul 1886 **Died:** 3 Nov 1951
Position: Forward
Debut: 11 Sep 1920 v Chelsea
Appearances: 10 **Goals scored:** 5
Seasons: 1920/21
Clubs: Newcastle United, Grimsby Town, Middlesbrough, Derby County, Manchester United, Heanor Town

After scoring a goal on his debut against Chelsea, following his £800 transfer from Derby in September 1920, Harry Leonard went on to score five goals in ten appearances and then completely disappear from view before joining Heanor Town in June 1921.

EDWARD 'EDDIE' LEWIS

Country: England
Born: 3 Jan 1935 **Died:** 2 May 2011
Position: Forward
Debut: 29 Nov 1952 v West Bromwich Albion
Appearances: 24 **Goals scored:** 11
Seasons: 1952/53 – 1955/56
Clubs: Goslings, Manchester United, Preston North End, West Ham United, Leyton Orient, Folkestone Town

A former Manchester and Lancashire schoolboy, Eddie Lewis signed for United upon leaving school. A member of the 1952/53 Youth Cup-winning team, he scored on his debut at West Bromwich after only seven minutes, soon after signing as a professional.

A well-built centre-forward, he stayed with United until December 1955, before joining Preston North End for £10,000, as he was unsurprisingly unable to oust Tommy Taylor as first-choice No.9.

LESLIE LIEVESLEY

Country: England
Born: Jul 1911 **Died:** 4 May 1949
Position: Half-back
Debut: 25 Mar 1932 v Charlton Athletic
Appearances: 2 **Goals scored:** 0
Seasons: 1931/32
Clubs: Doncaster Rovers, Manchester United, Chesterfield, Torquay United, Crystal Palace

Although Lievesley's career in the first team at Old Trafford lasted just two days, playing back-to-back fixtures on Good Friday and Easter Saturday, after the war he went on to become coach at Torino and was on the plane for the Superga air disaster on 4 May 1949, when the plane flew into a thunderstorm when approaching Turin. In all 31 people died, including 18 players and Lievesley. The tragedy devastated Italian football as the club had won the Scudetto for four consecutive seasons between 1946 and 1949, and many of its players were members of the national team as well.

WILFRED LIEVESLEY

Country: England
Born: 6 Oct 1902 **Died:** 21 Feb 1979
Position: Forward
Debut: 20 Jan 1923 v Leeds United
Appearances: 3 **Goals scored:** 0
Seasons: 1922/23
Clubs: Derby County, Manchester United, Exeter City, Wigan Borough, Cardiff City

ANDERS ROSENKRANTZ LINDEGAARD

Country: Denmark
Born: 13 Apr 1984
Position: Goalkeeper
Debut: 29 Jan 2011 v Southampton
Appearances: 26 **Goals scored:** 0
Seasons: 2010/11 – present
Clubs: Odense Boldklub, Kolding (loan), Aalesund, Manchester United

There was a time when many thought that Anders Lindegaard would become Manchester United's first-choice goalkeeper, following in the footsteps of fellow Dane Peter Schmeichel. Although he could hardly hope to emulate his countryman's legendary career, in the latter half of United's 20th title-winning season, he found himself regularly behind David De Gea in the club's pecking order.

He signed for United for an undisclosed fee during 2010/11 ahead of Edwin van der Sar's retirement, but injuries have done little to help his bid to be United's regular No.1. He won his first Premier League title in 2012/13 and has also won full international honours for Denmark.

OSCAR HORACE S. LINKSON

Country: England
Born: 16 Mar 1888 **Died:** 8 Aug 1916
Position: Full-back
Debut: 24 Oct 1908 v Nottingham Forest
Appearances: 59 **Goals scored:** 0
Seasons: 1908/09 – 1912/13
Clubs: Barnet Alston, Manchester United, Shelbourne

Oscar Linkson made his United debut as a 20-year-old in October 1908, but failed to command a regular place until season 1911/12, thus missing out on the FA Cup success in 1909 and the league title in 1911. After missing only five of the first 19 fixtures of 1912/13 season, he again faded from the scene, joining Shelbourne in August 1913. Having returned to England on the outbreak of war, he joined the 1st Football Battalion of the Middlesex Regiment, and was killed in action during the Somme offensive.

GEORGE TURNER LIVINGSTONE

Country: Scotland
Born: 5 May 1876 **Died:** 15 Jan 1950
Position: Forward
Debut: 23 Jan 1909 v Manchester City
Appearances: 46 **Goals scored:** 4
Seasons: 1908/09 – 1913/14
Clubs: Sinclair Swifts, Artizan Thistle, Heart of Midlothian, Sunderland, Celtic, Liverpool, Manchester City, Rangers, Manchester United

United's poor league form between January and April 1909 must have given new signing George Livingstone food for thought and led him to wonder if he had made the correct decision in leaving Rangers to join the Reds. He had made his United debut alongside former City team-mates Burgess, Meredith and Sandy Turnbull, ironically against Manchester City, scoring twice in a 3-1 win, but was later to be disappointed at missing out on a place in the FA Cup final line-up, as he had played in the league fixtures prior to both the semi-final and the final. Two seasons later, he was again to miss out on United's trophy success, as he could manage only ten games in the title-winning side of 1910/11.

Playing a fair percentage of his games in the United reserve side, he was appointed player-manager of the second string, a position that he was to hold until announcing his retirement during the First World War. He holds the unique status of having played for both sides in the Old Firm and in Manchester.

ARTHUR WILLIAM LOCHHEAD

Country: Scotland
Born: 8 Dec 1897 **Died:** 30 Dec 1966
Position: Forward
Debut: 27 Aug 1921 v Everton
Appearances: 153 **Goals scored:** 50
Seasons: 1921/22 – 1925/26
Clubs: Heart of Midlothian, Manchester United, Leicester City

Arriving at Old Trafford as part of the deal that took Tommy Miller to Hearts in July1921, Arthur Lochhead, valued at £2,300, initially struggled as United fought an unsuccessful relegation battle during his first season. In the Second Division, he scored 40 goals in three seasons, with United gaining promotion in 1924/25. It was thought that Lochhead's goals would play a major part in the club consolidating its place in the top flight, but he was transferred to Leicester City in October 1925 for a fee of £3,300, where he would go on to make more than 300 league appearances.

WILLIAM LONGAIR

Country: Scotland
Born: 19 Jul 1870 **Died:** 28 Nov 1926
Position: Half-back
Debut: 20 Apr 1895 v Notts County
Appearances: 1 **Goals scored:** 0
Seasons: 1894/95
Clubs: Dundee East End, Dundee, Newton Heath, Dundee, Sunderland, Burnley, Dundee, Brighton United, Dundee

LONGTON

Country: Unknown
Born: Unknown **Died:** Unknown
Position: Forward
Debut: 30 Oct 1886 v Fleetwood Rangers
Appearances: 1 **Goals scored:** 0
Seasons: 1886/87
Clubs: Newton Heath

THOMAS 'TOMMY' LOWRIE

Country: Scotland
Born: 14 Jan 1928 **Died:** 2009
Position: Half-back
Debut: 7 Apr 1948 v Manchester City
Appearances: 14 **Goals scored:** 0
Seasons: 1947/48 – 1950/51
Clubs: Troon Athletic, Manchester United, Aberdeen, Oldham Athletic

Tommy Lowrie was recommended to United by Jimmy Delaney who saw him play for Troon in a charity match. The energetic half-back made a big impression in his debut against Manchester City, showing much promise in the games that followed. However, with a strong playing staff, his first-team outings were limited. In his final league appearance, he was embarrassed by Len Shackleton, who goaded him to try to get the ball off him, and in March 1951 he returned north and joined Aberdeen.

GEORGE LYDON

Country: England
Born: 24 Jun 1902 **Died:** 12 Aug 1953
Position: Half-back
Debut: 25 Dec 1930 v Bolton Wanderers
Appearances: 3 **Goals scored:** 0
Seasons: 1930/31 – 1931/32
Clubs: Nelson United, Mossley, Manchester United, Southport

MARK JOHN LYNCH

Country: England
Born: 2 Sep 1981
Position: Full-back
Debut: 18 Mar 2003 v Deportivo de La Coruña
Appearances: 1 **Goals scored:** 0
Seasons: 2002/03
Clubs: Manchester United, St Johnstone (loan), Sunderland, Hull City, Yeovil Town, Rotherham United, Stockport County, Altrincham

DAVID LYNER

Country: Ireland
Born: 9 Jan 1893 **Died:** 5 Dec 1973
Position: Forward
Debut: 23 Sep 1922 v Coventry City
Appearances: 3 **Goals scored:** 0
Seasons: 1922/23
Clubs: Glentoran, Manchester United, Kilmarnock, Queen's Island, Dundela, Clydebank, Mid Rhondda, New Brighton, Glentoran, Queen's Island

SAMUEL 'SAMMY' LYNN

Country: England
Born: 25 Dec 1920 **Died:** Jan 1995
Position: Half-back
Debut: 3 Jan 1948 v Charlton Athletic
Appearances: 13 **Goals scored:** 0
Seasons: 1947/48 – 1949/50
Clubs: Manchester United, Bradford Park Avenue

Sammy Lynn came to United's notice in St Helens junior football, moving through the ranks before eventually making his debut in January 1948, almost ten years after making his reserve-team debut. A defender with Lancashire Schoolboys, it was as a half-back that he played his early United games, but, reverting back to centre-half, he found few opportunities up against Allenby Chilton and left to join Bradford Park Avenue in February 1951.

GEORGE LYONS

Country: England
Born: Apr 1884 **Died:** Unknown
Position: Forward
Debut: 23 Apr 1904 v Burton United
Appearances: 5 **Goals scored:** 0
Seasons: 1903/04 – 1905/06
Clubs: Black Lane Temperance, Manchester United, Oldham Athletic

NEIL McBAIN

Country: Scotland
Born: 15 Nov 1895 **Died:** 13 May 1974
Debut: 26 Nov 1921 v Aston Villa
Position: Half-back

Appearances: 43 **Goals scored:** 2
Seasons: 1921/22 – 1922/23
Clubs: Ayr United, Manchester United, Everton, St Johnstone, Liverpool, Watford, New Brighton

Neil McBain was a skilful centre-half, for whom United had to pay Ayr United £4,600 to secure his signature, quite a fee in the early days of the 1920s. Having had his career interrupted by the First World War, the stylish defender had attracted United with his skilful play. Arriving at Old Trafford in November 1921 saw one reporter of the period write: 'The introduction of McBain at centre-half, has had a wonderful effect. His defensive play is fine, but his judgement in working out attacks is even finer.' It was this ability that saw him win the first of three Scotland caps in April 1922.

In 1922/23 he switched to left-half, because of the arrival of the more robust Frank Barson. To everyone's surprise, McBain requested a transfer in January 1923. His reasons for doing so were never made public, though perhaps it was mainly due to his selection in the unfamiliar and unwanted role of inside-forward. When news of his impending transfer was announced, a vast number of United supporters held a protest meeting in a local hall, but it was to no avail. There were obviously many teams interested in such a talented individual and he decided to join Everton, with United receiving a fee of £4,200.

Astonishingly, 24 years later, McBain (by then manager of New Brighton) had to turn out as his club's goalkeeper in a game against Hartlepools United on 15 March 1947, setting a record as the oldest player ever to appear in a Football League game, at the age of 51 years and 120 days.

JAMES 'JIM' McCALLIOG

Country: Scotland
Born: 23 Sep 1946
Debut: 16 Mar 1974 v Birmingham City
Position: Midfield
Appearances: 37 (1) **Goals scored:** 7
Seasons: 1973/74 – 1974/75
Clubs: Chelsea, Sheffield Wednesday, Wolverhampton Wanderers, Manchester United, Southampton, Chicago Sting, Lyn Oslo, Lincoln City

McCalliog, a former Glasgow Schoolboy, had originally joined Leeds United as an apprentice in May 1963, but failed to make the grade at Elland Road. Four months later, he joined Chelsea under Tommy Docherty and, although winning Scottish Youth honours, he made only seven league appearances, scoring twice, before he was told that he was being released and made available for transfer, moving to Sheffield Wednesday in October 1965 for £37,500, then a record for a teenager.

A member of the Scotland side that defeated World Cup winners England 3-2 at Wembley in 1967 (scoring the third goal), he was to join Wolves in the summer of 1969 for £70,000, before his old manager Tommy Docherty paid £60,000 to take him to United in March 1974. Although his goals and performances almost helped United avoid relegation, he did not see out the Second Division campaign, joining Southampton for £40,000 in February 1975 and coming back to haunt United at Wembley in the 1976 FA Cup final.

PATRICK McCARTHY

Country: Wales
Born: Apr 1888 **Died:** Unknown
Debut: 20 Jan 1912 v West Bromwich Albion
Position: Forward
Appearances: 1 **Goals scored:** 0
Seasons: 1911/12
Clubs: Chester, Skelmersdale United, Manchester United

WILLIAM JOHN McCARTNEY

Country: Scotland
Born: 1866 **Died:** 18 Jan 1933
Debut: 8 Sep 1894 v Burton Wanderers
Position: Full-back
Appearances: 20 **Goals scored:** 1
Seasons: 1894/95
Clubs: Cartvale, Thistle, Rangers, Cowlairs, Newton Heath, Luton Town, Barnsley

John McCartney, a distinguished professional before his arrival in Manchester, having been a member of the Rangers side who had reached the semi-finals of the FA Cup in 1887, was a solidly built individual, of whom it was once written that 'charging him would be like a ball going against a billiard cushion'. Despite being given the captaincy, his spell at Clayton was brief, even though he took the Heathens to within touching distance of possible promotion. In April 1895, he joined Luton Town, where he again became club captain.

His career following his departure from Newton Heath was certainly one of note, as he then saw service as a player with Luton and Barnsley, where he went on to become manager, before returning to Scotland to take charge of St Mirren and then Hearts, where he had arguably the best years of his footballing career, before returning south to join Portsmouth and Luton for a second spell.

WILLIAM McCARTNEY

Country: Scotland
Born: Unknown **Died:** Unknown
Debut: 5 Sep 1903 v Bristol City
Position: Forward
Appearances: 13 **Goals scored:** 1
Seasons: 1903/04
Clubs: Rutherglen Glencairn, Ayr, Hibernian, Manchester United, West Ham United, Broxburn, Lochgelly United, Clyde

A Scottish international while with his previous club, Hibs, William McCartney was described as a 'man of more than ordinary capability'. His reputation, however, did not provide him with a regular place in the United starting line-up. Having turned professional in 1898, he joined Hibs in January 1900 and soon became a firm favourite with the green side of Edinburgh. Sadly, success did not follow the player south after his transfer to United in May 1903, as a mere 13 appearances and one goal were his contribution to his new club's 1903/04 season. During this time, he filled five different positions, including something of a surprise appearance at centre-half. In the summer of 1904, he joined West Ham United.

BRIAN JOHN McCLAIR

Country: Scotland
Born: 8 Dec 1963
Debut: 15 Aug 1987 v Southampton
Position: Forward
Appearances: 398 (73) **Goals scored:** 127
Seasons: 1987/88 – 1997/98
Clubs: Aston Villa, Motherwell, Celtic, Manchester United, Motherwell

Born in Airdrie, Brian McClair played for local sides St Edwards Boys Guild and Coatbridge YM before moving south of the border as an apprentice with Aston Villa in 1980, but, disenchanted, he returned to Scotland after 14 months to join Motherwell. With a doubt in his mind regarding a full-time career in football, he enrolled in a mathematics course at Glasgow University. His plans for the university degree lasted as long as his Motherwell playing career, just two years, as Celtic offered £75,000 to take him from Fir Park to the east end of Glasgow.

At Celtic Park he topped the club's scoring charts for the next four seasons, with 121 goals, winning title honours and Scottish Cup medals along with personal accolades as the Scottish PFA Player of the Year, the Scottish Writers' Player of the Year in 1986. He won his first international cap on 12 November 1986 against Luxembourg, in the same match as Kenny Dalglish won his last cap.

When Alex Ferguson tried to sign him in the summer of 1987, a transfer tribunal set the fee at £850,000, as Celtic boss Billy McNeill had valued him at £2 million. At the end of the hearing, the Celtic manager complained, 'We've lost the biggest asset in Scotland. They have got him for a song.' Thirty-one goals in 48 games during his initial season would never be bettered, but his contribution to the United cause was never in doubt, and during the 1990s he took on a more deep-lying role, and up until the end of the 1992/93 season, he rarely missed a match. Thereafter he found himself more of a squad player, with a place on the bench increasingly his normal match-day position.

Awarded a testimonial against Celtic to mark his ten years at Old Trafford, McClair was given a free transfer at the end of season 1997/98, having won four Premier League titles, two FA Cup medals, one League Cup medal (scoring the only goal of the game) and one European Cup-Winners' Cup medal. He returned to Motherwell for a short spell, but when Brian Kidd left Old Trafford for Blackburn Rovers, he appointed Brian McClair as one of his coaching staff. Following Kidd's departure from Ewood Park, McClair was out of the game for a while, but prior to the start of season 2001/02 he returned to Manchester United as reserve-team coach and is now director of the club's Academy.

JAMES 'JIMMY' McCLELLAND

Country: Scotland
Born: 11 May 1903 **Died:** Unknown
Debut: 2 Sep 1936 v Huddersfield Town
Position: Forward
Appearances: 5 **Goals scored:** 1
Seasons: 1936/37
Clubs: Rosslyn, Raith Rovers, Southend United, Middlesbrough, Bolton Wanderers, Preston North End, Blackpool, Bradford Park Avenue, Manchester United

JAMES CLARK FULTON McCRAE

Country: Scotland
Born: 2 Sep 1894 **Died:** 3 Sep 1974
Debut: 16 Jan 1926 v Arsenal
Position: Midfield
Appearances: 13 **Goals scored:** 0
Seasons: 1925/26
Clubs: Clyde, West Ham United, Bury, Wigan Borough, New Brighton, Manchester United, Watford

James McCrae made his United debut at left-half, on 16 January 1926 against Arsenal, at Highbury, in the 3-2 defeat. Born into a footballing family in the Bridge of Weir, McCrae played with Clyde before joining the Grenadier Guards in the war. Afterwards, he played for West Ham United until a £750 fee took him to Bury, where he was to spend three years, before moving to Wigan Borough during September 1923. A year at New Brighton followed, before he became a Manchester United player in August 1925.

Following his debut, he was to play first-team football on only a further 12 occasions, all during 1925/26 (eight in the league and four during the FA Cup run). Prior to the start of season 1926/27 he moved back to the London area and joined Watford. He became the first ex-United player to coach at the World Cup, managing Egypt in the 1934 finals.

DAVID McCREERY

Country: Northern Ireland
Born: 16 Sep 1957
Debut: 15 Oct 1974 v Portsmouth
Position: Midfield
Appearances: 57 (53) **Goals scored:** 8
Seasons: 1974/75 – 1978/79
Clubs: Manchester United, Queens Park Rangers, Tulsa Roughnecks, Newcastle United, GIF Sundsvall, Heart of Midlothian, Hartlepool, Coleraine, Carlisle United, Hartlepool

David McCreery was one of the many unsung Manchester United heroes over the years, who, while not a big-money buy, was an integral cog in the wheel; he was able to play anywhere and always gave 100 per cent. The former Northern Ireland Schoolboy international from Belfast was one of scout Bob Bishop's discoveries and joined Manchester United straight from school in September 1972, signing amateur forms, after winning three schoolboy caps. He quickly settled at Old Trafford, signing professional forms in April 1974 and was soon making a name for himself in the United junior teams and the Northern Ireland Youth side.

He made his senior United debut as a 16-year-old substitute in a friendly against the Republic of Ireland at Old Trafford on 4 September 1974 with his league debut following a month later. Almost half of his appearances were as a substitute, including those in the 1976 and 1977 FA Cup finals, replacing Gordon Hill on both occasions, but the adaptable Northern Ireland international was never going to hold a regular first-team spot. With Ray Wilkins's arrival at United, Tommy Docherty, his old boss now at QPR, made what he called 'the bargain of the century' when he paid United £200,000 for the player in August 1979. He subsequently played for Newcastle United for seven years.

KENNETH 'KEN' MacDONALD

Country: Wales
Born: 24 Apr 1898 **Died:** Unknown
Debut: 3 Mar 1923 v Southampton
Position: Forward
Appearances: 9 **Goals scored:** 2
Seasons: 1922/23 – 1923/24
Clubs: Inverness Citadel, Clachnacuddin, Aberdeen, Caerau, Cardiff City, Manchester United, Bradford Park Avenue, Hull City, Halifax Town, Coleraine, Walker Celtic, Blyth Spartans

WILLIAM McDONALD

Country: Scotland
Born: 9 Jul 1905 **Died:** 1979
Debut: 23 Apr 1932 v Bradford City
Position: Forward
Appearances: 27 **Goals scored:** 4
Seasons: 1931/32 – 1933/34
Clubs: Coatbridge FC, Dundee, Broxburn United, Laws Scotia FC, Airdrieonians, Manchester United, Tranmere Rovers, Coventry City, Plymouth Argyle

The Coatbridge-born McDonald (in some sources he is named as MacDonald) had played most of his early football in Scotland turning out for his hometown club, Broxburn United, and Laws Scotia. He had, however, spent a few months with Dundee United during season 1925/26, returning to the professional game in May 1928 with Airdrieonians. Joining United in 1931 he was given special permission to play in the closing games of that season as they did not involve any championship or relegation issues. Much was expected of the player during season 1932/33, but despite featuring in the opening half-dozen games, he was to play in only 21 of the fixtures, scoring four goals. The following season, he made only four appearances and it came as no surprise that at the end of 1933/34 he left the club, joining Tranmere Rovers.

EDWARD JOHN 'TED' MacDOUGALL

Country: Scotland
Born: 8 Jan 1947
Debut: 7 Oct 1972 v West Bromwich Albion
Position: Forward
Appearances: 18 **Goals scored:** 5
Seasons: 1972/73
Clubs: Liverpool, York City, Bournemouth, Manchester United, West Ham United, Norwich City, Southampton, Bournemouth, Blackpool

Although born in Inverness, Ted MacDougall's family had moved to the Widnes area when he was just a youngster and, following a short spell with the local ICI Recs, he joined Liverpool in 1964, signing professional forms two years later. The closest he came to a first-team appearance was a place on the substitute's bench for one game and, due to this lack of first-team opportunities he readily agreed to the £5,000 move to York City in 1967. Two years later, he joined Bournemouth, where he soon hit the headlines, scoring nine of his team's 11 goals against Margate in the FA Cup (the best performance by any player in the FA Cup proper). In all, he scored 103 league goals in 146 games for the Cherries, earning him a £195,000 move to United.

He made his United debut at West Bromwich on 7 October 1972, but had to wait until the following Saturday, against Birmingham City at Old Trafford, before notching his first goal for his new club, scoring the only goal of the game. Despite his arrival, United continued to struggle, with MacDougall getting few breaks, although the second goal in a 2-0 win over Liverpool did endear him to the Old Trafford support. When Tommy Docherty joined in late December, he soon decided to move the striker on, and he transferred to West Ham in February 1973 for £170,000.

ROBERT 'BOB' McFARLANE

Country: Scotland
Born: Unknown **Died:** Oct 1898
Debut: 3 Oct 1891 v Manchester City
Position: Full-back
Appearances: 3 **Goals scored:** 0
Seasons: 1891/92
Clubs: Airdrieonians, Bootle, Sunderland Albion, Newton Heath, Airdrieonians

NOEL WILLIAM McFARLANE

Country: Republic of Ireland
Born: 20 Dec 1934 **Died:** Unknown
Debut: 13 Feb 1954 v Tottenham Hotspur
Position: Forward
Appearances: 1 **Goals scored:** 0
Seasons: 1953/54
Clubs: Manchester United, Waterford, Altrincham, Hyde United

DAVID McFETTERIDGE

Country: Scotland
Born: Unknown **Died:** Unknown
Debut: 13 Apr 1895 v Newcastle United
Position: Forward
Appearances: 1 **Goals scored:** 0
Seasons: 1894/95
Clubs: Bolton Wanderers, Cowlairs, Newton Heath, Stockport County

SCOTT THOMAS McGARVEY

Country: Scotland
Born: 22 Apr 1963
Debut: 13 Sep 1980 v Leicester City
Position: Forward
Appearances: 13 (12) **Goals scored:** 3
Seasons: 1980/81 – 1982/83
Clubs: Manchester United, Wolverhampton Wanderers (loan), Portsmouth, Carlisle United, Grimsby Town, Bristol City, Oldham Athletic, Wigan Athletic (loan), Mazda, Aris Limassol, Derry City, Barrow, Witton Albion

Glasgow-born McGarvey was a member of the Celtic Boys Club side before joining United as an associated schoolboy in November 1978, signing professional forms in April 1980. Ideally built for a forward at 5'11" and weighing 11st 9lb, McGarvey earned a favourable reputation at junior and reserve-team level, with his displays earning him selection for the Scotland Under-21 side in 1982. By then, he had appeared in the Manchester United first team, with a substitute appearance against Leicester City, at Old Trafford, on 13 September 1980.

The following campaign saw him make his first start, but season 1982/83 found him knocked back in the pecking order by the emergence of Norman Whiteside, making only three full appearances, plus four more as substitute, scoring once. A lack of first-team opportunities saw him join Wolves on loan in March 1984 and that summer he joined Portsmouth in an £85,000 deal.

PATRICK COLM McGIBBON

Country: Northern Ireland
Born: 6 Sep 1973
Debut: 20 Sep 1995 v York City
Position: Defender
Appearances: 1 **Goals scored:** 0
Seasons: 1995/96
Clubs: Portadown, Manchester United, Swansea City (loan), Wigan Athletic, Scunthorpe United (loan), Tranmere Rovers, Portadown, Glentoran

CHARLES 'CHARLIE' McGILLIVRAY

Country: Scotland
Born: 5 July 1912 **Died:** 7 Nov 1986
Debut: 26 Aug 1933 v Plymouth Argyle
Position: Forward
Appearances: 9 **Goals scored:** 0
Seasons: 1933/34
Clubs: Ayr United, Glasgow Celtic, Manchester United, Motherwell, Dundee, Dundee United

JOHN McGILLIVRAY

Country: England
Born: Apr 1886 **Died:** Unknown
Debut: 11 Jan 1908 v Blackpool
Position: Midfield
Appearances: 4 **Goals scored:** 0
Seasons: 1907/08 – 1908/09
Clubs: Berry's Association, Manchester United, Southport Central, Stoke, Dartford

WILLIAM 'BILLY' McGLEN

Country: England
Born: 27 Apr 1921 **Died:** 23 Dec 1999
Debut: 31 Aug 1946 v Grimsby Town
Position: Full-back, midfield
Appearances: 122 **Goals scored:** 2
Seasons: 1946/47 – 1951/52
Clubs: Blyth Spartans, Manchester United, Lincoln City, Oldham Athletic

Having learnt his football in the north-east with Blyth Spartans, Billy McGlen was one of Matt Busby's first signings when he joined United in January 1946, stepping immediately into the first team once football got back to normality in 1946/47 when he held down the left-back position for most of the season. He made a big impression until a cartilage operation put him of contention, then shortly after returning to the first team during 1947/48 injury again forced him to the sidelines. During the next few seasons, he was in and out of the team, but proved to be a valuable utility man, with a strong tackle, good heading ability and his never-say-die attitude. At the end of season 1951/52, he was transferred to Lincoln City for £8,000.

CHRISTOPHER ROLAND 'CHRIS' McGRATH

Country: Northern Ireland
Born: 29 Nov 1954
Debut: 23 Oct 1976 v Norwich City
Position: Midfield
Appearances: 15 (19) **Goals scored:** 1
Seasons: 1976/77 – 1980/81
Clubs: Tottenham Hotspur, Millwall (loan), Manchester United, Tulsa Roughnecks, South China

A Northern Ireland international, Chris McGrath was struggling to get into the Tottenham Hotspur first team in the opening months of 1976/77, when he was surprisingly transferred to United for £30,000. If he thought that the move to United would revitalise his career, then he was quite a bit off the mark, as he made only two first-team starts during the remainder of that season.

The departure of Tommy Docherty was something of a blessing for Chris McGrath, as under the new manager Dave Sexton he was involved in 14 of the opening 18 fixtures of 1977/78 – five as substitute. But 1978/79 saw him back in the reserves and a broken leg during 1979/80 set his career back further, and when the chance of a stint on the American circuit materialised, he took it, joining Tulsa Roughnecks, with United recouping their £30,000 outlay.

PAUL McGRATH

Country: Republic of Ireland
Born: 4 Dec 1959
Debut: 10 Nov 1982 v Bradford City
Position: Defender
Appearances: 192 (7) **Goals scored:** 16
Seasons: 1982/83 – 1988/89
Clubs: St Patrick's Athletic, Manchester United, Aston Villa, Derby County, Sheffield United

Born in Ealing, London, to an Irish mother and a Nigerian father, Paul McGrath spent the first 16 years of his life with foster parents, having returned to Dublin as a six-week-old baby. His love for football took him to Pearce Rovers, Dalkey United and then on to St Patrick's Athletic, where he was voted the PFAI Player of the Year in 1982, before being snapped up by Manchester United for a bargain fee of around £30,000 in April 1982, following recommendations by scout Billy Behan.

The very talented 22-year-old, who showed a combination of strength and absolute confidence on the ball, was thrust into the first-team picture prior to the start of season 1982/83, with a place in the side to play Aldershot in a friendly in aid of the South Atlantic Fund. An injury prevented him from making an early competitive debut, and he had to wait until 10 November for this, against Bradford City in the League Cup.

It wasn't until season 1984/85 that he became something of a first-team regular, as well as making his Republic of Ireland debut, going on to win an FA Cup winner's medal against Everton, when he was named Man of the Match after shoring up United's defence following the dismissal of Kevin Moran. But injuries soon began to play a major part in his career and off-field activities did not exactly endear him to Alex Ferguson when he took over as United manager.

Due to a recurring knee injury, he was advised to retire and accept an insurance pay-out, but the big central defender was determined to carry on. A number of clubs showed an interest in him, with Aston Villa eventually securing his signature for a fee of £450,000. 'Having listened to medical advice, I decided it was worth taking a chance,' said the Villa manager Graham Taylor. He was rewarded with seven years of service, during which McGrath even became the PFA Player of the Year in 1994.

WILFRED 'WILF' McGUINNESS

Country: England
Born: 25 Oct 1937
Debut: 8 Oct 1955 v Wolverhampton Wanderers
Position: Wing-half
Appearances: 85 **Goals scored:** 2
Seasons: 1955/56 – 1959/60
Clubs: Manchester United

The former captain of Manchester, Lancashire and England Schoolboys, Wilf McGuinness walked through the Old Trafford doors on the same day as Bobby Charlton and, although not blessed with similar talent, no one could deny the Manchester-born youngster's determination, especially as he was often competing with the peerless Duncan Edwards for a place in the United side.

Making his debut in October 1955, he won a First Division Championship medal in 1956/57, but was, perhaps fortunately, injured at the time of the Munich disaster. He became an important cog in the team during the rebuilding that followed, but broke his leg during a Central League match in December 1959 – an injury that was to bring his career to an end, although he was named as substitute against Leicester City in November 1966. Sadly, a comeback was to be little more than a dream and he was finally forced to give up all thoughts of playing again.

Moving into coaching with United and then England at youth team level, he was a part of Alf Ramsey's backroom staff during the 1966 World Cup. In June 1969, aged only 31, he was named as Sir Matt Busby's successor, but despite reaching three cup semi-finals, he was to find himself demoted to trainer/coach of the reserve team in December 1970, leaving the club two months later to take up a managerial post in

Greece. He continues to be a popular figure at the club, and his son Paul coached United to FA Youth Cup success in 2011 – a trophy his father had won more than 50 years earlier.

SAMUEL BAXTER 'SAMMY' McILROY

Country: Northern Ireland
Born: 2 Aug 1954
Debut: 6 Nov 1971 v Manchester City
Position: Midfield
Appearances: 391 (28) **Goals scored:** 71
Seasons: 1971/72 – 1981/82
Clubs: Manchester United, Stoke City, Manchester City, Orgryte IS, Bury, Admira Wacker (loan), Preston North End, Northwich Victoria

Belfast-born Sammy McIlroy's talents first shone through while playing for Ashfield Secondary School in his native city and also the Northern Ireland Schoolboy side, whom he represented four times. On Bob Bishop's recommendation, with the United scout having paid for the slimly built youngster's first pair of football boots, United despatched chief scout Joe Armstrong to the McIlroy home to secure his signature on his 15th birthday, famously becoming Sir Matt Busby's last signing.

The young Irishman progressed quickly, making his debut in January 1971 in a friendly against Bohemians, with his league debut coming the following November in a daunting local 'derby' against City at Maine Road, scoring in the pulsating 3-3 draw. Content with being used in a substitute role, with an occasional start thrown in, McIlroy's life was thrown into complete disarray when he was seriously injured in a car crash in January 1973, keeping him out of the game for the remainder of that season.

But, returning to full fitness, he claimed a regular place as United stuttered towards relegation and the Second Division. From then on, he was an almost ever-present, missing only nine league games between seasons 1974/75 and 1979/80, winning a Second Division Championship medal and FA Cup winner's and runner-up medals. Missing the final seven games of 1980/81, many thought that his days at United were numbered, especially with the signing of Bryan Robson from West Bromwich Albion. McIlroy, however, had other ideas and on the day that Robson strode onto the Old Trafford pitch to sign for United, he hit a superb hat-trick in the 5-0 victory over Wolverhampton Wanderers.

Appearances were limited following Robson's arrival, and in February 1982 McIlroy bade Manchester farewell and signed for Stoke City for a club record fee of £350,000, a mark of how much he still had to offer. That summer he played for Northern Ireland in the World Cup, helping to beat the host nation Spain. The goalscoring midfielder had stamina and skill, and went on to captain his country in the 1986 World Cup finals.

EDWARD 'EDDIE' JOSEPH McILVENNY

Country: Scotland
Born: 21 Oct 1924 **Died:** 18 May 1989
Debut: 19 Aug 1950 v Fulham
Position: Half-back
Appearances: 2 **Goals scored:** 0
Seasons: 1950/51
Clubs: Morton, Wrexham, Fairhill Club (USA) Philadelphia Nationals, Manchester United, Waterford United

Although he played only twice for United, at the beginning of the 1950/51 season, McIlvenny remained with United until the end of season 1952/53, when he was given a free transfer, moving to League of Ireland side Waterford where he was eventually to become player-manager. But that tells only a small part of the story of the Greenock-born half-back, who emigrated to the USA in 1949. He caught Matt Busby's attention during United's summer tour of the USA in 1950, but it was the events of 29 June 1950 that were to earn him lasting fame. For on that day, he captained the USA side to their 1-0 victory over England in the World Cup at Belo Horizonte, beating a side that included Tom Finney, Wilf Mannion, Stan Mortensen, Alf Ramsey and Billy Wright, among others.

WILLIAM 'BILL' McKAY

Country: Scotland
Born: 24 Aug 1906 **Died:** Unknown
Debut: 17 Mar 1934 v Fulham

Position: Midfield
Appearances: 182 **Goals scored:** 15
Seasons: 1933/34 – 1938/39
Clubs: East Stirlingshire, Hamilton Academical, Bolton Wanderers, Manchester United, Stalybridge Celtic

Bill McKay hailed from West Benhar, amid the Lanarkshire coalfields, and was a versatile player who could quickly settle in any position. He was also renowned for turning up on match days resplendent in an immaculate three-piece suit and black bowler hat.

In 1925 he joined East Stirlingshire from Shotts Battlefield, spending two years with them before Hamilton Academical managed to prise him away.

With Hamilton, where he played inside-right, 23 goals in 81 appearances over a two-year period, was a satisfactory return and enough to earn him a move south to Bolton Wanderers in 1929. Strangely, his Bolton debut was a 1-1 draw against United at Old Trafford in December 1929 and he went on to play over 100 games for the Trotters, scoring 17 goals.

As United faced a battle to avoid relegation from the Second Division in 1933/34, Scott Duncan signed him up, hoping he could both bolster his defence and be a creator of goalscoring opportunities. Described as 'a soccer tactician, who made full use of every ball', he moved the short distance to Manchester and played his part in the club's rescue mission, helping them to promotion in 1936 and again in 1938, when he scored four goals in the last four games of the season. He served United well up until the outbreak of the Second World War, and afterwards joined Stalybridge Celtic in 1946.

COLIN McKEE

Country: Scotland
Born: 22 Aug 1973
Debut: 8 May 1994 v Coventry City
Position: Forward
Appearances: 1 **Goals scored:** 0
Seasons: 1993/94
Clubs: Manchester United, Bury (loan), Kilmarnock, Partick Thistle, Falkirk, Queen of the South, Ross County, Stirling Albion, Vikingur (loan), Queen's Park, Fauldhouse United

GEORGE HERBERT McLACHLAN

Country: Scotland
Born: 21 Sep 1902 **Died:** Unknown
Debut: 21 Dec 1929 v Leeds United
Position: Winger
Appearances: 116 **Goals scored:** 4
Seasons: 1929/30 – 1932/33
Clubs: Clyde, King's Park Strollers (loan), Cardiff City, Manchester United, Chester, Le Havre

One individual who could claim his place in football history prior to his arriving at Manchester United was George McLachlan. His name will be unknown to most of the present-day Old Trafford regulars, but mention it around Cardiff and it will be recalled that McLachlan was a member of the Cardiff City team who defeated Arsenal 1-0 in the 1927 FA Cup final, to take the famous trophy out of England for the first and only time.

With Clyde, McLachlan was on the verge of Scottish international honours, but a broken leg killed the dream; however, regaining full fitness, he joined Cardiff for £2,000 in November 1925. Following the FA Cup success, he was signed by United for a fee that the record books mention as 'not to exceed £2,500' in December 1929 and, although normally an outside-left, he was switched to left-half during 1930/31, playing every game of that relegation campaign, captaining the side the following season. In 1933, he moved to Chester for £250.

HUGH 'HUGHIE' McLENAHAN

Country: England
Born: 23 Mar 1909 **Died:** May 1988
Debut: 4 Feb 1928 v Tottenham Hotspur
Position: Half-back
Appearances: 116 **Goals scored:** 12
Seasons: 1927/28 – 1936/37
Clubs: Stockport County, Manchester United, Notts County

Hughie McLenahan was a Gorton-born England Schoolboy international, who was expected to sign for United upon leaving school, but somehow escaped their clutches and joined Stockport County as an amateur in February 1927. Word, however, filtered out that the talented youngster was not happy at Edgeley Park, and when it became known that County were arranging a fund-raising bazaar, United's jack-of-all-trades, Louis Rocca, famously arranged for three freezers of ice-cream from his family's business to be sent to Stockport, with negotiations for McLenahan's transfer included as part of the 'deal'.

McLenahan was to play a big part in United's First Division fight for survival in his debut season of 1927/28, but in only the second game of the following season at Aston Villa, he suffered a broken leg and was sidelined until October 1929. Moving to inside-forward towards the end of season 1929/30, he scored six goals in five games, once again helping United avoid relegation.

Unfortunately, his United career was something of a stop-start affair and in December 1936, he joined Notts County for a fee of £1,000.

SAMUEL THOMAS 'SAMMY' McMILLAN

Country: Northern Ireland
Born: 20 Sep 1941
Debut: 4 Nov 1961 v Sheffield Wednesday
Position: Forward
Appearances: 15 **Goals scored:** 6
Seasons: 1961/62 – 1962/63
Clubs: Manchester United, Wrexham, Southend United, Chester, Stockport County

Sammy McMillan joined United as an amateur in 1957, signing professional forms two years later. The highly talented youngster made his first-team debut on 4 November 1961, playing outside-left against Sheffield Wednesday away. As Busby juggled his side in pursuit of a winning formula, McMillan also played in the following two games, scoring in the second of those, a 4-1 defeat at Ipswich Town, but was then dropped back to the reserves.

Towards the end of that season, he reappeared to play in eight of the final nine fixtures, during which time he scored five goals, with doubles against Leicester City and Sheffield United. However, there was little hope of McMillan securing a regular place in the side, though he did win two caps for Northern Ireland in 1962. On Christmas Eve 1963, he moved to Wrexham for a fee of £8,000.

WALTER S. McMILLEN

Country: Ireland
Born: 24 Nov 1913 **Died:** 11 May 1987
Debut: 16 Sep 1933 v Brentford
Position: Half-back
Appearances: 29 **Goals scored:** 2
Seasons: 1933/34 – 1934/35
Clubs: Carrickfergus, Cliftonville, Manchester United, Chesterfield, Tonbridge

Having failed to impress during a trial with Arsenal, the Belfast-born Irish amateur international Walter McMillen was delighted to be given a second chance to prove himself with Manchester United, crossing the Irish Sea for Manchester in August 1933. His emergence into the United first team brought him his first full cap against England on 14 October 1933. Over the next couple of seasons, he was to win a further two caps for his country, including one game where he had to go in goal and made a series of fine saves to help Ireland beat Scotland. But his United opportunities were limited, mainly due to injury rather than ability. He made his last appearance for United against Burnley at Old Trafford, on 27 March 1935, scoring in the 4-3 defeat. He joined Chesterfield in December 1936 for around £200.

JAMES RANKIN McNAUGHT

Country: Scotland
Born: 8 Jun 1870 **Died:** 1 Mar 1919
Debut: 2 Sep 1893 v Burnley
Position: Half-back
Appearances: 162 **Goals scored:** 12
Seasons: 1893/94 – 1897/98
Clubs: Dumbarton, Linfield, Newton Heath, Tottenham Hotspur, Maidstone United

James McNaught joined Newton Heath towards the end of season 1892/93 and it was hoped that his presence would boost the end-of-season fight for survival. As it turned out, he injured his shoulder in a friendly against Ardwick shortly after signing and missed the vital fixtures. Known as 'the little wonder', he was one of the finest ball players ever seen at Clayton. Although only 5'6", he preferred to play at the back and in his second season he played all but two of the league fixtures in the centre-half position.

His versatility, however, caught up with him during 1896/97, when he made only one appearance in his favoured position, with the other 41 split between the wing-half and inside-forward positions. The signing of Caesar Jenkyns, a notable centre-half, also played a significant part in McNaught switching positions. However, in his final season with Newton Heath, he again featured mainly as a centre-half. Sadly international honours passed by the player. At the end of season 1897/98, Southern League Tottenham Hotspur made a move for his services, offering him a £50 signing-on fee and £4.10/- (£4.50p) per week, a 10/- (50p) increase on his Newton Heath wage. Much to the despair of the Heathens' support and directors he accepted the terms and went on to enjoy a successful nine years in the south, winning a Southern League Championship medal in 1900, but missing out on an FA Cup medal a year later.

THOMAS 'TOMMY' McNULTY

Country: England
Born: 30 Dec 1929 **Died:** Apr 1979
Debut: 15 Apr 1950 v Portsmouth
Position: Full-back
Appearances: 60 **Goals scored:** 0
Seasons: 1949/50 – 1953/54
Clubs: Manchester United, Liverpool

One of the many local players to have been carefully groomed in the junior and Central League sides, Tommy McNulty made his league debut at the end of the 1949/50 season, but rarely played until the late autumn of 1951. When he got his chance, along with Roger Byrne in the other full-back position, not only did he keep his place, but he forced Matt Busby to move captain Johnny Carey to right-half to accommodate the Salford-born player. McNulty won a league title medal that season, but in February 1954 Busby sold the speedy right-back to Liverpool in a £7,000 deal.

FRANCIS COMBER 'FRANK' McPHERSON

Country: England
Born: 14 May 1901 **Died:** 5 Mar 1953
Debut: 25 Aug 1923 v Bristol City
Position: Forward
Appearances: 175 **Goals scored:** 52
Seasons: 1923/24 – 1927/28
Clubs: Barrow, Manchester United, Manchester Central, Watford, Reading, Watford, Barrow

Frank McPherson was a highly talented winger-cum-centre-forward with a distinctive burst of speed, who was signed by United as a 20-year-old from Barrow in May 1922. Following a season in the reserves, he broke into the first team at outside-left, but when switched to centre-forward, in October 1925, he began finding the net on a regular basis, with 16 in 22 games. In the opening four fixtures of 1926/27, he scored seven times, but despite this, he was far from being a terrace favourite. Upon leaving United in the summer of 1928, he spent a couple of months with Manchester Central before joining Watford, where he was to score 60 goals in 68 games.

GORDON McQUEEN

Country: Scotland
Born: 26 Jun 1952
Debut: 25 Feb 1978 v Liverpool
Position: Centre-back
Appearances: 229 **Goals scored:** 26
Seasons: 1977/78 – 1983/84
Clubs: St Mirren, Leeds United, Manchester United, Seiko SA

Born in Kilbirnie, Ayrshire, Gordon McQueen had trials with both Rangers and Liverpool before joining St Mirren in May 1970.

With the Paisley side, he made over 50 appearances between 1970/71 and 1972/73, before joining Leeds United, to be groomed as Jackie Charlton's successor in a deal of around £35,000. His career ran along similar lines to that of Joe Jordan, winning his first full cap in 1974 (replacing Jim Holton in the Scotland side against Belgium on 1 June) and adding the same medals to the trophy cabinet as his friend and team-mate.

At 6'3", he was a towering presence in the penalty area at either end of the pitch and a few weeks after signing Jordan, Dave Sexton went back to Leeds for McQueen, paying out £495,000 for his signature. On joining the club, he famously commented: 'Ninety-nine per cent of players want to play for Manchester United, and the rest are liars.'

Alongside Martin Buchan and later Kevin Moran, he formed a formidable rearguard for United. Injuries and suspensions kept him out of the side from time to time, following his debut at Liverpool, but his career was to span the reigns of both Sexton and his replacement, Ron Atkinson. He won an FA Cup medal in 1983, but in January 1984 at Anfield, he sustained an injury that saw him miss the remainder of that season and virtually ended his United playing career. He managed only another 12 games, before leaving for Hong Kong where he became player-coach of Seiko in August 1985. More recently he has been a TV pundit, working for Sky Sports and MUTV.

HENRY 'HARRY' McSHANE

Country: Scotland
Born: 8 Apr 1920 **Died:** 7 Nov 2012
Debut: 13 Sep 1950 v Aston Villa
Position: Winger
Appearances: 57 **Goals scored:** 8
Seasons: 1950/51 – 1953/54
Clubs: Blackburn Rovers, Huddersfield Town, Bolton Wanderers, Manchester United, Oldham Athletic, Chorley, Wellington Town, Droylsden

Born in the same mining village as Matt Busby, Harry McShane was to begin his playing career with Bellshill Athletic, before being snapped up on amateur forms by Blackburn Rovers in January 1937. Signing as a professional that same year, he made only two league appearances before the outbreak of World War Two interrupted his career. Due to the hostilities, a large part of what could have been a promising career passed him by, and it was not until September 1946, having now signed for Huddersfield Town, that he reappeared in a Football League fixture.

His stay in Yorkshire lasted less than a year, as he returned to Lancashire in the summer of 1947, joining Bolton Wanderers. McShane had the ability to perform well in either of the wing positions, but preferred outside-left and it was his reluctance to perform on the right side of the forward line that led to his departure from Burnden Park, in September 1950, as part of an exchange deal which saw United's John Ball, along with £4,500, going in the opposite direction.

Brought in to replace Charlie Mitten, he helped United to the runners-up spot in 1950/51 but picked up an injury early the following title-winning season. By the time he recovered, the speedy wing-man found David Pegg and Jack Rowley both competing for his position, and so in February 1954 he moved to Oldham Athletic for £750. He later worked as a scout for United, and was the father of actor Ian McShane.

LUIGI 'LOU' MACARI

Country: Scotland
Born: 4 Jun 1949
Debut: 20 Jan 1973 v West Ham United
Position: Forward/Midfield
Appearances: 374 (27) **Goals scored:** 97
Seasons: 1972/73 – 1983/84
Clubs: Celtic, Manchester United, Swindon Town

Perhaps better known by today's match-going supporters for the chip shop that bears his name, rather than his on-field exploits, Lou Macari was born in Edinburgh to Italian parents, winning Scottish Schoolboy honours before joining Celtic in July 1966 and going on to enjoy an honour-strewn career with the Glasgow club, as well as winning international honours with Scotland.

Prior to United sealing the record-breaking £200,000 transfer, Macari could have moved to the league leaders of that time, Liverpool, and indeed it was at Anfield, where he was due to sign the following day, that a chance meeting with United assistant manager Pat Crerand saw him change his mind and, perhaps surprisingly, opt for a move to the club sitting at the opposite end of the table. He was one of several Scots to join the club in the weeks after Tommy Docherty took charge.

Although small in stature, Macari was big in heart and he set about repaying his transfer fee almost immediately, scoring an 80th-minute equaliser against West Ham on his debut, earning United a 2-2 draw and adding a further four as they fought to avoid relegation. There was little he could do to help avoid the drop to Division Two during the following campaign, scoring a meagre five goals in 35 appearances.

On returning to Division One a year later, and playing more in a midfield role, Macari finished only one goal behind leading scorer Stuart Pearson with 12. He played a major part in the FA Cup success of 1977 – his shot at the Liverpool goal being deflected off Jimmy Greenhoff's chest to give United their 2-1 win. After Docherty left the club in the summer of 1977, Macari continued to play a key role under new boss Dave Sexton, rarely missing a game.

It was only with the arrival of Ron Atkinson in 1981/82 that he began to be moved to the fringes of the action, though he stayed on until the end of 1983/84. Despite a few ups and downs, he spent over 11 years at Old Trafford, earning a testimonial against his former club Celtic, a game that saw 40,140 pay £85,000, with Macari turning out in the colours of both clubs.

Upon leaving United he became player-manager of Swindon Town, kicking off a long and eventful career in management.

FEDRICO 'KIKO' MACHEDA

Country: Italy
Born: 22 Aug 1991
Debut: 5 Apr 2009 v Aston Villa
Position: Forward
Appearances: 15 (21) **Goals scored:** 5
Seasons: 2008/09 – present
Clubs: Manchester United, Sampdoria (loan), Queens Park Rangers (loan), VfB Stuttgart (loan)

He may never accumulate a vast number of appearances in the red of Manchester United, but the mere mention of his name will always conjure up fond memories due to his injury-time goal against Aston Villa at Old Trafford on his debut, a wonder strike that played a crucial part in United securing the Premier League title that season, as they came back from 2-1 down to snatch victory at the very end.

Born in Rome, Macheda was to find the net on countless occasions in United's reserve side, after joining the club from Lazio as a 16-year-old in 2007. Since that debut, first-team opportunities have been in short supply, with the likes of Wayne Rooney, Dimitar Berbatov, Chicharito, Danny Welbeck and, more recently, Robin van Persie in front of him in the pecking order.

CHARLES MACKIE

Country: Scotland
Born: 1882 **Died:** Unknown
Debut: 3 Sep 1904 v Port Vale
Position: Forward
Appearances: 7 **Goals scored:** 4
Seasons: 1904/05
Clubs: Aberdeen, Manchester United, West Ham United, Aberdeen, Lochgelly United

GUILIANO 'JULES' MAIORANA

Country: England
Born: 18 Apr 1969
Debut: 14 Jan 1989 v Millwall
Position: Left winger
Appearances: 2 (6) **Goals scored:** 0
Seasons: 1988/89 – 1993/94
Clubs: Histon, Manchester United, Ljungskile

THOMAS RONALD 'TOM' MANLEY

Country: England
Born: 7 Oct 1912 **Died:** 4 Jul 1988
Debut: 5 Dec 1931 v Millwall
Position: Half-back/Winger
Appearances: 195 **Goals scored:** 41
Seasons: 1931/32 – 1938/39
Clubs: Manchester United, Brentford

Tommy Manley joined United as an amateur from Northwich Victoria in September 1930, making his debut in December the following year. He appeared mainly as a half-back, but it was as an outside-left that he wrote his name in the United history books, scoring one of the vital goals in the 2-0 victory over Millwall in May1934 that prevented a drop into the Third Division. His goals, 14 in 31 appearances, also helped towards the club winning the Second Division title in season 1935/36. In July 1939, he left to join Brentford, but returned to the United ranks as a wartime guest.

FRANK DRURY MANN

Country: England
Born: 17 Mar 1891 **Died:** Jul 1966
Debut: 17 Mar 1923 v Bradford City
Position: Half-back
Appearances: 197 **Goals scored:** 5
Seasons: 1922/23 – 1929/30
Clubs: Aston Villa, Huddersfield Town, Manchester United, Mossley

Frank Mann played as an amateur for around five years with the likes of Newark Town, Leeds City, Lincoln City and Aston Villa before turning professional with the Midlands club in May 1911. In July of the following year, he joined Huddersfield Town and was their top scorer for two seasons when they finished runners-up in both the league and the FA Cup, claiming a winner's medal in the latter in 1922. A fee of £1,750 took him to Old Trafford at the age of 32 and he was to prove a good investment, as he gave eight years of service to the club, helping them to promotion in 1925. Upon leaving United in August 1930, he returned to the non-league ranks.

HERBERT 'HARRY' MANN

Country: England
Born: 30 Dec 1907 **Died:** 24 Apr 1977
Debut: 29 Aug 1931 v Bradford Park Avenue
Position: Forward
Appearances: 13 **Goals scored:** 2
Seasons: 1931/32 – 1933/34
Clubs: Griff Colliery, Derby County, Grantham Town, Manchester United, Ripley Town

Harry Mann's signing from Grantham Town in May 1931 was seen as something of a gamble. It was one that did not pay off and he was dropped following his debut, a 3-1 defeat at Bradford Park Avenue in the opening match of 1931/32. His performances did little to merit an extended run in the team and he joined Ripley Town in November 1933.

THOMAS 'TOM' MANNS

Country: England
Born: Jan 1911 **Died:** Unknown
Debut: 3 Feb 1934 v Burnley
Position: Wing-half
Appearances: 2 **Goals scored:** 0
Seasons: 1933/34
Clubs: Burnley, Manchester United, Clapton Orient

MATEUS ALBERTO CONTREIRAS 'MANUCHO' CONCLAVES

Country: Angola
Born: 7 Mar 1983
Debut: 23 Sep 2008 v Middlesbrough
Position: Forward
Appearances: 0 (3) **Goals scored:** 0
Seasons: 2008/09
Clubs: Benfica de Luanda, Petro Atletico, Manchester United, Panathinaikos (loan), Hull City (loan), Real Valladolid, Bucaspor (loan), Manisaspor (loan)

PHILIP MARSH

Country: England
Born: 15 Nov 1986
Debut: 25 Oct 2006 v Crewe Alexandra
Position: Forward
Appearances: 1 **Goals scored:** 0
Seasons: 2006/07
Clubs: Manchester United, Blackpool, Northwich Victoria, Hyde United, Leigh Genesis, FC United of Manchester, Stalybridge Celtic, Forest Green Rovers, Hereford United (loan), Guiseley

ARTHUR GEORGE MARSHALL

Country: England
Born: Oct 1881 **Died:** Unknown
Debut: 9 Mar 1903 v Woolwich Arsenal
Position: Full-back
Appearances: 6 **Goals scored:** 0

Seasons: 1902/03
Clubs: Everton, Chester City, Crewe Alexandra, Leicester Fosse, Stockport County, Manchester United, Portsmouth

LEE ANDREW MARTIN

Country: England
Born: 5 Feb 1968
Debut: 9 May 1988 v Wimbledon
Position: Full-back
Appearances: 84 (25) **Goals scored:** 2
Seasons: 1987/88 – 1993/94
Clubs: Manchester United, Celtic, Bristol Rovers, Huddersfield Town (loan)

Lee Martin was a full-back who was to score only two goals during the course of his eight years as a professional with the club, one of those especially noteworthy as it was to bring Alex Ferguson his first trophy as manager of Manchester United. Joining the club as a trainee in June 1985, three years after signing associate schoolboy forms, he worked his way through the ranks, making his first-team debut against Wimbledon on the final day of season 1987/88.

A solid and adaptable defender, he played in the opening fixture of the following season, but failed to command a regular place until 1989/90, a season that saw him score that dramatic Wembley winner, in the FA Cup final replay against Crystal Palace. Despite this, the arrival of Denis Irwin and then Paul Parker meant that he found himself somewhat on the fringes of things, with his time spent mainly in the reserves. It came as no surprise that he finally left the club in January 1994 and joined Celtic, then managed by Lou Macari, for a fee of £350,000.

LEE ROBERT MARTIN

Country: England
Born: 9 Feb 1987
Debut: 26 Oct 2005 v Barnet
Position: Midfield
Appearances: 3 **Goals scored:** 0
Seasons: 2005/06 – 2008/09

Clubs: Manchester United, Royal Antwerp (loan), Rangers (loan), Stoke City (loan), Plymouth Argyle (loan), Sheffield United (loan), Nottingham Forest (loan), Ipswich Town, Charlton Athletic (loan), Millwall

MICHAEL PAUL 'MICK' MARTIN

Country: Republic of Ireland
Born: 9 Jul 1951
Debut: 24 Jan 1973 v Everton
Position: Midfield
Appearances: 36 (7) **Goals scored:** 2
Seasons: 1972/73 – 1974/75
Clubs: Bohemians, Manchester United, West Bromwich Albion, Newcastle United, Vancouver Whitecaps, Cardiff City, Peterborough United, Rotherham United, Preston North End

Son of the famous Aston Villa and Republic of Ireland player Con Martin, Mick was a product of the famous Home Farm club, but from there moved to Bohemians, where he won League of Ireland representative honours. Before crossing the sea to England, he won six full caps, making his debut in a 6-0 defeat against Austria in Linz in October 1971. Originally a defender, it was as a midfield player that Tommy Docherty signed him in a £20,000 deal.

One week after signing, Martin was thrown in at the deep end against Everton and went on to play in the remaining 15 games of 1972/73, including two as a substitute, scoring two goals. During the relegation season of 1973/74 his 12 appearances were scattered throughout the campaign and were even fewer the following season, playing only seven times as United swept through the Second Division to win the Championship.

On 3 October 1975, he joined West Bromwich Albion on loan, under the managership of Republic of Ireland boss Johnny Giles. The move became permanent two months later, with United receiving around £35,000. Martin went on to win 52 caps for his country, and eventually retired from the game in 1987.

WILLIAM MATHIESON

Country: Scotland
Born: 1870 **Died:** Unknown
Debut: 3 Sep 1892 v Blackburn Rovers
Position: Forward
Appearances: 10 **Goals scored:** 2
Seasons: 1892/93 – 1893/94
Clubs: Glasgow Thistle, Clydesdale, Newton Heath, Rotherham Town

A Glaswegian who had previously been with Clydesdale, William Mathieson moved south to join Newton Heath in the latter stages of season 1891/92, playing in the final three games of that particular season at outside-left, scoring in the second of those, against Lincoln City. He made his official debut in the Heathens' first-ever game in the Football League. Unfortunately, he was not cut out for the more physical English game. In the close season of 1894 he moved to Rotherham Town.

DAVID MAY

Country: England
Born: 24 Jun 1970
Debut: 14 Aug 1994 v Blackburn Rovers
Position: Defender
Appearances: 98 (20) **Goals scored:** 8
Seasons: 1994/95 – 2002/03
Clubs: Blackburn Rovers, Manchester United, Huddersfield Town (loan), Burnley

Oldham-born David May joined Blackburn Rovers in 1986, making over 150 appearances before moving across Lancashire to Manchester in July 1994 for a fee of £1.4 million. Capable of playing at both full-back and in central defence, May was to win two Premiership medals, in 1996 and 1997, two FA Cup winner's medals in 1996 and 1999, and a Champions League medal in 1999. A third Premier League medal might have been added to the total, but he was to play in only six games during that memorable Treble-winning campaign. Renowned for his 'over the top' celebrations in Barcelona following the 1999 Champions League triumph, he endeared himself to the United support forever. But, following that season, his appearances became even more sporadic due to injuries and, at the end of his contract in 2003, he was given a free transfer, subsequently joining Burnley.

THOMAS 'TOMMY' MEEHAN

Country: England
Born: Jun 1896 **Died:** 18 Aug 1924
Debut: 1 Sep 1919 v Sheffield Wednesday
Position: Half-back
Appearances: 53 **Goals scored:** 6
Seasons: 1919/20 – 1920/21
Clubs: Rochdale, Manchester United, Chelsea

Tommy Meehan joined United from Rochdale in June 1917, with the adaptable Harpurhey-born player stepping into the first team as an inside-forward when league football got back to normal following the First World War. Despite being highly thought of as a player, receiving creditable reviews in the press, he was surprisingly allowed to leave United, with Chelsea paying £3,300 for his services in December 1920. At Stamford Bridge, he was to gain a full England cap. Sadly, his career came to a premature end, when, at the age of only 28, he contracted encephalitis lethargica and died in hospital. A benefit match for his family raised £1,580.

JOHN 'JACK' MELLOR

Country: England
Born: Jul 1906 **Died:** Unknown
Debut: 15 Sep 1930 v Huddersfield Town
Position: Full-back
Appearances: 122 **Goals scored:** 0
Seasons: 1930/31 – 1936/37
Clubs: Witton Albion, Manchester United, Cardiff City

A schoolboy rugby player who tried the union code with Oldham, Jack Mellor switched to the round-ball game in local leagues and then with Witton Albion. Joining United in May 1929, he succeeded Charlie Moore at right-back in 1930/31, going on to be something of an ever-present until September 1933, when loss of form saw him lose his place in the side and he rarely appeared at first-team level again, leaving the club in January 1937 to join Cardiff City. Only two outfield players in the club's history have played more times for United without scoring.

ALEXANDER WILLIAM MENZIES

Country: Scotland
Born: 25 Nov 1882 **Died:** Unknown
Debut: 17 Nov 1906 v Sheffield Wednesday
Position: Forward
Appearances: 25 **Goals scored:** 4
Seasons: 1906/07 – 1907/08
Clubs: Blantyre Victoria, Heart of Midlothian, Motherwell (loan), Arthurlie, Heart of Midlothian, Manchester United, Luton Town, Dundee

Lanarkshire-born Menzies began his career with local side Blantyre Victoria in 1901, before signing for Hearts in December 1902. The gifted centre-forward won a Scottish Cup medal in 1906, as well selection for the Scottish international side to face England.

United brought him south in November 1906, paying Hearts £500 for his services and, following his excellent debut display, when he scored against Sheffield Wednesday, he should have gone on to make a name for himself. Instead, he drifted in and out of the side for the remainder of that season. He began season 1907/08 as first-choice centre-forward, playing in the opening five games, but his failure to score and the arrival of Jimmy Turnbull saw him demoted to the reserves and he soon left to join Luton Town.

WILLIAM HENRY 'BILLY' MEREDITH

Country: Wales
Born: 30 July 1874 **Died:** 19 Apr 1958
Debut: 1 Jan 1907 v Aston Villa
Position: Winger
Appearances: 335 **Goals scored:** 36
Seasons: 1906/07 – 1920/21
Clubs: Chirk, Northwich Victoria, Manchester City, Manchester United, Manchester City

Billy Meredith was arguably football's first superstar – a crowd puller and entertainer supreme. Born in Chirk, North Wales, in 1874, his elder brothers were all keen footballers, so it was only natural that the youngster would follow suit. As a 12-year-old, he went to work down the mines while continuing to hone his footballing skills, joining his local club with whom he played in the 1893 Welsh Cup final. Invited to play a handful of games with struggling Football League side Northwich Victoria, his ability did not go unnoticed and Manchester City won the chase to sign him in October 1894.

Remaining an amateur, it did not take long for the slimly built, bandy-legged individual, with the trademark toothpick protruding from the corner of his mouth, to become a firm favourite with the Hyde Road side, with his dribbling skills, exciting wing-play, pinpoint centres and his ability to score goals all giving the team a new dimension. Finishing top scorer in his first season, Meredith, who went on to make 48 appearances for Wales, led City to FA Cup success, scoring the only goal in the 1904 final as the club picked up its first major honour.

He had previously won two Second Division Championship medals, in 1899 and 1903, as he went on to accumulate some 358 appearances, scoring 149 goals, before he got caught up in a bribery scandal and, despite pleading his innocence, was banned for 18 months. Although a disaster for City, as a number of other players were also banned, it came as a bigger blow when the Welshman signed for neighbours United in October 1906, although he was unable to play for them until 1 January, making his debut alongside former City team-mates Herbert Burgess, Jimmy Bannister and Sandy Turnbull.

In the red of United, where he became a founder member of the Professional Footballers' Association, campaigning for better pay and treatment for his fellow professionals, he strode to greater heights, winning a second FA Cup winner's medal in 1909 and First Division Championship medals in 1908 and 1911, making 335 appearances and scoring 36 goals. The crowds he helped attract was one of the reasons why club chairman John Henry Davies built Old Trafford, which opened in February 1910. On 7 May 1921, at the age of 46 years and 281 days, he set a record as the oldest player ever to appear for United.

That summer, he returned to City after being given a free transfer, playing a further 32 games, including the 1924 FA Cup semi-final at the age of 49, before retiring. On top of the 736 competitive fixtures he played in his career, he also took part in countless charity games, his presence always attracting a favourable crowd. Following his retirement, he moved into coaching, being involved with the fledgling Manchester Central club and also back at Old Trafford with United, and he also ran the Stretford Road Hotel.

JOHN WILLIAM 'JACK' MEW

Country: England
Born: 30 Mar 1889 **Died:** 16 Jan 1963
Debut: 26 Oct 1912 v Middlesbrough
Position: Goalkeeper
Appearances: 199 **Goals scored:** 0
Seasons: 1912/13 – 1925/26
Clubs: Manchester United, Barrow

A Central League Championship winner in his second season with United, Jack Mew was a more than capable custodian, who went on to represent the Football League, winning one England cap against Ireland in 1923 – keeping a clean sheet – and touring South Africa with the FA.

He joined United in July 1912, but it wasn't until the immediate post-First World War years that he became United's first-choice keeper, missing only four games in four seasons, a period that saw United relegated in 1922 despite his best efforts in goal. Awarded two benefits with the club, earning him around £1,700, he was to join Barrow in September 1926 before taking up coaching posts abroad. Only nine other men have kept goal for United for often than Mew.

ROBERT 'BOB' MILARVIE

Country: Scotland
Born: 1864 **Died:** Nov 1912
Debut: 4 Oct 1890 v Higher Walton
Position: Forward
Appearances: 1 **Goals scored:** 0
Seasons: 1890/91
Clubs: Hibernian, Stoke City, Burslem Port Vale, Derby County, Newton Heath, Ardwick

GEORGE MILLAR

Country: Scotland
Born: 1874 **Died:** Unknown
Debut: 22 Dec 1894 v Lincoln City
Position: Forward
Appearances: 7 **Goals scored:** 5
Seasons: 1894/95
Clubs: Glasgow Perthshire, Newton Heath, Chatham Town

JAMES 'JOCK' MILLER

Country: Scotland
Born: Unknown **Died:** Unknown
Debut: 15 Mar 1924 v Hull City
Position: Forward
Appearances: 4 **Goals scored:** 1
Seasons: 1923/24
Clubs: Port Glasgow Athletic, Blantyre Victoria, Hamilton Academical, St Mirren, Morton, Grimsby Town, Manchester United, York City, Boston Town, Shirebrook

WILLIAM PETER 'LIAM' MILLER

Country: Republic of Ireland
Born: 13 Feb 1981
Debut: 11 Aug 2004 v Dinamo Bucharest
Position: Midfield
Appearances: 11 (11) **Goals scored:** 2
Seasons: 2004/05 – 2005/06
Clubs: Celtic, AGF Aarhus (loan), Manchester United, Leeds United (loan), Sunderland, Queens Park Rangers, Hibernian, Perth Glory, Brisbane Roar

A former Celtic player, Liam Miller was signed on a free transfer under the Bosman ruling in July 2004. Having enjoyed a promising career with the Parkhead side, where he was tipped for success, his time in the red of United came as something of a disappointment, making only 22 appearances over the course of two seasons. A loan to Leeds United was followed by a free transfer to Sunderland in 2006, managed at the time by Roy Keane.

THOMAS 'TOMMY' MILLER

Country: Scotland
Born: 30 Jun 1890 **Died:** 3 Sep 1958
Debut: 25 Sep 1920 v Tottenham Hotspur
Position: Forward
Appearances: 27 **Goals scored:** 8
Seasons: 1920/21
Clubs: Larkhall Hearts, Glenview, Third Lanark, Lanark United, Hamilton Academical, Liverpool, Manchester United, Heart of Midlothian, Torquay United, Hamilton Academical, Raith Rovers

In September 1920, Manchester United made something of a controversial signing, when they secured Tommy Miller, a member of Liverpool's 1914 FA Cup final side, for £2,000. The player had been one of the four Liverpool players involved in the notorious match against United, on 2 April 1915, which was fixed. However, because of his army service, he was, along with his team-mates, given the opportunity to apologise for his misdemeanours and returned to the Liverpool ranks after the war, scoring some 15 goals in his first 24 games during that post-war season. His performances also earned him a Scottish international cap against England, when he scored twice on debut.

He soon settled and even captained the United side on occasion, but unfortunately things took a downward turn and, despite gaining further international honours, he decided to return to Scotland, joining Heart of Midlothian in a player-exchange deal which gave United £550 plus Arthur Lochhead.

RALPH MILNE

Country: Scotland
Born: 13 May 1961
Debut: 19 Nov 1988 v Southampton
Position: Winger
Appearances: 26 (4) **Goals scored:** 3
Seasons: 1988/89 – 1989/90
Clubs: Dundee United, Charlton Athletic, Bristol City, Manchester United, West Ham United (loan), Sing Tao

As a United player, Ralph Milne came in for much criticism from some fans. Few realised that he was a very experienced individual, having played at the highest level both at home and abroad with Dundee United. His Tannadice career spanned the best part of ten years and it was no coincidence that it was also the club's most successful spell in their history. Milne helped them to a Scottish title in 1983, three Scottish Cup runners-up medals, and was also the club's top scorer in Europe with 15 goals.

He moved south to Charlton Athletic for £125,000 in January 1987, joining Bristol City a year later. His move to Old Trafford, as Alex Ferguson strove towards stability within the ranks, was something of a gamble, which unfortunately didn't pay off, but he saw out his three-year deal. He was released on a free transfer in 1991, eventually moving to Hong Kong, to join Sing Tao FC. The £175,000 paid by Alex Ferguson to Bristol City for Milne's signature was the last cheque that he would sign for a Scottish-born player.

ANDREW 'ANDY' MITCHELL

Country: Scotland
Born: Unknown **Died:** Unknown
Debut: 10 Sep 1892 v Burnley
Position: Full-back
Appearances: 61 **Goals scored:** 0
Seasons: 1892/93 – 1893/94
Clubs: Airdrieonians, Newton Heath, Burton Swifts

Andrew Mitchell had been signed from Airdrieonians in September 1892 in what could be considered strange circumstances. The regular Newton Heath right-back during the successful Alliance season of 1891/92, Bob McFarlane, had returned home for what was meant to be a holiday (while being paid by Newton Heath), and was approached and successfully signed by his former club Airdrieonians, with the Newton Heath officials immediately signing Andrew Mitchell, the player he would have partnered at Airdrieonians, as his replacement.

The 22-year-old Mitchell made an early impression on all who saw him play, with his firm tackling and fine distribution, making an unbroken 49-game league and cup run in the team. Following the club's relegation into the Second Division at the end of season 1893/94, Mitchell moved to Burton Swifts.

ANDY MITCHELL

Country: England
Born: 20 Apr 1907 **Died:** 3 Dec 1971
Debut: 18 Mar 1933 v Notts County
Position: Winger
Appearances: 1 **Goals scored:** 0
Seasons: 1932/33
Clubs: Coxhoe Albion, Ferryhill Athletic, Crook Town, Sunderland, Notts County, Darlington, Manchester United, Hull City, Northampton, Rossendale United

JOHN MITCHELL

Country: Unknown
Born: Unknown **Died:** Unknown
Debut: 30 Oct 1886 v Fleetwood Rangers
Position: Full-back
Appearances: 3 **Goals scored:** 0
Seasons: 1886/87 & 1890/91
Clubs: Newton Heath, Bolton Wanderers, Newton Heath

CHARLES 'CHARLIE' MITTEN

Country: England
Born: 17 Jan 1921 **Died:** 2 Jan 2002
Debut: 31 Aug 1946 v Grimsby Town
Position: Winger
Appearances: 162 **Goals scored:** 61
Seasons: 1946/47 – 1949/50
Clubs: Manchester United, Santa Fe, Fulham, Mansfield Town

Born in Rangoon, Burma, where his sergeant-major father was stationed, Charlie Mitten was spotted playing in Perthshire junior football and signed by United in August 1936, progressing through the junior ranks, while working as an office boy at Old Trafford, before making his unofficial first-team debut in November 1939. During the war, he served in the RAF.

Selected as 12th man for Scotland in the Bolton disaster-fund match against England at Maine Road in 1946, he was surprisingly overlooked at international level by both countries, despite his performances with United in both the league and FA Cup. In the latter, he was a member of United's triumphant 1948 side, who defeated Blackpool 4-2 at Wembley. Although basically an outside-left, he was a noted goalscorer and during season 1948/49 had the distinction of scoring a hat-trick of penalties in a four-goal haul against Aston Villa, a season that saw him score 23 goals in both domestic competitions.

During United's summer tour of America in 1950, he was approached with an offer to play in Bogota; accepting the opportunity due to the money on offer – a reported signing-on fee of £5,000 plus £40 per week wages (his United pay was £12 per week). The 'Bogota Bandit' was duly suspended by the FA and fined £250, upon his somewhat disillusioned return home a year later. Unwanted at United, Fulham offered him the chance to resurrect his career, signing him up for £22,000.

HENRY HERBERT 'HARRY' MOGER

Country: England
Born: Sep 1879 **Died:** 16 Jun 1927
Debut: 10 Oct 1903 v Barnsley
Position: Goalkeeper
Appearances: 266 **Goals scored:** 0
Seasons: 1903/04 – 1911/12
Clubs: Freemantle, Southampton, Manchester United

At 6'3" and 12st 12lbs, Harry Moger was the ideal height and build for a goalkeeper and, after a somewhat unconvincing start to his United career, he went on to become one the best keepers to play for the club. Southampton-born, he began his career playing locally before moving north in May 1903 to start a nine-year stay with the Reds, during which he was to help United to both league (1908 and 1911) and FA Cup (1909) success. But like numerous others who played for the club, domestic success failed to bring international honours.

In the latter half of the second title-winning campaign, he lost his place to Hugh Edmonds and spent his final season at United mainly in the reserves, retiring from the game in the summer of 1912. Coincidentally, he played exactly the same number of times for United – 266 – as Edwin van der Sar.

IAN MOIR

Country: Scotland
Born: 30 Jun 1943
Debut: 1 Oct 1960 v Bolton Wanderers
Position: Winger
Appearances: 45 **Goals scored:** 5
Seasons: 1960/61 – 1964/65
Clubs: Manchester United, Blackpool, Chester City, Wrexham, Shrewsbury Town, Wrexham, Arcadia Shepherds, Oswestry Town, Colwyn Bay

Ian Moir had been expected to sign for this hometown club Aberdeen, having trained with them as a schoolboy, but United persuaded him to sign amateur forms for them as a 15-year-old in 1958. He turned professional two years later, and was soon producing some notable performances in the Central League side. A rather indifferent start to United's1960/61 season forced Matt Busby to ring the changes for the trip to Bolton on 1 October, with Moir making a favourable debut in the 1-1 draw. Although he did not retain his place, the slimly built, tricky youngster did return to the first-team scene before the end of the season and played in seven of the last 12 fixtures, scoring his first senior goal in the 1-1 home draw with Arsenal.

However, with the emergence of a certain George Best and the tendency of Busby to reshuffle the forward line, he more often than not found himself in and out of the first-team picture and, with the signing of John Connelly from Burnley in 1964, he was transferred to Blackpool for a fee of £30,000.

ARCHIBALD 'ARCHIE' MONTGOMERY

Country: Scotland
Born: 27 Jan 1873 **Died:** 5 Jan 1922
Debut: 16 Sep 1905 v Glossop
Position: Goalkeeper

Appearances: 3 **Goals scored:** 0
Seasons: 1905/06
Clubs: Rangers, Bury, Manchester United

JAMES MONTGOMERY

Country: England
Born: 1890 **Died:** 14 Nov 1960
Debut: 13 Mar 1915 v Bradford City
Position: Half-back
Appearances: 27 **Goals scored:** 1
Seasons: 1914/15 – 1920/21
Clubs: Glossop North End, Manchester United

Defender James Montgomery joined United at the right time, as his arrival in March 1915, at a time when relegation was more than a possibility, brought some stability to the half-back line. After the war, during which he was gassed, he perhaps understandably failed to consolidate his place in the side and was only something of a bit-part player, taking on a coaching position, until he left the club to join Crewe in 1921.

JOHN MOODY

Country: England
Born: 1 Nov 1904 **Died:** 23 Apr 1963
Debut: 26 Mar 1932 v Oldham Athletic
Position: Goalkeeper
Appearances: 51 **Goals scored:** 0
Seasons: 1931/32 – 1932/33
Clubs: Arsenal, Bradford Park Avenue, Doncaster Rovers, Manchester United, Chesterfield

A talented goalkeeper signed from Doncaster Rovers in February 1932, John Moody succeeded Alf Steward between the sticks, turning in promising performances following his debut a few weeks later. Having played in all 42 league fixtures the following season, the only ever-present, it came as something of a surprise that he was allowed to leave at the end of that 1932/33 season, joining Chesterfield. It turned out to be a huge mistake on the club's behalf, as United were almost relegated the following season, with his new club Chesterfield conceding only 43 goals in their 42 games, the best record in the Football League. United on the other hand had conceded 85!

CHARLES WILLIAM 'CHARLIE' MOORE

Country: England
Born: 3 Jun 1898 **Died:** 9 Mar 1966
Debut: 30 Aug 1919 v Derby County
Position: Full-back
Appearances: 328 **Goals scored:** 0
Seasons: 1919/20 – 1920/21 & 1922/23 – 1929/30
Clubs: Hednesford Town, Manchester United

Charlie Moore joined United as a 21-year-old from non-league side Hednesford Town at the end of the 1918/19 season, making his debut on the opening day of the following campaign. He was a strong, dependable full-back, whose career was almost brought to a premature end due to an ankle injury, but which went on to span some 11 years and over 320 appearances. The injury, which saw him released by the club in the summer of 1921 with an insurance pay-out agreed, was soon overcome and he returned to training, resuming his first-team role in September 1922 and reclaiming his place on a permanent basis at the start of season 1923/24, playing every game that season – the only member of the squad to do so.

He was completely overlooked for international recognition, while his club loyalty also failed to bring him anything in the way of silverware. He does, however, have the distinction of being the United player who has made the most appearances for the club without scoring a goal. By the outbreak of the Second World War, only three men had played more times for United than this stalwart defender from Staffordshire.

GRAHAM MOORE

Country: Wales
Born: 7 Mar 1941
Debut: 9 Nov 1963 v Tottenham Hotspur
Position: Forward
Appearances: 19 **Goals scored:** 5

Seasons: 1963/64
Clubs: Cardiff City, Chelsea, Manchester United, Northampton Town, Charlton Athletic, Doncaster Rovers

Graham Moore was seen by Matt Busby as a player who could play an influential part in his continued rebuilding after Munich, following his £35,000 transfer from Chelsea in November 1963. He had sprung to prominence with Cardiff City, before his £35,000 move to Stamford Bridge in December 1961, where he was to help the Londoners to promotion into the First Division. The Welsh international's move to Old Trafford failed to bring the hoped-for springboard to success, as injuries restricted him to only 19 appearances over the course of two years before he joined Northampton Town. He would play on for another decade.

KEVIN BERNARD MORAN

Country: Republic of Ireland
Born: 29 Apr 1956
Debut: 30 Apr 1979 v Southampton
Position: Centre-back
Appearances: 284 (5) **Goals scored:** 24
Seasons: 1978/99 – 1987/88
Clubs: Bohemians, Pegasus, Manchester United, Sporting Gijon, Blackburn Rovers

It is debatable if any player has shed more blood, or has received more stitches while playing for United, than Kevin Moran. Like fellow Dubliner and former United captain Johnny Carey, Moran was a devotee of Gaelic football and not just a mere bit player, but one of the top players in the history of the Irish game, playing in three All-Ireland finals and winning the 'Sam Maguire' twice, in 1976 and 1977.

A switch to the round-ball game, with Bohemians, saw him quickly adapt to the difference in rules, tactics and play, with his talents being spotted by United after moving into college football with Pegasus. In February 1978, contained at the end of an article on Joe Jordan, the *Manchester Evening News* reported – 'Reds Swoop For Moran', a completely out-of-the-blue signing, as his trials with United had been kept quiet due to his involvement in the Gaelic game. The club, however, allowed him to return to Ireland to play in the 1978 final.

Arriving at Old Trafford, under the guidance of Dave Sexton, who gave him his debut a year after signing, Moran had many rough edges to be smoothed down and the club's coaching staff immediately set about preparing the footballing novice, who was to emerge as a defender of awesome determination. Because of his playing style, Moran was always going to miss games through injury or suspension. The fear of either made little difference to his game, as he gave 100 per cent on every occasion.

Moran's physical attributes, while a big asset to both Manchester United and the Republic of Ireland, almost brought an end to not just his footballing career, but also his life. On 1 January 1987, while playing for United against Newcastle United at Old Trafford, Moran was hit in the face during a goalmouth scramble. As he fell to the ground, no one realised how series the incident would become. United's physiotherapist, Jimmy McGregor, was quickly on the scene as usual, but upon seeing the stunned Moran, he realised that the Irishman was in the process of swallowing his tongue. A hush enveloped Old Trafford, as the crowd realised that something was seriously wrong with the big defender, as there was no sign of movement for some three or four minutes. McGregor thankfully reacted quickly, having experienced similar incidents previously, and Moran was actually able to walk off the pitch unaided. Typical of the player, he wanted to return to the fray, but was stopped by the club doctor, as he was suffering from mild concussion.

In May 1985, Kevin Moran earned himself much unwanted publicity by becoming the first player ever to be sent off in an FA Cup final, following a mistimed challenge of Everton's Peter Reid, and thus he was the first player to climb the steps up to the Royal Box and not receive a medal, though he had won one in 1983.

After the signing of Steve Bruce – another tough central defender – 1988 saw Moran, at the age of 32, bring the curtain down on his United career, having been awarded a free transfer for his services to the club. He was also given a testimonial against Manchester City on 21 August of that year, before joining Sporting Gijon and subsequently helping Blackburn Rovers back to the top flight. He also won 71 caps for the Republic of Ireland between 1980 and 1994.

HUGH MORGAN

Country: Scotland
Born: 1875 **Died:** Unknown
Debut: 15 Dec 1900 v Lincoln City
Position: Forward
Appearances: 23 **Goals scored:** 4
Seasons: 1900/01
Clubs: Harthill Thistle, Airdrieonians, Sunderland, Bolton Wanderers, Newton Heath, Manchester City, Accrington Stanley, Blackpool

Hugh Morgan was player with a CV better than most, helping Sunderland to secure the runners-up spot in the Football League at the end of season 1897/98. Bolton, attracted by his talents, paid the pricey sum of £250 for his signature in February 1899 and his presence helped towards his club winning promotion the following season, after they had been relegated from the top flight soon after his arrival. It was from Bolton Wanderers that he joined Newton Heath in December 1900, scoring on his debut against Lincoln City. His stay at the club was rather brief, however, moving across Manchester the following summer to join City.

WILLIAM HENRY 'BILLY' MORGAN

Country: England
Born: 1878 **Died:** 5 Jun 1939
Debut: 2 Mar 1897 v Darwen
Position: Half-back
Appearances: 152 **Goals scored:** 7
Seasons: 1896/97 – 1902/03
Clubs: Horwich, Newton Heath, Bolton Wanderers, Watford, Leicester Fosse, New Brompton

Billy Morgan was born in Barrow in Furness and joined Newton Heath in 1897. He became a regular between 1899/00 and 1901/02, making more than 100 appearances in that time. In total he would play for half a dozen seasons for the club, in a career that spanned the demise of Newton Heath and the birth of Manchester United. He began as a centre-half, but later occupied both wing-half positions before his departure to Bolton in March 1903. His total of 143 appearances in Second Division games puts him in the top ten of that particular list at United.

WILLIAM 'WILLIE' MORGAN

Country: Scotland
Born: 2 Oct 1944
Debut: 28 Aug 1968 v Tottenham Hotspur
Position: Winger
Appearances: 293 (3) **Goals scored:** 34
Seasons: 1968/69 – 1974/75
Clubs: Burnley, Manchester United, Burnley, Bolton Wanderers, Chicago Sting (loan), Minnesota Kicks (loan), Blackpool

Willie Morgan was born in Sauchie, near Alloa, and joined Burnley from Fishcross Boys Club in May 1960, signing professional forms in October of the following year. He made his initial breakthrough at Turf Moor in April 1963, but following John Connelly's transfer to United during season 1963/64, he came more to the fore and slowly began to make a name for himself. His dribbling skills and natural talent earned him Scotland Under-23 caps and one full cap, against Northern Ireland in 1967.

However, he had also caught the eye of United manager Matt Busby, scoring in his team's 6-1 thrashing of United on Boxing Day 1963. It was a performance that Busby remembered and prompted the move to Old Trafford immediately following the European Cup final success in 1968, taking over the No.7 shirt, with George Best moving over to the left side. More of a goal-maker than a goal-taker, he scored only 34 goals in 296 games, and was to find himself out of favour for a while during Wilf McGuinness's short reign as manager.

But, with the appointment of Frank O'Farrell into the United hot seat, coupled with the decline of Best, he found himself back in the frame during 1971/72, while also receiving a recall to the Scotland set-up. Morgan enjoyed perhaps his best spell at the club following Tommy Docherty's arrival, when he was employed more in a midfield role. He won a Second Division Championship medal in 1974/75, but his relationship with Docherty hit a sour note in October 1974 when he was substituted, much to his disgust, against Southampton. With the arrival of Steve Coppell, Morgan was allowed to leave United and rejoin his previous club Burnley, for what was only a brief reacquaintance, before he moved across Lancashire to join Bolton Wanderers.

KENNETH GODFREY 'KENNY' MORGANS

Country: Wales
Born: 16 Mar 1939 **Died:** 18 Nov 2012
Debut: 21 Dec 1957 v Leicester City
Position: Winger
Appearances: 23 **Goals scored:** 0
Seasons: 1957/58 – 1960/61
Clubs: Manchester United, Swansea Town, Newport County, Barry Town

Had he been a year, or even a few months older, then Kenny Morgans may well have found himself in Cardiff instead of Belgrade on a cold February afternoon in 1958, playing for Wales in a World Cup tie, rather than a European Cup tie with United. At 18, he was the youngest of the 'Babes', and had made his debut only the previous December; having joined United as a junior in January 1955 as a Swansea schoolboy, he had captained the FA Youth Cup-winning side of 1957.

Having turned professional in April 1956, he had only played half a dozen league games at the time of the Munich crash and was destined for a long and successful career with United, having taken the place of Johnny Berry on the right wing. Alas, it was not to be. The last survivor to be found and pulled from the wreckage, he was to make only four further appearances for United after that season, before returning to Swansea and joining his local side.

JOHN 'JOHNNY' MORRIS

Country: England
Born: 27 Sep 1923 **Died:** 6 Apr 2011
Debut: 26 Oct 1946 v Sunderland
Position: Forward
Appearances: 93 **Goals scored:** 35
Seasons: 1946/47 – 1948/49
Clubs: Manchester United, Derby County, Leicester City, Corby Town

Radcliffe-born Johnny Morris joined the club as a junior in August 1939 from amateur side St John's, becoming one of the original members of the MUJACs (the Manchester United Junior Athletic Club, the Reds' first foray into a youth policy). Originally a centre-half, he was a member of Tommy Walker's army touring side during the Second

World War, making his initial United appearances during season 1941/42 mainly as an inside-forward, the position where he was to come to the fore in the first of Matt Busby's great sides.

Upon the resumption of league football following the war, it took Morris only a few weeks to claim his place in the United first team, going on to form a formidable partnership with Jimmy Delaney on the right wing. In March 1948 he won Football League honours, and it was disappointing to player and supporters alike that only one other Football League cap was to follow, though he did also pick up three England caps in 1949. With United, however, he played his part in the 1948 FA Cup success, scoring important goals in the third- and fourth-round ties, but by the time of the first post-war league success in 1952, he had left the club, having fallen out with Matt Busby and joined Derby County in March 1949 for a fee of £25,000.

RAVEL RYAN MORRISON

Country: England
Born: 2 Feb 1993
Debut: 26 Oct 2010 v Wolverhampton Wanderers
Position: Midfield
Appearances: 0 (3) **Goals scored:** 0
Seasons: 2010/11 – 2011/12
Clubs: Manchester United, West Ham United, Birmingham City (loan)

THOMAS 'TOMMY' MORRISON

Country: Ireland
Born: 16 Dec 1874 **Died:** 26 Mar 1940
Debut: 25 Dec 1902 v Manchester City
Position: Forward
Appearances: 36 **Goals scored:** 8
Seasons: 1902/03 – 1903/04
Clubs: Glentoran, Burnley, Celtic, Burnley, Manchester United, Colne, Burnley, Glentoran

Beginning his junior career with Stormont, Belfast-born Morrison moved to Glentoran in August 1891, winning the first of his seven Irish caps against England four years later. In February 1894, he crossed the

Irish Sea and joined Burnley, but his stay amid the cotton mills lasted only 14 months before he moved to Glasgow to join Celtic. A £300 transfer took him back to Burnley less than two years later. In December 1902, he made the relatively short journey to Manchester, playing his first three games for his new club on consecutive days – 25, 26 and 27 December. His debut not only made him the first Irish player to play for Manchester United (as opposed to Newton Heath), it was also the occasion of the biggest crowd ever at Bank Street. Seven goals from 20 outings in that first season wasn't a bad return, but he failed to gain a permanent place in the side and was not retained at the end of season 1903/04; he subsequently joined non-league side Colne.

BENJAMIN W. MORTON

Country: England
Born: 28 Aug 1910 **Died:** Nov 1962
Debut: 16 Nov 1935 v West Ham United
Position: Forward
Appearances: 1 **Goals scored:** 0
Seasons: 1935/36
Clubs: Stourbridge, Wolverhampton Wanderers, Manchester United, Torquay United, Swindon Town

REMI MARK MOSES

Country: England
Born: 14 Nov 1960
Debut: 19 Sep 1981 v Swansea City
Position: Midfield
Appearances: 188 (11) **Goals scored:** 12
Seasons: 1981/82 – 1987/88
Clubs: West Bromwich Albion, Manchester United

Despite being born in Manchester, Remi Moses escaped the clutches of both the local clubs, joining West Bromwich Albion in July 1977. Although only 5'6" tall, Moses made up for his lack of inches with his combative midfield play, which was to earn him England Under-21 honours. He had been a crucial part of a strong West Brom side, and it came as no surprise that when Ron Atkinson left The Hawthorns to take over at United, he raided his former club to bring in Moses as part of a double £2 million transfer that took him and Bryan Robson to Old Trafford in September 1981.

Unfortunately, his time at United was blighted by injuries, meaning he missed both of the club's FA Cup final successes in 1983 and 1985. In the end, a promising career was brought to a premature end, as injuries forced him to retire from the game in June 1988 at the age of 27.

ARNOLD JOHANNUS HYACINTHUS MUHREN

Country: Netherlands
Born: 2 Jun 1951
Debut: 28 Aug 1982 v Birmingham City
Position: Midfield
Appearances: 93 (5) **Goals scored:** 18
Seasons: 1982/83 – 1984/85
Clubs: Volendam, Ajax, FC Twente, Ipswich Town, Manchester United, Ajax

A member of Bobby Robson's highly talented Ipswich side of the late 1970s, Dutch international Arnold Muhren was a pencil-thin midfield player of immense talent with a cultured left foot. His distribution skills ensured that those around him could always rely on receiving the perfect pass to set them up. An integral part of the Portman Road UEFA Cup-winning side of 1981, he had already won the European Cup with Ajax in 1973. He joined United in August 1982, quickly fitting into the side alongside Bryan Robson and went on to score the fourth goal in the FA Cup final replay against Brighton, cancelling out the disappointment of having lost to Liverpool in the Milk Cup final two months earlier.

Missing from the United ranks through injury in the latter stages of 1983/84, United's title challenge stuttered to a halt, as did Muhren's Old Trafford career and he returned to Holland in the summer of 1985, rejoining Ajax where he was to win a European Cup-Winners' Cup medal in 1987.

PHILIP PATRICK STEPHEN 'PHIL' MULRYNE

Country: Northern Ireland
Born: 1 Jan 1978
Debut: 14 Oct 1997 v Ipswich Town

Position: Midfield
Appearances: 4 (1) **Goals scored:** 0
Seasons: 1997/98 – 1998/99
Clubs: Manchester United, Norwich City, Cardiff City, Leyton Orient, King's Lynn

ROBERT D. MURRAY

Country: Scotland
Born: 27 Mar 1915 **Died:** Unknown
Debut: 28 Aug 1937 v Newcastle United
Position: Forward
Appearances: 4 **Goals scored:** 0
Seasons: 1937/38
Clubs: Heart of Midlothian, Manchester United, Bath City, Colchester United

GEORGE MUTCH

Country: Scotland
Born: 21 Nov 1912 **Died:** 30 Mar 2001
Debut: 25 Aug 1934 v Bradford City
Position: Forward
Appearances: 120 **Goals scored:** 49
Seasons: 1934/35 – 1937/38
Clubs: Arbroath, Manchester United, Preston North End, Bury, Southport

Aberdeen-born George Mutch may have had his greatest moment in colours other than those of United, but he still had a good career at Old Trafford. Signed from Arbroath in May 1934 for a fee of £800, he scored a five-minute hat-trick against Barnsley on 8 September 1934, in what was only his fourth game for the club. The following season, as United strode to the Second Division title, he was an ever-present, scoring 21 goals in his 42 appearances.

A fee of £5,000 took him to Preston North End in September 1937 and it was at Deepdale that he won Scottish international honours and an FA Cup winner's medal. Against Huddersfield Town in that 1938 Wembley final (the first to be shown on television), he was brought down inside the area with only 60 seconds remaining and the score at

0-0. Although dazed by his fall, he got up and took the spot-kick, scoring the only goal of the game.

JOSEPH 'JOE' MYERSCOUGH

Country: England
Born: 8 Aug 1893 **Died:** 29 Jul 1975
Debut: 4 Sep 1920 v Bolton Wanderers
Position: Forward
Appearances: 34 **Goals scored:** 8
Seasons: 1920/21 – 1922/23
Clubs: Lancaster Town, Manchester United, Bradford Park Avenue

A regular goalscorer with Lancaster Town prior to joining United in May 1920, Joe Myerscough won a Central League medal with his new club in his first season. Four goals in two games against Bradford Park Avenue in December 1920 did not go unnoticed and as his United career stuttered along, he was signed by the Yorkshire club, along with team-mate Ken MacDonald in October 1923, for a combined fee of £1,500.

LUIS CARLOS ALMEIDA DA CUNHA 'NANI'

Country: Portugal
Born: 17 Nov 1986
Debut: 5 Aug 2007 v Chelsea
Position: Winger
Appearances: 168 (47) **Goals scored:** 40
Seasons: 2007/08 – present
Clubs: Sporting Lisbon, Manchester United

There is no doubting the ability of the Portuguese winger, who on his day is a match for anyone, but instead of rising to take over the mantle from fellow countryman Cristiano Ronaldo as a regular match-winning winger, a run of injuries has meant that many of the Old Trafford faithful have been frustrated not to have seen more of him at his very best – for when they do, he appears almost unstoppable.

Signed from Sporting Lisbon in July 2007 for a fee of £17 million, Nani had the perfect balance for a winger and, with goals added to his wide repertoire, he looked set to become a long-term favourite at the club. His performances were recognised by supporters and team-mates alike, with the latter naming him their Player of the Year in 2011.

His round-off and back somersault after scoring has become something of a forgotten celebration, with injuries as much as lack of form curtailing his appearances. Just when he looked to be about to prove that he had what it takes to shine on the European stage, he received an unmerited red card in the Champions League against Real Madrid at Old Trafford. He has now won four Premier League titles, the League Cup and the Champions League, as well as 66 caps for his country. The arrival of Wilfried Zaha at Old Trafford will only add to the pressure on him for one of the slots out wide, as he will also be competing with Ashley Young and Antonio Valencia.

DANIEL ANTHONY NARDIELLO

Country: Wales
Born: 22 Oct 1982
Debut: 5 Nov 2001 v Arsenal
Position: Forward
Appearances: 1 (3) **Goals scored:** 0
Seasons: 2001/02 – 2003/04
Clubs: Manchester United, Swansea City (loan), Barnsley, Queens Park Rangers, Barnsley (loan), Blackpool, Hartlepool (loan), Bury (loan), Oldham Athletic (loan), Exeter City, Rotherham United

GARY ALEXANDER NEVILLE

Country: England
Born: 18 Feb 1975
Debut: 16 Sep 1992 v Torpedo Moscow
Position: Full-back

Appearances: 566 (36) **Goals scored:** 7
Seasons: 1992/93 – 2010/11
Clubs: Manchester United

The elder of the Neville brothers, Gary, like brother Phil, was one of a golden age of young players to progress through the Old Trafford ranks during the early years of Alex Ferguson's reign as United manager. Bury-born Gary was a dyed-in-the-wool Red from day one, and his passion and enthusiasm for the club were shown clearly in his play throughout his career, with his goal celebrations against certain clubs being particularly noteworthy, and occasionally landing him in trouble with the authorities – something that hardly worried those on the Stretford End.

Joining United straight from school in 1991 at the age of 16, he became a member of the esteemed Class of '92 United youth side, alongside the likes of Ryan Giggs, David Beckham, Nicky Butt and Paul Scholes, going on to win England Youth honours the following year. Ferguson introduced the converted midfield player into the limelight as a substitute in a UEFA Cup tie against Torpedo Moscow in September 1992 for his initial appearance, but the youngster had to wait until May 1994 before making his full league debut against Coventry City, when several players were rested ahead of the FA Cup final.

Injuries, notably to Paul Parker, stretched United's defensive options in the early stages of season 1994/95, giving Gary an opportunity that he grasped with both hands, and he was to remain something of a permanent fixture in the side over the course of the next 16 years, going on to win eight Premier League titles, three FA Cups, two League Cups, two Champions Leagues, one FIFA World Club Cup, one Inter-Continental Cup, and three FA Community Shields, alongside 85 England appearances. Indeed, of that talented group of youngsters coming through the ranks, he was the first to win a full international cap on 3 June 1995.

A no-nonsense defender, despite his lack of inches he could easily adapt to a more central defensive role, as he did often during the Treble-winning season. His lack of goals – just seven – showed where his role in the team lay, but he was more than capable at going forward in support of his forwards, forming an excellent understanding with David Beckham, and was a great crosser of the ball.

Having taken over as club captain after the departure of Roy Keane, he subsequently suffered from injury problems. Having played more than 600 times for the club, he was critical of his own performance against

West Bromwich Albion at The Hawthorns on New Year's Day 2011 and decided the time had come to hang up his boots. He brought down the curtain on his United days with a testimonial against Juventus in May 2011 that featured many of the players he had started with some 20 years earlier.

He was not, however, out of the limelight for long, as he was brought into the England set-up under Roy Hodgson and became a highly acclaimed analyst on Sky Sports.

PHILIP JOHN 'PHIL' NEVILLE

Country: England
Born: 21 Jan 1977
Debut: 28 Jan 1995 v Wrexham
Position: Full-back/Midfield
Appearances: 301 (85) **Goals scored:** 89
Seasons: 1994/95 – 2004/05
Clubs: Manchester United, Everton

Philip, Gary Neville's younger brother, was widely tipped to have a big future in cricket rather than football, as he was seen by Lancashire as a future England player. He was, but in the end opted for the bigger Old Trafford stage, a decision that was to prove the correct one to make.

Captain of the United Youth Cup team of 1994/95, Phil Neville was called into the United senior XI to face Wrexham in January 1995, appearing on a more regular basis the following season, winning Premier League and FA Cup medals as United clinched the Double, and making his England debut during that season, on his 19th birthday. Highly thought of by his manager, it was not uncommon to see the Neville brothers on either side of the United back four, but the younger of the two Bury-born youngsters could often be found in the midfield, where he was equally at home, and he was occasionally deployed to do a man-marking job when the manager felt that someone in the opposition had the potential to hurt the team.

In the end, despite winning six Premier League titles, three FA Cup medals, and being part of the Champions League side in 1999, it was perhaps his versatility that was to prove his downfall. Sir Alex Ferguson was unable to provide him with a regular place in his starting line-ups, and ten years after making his first-team debut, the 59-times capped England international decided that a move was in his best interests and he joined Everton in August 2005 for around £3.5 million, almost immediately taking on the role of club captain.

At his new club, he went on to pass 500 Premier League appearances, helping David Moyes's side to achieve consistently well. When Moyes moved to United in the summer of 2013, he brought Phil Neville with him to be first team coach.

GEORGE WILLIAM NEVIN

Born: 16 Dec 1907 **Died:** Jan 1973
Debut: 6 Jan 1934 v Lincoln City
Position: Full-back
Appearances: 5 **Goals scored:** 0
Seasons: 1933/34
Clubs: Newcastle United, Sheffield Wednesday, Manchester United, Sheffield Wednesday, Burnley, Lincoln City, Rochdale

ERIK NEVLAND

Country: Norway
Born: 10 Nov 1977
Debut: 14 Oct 1997 v Ipswich Town
Position: Forward
Appearances: 2 (4) **Goals scored:** 1
Seasons: 1997/98 – 1998/99
Clubs: Viking FK, Manchester United, IFK Goteborg (loan), Viking FK, FC Groningen, Fulham, Viking FK

PERCY NEWTON

Country: England
Born: Jan 1904 **Died:** Oct 1993
Debut: 3 Feb 1934 v Burnley
Position: Full-back
Appearances: 2 **Goals scored:** 0
Seasons: 1933/34
Clubs: Sandbach Ramblers, Manchester United, Tranmere Rovers

JAMES MICHAEL 'JIMMY' NICHOLL

Country: Northern Ireland
Born: 28 Feb 1956
Debut: 5 Apr 1975 v Southampton
Position: Full-back
Appearances: 235 (13) **Goals scored:** 6
Seasons: 1974/75 – 1981/82
Clubs: Manchester United, Sunderland (loan), Toronto Blizzard, Sunderland, Toronto Blizzard, Rangers, West Bromwich Albion, Rangers, Dunfermline Athletic, Raith Rovers, Bath City

Canadian-born Jimmy Nicholl moved to Belfast with his parents in 1957 and played his early football with the 7th Newton Abbey Boys Brigade side and Glymower Wolves Boys Club. Spotted by Bob Bishop, he crossed the Irish Sea in November 1971 to join United, progressing through the ranks to become captain of the youth team. He was called into the first team for his initial appearance in a friendly against Rangers on 9 March 1974.

However, it wasn't until September 1975 that he made his first start, winning his first international cap six months later. A skilful player, he had good distribution skills and always seemed calm under pressure. By the start of 1976/77, he had replaced Alex Forsyth as United's first-choice right-back, and ended the campaign picking up an FA Cup winner's medal. He was ever-present in 1979/80, helping the Reds to the runners-up spot, their best finish since 1968, but following the signing of John Gidman in August 1981, he found himself out of new manager Ron Atkinson's plans, going on loan to Sunderland in December.

The Roker Park side could not afford to buy him, while United offered him £35,000 to leave the club, but it was not until April 1983 that he eventually left Old Trafford, moving back to Canada, joining Toronto Blizzard for £250,000. The Northern Ireland international would win 73 caps for his country, and spent six years at the end of his career as player-manager of Raith Rovers, continuing until he was 40.

JAMES JOSEPH 'JIMMY' NICHOLSON

Country: Northern Ireland
Born: 27 Feb 1943
Debut: 24 Aug 1960 v Everton

Position: Half-back
Appearances: 68 **Goals scored:** 6
Seasons: 1960/61 – 1962/63
Clubs: Manchester United, Huddersfield Town, Bury, Mossley, Stalybridge Celtic

Discovered by United scout Bob Harpur while playing for Boyland Youth, the Northern Ireland Schoolboy international joined United on amateur forms in May 1958 and before he had turned 16 had won Irish Youth and Under-23 caps. He made his United debut in August 1960, six months after signing professional forms, and the talented half-back went on to progress to the full Northern Ireland international side, eventually winning 41 caps. But injuries and, perhaps more to the point, the signing of Pat Crerand, saw his first-team appearances limited, so in December 1964 he reluctantly left Manchester United and joined Huddersfield Town for something of a bargain fee of only £7,500.

An own goal on his Town debut was not the best of starts, but over a period of nine years, Jimmy Nicholson was to make over 400 appearances for the Leeds Road side and in season 1969/70, as club captain, he played a major part in guiding Huddersfield to the Second Division title.

GEORGE NICOL

Country: Scotland
Born: 14 Dec 1903 **Died:** 18 Dec 1968
Debut: 11 Feb 1928 v Leicester City
Position: Forward
Appearances: 7 **Goals scored:** 2
Seasons: 1927/28 – 1928/29
Clubs: Saltcoats Victoria, Manchester United, Brighton & Hove Albion, Glenavon, Gillingham, RC Roubaix

ROBERT 'BOBBY' NOBLE

Country: England
Born: 18 Dec 1945
Debut: 9 Apr 1966 v Leicester City
Position: Full-back

Appearances: 33 **Goals scored:** 0
Seasons: 1965/66 – 1966/67
Clubs: Manchester United

Bobby Noble was part of the 1964 FA Youth Cup-winning side, along with George Best. Born in Stockport, the young full-back had pace and skill, but faced tough competition to break into the side when Shay Brennan, Noel Cantwell and Tony Dunne were also available. During 1966/67, he became a regular at left-back, helping the club to the title. But before that was achieved, he crashed his car after a 0-0 draw with Sunderland. The injuries nearly cost him his life, but they were to end his hugely promising playing career.

JOSEPH PATRICK 'JOE' NORTON

Country: England
Born: Jul 1890 **Died:** Unknown
Debut: 24 Jan 1914 v Oldham Athletic
Position: Forward
Appearances: 37 **Goals scored:** 3
Seasons: 1913/14 – 1914/15
Clubs: Stockport County, Nuneaton Town, Manchester United, Leicester City, Bristol Rovers, Swindon Town

Signed from Nuneaton Town in December 1913 for £195 as the replacement for George Wall, he was to find his Manchester United career brought to an early end by the First World War. Despite success with Nottingham Forest as a guest player during the hostilities, he was transferred listed by United in May 1919, with a £100 price tag alongside his name and subsequently joined Leicester City prior to the start of season 1919/20.

ALEXANDER McKEACHIE 'ALEX' NOTMAN

Country: Scotland
Born: 10 Dec 1979
Debut: 2 Dec 1998 v Tottenham Hotspur
Position: Forward
Appearances: 0 (1) **Goals scored:** 0

Seasons: 1998/99
Clubs: Manchester United, Aberdeen (loan), Sheffield United (loan), Norwich City, King's Lynn, Boston United

THOMAS ALBERT B. NUTTALL

Country: England
Born: Jan 1889 **Died:** Oct 1963
Debut: 23 Mar 1912 v Liverpool
Position: Forward
Appearances: 16 **Goals scored:** 4
Seasons: 1911/12 – 1912/13
Clubs: Heywood United, Manchester United, Everton

With his father as assistant trainer, Tom Nuttall had a helping hand towards a career with United, but ten goals in three successive reserve-team outings, after joining the club in May 1910 from Heywood United, showed that he didn't need any extra help. Two goals in six appearances towards the end of season 1911/12 looked promising, but after a further ten appearances in the early stages of the following season, he failed to feature at first-team level again, leaving Old Trafford in May 1913 to join Everton for a fee of £250, having been released by the club.

GABRIEL ANTOINE OBERTAN

Country: France
Born: 26 Feb 1989
Debut: 27 Oct 2009 v Barnsley
Position: Winger
Appearances: 13 (15) **Goals scored:** 1
Seasons: 2009/10 – 2010/11
Clubs: Bordeaux, Lorient (loan), Manchester United, Newcastle United

Signed by United for an undisclosed fee in July 2009, Frenchman Gabriel Obertan sprang to prominence during the 2009 Toulon Under-21 tournament, claiming the man-of-the-match award in the final. Having represented his country at every level prior to this, it was considered that he had a bright future in the game and it was during a spell at the renowned Clairefontaine academy that he was spotted by Bordeaux. Under the guidance of former United player Laurent Blanc he progressed, more so after a loan spell with Lorient, and in the summer of 2009 he crossed the Channel to join United. First-team appearances, however, were limited for the speedy wingman, although he would often shine in reserve outings, and injuries did little to help his prospects. So, in August 2011 following the signing of Ashley Young, he was allowed to join Newcastle United, again for an undisclosed fee.

GEORGE W. O'BRIEN

Country: England
Born: Unknown **Died:** Unknown
Debut: 7 Apr 1902 v Middlesbrough
Position: Winger
Appearances: 1 **Goals scored:** 0
Seasons: 1901/02
Clubs: Newton Heath

WILLIAM FRANCIS 'LIAM' O'BRIEN

Country: Republic of Ireland
Born: 5 Sep 1964
Debut: 20 Dec 1986 v Leicester City
Position: Midfield
Appearances: 17 (19) **Goals scored:** 2
Seasons: 1986/87 – 1988/89
Clubs: Bohemians, Shamrock Rovers, Manchester United, Newcastle United, Tranmere Rovers, Cork City, Bohemians

Signed only a few weeks before Alex Ferguson's arrival for a fee of £40,000 (plus the promise of two friendly fixtures) from Shamrock Rovers, Liam O'Brien had originally been with the Dublin-based Stella Maris club, before joining Bohemians. Moving to Shamrock Rovers in

1983, he won the League of Ireland title for three years in succession while there. Despite standing just over six foot tall, O'Brien possessed a sublime talent, which was soon attracting covetous glances from across the Irish Sea, and in October 1986 he ended up being Ron Atkinson's last signing for United.

The adjustment to full-time football came naturally and Alex Ferguson had 'absolutely no doubts about him', when announcing that he was giving him his debut against Leicester City on 20 December 1986. With only two full appearances under his belt, O'Brien suddenly hit the headlines, but for the wrong reasons, being sent off after only 85 seconds following a mistimed tackle at Southampton on 3 January 1987. Despite the manager's praise, the Republic of Ireland international couldn't earn a regular place in the side, so he was allowed to join Newcastle United for £275,000 in the autumn of 1988.

PATRICK JOSEPH O'CONNELL

Country: Ireland
Born: 8 Mar 1887 **Died:** 27 Feb 1959
Debut: 2 Sep 1914 v Oldham Athletic
Position: Defender
Appearances: 35 **Goals scored:** 2
Seasons: 1914/15
Clubs: Belfast Celtic, Sheffield Wednesday, Hull City, Manchester United, Dumbarton, Ashington

Although born in Dublin, O'Connell had played with Belfast Celtic before joining Sheffield Wednesday in October 1908 and it was with the Hillsborough side that he won the first of his five Ireland caps. Joining Hull City in the summer of 1912, he made around 60 appearances with the Tigers before moving to United in May 1914. He soon established himself in the United side, becoming captain, during that first wartime season. Controversially, he missed a penalty in the 'fixed' game against Liverpool in April 1915, but was not charged by the FA.

When football returned to normality for the start of season 1919/20, O'Connell signed for Dumbarton. However, it was as a manager that he was to make his biggest mark on the game, becoming one of the most influential bosses in Spain between the wars, and helping to save

Barcelona from going bust in the 1930s during the Spanish Civil War, thus earning the nickname Don Patricio.

JOHN ANDREW O'KANE

Country: England
Born: 15 Nov 1974
Debut: 21 Sep 1994 v Port Vale
Position: Full-back
Appearances: 5 (2) **Goals scored:** 0
Seasons: 1994/95 – 1996/97
Clubs: Manchester United, Bury (loan), Bradford City (loan), Everton, Burnley (loan), Bolton Wanderers, Blackpool, Hyde United

ROBERT LESLIE 'LES' OLIVE

Country: England
Born: 27 Apr 1928 **Died:** 20 May 2006
Debut: 11 Apr 1953 v Newcastle United
Position: Goalkeeper
Appearances: 2 **Goals scored:** 0
Seasons: 1952/53
Clubs: Manchester United

A highly respected individual, Les Olive joined the United office staff upon leaving school as a 14-year-old in September 1942.

Three years later, he was to join the RAF, but returned to Old Trafford in 1948 turning out for the 'A' and 'B' teams when not working in the ticket office. By season 1952/53 he was a member of the Central League side, having played in every position except outside-left. In April 1953, he suddenly found himself thrust into the first team as a replacement goalkeeper due to a spate of injuries, making his debut at Newcastle and keeping his place the following week.

In March 1955, he was appointed assistant secretary and, due to his efficient running of things following Walter Crickmer's death at Munich, he was given the position on a permanent basis. It was a role that he was to fulfil until 1988, when he was made a director of the club, a position he held until his death in May 2006, after more than 60 years of service.

JESPER OLSEN

Country: Denmark
Born: 20 Mar 1961
Debut: 25 Aug 1984 v Watford
Position: Winger
Appearances: 149 (27) **Goals scored:** 24
Seasons: 1984/85 – 1987/88
Clubs: Naestved, Ajax, Manchester United, Bordeaux, Caen

He was born in Denmark, but it was as an Ajax player that Jesper Olsen sprang to prominence. The young, diminutive winger joined United from the Dutch club in July 1984 for a fee of £700,000. In those days, foreign signings at Old Trafford were still comparatively rare, with only Nikki Jovanovic and Arnold Muhren preceding him.

He made his debut in the same game as Gordon Strachan, and manager Ron Atkinson's plan was to have the pair of them working out wide, while Bryan Robson and Remi Moses worked in the centre of midfield. In his debut season, when United beat Everton 1-0 in the final, he added an FA Cup winner's medal to his two Dutch titles and a Dutch Cup winner's medal. Swift of foot and certainly talented, although perhaps a little on the light side for the physical element of the English game, he followed it up with his most prolific season in 1985/86 when he scored 13 goals in all competitions, including all three against Atkinson's old club West Brom. Unfortunately, he was unable to build on that, and it was of little surprise when he left United, joining Bordeaux in November 1988 for £400,000.

THOMAS PATRICK 'TOMMY' O'NEIL

Country: England
Born: 25 Oct 1952 **Died:** May 2006
Debut: 5 May 1971 v Manchester City
Position: Full-back
Appearances: 68 **Goals scored:** 0
Seasons: 1970/71 – 1972/73
Clubs: Manchester United, Blackpool (loan), Southport, Tranmere Rovers, Halifax Town

Tommy O'Neil had the unusual distinction of double international recognition as a schoolboy, playing for England at both rugby league and football. He joined United as an apprentice in August 1968 and, after turning professional a year later, made his league debut against Manchester City in the final match of season 1970/71. The following season, he began as first-choice right-back, missing only a handful of games, keeping his place during the opening months of the following campaign, but an injury in December 1972 brought an end to his United career. Initially joining Blackpool on loan, he was given a free transfer at the end of 1972/73 and moved to Southport.

T. O'SHAUGHNESSEY

Country: Unknown
Born: Unknown **Died:** Unknown
Debut: 25 Oct 1890 v Bootle Reserves
Position: Forward
Appearances: 1 **Goals scored:** 0
Seasons: 1890/91
Clubs: Newton Heath

JOHN FRANCIS O'SHEA

Country: Republic of Ireland
Born: 30 Apr 1981
Debut: 13 Oct 1999 v Aston Villa
Position: Defender/Midfield
Appearances: 301 (92) **Goals scored:** 15
Seasons: 1999/2000 – 2010/11
Clubs: Manchester United, Bournemouth (loan), Royal Antwerp (loan), Sunderland

A Republic of Ireland international at Under-16, Youth and Under-21 level, Waterford-born John O'Shea joined Manchester United on 3 August 1998 and by the end of his first season had progressed to the reserve side with little difficulty. Although he had made his United debut in the League Cup against Aston Villa in October 1999, United were well off for central defenders, with Stam, Silvestre and Berg all regulars, so he was dispatched to the south coast for a loan spell with

Bournemouth, where he made a big impact during his ten league outings.

A further loan spell at Royal Antwerp added to his experience and, with Stam and Berg having left the club, he now had a better chance to grab first-team football and in November 2001 he made his league debut, three months after his first full international start. The following season, he was a regular in the starting line-up, often in the centre of defence alongside new signing Rio Ferdinand, but he also turned out in either full-back slot or in the midfield, his adaptability helping the Reds to the Premier League title.

The next campaign, he made more starting appearances than anyone else, and his first goal for the club was the only one in the match against Wolverhampton on 27 August 2003. An excellent utility player, he was even to take over from an injured Edwin van der Sar in February 2007 at Tottenham; it was perhaps this ability that was to prove his downfall, as, like Phil Neville, he began to find it difficult to hold down a regular first-team place. Despite that, Sir Alex Ferguson used him as a starter in the Champions League campaign of 2008/09 more than anyone else, a reflection of his experience and calmness in the high-pressure situations.

A winning goal at Anfield against Liverpool in March 2007 was a definite highlight, and when he had to play as an emergency striker the following season, it mean he had played in every position for the club. As he reached 30, the starting appearances grew fewer, so in July 2011, he was signed for Sunderland by former United captain Steve Bruce. By then, he had won all the major club honours, including the 2008 Champions League and the Club World Cup.

GEORGE ALFRED OWEN

Country: Wales
Born: 1865 **Died:** 29 Jan 1922
Debut: 18 Jan 1890 v Preston North End
Position: Forward
Appearances: 1 **Goals scored:** 0
Seasons: 1889/90
Clubs: Chirk, Newton Heath, West Manchester, Chirk, Druids, Chirk

JOHN 'JACK' OWEN

Country: Wales
Born: 1866 **Died:** Unknown
Debut: 18 Jan 1890 v Preston North End
Position: Half-back
Appearances: 6 **Goals scored:** 0
Seasons: 1889/90 – 1891/92
Clubs: Chirk, Newton Heath

The brother of George (above), Jack Owen was the only man to play in all six of Newton Heath's official fixtures before the club joined the Football League. Like his brother, he was one of the club's earliest internationals.

MICHAEL JAMES OWEN

Country: England
Born: 14 Dec 1979
Debut: 9 Aug 2009 v Chelsea
Position: Forward
Appearances: 15 (33) **Goals scored:** 17
Seasons: 2009/10 – 2011/12
Clubs: Liverpool, Real Madrid, Newcastle United, Manchester United, Stoke City

Michael Owen had had a notable and distinguished career prior to joining United in July 2009, in what was something of a surprise signing by Sir Alex Ferguson. The former Liverpool player's best days appeared to be behind him after a series of injuries had left him struggling for a run of games, but he was still a good, experienced addition to the United squad.

In 2001, the former BBC Sports Personality of the Year had won five trophies with Liverpool, and in 2004 he had a season with Real Madrid, before moving on to spend four years at Newcastle United. However, despite all of that, it was not until he joined United that he could get his hands on a title-winner's medal, being part of the squad that lifted the Premiership trophy in 2010/11.

With United, injuries meant his opportunities were not as frequent as he might have liked, and his five league goals were considerably fewer than he would normally have been expected to score. However, one of them ensured he will forever be remembered by the United faithful. It came, of course, in the sixth minute of stoppage time against Manchester City at Old Trafford on 20 September 2009, as United won out in a stunning 4-3 derby triumph. At the end of season 2011/12, he was released by the club, joining Stoke City on a one-year deal, and retired at the end of that campaign.

W. OWEN

Country: Wales
Born: Unknown **Died:** Unknown
Debut: 15 Oct 1898 v Small Heath
Position: Winger
Appearances: 1 **Goals scored:** 0
Seasons: 1898/99
Clubs: Newton Heath

WILLIAM 'BILL' OWEN

Country: England
Born: 17 Sep 1906 **Died:** 26 Mar 1981
Debut: 22 Sep 1934 v Norwich City
Position: Outside-left
Appearances: 17 **Goals scored:** 1
Seasons: 1934/35 – 1935/36
Clubs: Northwich Victoria, Macclesfield Town, Manchester United, Reading, Exeter City, Newport County

Bill Owen joined United in May 1934. Fifteen games scattered throughout his first season hinted that he might have a chance at this higher level, but the following campaign brought only a mere two outings and he was released and joined Reading in January 1936.

LOUIS ANTONIO PAGE

Country: England
Born: 27 Mar 1899 **Died:** 11 Oct 1959
Debut: 25 Mar 1932 v Charlton Athletic
Position: Forward
Appearances: 12 **Goals scored:** 0
Seasons: 1931/32 – 1932/33
Clubs: Stoke City, Northampton Town, Burnley, Manchester United, Port Vale, Yeovil & Petters United

Something of an all-round sportsman, Louis Page represented England at both football and baseball, winning seven caps at the former during 1927, as well as playing once for the Football League. Kicking off his professional career with Stoke immediately after the First World War and joining Northampton Town in 1922, it wasn't until he became a Burnley player that he really hit the headlines, being considered as one of the outstanding wing men of the period, scoring 115 goals in 259 games for the Turf Moor side, including six in one game. When Scott Duncan paid £1,000 for him in March 1932, his best days were behind him, and even although he was appointed captain at the start of season 1932/33, he was to start only three games and was transferred to Port Vale two months into the season.

GARY ANDREW PALLISTER

Country: England
Born: 30 June 1965
Debut: 30 Aug 1989 v Norwich City
Position: Centre-back
Appearances: 433 (4) **Goals scored:** 15
Seasons: 1989/90 – 1997/98
Clubs: Middlesbrough, Darlington (loan), Manchester United, Middlesbrough

Had Darlington been able to afford the £4,000 Middlesbrough required in November 1985 for the loan deal of their 21-year-old Gary Pallister to become permanent, then there is no telling what direction the tall centre-half's footballing career might have taken. As it turned out, he returned to Ayresome Park, became a first-team regular and in August 1989 joined the Alex Ferguson revolution at Old Trafford, with Middlesbrough receiving almost £2.3 million more than they had wanted from Darlington.

United's then record signing forged a formidable partnership alongside Steve Bruce, as the pair earned the nicknames 'Dolly and Daisy'. In their first season together, they helped United to win their first trophy under Alex Ferguson, with the FA Cup duly wrapped up after a replay against Crystal Palace. They followed it up with more trophies, before they took United to their first league title in 26 years during 1992/93, when both men were ever-present. Having won the title when Aston Villa slipped up, the following day's celebrations against Blackburn Rovers were made complete when Pallister, the only player in the side not to have scored during that campaign, fired home a free-kick from just outside the box.

During his time at United, he would win four Premier League titles, three FA Cup winner's medals, as well as a League Cup, European Cup-Winners' Cup and Super Cup winner's medals. He also picked up a total of 22 England caps, which many felt could have been a much higher total, and was voted the PFA Player of the Year in 1992. An unflappable presence in the United defence, adding the brain to the brawn of Bruce, he was arguably the more skilful of the pair, and certainly had more pace. The understanding they shared undoubtedly made Pallister and Bruce one of the all-time great defensive partnerships at the club. Pallister enjoyed nine years at Old Trafford, making 437 appearances. In 1998, with the arrival of Jaap Stam, he moved back to Middlesbrough for a fee of £1.95 million, giving them three more years of excellent service.

ALBERT ARTHUR PAPE

Country: England
Born: 13 Jun 1897 **Died:** 18 Nov 1955
Debut: 7 Feb 1925 v Clapton Orient
Position: Forward
Appearances: 18 **Goals scored:** 5

Seasons: 1924/25 – 1925/26
Clubs: Rotherham County, Notts County, Clapton Orient, Manchester United, Fulham, Rhyl Athletic, Hurst, Darwen, Manchester Central, Hartlepools United, Halifax Town, Burscough Rangers, Horwich RMI, Nelson

On the morning of 7 February 1925, Albert Pape travelled to Manchester with his Clapton Orient team-mates, looking forward to running out at Old Trafford against United, but upon his arrival at the ground he became the centre of an astonishing transfer that would find him in the home dressing room rather than the away one. Negotiations between the two clubs were concluded quickly, with a fee of £1,070 agreed. Pape announced that he was happy to move and the details were sent to the FA and the Football League, and the player was allowed to turn out against his former team-mates. Rather ironically, he scored United's third goal in their 4–2 win.

He was to score a further four goals as United secured the runners-up place in the Second Division and promotion to the top flight, but he was to make only two appearances in the First Division, as he was sold to Fulham in October 1925. Strangely, he did not move to London following the transfer, but continued to live in Bolton and trained at Old Trafford with United.

JI-SUNG PARK

Country: South Korea
Born: 25 Feb 1981
Debut: 9 Aug 2005 v Debrecen
Position: Midfield
Appearances: 146 (59) **Goals scored:** 27
Seasons: 2005/06 – 2011/12
Clubs: Kyoto Purple Sanga, PSV Eindhoven, Manchester United, Queens Park Rangers, PSV Eindhoven (loan)

Upon joining United, Ji-Sung Park had much to prove, as many critics believed that he had been signed as nothing more than a marketing ploy in order to build the club's profile in his native South Korea. They were, however, to be proved wrong, as the effervescent midfielder showed himself a worthy addition to the United squad in his seven years at the club. Signed for £4 million from PSV Eindhoven in 2005, who he had helped to the Champions League semi-finals, Park undoubtedly did shift a few shirts, but as a player he put in a number of excellent displays, with his unselfish running giving the team something of an extra dimension, as did his ability to perform as an emergency full-back if called upon.

In his native South Korea, he was an undoubted superstar, playing in three World Cup final tournaments and winning 100 caps, with his performances for his country earning him the accolade of getting a road named after him in his home town of Suwon. At United, his initial role was on the left side of midfield, where he provided an alternative to Ryan Giggs.

A knee injury in 2007 saw him out of action for a long spell, but he still managed to become the first South Korean to win a Premier League title that year. It took a while before he returned to full fitness, but was sadly left out of the squad in the 2008 Champions League final. The following season, he played a more central role, often used to shackle the opposing midfield, where his energy was invaluable. He was to win four Premier League medals, three League Cups and a FIFA Club World Cup winner's medal, but competition for first-team places was soon to become much tougher and, despite having played in just over 200 games for United, the manager could not guarantee him a starting place, or even a place on the bench and he decided that it was perhaps best to move on, signing for Queens Park Rangers for an undisclosed fee in July 2012.

PAUL ANDREW PARKER

Country: England
Born: 4 Apr 1964
Debut: 17 Aug 1991 v Notts County
Position: Full-back
Appearances: 137 (9) **Goals scored:** 2
Seasons: 1991/92 – 1995/96
Clubs: Fulham, Queens Park Rangers, Manchester United, Derby County, Sheffield United, Fulham, Chelsea

Whatever Paul Parker was lacking in inches, he certainly made up for in grit and determination as a speedy and cultured full-back with

Fulham, Queens Park Rangers, United and England. London-born, he joined Fulham as a schoolboy, spending seven years with the Craven Cottage side before moving across the capital to Loftus Road as part of a £500,000 double signing and in his four years at QPR he was to become an England regular, going on to win 19 caps.

A £1.7 million fee took him to Old Trafford in August 1991, where he formed the final piece of the defensive jigsaw, along with Steve Bruce, Denis Irwin, Gary Pallister and Peter Schmeichel (who made his debut for United on the same day). Despite an injury disrupting his first season with United, he went on to win two Premier League, one FA Cup and a League Cup winner's medals with the club. Despite his height (5'7"), he was good in the air and enjoyed moving forward in attack, but was far from being a noted goalscorer, managing only two in his five years at Old Trafford. Injuries were to prove to be his downfall and, along with the emergence of Gary Neville at the club, his first-team days were truly numbered and he was allowed to leave in the summer of 1996, joining Derby County.

SAMUEL 'SAM' PARKER

Country: Scotland
Born: 1872 **Died:** Unknown
Debut: 13 Jan 1894 v Sheffield Wednesday
Position: Forward
Appearances: 12 **Goals scored:** 0
Seasons: 1893/94
Clubs: Hurlford, Newton Heath, Burnley, Southport Central, Hurlford, Kilmarnock Athletic

Samuel Parker was born in the Ayrshire village of Hurlford and joined Newton Heath from his local club. Following the move, he failed to make a similar impression on club officials and spectators alike, with his 12 appearances failing to produce any of the hoped-for goals. Season 1894/95 found him in the reserve side and, with only a few weeks of the campaign played, he was transferred to Burnley, but was again moved on quickly.

THOMAS ALBERT 'TOMMY' PARKER

Country: England
Born: 22 Nov 1906 **Died:** 11 Nov 1964
Debut: 11 Oct 1930 v West Ham United
Position: Defender
Appearances: 17 **Goals scored:** 0
Seasons: 1930/31 – 1931/32
Clubs: Manchester United, Bristol City, Carlisle United, Stalybridge Celtic

Tommy Parker was as an amateur during United's poor start to season 1930/31, but was to make little difference to the defence, as they leaked 11 goals in his first three games, winning only one of the nine games in which he featured that season. Indeed, in the 17 games he played between October 1930 and January 1932, United won only three. Transfer-listed at the end of season 1931/32, he joined Bristol City, becoming a first-team regular.

ROBERT PARKINSON

Country: England
Born: 27 Apr 1873 **Died:** Unknown
Debut: 11 Nov 1899 v Barnsley
Position: Forward
Appearances: 15 **Goals scored:** 7
Seasons: 1899/1900
Clubs: Rotherham Town, Luton Town, Blackpool, Warmley, Nottingham Forest, Newton Heath, Watford, Swindon Town

Signed from Nottingham Forest's reserve side in November 1899, Robert Parkinson's introduction to the Newton Heath side produced something of an upturn in fortune, as he scored seven goals in 15 outings (including five in five), but a breach of club discipline, which was never revealed, saw him suspended, put up for sale in March 1900 and transferred to Blackburn Rovers, although he was never to appear in their first team.

EDWARD 'TEDDY' PARTRIDGE

Country: England
Born: 13 Feb 1891 **Died:** Jun 1970
Debut: 9 Oct 1920 v Oldham Athletic
Position: Winger
Appearances: 160 **Goals scored:** 18
Seasons: 1920/21 – 1928/29
Clubs: Ebbw Vale, Manchester United, Halifax Town, Manchester Central, Altrincham, Crewe

Yet another former miner within the ranks, Teddy Partridge was signed as a 29-year-old from Ebbw Vale in June 1920 for a £19 signing-on fee. He enjoyed a favourable first season, becoming the joint top scorer, with seven goals in 28 appearances. He was a first-team regular for the majority of his first three seasons at Old Trafford, but his enthusiastic performances were not enough to deflect criticism from the terraces, as fans grew disappointed about his decline in goals scored. However, despite making only nine outings over the next three seasons, he clawed his way back into the side on a regular basis and was given a benefit match in March 1928 for his services to the club. The following year he left United, joining Halifax Town.

STEVEN WILLIAM 'STEVE' PATERSON

Country: Scotland
Born: 8 Apr 1958
Debut: 29 Sep 1976 v Ajax Amsterdam
Position: Defender
Appearances: 5 (5) **Goals scored:** 0
Seasons: 1976/77 – 1979/80
Clubs: Nairn County, Manchester United, Buckie Thistle, Peterhead, Nairn County, Sydney Olympic, Hong Kong Rangers, Yomiuri

Steve Paterson was to make more of a name for himself as a manager than as a player. He signed for United as an 18-year-old from Nairn County, and few can have had more illustrious debuts than the 6'2" central defender from Mostodloch, near Elgin, coming on as a substitute in the UEFA Cup first round second leg tie against Ajax at Old Trafford.

His second outing was even more daunting, again as a substitute, this time against Juventus a few weeks later.

An ankle injury and the signing of Gordon McQueen did little to help his claims for a first-team place and he was released by United in the summer of 1980, with United having picked up £50,000 insurance from his ankle injury. He was promptly offered a contract by Sheffield Wednesday, but failed the medical. He later became a manager back in Scotland with the likes of Elgin City and Inverness Caledonian Thistle, engineering a notable Scottish Cup victory over Celtic at Parkhead that sparked the famous headline: 'Super Caley Go Ballistic, Celtic Are Atrocious'.

ERNEST PAYNE

Country: England
Born: 23 Dec 1884 **Died:** 10 Sep 1961
Debut: 27 Feb 1909 v Nottingham Forest
Position: Winger
Appearances: 2 **Goals scored:** 1
Seasons: 1908/09
Clubs: Worcester City, Manchester United

While Payne's brief career at United was unimpressive – 'he was a very weak spot indeed,' said one newspaper – he did have the unique distinction of winning a gold medal in the 1908 London Olympics in cycling.

STEPHEN 'STEVE' PEARS

Country: England
Born: 22 Jan 1962
Debut: 12 Jan 1985 v Coventry City
Position: Goalkeeper
Appearances: 5 **Goals scored:** 0
Seasons: 1984/85
Clubs: Manchester United, Middlesbrough, Liverpool, Hartlepool

Although Pears could not displace Gary Bailey, he went on to become Middlesbrough's keeper for a decade between 1985 and 1995.

MARK PEARSON

Country: England
Born: 28 Oct 1939
Debut: 19 Feb 1958 v Sheffield Wednesday
Position: Forward
Appearances: 80 **Goals scored:** 14
Seasons: 1957/58 – 1962/63
Clubs: Manchester United, Sheffield Wednesday, Fulham, Halifax Town, Bacup Borough

Mark Pearson played for Derbyshire and England Boys before joining United straight from school, progressing into the United and England youth set-up before making his United debut at inside-left in the FA Cup against Sheffield Wednesday in the aftermath of the Munich disaster. He was to come in for some criticism for his rugged style of play, but this was because he was such a good tackler (and perhaps because he was labelled by Burnley chairman Bob Lord as a 'teddy boy'), as he did show that he had the makings of a good player. The following season, due to injury problems and the form of Albert Quixall and Bobby Charlton, his appearances were limited, but he always made the most of those that he was given. However, he decided that a move was perhaps best and joined Sheffield Wednesday in October 1963 for a fee of £20,000.

STANLEY CLARE 'STAN' PEARSON

Country: England
Born: 11 Jan 1919 **Died:** 20 Feb 1997
Debut: 13 Nov 1937 v Chesterfield
Position: Inside-forward
Appearances: 343 **Goals scored:** 148
Seasons: 1937/38 – 1953/54
Clubs: Manchester United, Bury, Chester

A former Salford Schoolboy, Stan Pearson joined the United groundstaff at the age of 17 in May 1936, making his debut at Chesterfield in November the following year a few months after signing professional forms. He remained a bit-part player before the war, but was then called up to serve in the army in India. On the resumption of league football in 1946/47, he was the only player to appear in every game that season, scoring 19 goals and formed a formidable strike partnership with Jack Rowley as the Reds finished as runners-up.

The next season, he proved even more prolific, his form earning him the first of eight England caps. He was especially lethal in front of goal in United's FA Cup run, scoring seven goals on the way to Wembley, taking United to the final with a hat-trick against Derby County in the semi-final. He was also to score United's first in the 4–2 win over Blackpool beneath the twin towers. A deserved League Championship medal finally arrived in 1952, by which stage this gentle easygoing character had missed just ten games since the war – a remarkable record. On the departure of Johnny Carey in 1953, he was named as club captain, a fitting honour for the quick forward with a deceptive body swerve and tricky footwork.

For someone who was never the main goalscorer, his strike-rate was impressive, and only four players in the club's history have scored more hat-tricks than his total of six. However, age eventually caught up with him and, more than 15 years after his debut (only six players have spent longer in the first team at United than he did), he moved to Bury in 1954, with the Shakers paying £4,500 for his services.

STUART JAMES PEARSON

Country: England
Born: 21 Jun 1949
Debut: 17 Aug 1974 v Leyton Orient
Position: Centre-forward
Appearances: 179 (1) **Goals scored:** 66
Seasons: 1974/75 – 1978/79
Clubs: Hull City, Manchester United, West Ham United

It can be argued that it was the lack of goals that sent United down into the Second Division in 1974, a mere 38 in 42 league fixtures (the club's defence was the seventh best that season), so it was of little surprise that Tommy Docherty went out and bought a goalscorer that summer, going back to one of his former clubs, Hull City, and paying £200,000 for Stuart Pearson.

Pearson had scored 44 in 129 league games for Hull and soon settled into his new surroundings, scoring 17 goals in 31 league games as United took the Second Division by storm, a total that would have been more had he not missed a few matches through injury. Season 1975/76 brought him England Under-23 and full international honours, while his goals helped establish United in the top flight once again.

He appeared in the 1976 and 1977 FA Cup finals, scoring the opening goal in the latter 2-1 success over Liverpool. His upraised arm and clenched-fist salute became his trademark after scoring, and he became a big terrace favourite at Old Trafford, as well as England's first-choice centre-forward. He was a hard-working player with pace and a great touch, and he formeda very effective partnership with Jimmy Greenhoff.

However, it was not to be the signing of Joe Jordan from Leeds that was the biggest threat to Pearson's first-team place, but injury, as he missed the first half of 1978/79, only to be injured again during his second comeback game. Although he was offered a new deal at the end of this season, he felt that he would perhaps be better off elsewhere and moved to West Ham United for £220,000 in August 1979.

JOHN HOPE 'JACK' PEDDIE

Country: Scotland
Born: 21 Mar 1877 **Died:** 20 Oct 1928
Debut: 6 Sep 1902 v Gainsborough Trinity
Position: Forward
Appearances: 121 **Goals scored:** 58
Seasons: 1902/03 & 1904/05 – 1906/07
Clubs: Third Lanark, Newcastle United, Manchester United, Plymouth Argyle, Manchester United, Heart of Midlothian

Jack Peddie, a Glasgow-born forward, came into the United side for the opening fixture of 1902/03 and was described as 'both a provider and a goal scorer, possessing a dynamic shot'. Both attributes were first class, but he appeared to be something of an easy-going, laid-back individual, producing both praise and scorn from the supporters throughout his career.

Newcastle fans were dismayed when the man who had scored 80 goals in 137 appearances (including 17 in his first 20 games) was transferred from Tyneside to Manchester United in June 1902, but with goalscoring being his forte, it is rather strange to note that it took him some eight games to get his name on the United scoresheet for the first time – a double against Lincoln City on 8 November. Despite the delayed start, he still finished the club's top goalscorer that season, with 15 to his credit.

At the end of 1902/03, he moved to Plymouth Argyle, who had just turned professional, before he returned to the United ranks in the summer of 1904. Once again, he was a regular in the side and he was to better his previous scoring rate, notching 17 in 32 outings. This included two hat-tricks, against Leicester Fosse and Burton United. Season 1905/06 also saw Peddie play a big part in the club's promotion back into the First Division after two years of finishing in third place. As season 1906/07 got under way, he was once again an ever-present in the side, with half a dozen goals to his credit after 16 appearances. However, shortly after the turn of the year, along with team-mates William Yates and Richard Wombwell, he was transferred to Heart of Midlothian. He was later to emigrate to the USA, where he died in October 1928.

JOHN 'JACK' PEDEN

Country: Ireland
Born: 11 Mar 1865 **Died:** Sep 1944
Debut: 2 Sep 1893 v Burnley
Position: Outside-left
Appearances: 32 **Goals scored:** 8
Seasons: 1893/94
Clubs: Linfield, Newton Heath, Sheffield United, Distillery, Linfield

Jack Peden has the distinction of being the first professional Irish player to represent the club, crossing the Irish Sea to join Newton Heath in February 1893, having played for Linfield, where he won international recognition. It was not until the opening day of season 1893/94 that his name appeared in the Heathens' line-up for the first time, making his debut against Burnley at Bank Street, Clayton, the first league fixture to be played on the ground.

Peden enthralled the Manchester public, who carried him off the pitch after his debut, but the club won only six of the 30 fixtures, which resulted in relegation to the Second Division, after only two years in the top flight. However, despite this, Peden was a success, playing in all but two of the games and scoring seven goals and another in the FA Cup. He left Manchester in the summer of 1894, crossing the Pennines to join First Division Sheffield United for a fee of £30.

DAVID PEGG

Country: England
Born: 20 Sep 1935 **Died:** 6 Feb 1958
Debut: 6 Dec 1952 v Middlesbrough
Position: Winger
Appearances: 150 **Goals scored:** 28
Seasons: 1952/53 – 1957/58
Clubs: Manchester United

The Pennines, much to the dismay of Yorkshire football, provided little in the way of a barrier to prevent Matt Busby from crossing the border in the search for talented young footballers. The wily Scot had already signed Mark Jones and would add Tommy Taylor at a later date, but in September 1950, he snatched a talented forward by the name of David Pegg, who had played for Doncaster and Yorkshire Boys as well as England Schools.

Joining United from school, he was a member of the all-conquering United FA Youth Cup-winning team of 1953, by which time he had already made his first-team debut as a 17-year-old in December 1952, and kept his place for much of the rest of the season. Thereafter, however, he had to wait until 1955/56 before he could claim a regular starting place at outside-left, a season that not only saw United win the title but which also earned him England Under-23 honours.

Although a member of a champion team, the speedy, skilful winger with an eye for goal was unfortunate to be playing at a time when Stanley Matthews and Tom Finney were still around, forming a barrier between the young Yorkshireman and the full England side, hence he won only one full cap on 19 May 1957, just after the Reds had retained their title but missed out on the Double. More would have undoubtedly followed for the 22-year-old had it not been for the events that unfolded on the runway in Munich in February 1958.

ERNEST 'DICK' PEGG

Country: England
Born: Jul 1878 **Died:** 11 Jun 1916
Debut: 6 Sep 1902 v Gainsborough Trinity
Position: Forward

Appearances: 51 **Goals scored:** 20
Seasons: 1902/03 – 1903/04
Clubs: Loughborough Town, Kettering Town, Reading, Preston North End, Manchester United, Fulham, Barnsley

During his half century of appearances, Dick Pegg had the distinction of being the player who scored United's first hat-trick in league football, the club having been renamed ahead of the 1902/03 season, his goals coming in the 3-1 home win over Bradford City on 26 September 1903. Having been signed from Preston North End in June 1902, he played in all but six of United's league fixtures that season, scoring seven goals, with six more in the FA Cup. In his second season, his hat-trick came in his first outing of the campaign and two games later he netted a double, but those goals did little to consolidate his place in the team and he was soon to find himself out of favour, leaving for Fulham during the close season.

JAMES KENNETH 'KEN' PEGG

Country: England
Born: 4 Jan 1926 **Died:** 25 Aug 1999
Debut: 15 Nov 1947 v Derby County
Position: Goalkeeper
Appearances: 2 **Goals scored:** 0
Seasons: 1947/48
Clubs: Manchester United, Torquay United, York City

FRANCIS 'FRANK' PEPPER

Country: England
Born: Jul 1875 **Died:** 1914
Debut: 10 Dec 1898 v Blackpool
Position: Defender
Appearances: 8 **Goals scored:** 0
Seasons: 1898/99
Clubs: Sheffield United, Newton Heath, Barnsley, Doncaster Rovers

GEORGE PERRINS

Country: England
Born: 24 Feb 1873 **Died:** Unknown
Debut: 3 Sep 1892 v Blackburn Rovers
Position: Half-back
Appearances: 102 **Goals scored:** 0
Seasons: 1892/93 – 1895/96
Clubs: Birmingham St George's, Newton Heath, Luton Town, Chatham, Stockport County

One of those who made their debuts in Newton Heath's first game in the Football League, Perrins was a regular in the side for the club's first three seasons in the league. By October 1894, he had made more official appearances for the Heathens than any other player, losing that honour to Fred Erentz in November 1895. He is one of only seven outfield players to have made more than 100 appearances without scoring a goal for the club.

JAMES PETERS

Country: England
Born: Unknown **Died:** Unknown
Debut: 8 Sep 1894 v Burton Wanderers
Position: Outside-left
Appearances: 51 **Goals scored:** 14
Seasons: 1894/95 – 1895/96
Clubs: Heywood Central, Newton Heath, New Brompton, Sheppey United

James Peters was one of four players who scored two goals in the 9-0 victory over Walsall Town Swifts in April 1895. He had been signed from Heywood Central in June 1894 and made an impressive debut against St Bernard's in a friendly, claiming the outside-left spot as his own for the remainder of the season. Twelve months on, however, after playing 11 of the opening 14 fixtures, he lost his place in the side and was transferred to New Brompton (now Gillingham) prior to the start of season 1896/97.

MICHAEL CHRISTOPHER 'MIKE' PHELAN

Country: England
Born: 24 Sep 1962
Debut: 19 Aug 1989 v Arsenal
Position: Defender/Midfield
Appearances: 127 (19) **Goals scored:** 3
Seasons: 1989/90 – 1993/94
Clubs: Burnley, Norwich, Manchester United, West Bromwich Albion

Mike Phelan began his league career in the Third Division with Burnley in 1981, winning a Championship medal in his second season before joining Norwich City in May 1985. A Second Division Championship medal followed and, after joining United for a fee of £750,000 in July 1989, he was to complete the set in 1993 when United lifted the inaugural Premier League trophy.

Phelan was an ever-present in the league in his first campaign at United, was also a member of the side that won the FA Cup that year. He followed it up with the European Cup-Winners' Cup a year later and the Football League Cup in 1992. While never being a player of eye-catching ability, he was a defensive midfield player who always gave 100 per cent, and was the perfect utility player who was perhaps worthy of more than one England cap (against Italy in 1989).

At the end of season 1993/94, Alex Ferguson released him, but was never to forget him, as following two seasons at West Bromwich and a spell as assistant manager at Stockport County, he returned to Old Trafford as a coach, going on to be Ferguson's right-hand man in what were arguably the most successful years in the club's history. He became first-team coach in 2001, before being promoted to assistant manger in September 2008. He left the club soon after Sir Alex retired at the end of the 2012/13 season.

JOHN BARCLAY 'JACK' PICKEN

Country: Scotland
Born: 1880 **Died:** 31 Jul 1952
Debut: 2 Sep 1905 v Bristol City
Position: Forward
Appearances: 122 **Goals scored:** 46

Seasons: 1905/06 – 1910/11
Clubs: Bolton Wanderers, Plymouth Argyle, Manchester United, Burnley, Bristol City

Having spent his early career in his native Ayrshire with Hurlford Thistle and Kilmarnock Shawbank, Picken signed for Bolton Wanderers in August 1899, as a 19-year-old. By the end of his first season south of the border, he had helped Bolton to promotion and played a prominent part in their return to the First Division. A broken leg in November 1902, however, brought a temporary halt to what was certainly becoming a promising career. So Plymouth Argyle took something of a gamble when they signed him at the end of season 1902/03, but he scored 46 goals in 89 appearances for the Pilgrims over a two-year period to justify the faith shown in him.

When signed by United in the summer of 1905, Picken was described as 'a bustler with a deadly shot, who had been playing some rare fine games down south' and was considered by many to be a 'very good capture'. He scored on his debut on the opening day of season 1905/06 and ended the season as the top scorer with 25 goals to his credit as United won promotion to the First Division. The following season at the higher level, his goals dried up, with only four in 26 league games. As United strode to the league title in 1908, he managed only eight appearances, scoring just one goal, as Sandy Turnbull kept him out of the team. As a reward, the squad was taken on a tour of Europe that summer, only for Picken to be hit by stones thrown by supporters of Hungarian side Ferencvaros, following United's 7-0 victory.

Having missed out on a title medal in 1907/08 and the entire FA Cup run in 1909, he was delighted to make amends for this in 1911, as United once again won the Championship, with Picken contributing four goals in his 14 outings. His contribution to the United cause was not forgotten, as the game against Newcastle United on 15 October 1910 was set aside as a benefit match for both Picken and Dick Holden. Each man was guaranteed £300, and the attendance of over 50,000, paying gate receipts of £2,320, ensured that both players obtained that sum. In December 1911, he joined Burnley, later moving to Bristol City in October 1913, where he saw out his professional playing career.

KEVIN WILLIAM PILKINGTON

Country: England
Born: 8 Mar 1974
Debut: 19 Nov 1994 v Crystal Palace
Position: Goalkeeper
Appearances: 6 (2) **Goals scored:** 0
Seasons: 1994/95 – 1997/98
Clubs: Manchester United, Rochdale (loan), Rotherham United (loan), Celtic (loan), Port Vale, Aberystwyth Town, Wigan Athletic, Mansfield Town, Notts County, Luton Town, Mansfield Town (loan), Notts County

One of the famous 'Class of '92', Pilkington found his path to the first team blocked by Peter Schmeichel, and eventually moved on. Ironically, much later in his career, while at Notts County, he was to lose his place to Schmeichel's son Kasper. But, along with former team-mates David Beckham, Ryan Giggs and Paul Scholes, he still made a first-class appearance in 2012/13, coming on as a substitute for Notts County, where he is now the goalkeeping coach.

MICHAEL JOHN PINNER

Country: England
Born: 16 Feb 1934
Debut: 4 Feb 1961 v Aston Villa
Position: Goalkeeper
Appearances: 4 **Goals scored:** 0
Seasons: 1960/61
Clubs: Aston Villa, Sheffield Wednesday, Queens Park Rangers, Manchester United, Chelsea, Swansea Town, Leyton Orient, Lisburn Distillery

An amateur keeper who attended Cambridge University, was a qualified solicitor and played for Great Britain in the 1960 Olympics, Pinner helped out United when both Harry Gregg and Dave Gaskell were injured.

GERARD PIQUÉ BERNABEU

Country: Spain
Born: 2 Feb 1987
Debut: 26 Oct 2004 v Crewe Alexandra

Position: Defender
Appearances: 14 (9) **Goals scored:** 2
Seasons: 2004/05 – 2007/08
Clubs: Manchester United, Real Zaragoza (loan), Barcelona

Undoubtedly, Gerard Piqué is the individual who has achieved more than any other after leaving Manchester United. Barcelona-born Piqué came to Manchester in 2004, having refused a professional contract with the Catalan club and, following promising displays in the reserve side, he made his first-team debut in October 2004 against Crewe Alexandra in the League Cup.

Needing to beef out a little before he could be considered for a regular first-team place, he was loaned out to Real Zaragoza in August 2006. Returning to United the following season, despite developing physically, he still could not command a regular place in the side, with Rio Ferdinand and Nemanja Vidić the first-choice pairing.

So on 27 May 2008 he returned to Barcelona, signing a four-year deal, with United receiving £5 million. With the Spanish giants, he has won La Liga four times, the Champions League twice, as well as two Super Cups and two Club World Cups, while with the national side he claimed both World Cup in 2010 and the European Championship in 2012 – a haul that no other former United player could boast. As if that were not enough, he recently had a son with his girlfriend, the singer Shakira.

KAREL POBORSKY

Country: Czech Republic
Born: 30 Mar 1972
Debut: 11 Aug 1996 v Newcastle United
Position: Winger
Appearances: 28 (20) **Goals scored:** 6
Seasons: 1996/97 – 1997/98
Clubs: České Budějovice, Viktoria Zizkov, Slavia Prague, Manchester United, Benfica, Lazio, Sparta Prague, České Budějovice

One of the success stories of Euro 96, scoring an excellent goal for the Czech Republic against Portugal in the quarter-finals, Poborsky had done enough to make Alex Ferguson fork out £3.5 million to bring him to Old Trafford prior to the start of the 1996/97 season. Looking more like a diminutive rock star than a Premier League footballer, he struggled to overcome the language difficulties and this seemed to impact on him, as his United career stuttered along with only brief glimmers of his best form. With David Beckham's rapid emergence at the start of the season, following his wonder goal from the halfway line, it was perhaps always going to be difficult for him.

Having won the Premier League title in his first season at the club, in December 1997 he was sold to Benfica for around £2 million and away from the goldfish bowl of Old Trafford, he rekindled his career, before moving to Italian side Lazio and then back to his home country where he played for Sparta Prague and České Budějovice. He eventually became the Czech Republic's most-capped player with 118 appearances.

PAUL LABILE POGBA

Country: France
Born: 15 March 1993
Debut: 20 Sep 2011 v Leeds United
Position: Midfield
Appearances: 0 (7) **Goals scored:** 0
Seasons: 2009/10 – 2011/12
Clubs: Le Havre, Manchester United, Juventus

The promising young midfielder left United at the start of the 2012/13 season, and made an instant impact at Juventus, winning the Serie A title in his first year at the club.

WILLIAM 'BILLY' PORTER

Country: England
Born: Jul 1905 **Died:** 28 Apr 1946
Debut: 19 Jan 1935 v Barnsley
Position: Full-back
Appearances: 65 **Goals scored:** 0
Seasons: 1934/35 – 1937/38
Clubs: Oldham Athletic, Manchester United, Hyde United

After nine years and some 274 appearances at Boundary Park, Oldham, Billy Porter made the relatively short journey to Old Trafford in January 1935, taking over the left-back position from Tom Jones. During the Second Division Championship-winning season of 1935/36, he was an ever-present in the side, but he was injured in the opening fixture of the following season and struggled to get back into the team, making only four appearances during the next two seasons. During the wartime seasons he returned to the team as captain, often playing at centre-half, before moving into non-league football with Hyde United in 1944.

RODRIGO POSSEBON

Country: Brazil/Italy
Born: 13 Feb 1989
Debut: 17 Aug 2008 v Newcastle United
Position: Midfield
Appearances: 3 (5) **Goals scored:** 0
Seasons: 2008/09
Clubs: Internacional, Manchester United, Sporting Braga (loan), Santos, Vicenza, Criciuma, Mirassol

ARTHUR POTTS

Country: England
Born: 26 May 1888 **Died:** Jan 1981
Debut: 26 Dec 1913 v Everton
Position: Forward
Appearances: 29 **Goals scored:** 5
Seasons: 1913/14 – 1919/20
Clubs: Willenhall Swifts, Manchester United, Wolverhampton Wanderers, Walsall

Signed from Willenhall Swifts in May 1913, inside-forward Arthur Potts did not enjoy something of an extended run in the United side until December 1914, when he scored four goals in 16 appearances, but his career was to be interrupted by the First World War, leaving him with 29 appearances to his name.

JOHN 'JACK' POWELL

Country: Wales
Born: 25 Mar 1860 **Died:** 16 Mar 1947
Debut: 30 Oct 1886 v Fleetwood Rangers
Position: Full-back
Appearances: 4 **Goals scored:** 0
Seasons: 1886/87 – 1890/91
Clubs: Druids, Bolton Wanderers, Newton Heath

Along with Tom Burke, Jack Powell was the first player for Newton Heath to win an international cap while at the club, playing for Wales on 26 February 1887, a few months after the Heathens' first official fixture.

NICHOLAS EDWARD 'NICK' POWELL

Country: England
Born: 23 March 1994
Debut: 15 Sep 2012 v Wigan Athletic
Position: Midfield
Appearances: 2 (4) **Goals scored:** 1
Seasons: 2012/13 – present
Clubs: Crewe Alexandra, Manchester United, Wigan Athletic (loan)

Nick Powell is a product of the famed Crewe academy and helped his home-town side to League One via the play-offs, scoring in the Wembley final a few weeks before joining United in July 2012 for a fee reported to be around £6 million, in a deal agreed prior to Gresty Road side's promotion to League One. The England Under-21 international is clearly one for the future, although he was given an early taste of life at the top on the club's pre-season tour, before beginning his league career with a bang, scoring a notable goal on his debut against Wigan at Old Trafford in September 2012. Restricted mainly to reserve-team outings, it was nonetheless an impressive first campaign, with much more expected in the years ahead.

JOHN H. PRENTICE

Country: Scotland
Born: 19 Oct 1898 **Died:** 28 Jun 1966
Debut: 2 Apr 1920 v Bradford Park Avenue
Position: Winger
Appearances: 1 **Goals scored:** 0
Seasons: 1919/20
Clubs: Manchester United, Swansea Town, Tranmere Rovers

STEPHEN PRESTON

Country: England
Born: 1879 **Died:** Unknown
Debut: 7 Sep 1901 v Gainsborough Trinity
Position: Forward
Appearances: 34 **Goals scored:** 14
Seasons: 1901/02 – 1902/03
Clubs: Newton Heath, Manchester United, Stockport County

Gorton-born Stephen Preston was rather unusually spotted taking part in nothing more than a kick-about and impressed the watching Newton Heath director so much that he was immediately signed, taking his place at centre-forward in the opening game of 1901/02 and proceeding to score 11 goals in 30 appearances. He was, however, to be something of a one-season wonder, as he was to make only a further four appearances for the club, before moving to Stockport County in February 1903. Good enough for Newton Heath, but not good enough for Manchester United!

ALBERT J. PRINCE

Country: England
Born: 1895 **Died:** Unknown
Debut: 27 Feb 1915 v Everton
Position: Forward
Appearances: 1 **Goals scored:** 0
Seasons: 1914/15
Clubs: Manchester United, Stafford Rangers

D. PRINCE

Country: Unknown
Born: Unknown **Died:** Unknown
Debut: 4 Nov 1893 v Darwen
Position: Winger
Appearances: 2 **Goals scored:** 0
Seasons: 1893/94
Clubs: Newton Heath

WILLIAM PRUNIER

Country: France
Born: 14 Aug 1967
Debut: 30 Dec 1995 v Queens Park Rangers
Position: Defender
Appearances: 2 **Goals scored:** 0
Seasons: 1995/96
Clubs: Auxerre, Marseilles, Bordeaux, Manchester United, FC Copenhagen, Montpellier, Napoli, Heart of Midlothian, KV Kortrijk, Toulouse, Al-Siliya

DANIEL ADAM 'DANNY' PUGH

Country: England
Born: 19 Oct 1982
Debut: 18 Sep 2002 v Maccabi Haifa
Position: Midfield
Appearances: 3 (4) **Goals scored:** 0
Seasons: 2002/03 – 2003/04
Clubs: Manchester United, Leeds United, Preston North End, Stoke City, Preston North End (loan), Leeds United, Sheffield Wednesday (loan)

JAMES PUGH

Country: England
Born: Jul 1891 **Died:** Unknown
Debut: 29 Apr 1922 v Cardiff City
Position: Full-back
Appearances: 2 **Goals scored:** 0

Seasons: 1921/22 – 1922/23
Clubs: Brighton & Hove Albion, Hereford United, Bridgend Town, Abertillery, Manchester United, Wrexham

WILLIAM JOHN JOSEPH 'JACK' QUINN

Country: Scotland
Born: 1890 **Died:** Unknown
Debut: 3 Apr 1909 v Sheffield Wednesday
Position: Forward
Appearances: 2 **Goals scored:** 0
Seasons: 1908/09 – 1909/10
Clubs: Higher Broughton, Cheetham Hill, Manchester City, Manchester United, Nelson, Chorley, Eccles Borough, Grimsby Town, Clyde, Ayr United

ALBERT QUIXALL

Country: England
Born: 9 Aug 1933
Debut: 20 Sep 1958 v Tottenham Hotspur
Position: Inside-forward
Appearances: 184 **Goals scored:** 56
Seasons: 1958/59 – 1963/64
Clubs: Sheffield Wednesday, Manchester United, Oldham Athletic, Stockport County, Altrincham, Radcliffe Borough

Albert Quixall's footballing life began on the groundstaff of Sheffield Wednesday, with the former England Schoolboy making his debut for the Owls as a 17-year-old in 1951. Within three years, following a dazzling display in an inter-league match, he was making his full England debut against Wales, and in 1955/56 he played a leading role in Wednesday's Second Division title triumph.

His ball-playing skills won him many admirers and in September 1958, seven months after he had captained Sheffield Wednesday against United at Old Trafford in that memorable first game after Munich, Matt Busby paid what was then a record fee of £45,000 for his signature. Following his move across the Pennines, he took a little while to settle (perhaps unsurprisingly in that post-Munich season), despite a favourable debut against Tottenham, but turned in a series of consistent performances over the next few years, playing his part in the 1963 FA Cup win. An intelligent, creative inside-forward, he could sometimes struggle to get into games, and he found himself out of favour in 1963/64 and in the close season he was transferred to Third Division Oldham Athletic for £7,000.

PAUL STEPHEN RACHUBKA

Country: England
Born: 21 May 1981
Debut: 11 Jan 2000 v South Melbourne
Position: Goalkeeper
Appearances: 1 (2) **Goals scored:** 0
Seasons: 1999/2000 – 2000/01
Clubs: Manchester United, Royal Antwerp (loan), Oldham Athletic (loan), Charlton Athletic, Burnley (loan), Huddersfield Town (loan), Milton Keynes Dons (loan), Northampton Town (loan), Huddersfield Town, Peterborough United (loan), Blackpool, Leeds United, Tranmere Rovers (loan), Leyton Orient (loan), Accrington Stanley (loan)

GEORGE RADCLIFFE

Country: England
Born: Unknown **Died:** Unknown
Debut: 12 Apr 1899 v Luton Town

Position: Winger
Appearances: 1 **Goals scored:** 0
Seasons: 1898/99
Clubs: Newton Heath

CHARLES 'CHARLIE' RADFORD

Country: England
Born: 19 Mar 1900 **Died:** 14 Jul 1924
Debut: 7 May 1921 v Derby County
Position: Full-back
Appearances: 96 **Goals scored:** 1
Seasons: 1920/21 – 1923/24
Clubs: Walsall, Manchester United

A hard-tackling, no-nonsense, former England Schoolboy international, Charlie Radford was signed by John Robson from Walsall in May 1920. He spent his first year in the United second string before making his debut in the final game of season 1920/21, but with the following season only a month old, he found himself in the first-team picture, making 26 starts, going on to become the first-choice No.2. In March 1924, he missed the final eight games of the season due to a six-week suspension following a sending off against Nelson, but he was never to play football again, as he was tragically killed in a motorbike accident in Wolverhampton in July 1924.

ROBERT D. RAMSAY

Country: England
Born: Oct 1864 **Died:** Unknown
Debut: 4 Oct 1890 v Higher Walton
Position: Defender
Appearances: 1 **Goals scored:** 0
Seasons: 1890/91
Clubs: Burslem Port Vale, Stoke City, Newton Heath, West Manchester, Northwich Victoria

CHARLES WILLIAM 'CHARLIE' RAMSDEN

Country: England
Born: 11 Jun 1904 **Died:** 16 Feb 1975
Debut: 24 Sep 1927 v Tottenham Hotspur
Position: Winger
Appearances: 16 **Goals scored:** 3
Seasons: 1927/28 – 1930/31
Clubs: Rotherham United, Manchester United, Stockport County (loan), Manchester North End, Witton Albion

A Herbert Bamlett signing from Rotherham United in May 1927, the outside-right had managed 16 goals in 50 appearances for the Yorkshire side, but was to struggle in his attempts to secure a regular place in the United starting line-up. Making his debut against Tottenham in September 1927, he appeared in the following fixture, but failed to feature again that season, and was allowed to join Stockport County on loan. Having scored nine goals in 21 appearances with Stockport, he returned to United for season 1928/29, but was to play only a further 14 games, scoring twice, over the course of the next two seasons. Surprisingly, he did not leave Old Trafford until August 1932, when he moved into non-league football.

RATTIGAN

Country: England
Born: Apr 1868 **Died:** Unknown
Debut: 25 Oct 1890 v Bootle Reserves
Position: Midfield
Appearances: 1 **Goals scored:** 0
Seasons: 1890/91
Clubs: Newton Heath

WILLIAM EDWARD 'BILLY' RAWLINGS

Country: England
Born: 3 Jan 1896 **Died:** 25 Sep 1972
Debut: 14 Mar 1928 v Everton
Position: Forward
Appearances: 36 **Goals scored:** 19

Seasons: 1927/28 – 1929/30
Clubs: Southampton, Manchester United, Port Vale, New Milton, Newport (Isle of Wight)

Bill Rawlings joined United from Southampton in March 1928, where he had earned a name for himself with an impressive goalscoring record of 156 in 294 appearances, which was enough to win him England international honours. Costing United around £4,000, Rawlings continued his goalscoring exploits in the north-west, with the only goal of the match on his debut against Everton in March 1928 and, two games later, he scored a hat-trick against Burnley. His ten goals in 12 appearances helped United avoid being relegated to the Second Division.

Despite his goalscoring ability, he failed to gain a regular place in the team, but was always ready for action, as 14 September 1929 was to prove. That Friday night he received a phone call telling him that he was playing at Middlesbrough the following afternoon. Arriving at the ground 90 minutes prior to kick off, he went out and scored another hat-trick. Despite this, he was to make only three further appearances for United before moving to Port Vale.

THOMAS HERBERT 'BERT' READ

Country: England
Born: Unknown **Died:** Unknown
Debut: 6 Sep 1902 v Gainsborough Trinity
Position: Full-back
Appearances: 42 **Goals scored:** 0
Seasons: 1902/03 – 1903/04
Clubs: Stretford, Manchester City, Manchester United

A member of Manchester City's Second Division Championship-winning side of 1898/99, Bert Read joined the fledgling Manchester United in August 1902, following a serious injury which at one point looked as though it might end his playing career.

Doctors gave him a clean bill of health and he featured in 27 of United's 34 Second Division fixtures. However, the following season saw him manage only eight league outings, due to his knee injury flaring up once again, and he was forced to retire at the end of that 1903/04 campaign.

WILLIAM 'BILLY' REDMAN

Country: England
Born: 29 Jan 1928 **Died:** Dec 1994
Debut: 7 Oct 1950 v Sheffield Wednesday
Position: Full-back
Appearances: 38 **Goals scored:** 0
Seasons: 1950/51 – 1953/54
Clubs: Manchester United, Bury, Buxton

Signed as a 14-year-old, Billy Redman was a capable full-back, comfortable on either flank, fast on the recovery and a difficult player to beat. He was selected for his debut in 1946, against Portsmouth, but the fixture was postponed and it wasn't until four years later that he eventually made that initial appearance. He was unfortunate to find the likes of John Aston in front of him in the pecking order, but he enjoyed a good run in the side during the latter half of 1950/51, when Aston was moved to centre-forward, and then in the opening four months of the following season. After two consecutive defeats against Chelsea and Portsmouth, he was dropped in favour of Roger Byrne, a move that basically ended his United career. He joined Bury in June 1954.

HUBERT REDWOOD

Country: England
Born: Jul 1913 **Died:** 28 Sep 1943
Debut: 21 Dec 1935 v Tottenham Hotspur
Position: Full-back
Appearances: 93 **Goals scored:** 4
Seasons: 1935/36 – 1938/39
Clubs: New Brighton, Manchester United

Born in the rugby league stronghold of St Helens, Hubert Redwood played both the round- and the oval-ball game at school. He joined United as an amateur in May 1933, but did not make his league debut until September 1935 against Tottenham Hotspur, which turned out to be his only appearance that season. On the opening day of the following season, John Griffiths was unable to play, so Redwood claimed the No.2 shirt and, except for a gap of six games in October/November, he played in 21 of the opening 27 fixtures. It wasn't until November 1937 that he reappeared in the side, making the right-back position his own up until the outbreak of war in 1939. Although tipped for international recognition, it never materialised and his career was to come to an end in 1943 when, having contracted tuberculosis while serving in the army, he died at the age of only 30.

THOMAS JOSEPH 'TOMMY' REID

Country: Scotland
Born: 15 Aug 1905 **Died:** Jul 1972
Debut: 2 Feb 1929 v West Ham United
Position: Forward
Appearances: 101 **Goals scored:** 67
Seasons: 1928/29 – 1932/33
Clubs: Blantyre Victoria, Clydebank, Liverpool, Manchester United, Oldham Athletic, Barrow, Rhyl

Motherwell-born Tommy Reid was yet another product of the Scottish junior game, playing for Blantyre Victoria before signing for Clydebank in the close season of 1925. Soon afterwards, he was a Liverpool player following a £1,000 transfer. The robust leader of the attack made a big impression at Anfield, and it came as a surprise to many that Manchester United managed to prise him from the Merseysiders' grasp in February 1929.

At Old Trafford, he made an immediate impact, scoring on his debut, which was followed two games later with a double against his former employers. The encouraging start brought 14 goals from 17 games, but his second season was rather indifferent. In the relegation campaign of 1930/31, he was a rare highlight, ending up as the top scorer with 17 league goals, ten more than his nearest rival. He continued to score at a rate of two every three games (only Tommy Taylor and Ruud van Nistelrooy have been more prolific), before United allowed him to join near neighbours Oldham Athletic, initially on loan, in March 1933. Due to the Latics' financial difficulties in those economically tough times, it was their supporters' club that paid the £400 transfer fee. It was to be money well spent, as the new signing was to score ten goals in the final 13 games of that season.

CLATWORTHY 'CHARLIE' RENNOX

Country: Scotland
Born: 25 Feb 1897 **Died:** 1967
Debut: 14 Mar 1925 v Portsmouth
Position: Forward
Appearances: 68 **Goals scored:** 25
Seasons: 1924/25 – 1926/27
Clubs: Dykehead, Wishaw, Clapton Orient, Manchester United, Grimsby Town

Signed in March 1925 in an effort to make the final push for promotion more positive, Charlie Rennox made his debut against Portsmouth on 14 March, but was to play in only four of the remaining 11 fixtures. Born in Shotts, Lanarkshire, he had begun his career with two non-league Scottish sides, Dykehead and Wishaw. In June 1921, he headed for the bright lights of London to join Clapton Orient, where he played for three years before his move to United.

The name of Rennox was missing from the first three line-ups of the 1925/26 season, but on 7 September, he was re-introduced into the side, at inside-left, for the match at Villa Park, scoring in the 2-2 draw. From then on, he only missed an odd game through injury, finishing the season as leading scorer in the league, with 17 goals from his 34 appearances, including a hat-trick against Burnley on 26 September. The next season was less fruitful, and so in the summer of 1927, he left Old Trafford for Grimsby Town, but failed to make a first-team appearance for them before drifting into non-league football.

RICARDO LOPEZ FELIPE

Country: Spain
Born: 30 Dec 1971
Debut: 18 Sep 2002 v Maccabi Haifa
Position: Goalkeeper
Appearances: 3 (2) **Goals scored:** 0
Seasons: 2002/03
Clubs: Atlético Madrid, Valladolid, Manchester United, Racing Santander (loan), Osasuna

CHARLES HENRY 'CHARLIE' RICHARDS

Country: England
Born: Nov 1874 **Died:** Unknown
Debut: 6 Sep 1902 v Gainsborough Trinity
Position: Forward
Appearances: 11 **Goals scored:** 2
Seasons: 1902/03
Clubs: Gresley Rovers, Newstead Byron, Notts County, Nottingham Forest, Grimsby Town, Leicester Fosse, Manchester United, Doncaster Rovers

Despite playing only 11 games for Manchester United after joining the club in August 1902, Charlie Richards had the distinction of scoring the only goal in the game that gave the club their first victory under that name. Richards had previously represented both the Nottingham clubs, County and Forest, earning an FA Cup winner's medal with the latter in 1898. While at Grimsby Town, won a Second Division Championship medal and one England cap. His stay at United was brief, and he moved to Doncaster Rovers in March 1903.

WILLIAM 'BILLY' RICHARDS

Country: England
Born: 6 Oct 1874 **Died:** 12 Feb 1926
Debut: 21 Dec 1901 v Port Vale
Position: Forward
Appearances: 9 **Goals scored:** 1
Seasons: 1901/02
Clubs: West Bromwich Albion, Newton Heath, Stourbridge

KIERAN EDWARD RICHARDSON

Country: England
Born: 21 Oct 1984
Debut: 23 Oct 2002 v Olympiakos
Position: Winger/Midfield
Appearances: 44 (37) **Goals scored:** 11
Seasons: 2002/03 – 2006/07
Clubs: Manchester United, West Bromwich Albion (loan), Sunderland, Fulham

A self-confident, London-born wide player, Kieran Richardson certainly had all the attributes, and they were to win him international recognition, as he scored twice on his debut against the USA. Had it been someone other than Ryan Giggs who stood in his way, who knows what he might have achieved. Unfortunately, despite winning a Premier League medal in 2007 and a League Cup winner's medal in 2006 during his stay at Old Trafford, his best performances came while out on loan at West Bromwich Albion in 2004/05. There, under former United captain Bryan Robson, he played mostly in the centre of midfield and helped them to stay up in the top division against all the odds. During the summer of 2007, seeking more regular first-team action, he moved to Sunderland, then under the management of another former United captain, Roy Keane.

LANCELOT HOLLIDAY 'LANCE' RICHARDSON

Country: England
Born: Apr 1899 **Died:** 22 Feb 1958
Debut: 1 May 1926 v West Bromwich Albion
Position: Goalkeeper
Appearances: 42 **Goals scored:** 0
Seasons: 1925/26 – 1928/29
Clubs: Shildon Athletic, South Shields, Manchester United, Reading

Reputed to be a somewhat eccentric goalkeeper, Lance Richardson was bought from South Shields in April 1926 for £1,000 as a back-up for Alf Steward. It wasn't until September 1927 that he managed something of an extended run in the side, but, following 42 appearances over three years, he was transfer listed at the end of season 1928/29 and left to join Reading.

WILLIAM 'BILL' RIDDING

Country: England
Born: 4 Apr 1911 **Died:** 29 Sep 1981
Debut: 25 Dec 1931 v Wolverhampton Wanderers
Position: Forward
Appearances: 44 **Goals scored:** 14
Seasons: 1931/32 – 1933/34
Clubs: Tranmere Rovers, Manchester City, Manchester United, Northampton Town, Tranmere Rovers, Oldham Athletic

Bill Ridding had a perfect Christmas present in 1931, making his United debut at Old Trafford and helping the side to a 3-2 win over promotion-chasing Wolves. But it was during his second season at the club that he had his biggest impact, finishing as the leading scorer with 11 goals in 23 league games. Soon after that, injury brought his career to a premature end. However, after the war, he was to cross United's path again, as he became the manager of Bolton Wanderers between 1950 and 1968. In 1958, he was in charge when the Trotters beat United in the FA Cup final that season, in the aftermath of the Munich disaster.

JOSEPH ARTHUR 'JOE' RIDGWAY

Country: England
Born: 25 Apr 1873 **Died:** Unknown
Debut: 11 Jan 1896 v Rotherham United
Position: Goalkeeper
Appearances: 17 **Goals scored:** 0
Seasons: 1895/96 – 1897/98
Clubs: West Manchester, Newton Heath, Rochdale Town

A local-born goalkeeper Joe Ridgway's Newton Heath career amounted to only 17 appearances over six years. When his opportunity in the first team did arise, he would manage only a handful of games before being knocked backed by injury. He was something of a crowd pleaser, as he could often be seen venturing up-field in the hope that he could get on the end of a loose ball and either score or contribute to a goal.

JOHN JAMES 'JIMMY' RIMMER

Country: England
Born: 10 Feb 1948
Debut: 15 Apr 1968 v Fulham
Position: Goalkeeper
Appearances: 45 (1) **Goals scored:** 0
Seasons: 1967/68 – 1972/73
Clubs: Manchester United, Swansea City (loan), Arsenal, Aston Villa, Swansea City

Jimmy Rimmer was signed by United upon leaving school and graduated through the junior teams, including the FA Youth Cup-winning side of 1964, until he became a regular in the Central League side and understudy to Alex Stepney. Due to the form of Stepney, he had to wait until the tail end of the 1967/68 season for his first-team debut, and picked up a European Cup winner's medal as a reserve that year. He did, however, play in both legs of the 1969 European Cup semi-final against AC Milan. Season 1970/71 saw him claim the No.1 jersey, but it was only for a limited period, as Stepney soon reclaimed it.

A loan spell at Swansea in October 1973, under the guidance of former United keeper Harry Gregg, helped his career tremendously and he returned to United in February 1974. He was only there a matter of weeks before joining Arsenal for £40,000, replacing Bob Wilson, a move that brought not just regular first-team football but also an England cap. Three years at Highbury was followed by a move to Aston Villa, where he won further honours in the form of the First Division title in 1981, the European Cup in 1982 (he had to go off injured early on, thus earning two medals with a combined total of nine minutes of game time) and the 1982 Super Cup.

ANDREW TIMOTHY 'ANDY' RITCHIE

Country: England
Born: 28 Nov 1960
Debut: 26 Dec 1977 v Everton
Position: Forward
Appearances: 32 (10) **Goals scored:** 13
Seasons: 1977/78 – 1980/81
Clubs: Manchester United, Brighton & Hove Albion, Leeds United, Oldham Athletic, Scarborough, Oldham Athletic

Andy Ritchie was a local lad who played very little football until leaving Mosley Hall School, where he had to endure rugby as the main sport, but he did play enough to gain England Schoolboy honours. A regular scorer in the United junior and reserve sides, he made his debut on Boxing Day 1977, retaining his place for the following three games. An injury to Joe Jordan in December 1978 saw him back in the first-team spotlight against Derby County, scoring two in a 3-1 win, and he went on to score ten goals in 17 games, including a hat-trick against

Leeds. But those three goals stood for very little, as he found himself dropped for the following match in place of a fit-again Jordan.

Although relegated back to the reserve team, he could always be relied upon when required and he hit a second first-team hat-trick in April 1980 against Tottenham in what was only his sixth outing of the season. With the arrival of Gary Birtles in October 1980, he was sold to Brighton for £500,000 to fund part of the deal, with many fans disappointed to see the promising local lad moved on while still in his teens. He was soon back in the north with Leeds United, but it was as an Oldham Athletic player he is perhaps best remembered, where he was to achieve legendary status for his goalscoring exploits.

JOHN E. ROACH

Country: England
Born: Unknown **Died:** Unknown
Debut: 5 Jan 1946 v Accrington Stanley
Position: Full-back
Appearances: 2 **Goals scored:** 0
Seasons: 1945/46
Clubs: Manchester United

DAVID MIDDLETON ROBBIE

Country: Scotland
Born: 6 Oct 1899 **Died:** 4 Dec 1978
Debut: 28 Sep 1935 v Southampton
Position: Winger
Appearances: 1 **Goals scored:** 0
Seasons: 1935/36
Clubs: Renton, Bury, Plymouth Argyle, Manchester United, Margate, Luton Town, Plymouth Argyle

CHARLES 'CHARLIE' ROBERTS

Country: England
Born: 6 Apr 1883 **Died:** 7 Aug 1939
Debut: 23 Apr 1904 v Burton United
Position: Half-back

Appearances: 302 **Goals scored:** 23
Seasons: 1903/04 – 1912/13
Clubs: Bishop Auckland, Grimsby Town, Manchester United, Oldham Athletic

Charlie Roberts was one of the legendary figures of Manchester United's history and the captain who guided them to their first-ever honour. Having begun his career in north-east junior circles, Darlington-born Roberts was signed by Ernest Mangnall for £400 in April 1904 after less than a season on the books of Grimsby Town, with countless other clubs hot on the trail of the 20-year-old, including local rivals Manchester City. The manager saw him as the perfect bedrock for the team, and someone he could build a side around, as he planned (with new chairman and benefactor John Henry Davies) to make United one of the best sides in the game.

He was considered by many as being 'without a superior as a centre-half-back', with the *Cricket and Football Field* adding that 'he was one of the best centre-halves we have yet had. He tackles, places and controls the ball with exceptional ability'. He was to feature in two of the last three fixtures of 1903/04, making the centre-half slot his own from the start of the following campaign as well as taking over the captaincy.

His performances won him a place in the North v South international trial, earning him the first of three England caps, against Ireland, becoming the first player to win such an honour at the club. He was also to play for the Football League against the Scottish League, going on to win eight caps at this level. Season 1905/06 saw him guide the club to the runners-up spot in the Second Division and, two seasons later, he became the first Manchester United captain to lift the First Division trophy. He followed it up with taking the inaugural Charity Shield, and a year later United tasted FA Cup success, beating Bristol City 1-0 in the final at Crystal Palace. In 1911, United were champions again.

Despite his success with United, forging a superb half-back partnership with Dick Duckworth and Alec Bell, it was perhaps his strong involvement with the fledgling Professional Footballers' Association, becoming chairman, that prevented him from winning more than his trio of England caps. The union was set up in December 1907, and had to battle with the FA and the Football League for recognition. During the summer of 1909, any player who was still a part of the union was threatened with suspension, but the United players stayed strong, posing for a famous photograph that billed them as 'The Outcasts'.

After Old Trafford had been built during 1909/10, the club found itself increasingly heavily in debt, as even the backing from Davies struggled to cope with the costs of the new stadium. Mangnall was forced to sell some of his best players, and in August 1913 Roberts was transferred to Oldham Athletic for a record fee of £1,500.

ROBERT HENRY ANWYL ROBERTS

Country: England
Born: 1892 **Died:** Unknown
Debut: 27 Dec 1913 v Sheffield Wednesday
Position: Full-back
Appearances: 2 **Goals scored:** 0
Seasons: 1913/14
Clubs: Altrincham, Manchester United

W. A. 'BOGIE' ROBERTS

Country: Unknown
Born: Unknown **Died:** Unknown
Debut: 18 Feb 1899 v Loughborough Town
Position: Winger
Appearances: 10 **Goals scored:** 2
Seasons: 1898/99 – 1899/1900
Clubs: Newton Heath

ALEXANDER ROBERTSON

Country: Scotland
Born: Unknown **Died:** Unknown
Debut: 5 Sep 1903 v Bristol City
Position: Outside-left
Appearances: 34 **Goals scored:** 10
Seasons: 1903/04 – 1904/05
Clubs: Hibernian, Fair City Athletic (loan), Manchester United

Outside-left Alexander Robertson was signed from Hibernian, where he had won both Scottish Cup and Scottish League honours in 1901/02 and 1902/03 respectively. Although described as a 'splendid class man, for whom a place would have to be found', his United first-team career was limited to only 28 league appearances, along with six cup ties. He had a slightly overweight appearance, which would often catch out opponents, as he could be quite fleet of foot when the occasion demanded and he also made considerable contributions to the workrate of the team. After a couple of appearances in 1904/05 he was out of the side for good, despite remaining at the club until 1907, seemingly content to play in the reserve XI, whom he captained during 1905/06.

ALEXANDER 'SANDY' ROBERTSON

Country: Scotland
Born: 1878 **Died:** Unknown
Debut: 5 Sep 1903 v Bristol City
Position: Half-back
Appearances: 35 **Goals scored:** 1
Seasons: 1903/04 – 1905/06
Clubs: Dundee, Middlesbrough, Manchester United, Bradford Park Avenue

The Manchester United career of Alex 'Sandy' Robertson was almost over before it began. In the opening month of 1903/04, the United players were taken to Lytham St Anne's for some special training, and Robertson (along with his namesake Tom, a former team-mate at Dundee) shocked officials and team-mates alike by turning up at their hotel the worse for wear. Both players were immediately dismissed for serious misconduct, but Sandy was fortunate enough to be reinstated and was able to regain his first-team place, going on to make 26 appearances during that particular campaign.

He had begun his career in his home-town of Dundee, playing for both Dundee Violet and Dundee, before joining Middlesbrough in May 1900, helping them to the runners-up spot in Division Two and promotion to the top league in 1902. A year later, he joined United, making 24 league appearances that first campaign, but thereafter he was rarely selected. However, like his aforementioned namesake, he was content to remain at the club until May 1907 when he moved to Bradford Park Avenue.

THOMAS 'TOM' ROBERTSON

Country: Scotland
Born: 1875 **Died:** Unknown
Debut: 5 Sep 1903 v Bristol City
Position: Forward
Appearances: 3 **Goals scored:** 0
Seasons: 1903/04
Clubs: Motherwell, Fauldhouse, Heart of Midlothian, Liverpool, Heart of Midlothian, Dundee, Manchester United, Bathgate

WILLIAM S. ROBERTSON

Country: Scotland
Born: 20 Apr 1907 **Died:** 1980
Debut: 17 Mar 1934 v Fulham
Position: Half-back
Appearances: 50 **Goals scored:** 1
Seasons: 1933/34 – 1935/36
Clubs: Third Lanark, Ayr United, Stoke City, Manchester United, Reading

William Robertson was one of the few Scots who did not come direct from a Scottish League club, arriving at Old Trafford from Stoke City, having previously been with Third Lanark and Ayr United, moving to the Potteries in October 1929. With Stoke City, the Falkirk-born wing-half added to his collection of honours, with a Second Division Championship medal in 1932/33, playing in all but three of their fixtures.

His solid tackling played a big part in the nail-biting final few games of United's relegation-threatened 1933/34 season and he retained his place in the line-up the following campaign, missing only the odd game through injury. In 1935/36 he was dropped to the reserves, as James Brown took over the right-half berth and, with only one appearance by December, he decided his best option was a move to another club, eventually joining Reading in the southern section of the Third Division.

MARK GORDON ROBINS

Country: England
Born: 22 Dec 1969
Debut: 12 Oct 1988 v Rotherham United

Position: Forward
Appearances: 27 (43) **Goals scored:** 17
Seasons: 1988/89 – 1991/92
Clubs: Manchester United, Norwich City, Leicester City, Copenhagen (loan), Reading (loan), CD Ourense, Panionios, Manchester City (loan), Walsall, Rotherham United, Bristol City (loan), Sheffield Wednesday, Burton Albion

Despite scoring the winning goal of the 1990 FA Cup semi-final replay that took United to Wembley, Mark Robins will always be tagged as the 'man who saved Alex Ferguson's job', when he scored the only goal in the third round of that season's competition against Nottingham Forest. The club has always stated that Ferguson's position was not under threat, as the board could see the work he was doing to put the club on the right path, but Robins was assured of at least one claim to fame.

A product of Boundary Park, where the Nevilles, Nicky Butt and Paul Scholes all played, he joined United as a schoolboy in February 1984, moving through the ranks as a clinical finisher at all levels, before making his first-team debut in the League Cup against Rotherham United in October 1988. Small in stature, but a real handful for defenders, he was unfortunate that he could never hold down a regular first-team place, with 43 of his 70 United appearances coming as a substitute. Knee operations were also to curtail his United appearances and, in August 1992, he joined Norwich City for a fee of £800,000. More recently, he has been a manager of various clubs, taking charge of Huddersfield Town during 2012/13.

JAMES WILSON ROBINSON

Country: Ireland
Born: 8 Jan 1898 **Died:** Unknown
Debut: 3 Jan 1920 v Chelsea
Position: Outside-left
Appearances: 21 **Goals scored:** 3
Seasons: 1919/20 – 1921/22
Clubs: Manchester United, Tranmere Rovers

Robinson began his playing career in Belfast junior football and was an Irish junior international when signed by United in the summer of 1919. His debut against Chelsea, a 2-0 defeat, was a rather poor affair, with one correspondent of the time writing: 'Robinson, who filled the outside-left berth, has still a lot to learn.' Unfortunately, he was never to get a good run in the side, with half a dozen the best he could ever muster. Given a free transfer at the end of season 1921/22, he was signed by Tranmere Rovers, but fared little better on the banks of the Mersey in Birkenhead, making only half a dozen appearances over a two-year period.

MATTHEW 'MATT' ROBINSON

Country: England
Born: 21 Apr 1907 **Died:** Aug 1987
Debut: 26 Sep 1931 v Chesterfield
Position: Outside-left
Appearances: 10 **Goals scored:** 0
Seasons: 1931/32
Clubs: Cardiff City, Manchester United, Chester City

Signed on a one-month trial from Cardiff City during season 1931/32, he did enough to win a permanent contract, but during his run of ten straight games, playing all but one at outside-left, which was not his usual position, he failed to show that he was worth a further extension and was allowed to leave before the end of the campaign and joined Chester.

BRYAN ROBSON

Country: England
Born: 11 Jan 1957
Debut: 7 Oct 1981 v Tottenham Hotspur
Position: Midfield
Appearances: 437 (24) **Goals scored:** 99
Seasons: 1981/82 – 1993/94
Clubs: West Bromwich Albion, Manchester United, Middlesbrough

Bryan Robson, a midfield leader in the true sense, was more than just the United captain during the 1980s and early 1990s. Following his record-breaking £1.5 million transfer from West Bromwich Albion in October 1981, he quickly became the talisman of the side, and if his name wasn't on the team-sheet, then many fans feared that an afternoon of doom and gloom would almost inevitably follow.

Born in Chester-le-Street in the north-east, he signed apprentice forms with West Bromwich Albion in 1972, turning professional two years later and making his debut at York City on 12 April 1975. He opened his scoring account the following week against Cardiff at The Hawthorns. In his early days, he could be found either as a full-back or at centre-half, before moving forward into a midfield role. At one point, it looked as though his career might be over before it had really begun, as he suffered three broken legs during season 1976/77, West Brom's first back in the top flight.

Recovering fully, although the injury jinx was to remain with him throughout his career, Robson became an established part of the side only when Ron Atkinson took charge in 1978. He helped the club to third in the table in 1979, and the following season won his first England cap. When Atkinson succeeded Tommy Docherty as Manchester United's manager, it was a foregone conclusion that he would return to his former club to sign his captain.

Robson made his debut in the red of United in a 1-0 League Cup defeat against Tottenham at White Hart Lane, with his league debut following three days later in a 0-0 draw against Manchester City at Maine Road; but from that modest start grew something truly spectacular. Robson was a dynamic individual, whose stamina at times seemed almost unnatural; he always led by example, putting his body into situations that others would avoid – his bravery leading to regular appearances on the treatment table, with his enthusiasm, whether in the red of United or the white of England, never faltering. Arguably his best performance came in a compelling game at Old Trafford against Barcelona in the quarter-finals of the Cup-Winners' Cup, when he inspired the Reds to overcome a 2-0 deficit, scoring twice in a 3-0 win over the Maradona-led opposition.

Winning 90 England caps, he represented them in the World Cups of 1982, 1986 and 1990, scoring the fastest goal of the 1982 tournament after only 27 seconds against France. But it is with United where he is best remembered, guiding the club to FA Cup success in 1983, 1985 and 1990, the European Cup-Winners' Cup and Super Cup in 1991, the League Cup in 1992, and the Premier League title in 1993 and 1994. He was also to lift the FA Charity Shield on three occasions.

By the time he finally picked up the long-deserved league title honours, his battle-scarred body was carrying the aches and pains of the endeavours that he had put in at stadiums across the globe and was increasingly used as a bit-part player, with Roy Keane his natural successor. In

May 1994, he decided that it was time to hang up the red No.7 shirt and call time on his playing career at Old Trafford, moving back to his native north-east to take over the role of player-manager with Middlesbrough, where he stayed in charge until 2001. Today, 'Captain Marvel' is one of the Manchester United ambassadors and a name that will live forever in the history of the club.

LEE PAUL ROCHE

Country: England
Born: 28 Oct 1980
Debut: 5 Nov 2001 v Arsenal
Position: Full-back
Appearances: 2 (1) **Goals scored:** 0
Seasons: 2001/02 – 2002/03
Clubs: Manchester United, Wrexham (loan), Burnley, Wrexham, Droylsden

PATRICK JOSEPH CHRISTOPHER 'PADDY' ROCHE

Country: Republic of Ireland
Born: 4 Jan 1951
Debut: 8 Feb 1975 v Oxford United
Position: Goalkeeper
Appearances: 53 **Goals scored:** 0
Seasons: 1974/75 – 1981/82
Clubs: Shelbourne, Manchester United, Brentford, Halifax Town, Chester City, Northwich Victoria

Dublin-born Roche kicked off his career with Shelbourne, winning Republic of Ireland international honours, before a fee of £15,000 made him Tommy Docherty's tenth signing in October 1973. His early days at the club were spent as understudy to Alex Stepney, making the odd substitute appearance in friendly fixtures before receiving his first-team call-up on 8 February 1975 at Oxford United, a match United lost 1-0, but he kept a clean sheet the next match. He was not to feature in the first team again until November 1975, keeping a clean sheet against Norwich City at home, before disaster struck seven days later at Anfield when United lost 3-1, with Roche perhaps unfairly criticised for a slip that led to one of Liverpool's goals.

He redeemed himself with a clean sheet seven days later against Aston Villa, but another 3-1 defeat, this time at Highbury, saw Roche make another error. It was a difficult time for him, both on and off the pitch, and he was often unfairly maligned by some fans. It wasn't until he joined Halifax Town, after a spell at Brentford, that he enjoyed his best football, proving himself as a more than capable keeper.

MARTYN ROGERS

Country: England
Born: 26 Jan 1960 **Died:** Mar 1992
Debut: 22 Oct 1977 v West Bromwich Albion
Position: Full-back
Appearances: 1 **Goals scored:** 0
Seasons: 1977/78
Clubs: Manchester United, Queens Park Rangers

CRISTIANO RONALDO DOS SANTOS AVEIRO

Country: Portugal
Born: 5 Feb 1985
Debut: 16 Aug 2003 v Bolton Wanderers
Position: Winger/Forward
Appearances: 244 (48) **Goals scored:** 118
Seasons: 2003/04 – 2008/09
Clubs: Sporting Lisbon, Manchester United, Real Madrid

Ronaldo arrived at Old Trafford in August 2003 as something of an unknown, although the £12.24 million paid to Sporting Lisbon for the 18-year-old should have alerted the masses that he must have possessed a certain something, while those who witnessed his debut, when he came on as a 60th-minute substitute against Bolton Wanderers, made their way home still wondering what the youngster with the highlighted hair and the countless step-overs was all about. By the time he left in June 2009, those fans had their answer.

Born in Madeira, Ronaldo took his first footballing steps with amateur side Andorinha as an eight-year-old, moving to Nacional in 1995, before a three-day trial earned him a contract with Sporting Lisbon in 2002. It was after a friendly between Sporting and United in the Portuguese capital that the United players talked of little else than his performance on the flight home. Sir Alex Ferguson and his staff had by then done their homework and, with other clubs including Arsenal and Liverpool already alerted to his potential, a deal was quickly put in place.

To many critics in those early days at United, he was considered little more than a show-pony, a player who would go to ground at the merest of touches. But by the time of his departure after six seasons at the club, opponents and opposition supporters had grown to have a grudging admiration for the Portuguese international who could always be expected to entertain, be it with a mazy run, his step-overs conjuring up yet another goal, or one of his trademark free-kicks that seemed to arrow unerringly into the net. He had become the complete footballer, having developed into a supreme athlete who was undoubtedly one of the greatest individuals to represent Manchester United. The greatest of all? That is for others to decide.

In his first season, he scored a goal in United's 3-0 FA Cup win over Millwall, but began to feature in the side much more the next campaign. He was on the scoresheet again in the League Cup final of 2006 as he picked up his second medal with United in a season when his goal tally reached double figures for the first time. After a World Cup tangle with Wayne Rooney that finished with his United team-mate sent off, many suggested he might have to leave the country, but the two players took charge of United's title surge in 2007.

The next season was his best at the club, as he scored an astonishing 42 goals in all competitions, inspiring United to another Premier League title as well as the Champions League trophy – another final in which he scored, though he did miss a penalty in the shoot-out to show he was human. He became the first United player since George Best in 1968 to be named European Footballer of the Year in December 2008 and a year later he went one step further to become the first Premiership player to win the FIFA World Player of the Year. In his final campaign with the Reds, he added the League Cup to another Premier League trophy and left the club as arguably the hottest property in world football, United accepting a world-record fee of £80 million from Real Madrid.

There were also games when, like every other player, he could perhaps have performed better, but had it not been for Cristiano Ronaldo it is debatable whether Manchester United's list of honours would read as they do today. He left talking of Sir Alex Ferguson as being his 'father in sport, one of the most important factors and most influential in my career'. On his return, in the Champions League in 2013, he received a warm welcome from the Old Trafford faithful, and seemed almost sad to have scored the goal that knocked United out of the competition.

WAYNE MARK ROONEY

Country: England
Born: 24 Oct 1985
Debut: 28 Sep 2004 v Fenerbahce
Position: Forward
Appearances: 360 (42) **Goals scored:** 197
Seasons: 2004/05 – present
Clubs: Everton, Manchester United

Wayne Rooney sprang to prominence as a 16-year-old when he scored for Everton against Arsenal at Goodison Park in 2002 and was soon to become one of the brightest talents in the English game – so much so, that Sir Alex Ferguson paid the Merseysiders a reported £25.6 million in August 2004 to sign him up after the player had turned down a £12,000 a week contract with Everton and a £20 million move to Newcastle.

Having impressed during the European Championships of 2004, the record fee for a teenager was quickly put into context when he marked his United debut against Fenerbahce with a stunning hat-trick, entering the record books as the youngest to do so in the Champions League. Named as PFA Young Player of the Year at the end of 2004/05, his inexperience occasionally shone through, with rash challenges and sendings-off blotting his copybook early in his time with the club, but he was to score twice as United defeated Wigan in the 2006 League Cup final.

It was his first winner's medal at United, but there were to be many more in the years that followed. His 14 league goals helped United to the Premier League title in 2007, a campaign in which he played more games than anyone else. A fractured metatarsal on the opening day of season 2007/08 was followed by an ankle injury, but these setbacks did little to dent his contribution to United's success in both the Premier and Champions Leagues. In October 2008 Rooney became the youngest player to reach 200 league appearances.

PFA Player of the Year in 2010, he scored 33 goals in the season following the departure of Ronaldo and Carlos Tevez. The start of the 2010/11 campaign saw him ask for a transfer, but he decided to stay and returned to something of his best form before going on to win his fourth Premier League medal. In February 2012, he marked his 400th senior appearance with two goals at Anfield in United's 2-1 win, and finished with 34 goals in all competitions. Following the signing of Robin van Persie at the start of season 2012/13, he was sometimes used in a deeper role, but still went on to win yet another Premier League medal.

Arguably the most naturally talented English player since Paul Gascoigne, Rooney has the ability to play almost anywhere on the pitch: he has a wide passing range, can score thunderbolt goals, has improved his heading and has developed into a greater goalscorer, as well as a scorer of great goals. He has also been central to England's hopes in major competitions, though has often found the tournaments have coincided with injuries or suspensions.

The summer of 2013 saw his future at United remain in the balance for some time, with a move to Chelsea looking likely. But in the end, with the club unwilling to sell, he decided to remain at United.

GIUSEPPE ROSSI

Country: Italy
Born: 1 Feb 1987
Debut: 10 Nov 2004 v Crystal Palace
Position: Forward
Appearances: 6 (8) **Goals scored:** 4
Seasons: 2004/05 – 2005/06
Clubs: Manchester United, Newcastle United (loan), Parma (loan), Villarreal, Fiorentina

An Italian-American, Giuseppe Rossi arrived in Manchester as a 16-year-old from Parma and immediately impressed at reserve-team level, making up for his lack of inches by scoring goals with regularity. He made his league debut at Sunderland in October 2005, scoring of course, but was unfortunate in that there was such strong competition for the forward positions at the club at this time, with van Nistelrooy, Rooney, Saha and Ronaldo all available. It was obvious that, despite his talents, he was going to struggle to command a regular first-team place.

At the start of 2006/07 he joined Newcastle United on loan, before a similar, more successful deal with Parma. In July 2007, he was on the move again, joining Villarreal on a permanent transfer for a fee reported to be around £6.6 million, which included a first-refusal buy-back option. However, the Italian international joined Fiorentina in 2013.

CHARLES ROTHWELL

Country: England
Born: Unknown **Died:** Unknown
Debut: 2 Dec 1893 v Everton
Position: Forward
Appearances: 3 **Goals scored:** 3
Seasons: 1893/94 – 1896/97
Clubs: Newton Heath

HERBERT 'BERT' ROTHWELL

Country: England
Born: 1880 **Died:** Unknown
Debut: 25 Oct 1902 v Arsenal
Position: Full-back
Appearances: 28 **Goals scored:** 0
Seasons: 1902/03
Clubs: Glossop North End, Manchester United, Manchester City

Bert Rothwell played in the Football League with Glossop North End before joining United in October 1902. A regular during season 1902/03, he lost his place to Robert Bonthron at the start of 1903/04 and joined City in December 1903 before returning to the amateur ranks.

WILLIAM GEORGE ROUGHTON

Country: England
Born: 11 May 1909 **Died:** 7 Jun 1989
Debut: 12 Sep 1936 v Manchester City
Position: Full-back
Appearances: 92 **Goals scored:** 0
Seasons: 1936/37 – 1938/39
Clubs: Huddersfield Town, Manchester United

Although born in Manchester, George Roughton was to begin his professional career with Huddersfield Town in 1928, enjoying eight years at Leeds Road before moving to Old Trafford in September 1936. Despite suffering relegation in his first season, when he missed only half a dozen games, he was a key part in the Second Division promotion-winning campaign of 1937/38. He was much less regular in the side during the next season, but the war was to bring an end to his United career and he moved into management with Exeter City and later Southampton.

ELIJAH ROUND

Country: England
Born: Jan 1882 **Died:** Unknown
Debut: 9 Oct 1909 v Liverpool
Position: Goalkeeper
Appearances: 2 **Goals scored:** 0
Seasons: 1909/10
Clubs: Barnsley, Oldham Athletic, Manchester United, Worksop Town, Mexborough

JOCELYN A. 'JOSH' ROWE

Country: England
Born: Unknown **Died:** Unknown
Debut: 5 Mar 1914 v Preston North End
Position: Full-back
Appearances: 1 **Goals scored:** 0
Seasons: 1913/14
Clubs: Bohemians, Manchester United, Bohemians

HENRY BOWATER 'HARRY' ROWLEY

Country: England
Born: 23 Jan 1904 **Died:** 19 Dec 1985
Debut: 27 Oct 1928 v Huddersfield Town
Position: Inside-forward
Appearances: 180 **Goals scored:** 55
Seasons: 1928/29 – 1931/32 & 1934/35 – 1936/37
Clubs: Southend United (trial), Shrewsbury Town, Manchester United, Manchester City, Oldham Athletic (loan), Manchester United, Burton Albion

One of the few players to sign for United twice, inside-forward Harry Rowley first joined United in May 1928 from Shrewsbury Town for a fee of £100, having scored 30 goals for the Stags during season 1927/28, but after 96 appearances, scoring 24 goals, he was allowed to leave only a matter of weeks into season 1931/32, joining City in exchange for Bill Ridding, following relegation to the Second Division at the end of the previous campaign.

Failing to make anything of his move across Manchester, he was loaned to Oldham, where he was to regain some of his earlier form, so much so that United perhaps surprisingly paid £1,375 for his signature in December 1934. In his second spell with the club, he made a further 84 appearances, scoring 31 goals, helping United to the Second Division title in 1935/36, although they were to drop back down again the following season, after which he left to become player-manager of Burton Albion.

JOHN FREDERICK 'JACK' ROWLEY

Country: England
Born: 7 Oct 1920 **Died:** 27 June 1998
Debut: 23 Oct 1937 v Sheffield Wednesday
Position: Forward
Appearances: 424 **Goals scored:** 211
Seasons: 1937/38 – 1954/55
Clubs: Wolverhampton Wanderers, Bournemouth, Manchester United, Plymouth Argyle

Jack Rowley was a member of a footballing family, with two brothers who were also professionals (his brother Arthur holds the record for the most league goals in a career, with 424), along with his father who was also an ex-player. He was born in Wolverhampton and duly signed by Wanderers as a 15-year-old, moving to Bournemouth. He scored ten times in his first 11 games, before subsequently finding his way to Old Trafford in November 1937 for a fee of £3,500. During the Second World War he guested for numerous clubs, and set individual scoring records when he scored eight for Wolves against Derby and seven for Spurs against Luton Town.

He won his first representative honour in 1944 when he played against Wales in a wartime international and in 1948 and 1949 he represented the Football League and the full England side, eventually winning six caps. Having lost much of his career to the war, he seemed anxious to make up for lost time during the 1946/47 season when he broke Sandy Turnbull's long-standing record of 25 league goals in one season, netting 26. It wasn't quite enough to bring the title to United, who ended up a point behind Liverpool. Gaining an FA Cup winner's medal in 1948 (when he scored two goals in the final) and a League Championship medal in 1951/52, when he broke his own record by scoring 30 league goals, he was able to play in any forward position. He possessed one of the most powerful shots in the game as well as being an excellent header of the ball.

Only Ryan Giggs, Gary Neville and Paul Scholes have achieved a longer career in the first team than his 17 years and 119 days, while only Bobby Charlton and Denis Law have scored more goals for United, with just Denis Law beating his career record of 12 hat-tricks for the club. When the all-time great strikers of United are discussed, his name is often missing from the list of candidates, but his record suggests he should certainly be included. He eventually left the club to join Plymouth Argyle as player-manager in February 1955 on a free transfer.

EZRA JOHN ROYALS

Country: England
Born: Jan 1882 **Died:** Unknown
Debut: 23 Mar 1912 v Liverpool
Position: Goalkeeper
Appearances: 7 **Goals scored:** 0
Seasons: 1911/12 – 1913/14
Clubs: Chesterton White Star, Manchester United, Northwich Victoria

JAMES 'JIMMY' RYAN

Country: Scotland
Born: 12 May 1945
Debut: 4 May 1966 v West Bromwich Albion
Position: Winger
Appearances: 24 (3) **Goals scored:** 4
Seasons: 1965/66 – 1969/70
Clubs: Manchester United, Luton Town, Dallas Tornado

Signed on amateur forms from Scottish junior side Cowie Hearts, Jimmy Ryan turned professional six weeks later. He was a talented winger who had all the attributes to do well in the game, but at Old Trafford he found his path blocked due to a surplus of forwards at the club. Following his debut in May 1966, he was never to enjoy an extended run in the side and at the end of 1969/70 he was given a free transfer. Moving to Luton Town, he soon established himself and was an important member of the side that gained promotion to the First Division in 1974.

He returned to United in 1991 as manager of the reserves, and eventually worked his way up to assistant manager, even once taking charge of the first team during 1998/99, when Alex Ferguson was away at a family funeral. The 3-2 defeat to Middlesbrough that day proved to be a turning point in United's season, as they would go on to the end of the campaign without defeat. He retired from the club at the end of the 2011/12 season.

DAVID SADLER

Country: England
Born: 5 Feb 1946
Debut: 24 Aug 1963 v Sheffield Wednesday
Position: Forward/Defender
Appearances: 328 (7) **Goals scored:** 27
Seasons: 1963/64 – 1973/74
Clubs: Manchester United, Miami Toros (loan), Preston North End

One of the most sought-after teenagers in British football, England amateur international David Sadler joined United from junior football at Maidstone United in November 1962, forsaking a career in banking for the make-or-break world of professional football. He began season 1963/64 as first-choice centre-forward, playing in the first dozen games, scoring three times, but was soon back in the reserves, although a hat-trick in the second leg of the 1963/64 FA Youth Cup final against Swindon Town nudged him back into the limelight.

Despite his creditable performances up front over the course of the following three seasons, there was still some debate as to Sadler's best position. Ending 1966/67 in the No. 9 shirt, he started the following campaign on the bench before finding himself at inside-forward, centre-half and wing-half over the course of the next ten games.

His versatility was a bonus to Matt Busby, but the United manager felt that it was in a defensive role he was best suited as he read the game well and it was in this position that he won full international honours, also winning Under-23 and Football League honours. Having learned his trade as a forward, he could often be found assisting his front men, with his goal in the 1968 European Cup semi-final in Madrid playing a major part in United's aggregate victory. His contribution in the final against Benfica is often overlooked, but it was his cross that created the all-important opening goal for Bobby Charlton.

Never a player to seek the limelight, happy to let others take that role, he was calm and dependable wherever he played and when Bobby Charlton left United for Preston North End, he was more than happy to take his former team-mate to Deepdale in November 1973 in a £20,000 deal, where his experience was invaluable.

CHARLES 'CHARLIE' SAGAR

Country: England
Born: 28 Mar 1878 **Died:** 4 Dec 1919
Debut: 2 Sep 1905 v Bristol City
Position: Forward
Appearances: 33 **Goals scored:** 24
Seasons: 1905/06 – 1906/07
Clubs: Turton Rovers, Bury, Manchester United, Atherton, Haslingden

Charlie Sagar came into prominence as a Bury player in the 1890s, winning his first England cap in 1900, and scoring on his debut against Ireland. He also appeared in the 1900 and 1903 FA Cup-winning sides, for in those days Bury was arguably the bigger club. He was signed for United by Ernest Mangnall in the close season of 1905 and (along with Wayne Rooney) is the only player to score a hat-trick on his first-team debut for United, notching 20 in his 23 outings in that 1905/06 season as United won promotion back into the First Division. A knee injury was to curtail his appearances over the next couple of seasons and he was released by the club in 1907.

LOUIS LAURENT SAHA

Country: France
Born: 8 Aug 1978
Debut: 31 Jan 2004 v Southampton
Position: Centre-forward
Appearances: 76 (48) **Goals scored:** 42
Seasons: 2003/04 – 2007/08
Clubs: FC Metz, Newcastle United (loan), Fulham, Manchester United, Everton, Tottenham Hotspur, Sunderland, Lazio

A prolific and skilful goalscorer, Louis Saha's performances for Fulham (where he scored 53 goals in 117 league appearances over four years) were enough to make Sir Alex Ferguson pay £12.8 million to take him to Old Trafford in January 2004. A goal on his debut against Southampton was the first of seven in ten starts, but despite this prolific beginning, his career at United was to be hampered by injuries which prevented him from fulfilling his potential. He did, however, win French international honours, picking up 20 caps, as well as two Premier League and one League Cup winner's medals.

Saha had all the attributes – he had pace, a fierce shot, was good in the air and when on song was extremely difficult to play against. But with competition for places up front always fierce at Old Trafford, it was decided to sell him to Everton for an undisclosed fee at the start of the 2008/09 season, who bought him on a cautious pay-as-you-play two-year deal. His 25-second FA Cup final goal in 2009 was the fastest ever in the history of the competition.

GEORGE DOUGLAS SAPSFORD

Country: England
Born: 10 Mar 1896 **Died:** 17 Oct 1970
Debut: 26 Apr 1920 v Notts County
Position: Forward

Appearances: 53 **Goals scored:** 17
Seasons: 1919/20 – 1921/22
Clubs: Manchester United, Preston North End, Southport

Broughton-born Sapsford joined United from Cheetham and District League football in April 1919, making his first-team debut towards the end of the following season. Not the most devastating of players, he was, however, a talented individual who could certainly have made a name for himself at Old Trafford. But instead of allowing him the opportunity to prove himself, the United directors were more interested in the £2,500 Preston North End offered in May 1922 for his signature. Having just been relegated, the club needed the money, so promptly sold him.

CARLO DOMENICO SARTORI

Country: Italy
Born: 10 Feb 1948
Debut: 9 Oct 1968 v Tottenham Hotspur
Position: Midfield
Appearances: 40 (16) **Goals scored:** 6
Seasons: 1968/69 – 1971/72
Clubs: Manchester United, Bologna, Spal, Lecce, Rimini, Trento

Although born in Italy, Carlo Sartori was brought up in Manchester and spotted while playing for Manchester Schools, joining United in July 1963. He made his first-team debut on 9 October 1968, coming on as a substitute to face Spurs in a 2-2 draw. Once in the first team, he played with great promise and was a handy type of player to have around due to his ability to play either up front or in midfield. Season 1969/70 proved to be his best at the club, with 27 appearances in league and cup fixtures. But with the pruning of the staff at the end of 1971/72, he was one of the players released and returned to Italy, joining Bologna for a fee of £50,000.

WILLIAM ISAAC SARVIS

Country: Wales
Born: Jul 1898 **Died:** 22 Mar 1968
Debut: 23 Sep 1922 v Coventry City

Position: Forward
Appearances: 1 **Goals scored:** 0
Seasons: 1922/23
Clubs: Aberdare Athletic, Merthyr Town, Manchester United, Bradford City, Walsall

JAMES EDWARD SAUNDERS

Country: England
Born: Oct 1878 **Died:** Unknown
Debut: 26 Dec 1901 v Lincoln City
Position: Goalkeeper
Appearances: 13 **Goals scored:** 0
Seasons: 1901/02 – 1902/03
Clubs: Glossop, Middlesbrough, Newton Heath, Manchester United, Nelson, Lincoln City, Chelsea, Watford

The career of James Saunders crossed the Newton Heath/Manchester United divide, but he was to play only twice for the latter.

When signed by the club, he was considered as 'a good understudy to Whitehouse', but opportunities to prove his worth were to be few and far between and he joined Lincoln City in October 1906.

ROBERT EDWARD 'TED' SAVAGE

Country: England
Born: Jan 1912 **Died:** 30 Jan 1964
Debut: 1 Jan 1938 v Newcastle United
Position: Half-back
Appearances: 5 **Goals scored:** 0
Seasons: 1937/38
Clubs: Lincoln City, Liverpool, Manchester United, Wrexham

F. SAWYER

Country: Unknown
Born: Unknown **Died:** Unknown
Debut: 14 Oct 1899 v Small Heath
Position: Forward

Appearances: 6 **Goals scored:** 0
Seasons: 1899/1900
Clubs: Newton Heath, Chorley

ALBERT JOSEPH SCANLON

Country: England
Born: 10 Oct 1935 **Died:** 22 Dec 2009
Debut: 20 Nov 1954 v Arsenal
Position: Outside-left
Appearances: 127 **Goals scored:** 35
Seasons: 1954/55 – 1960/61
Clubs: Manchester United, Newcastle United, Lincoln City, Mansfield Town, Belper Town

Albert Scanlon represented Manchester and Lancashire Schools before joining United in 1951 and, following the usual grooming in the junior and reserve sides, winning FA Youth Cup and later Central League medals, he made his league debut in November 1954 against Arsenal at Old Trafford. He took over the outside-left spot from Jack Rowley and was to prove a worthy successor with his boundless enthusiasm and powerful shot in either foot. In United's final league game before Munich, at Highbury, he set up three goals in the famous 5-4 victory.

In the Munich disaster, he was to suffer leg injuries, but made a fine recovery and soon regained his first-team spot, playing in all 42 league fixtures of 1958/59, scoring 16 goals, earning England Under-23 honours in the process. A great character, he was also tipped for a place in the full England side, but it was never to materialise, as his game began to lose some of the passion and consistency that it once possessed, and in November 1960 he moved to Newcastle United for a fee of £18,000.

PETER BOLESLAW SCHMEICHEL

Country: Denmark
Born: 18 Nov 1963
Debut: 17 Aug 1991 v Notts County
Position: Goalkeeper

Appearances: 398 **Goals scored:** 1
Seasons: 1991/92 – 1998/99
Clubs: Gladsaxe-Hero, Hvidovre, Brondby, Manchester United, Sporting Lisbon, Aston Villa, Manchester City

Peter Schmeichel's physical presence was an intimidating sight for any forward and an inspiration to his team-mates, with his agility somewhat surprising for a goalkeeper of his size. He was a commanding figure, who certainly made himself heard around the penalty area, and his distribution was an outstanding feature, his throws travelling as far as many could kick, prompting many counter-attacks. Signed from Brondby prior to the start of season 1991/92 for the bargain fee of £500,000, Schmeichel would always be a contender as the best pound-for-pound signing Sir Alex ever made, and it is perhaps not surprising that during each of his eight seasons with United they were to win silverware.

He was Danish Footballer of the Year in 1990 and their most-capped player with 129, during an international career that ran from 1987 to 2001, and was part of the side that won the European Championship in 1992. He won four championships and a Danish Cup with Brondby before coming to United, and once at Old Trafford was quick to show that he was not going to be fazed by the hustle and bustle of the English game, keeping a clean sheet in his first four games, going on to concede only four times in his first 13 outings.

It wasn't simply within the confines of his own penalty area that he used his size to his advantage, as he out-jumped everyone in the Rotor Volgograd goalmouth during the UEFA Cup tie at Old Trafford in September 1995, scoring United's second goal in the 2-2 draw that saw the Reds tumble out of the competition on away goals. It is worth noting that he scored ten goals during his career, including six in one season for Hvidovre.

His green jersey was again highly visible in the opposition area in Barcelona's Nou Camp on the evening of 26 May 1999, as United chased an equaliser in the Champions League final against Bayern Munich. Although on this occasion he did not connect with the ball, his presence was enough to distract the Germans and Teddy Sheringham snatched the equaliser. Minutes later, as stand-in captain in place of the suspended Roy Keane, he was hoisting the European Cup high in the Spanish air alongside Alex Ferguson, following Ole Gunnar Solskjaer's dramatic winner.

But it is for his work in his own penalty area that he will best be remembered. His penalty save against Dennis Bergkamp in the last moments of the FA Cup semi-final replay against Arsenal was so very important in the march towards the Treble. There were countless memorable saves, such as a crucial one in the Champions League against Rapid Vienna in December 1996, but Schmeichel wasn't flawless, nor was he injury free, and in mid-season 1998/99, with the Treble not even being considered as a possibility, he announced that he would be leaving Old Trafford at the end of that season. Even winning the Treble could not change his mind – but what a way to bow out.

ALFRED JOHN 'ALF' SCHOFIELD

Country: England
Born: 1873 **Died:** Unknown
Debut: 1 Sep 1900 v Glossop
Position: Outside-right
Appearances: 179 **Goals scored:** 35
Seasons: 1900/01 – 1906/07
Clubs: Everton, Newton Heath, Manchester United

A winger with excellent crossing ability, Schofield was signed from Everton in August 1900 after five years on Merseyside. Due to business interests in his native Liverpool, it is somewhat surprising that he was able to maintain such high standards of play, as training was far from being a priority. A Second Division title-winner with United in 1906, he was suddenly surplus to requirements a year later with the arrival of a certain Billy Meredith and he decided to call it a day.

GEORGE WILLIE SCHOFIELD

Country: England
Born: 6 Aug 1896 **Died:** Unknown
Debut: 4 Sep 1920 v Bolton Wanderers
Position: Outside-right
Appearances: 1 **Goals scored:** 0
Seasons: 1920/21 – 1921/22
Clubs: Manchester United, Crewe Alexandra

JOSEPH SCHOFIELD

Country: England
Born: 1881 **Died:** Unknown
Debut: 26 Mar 1904 v Grimsby Town
Position: Outside-left
Appearances: 2 **Goals scored:** 0
Seasons: 1903/04
Clubs: Brynn Central, Ashton Town, Manchester United, Stockport County, Luton Town

PERCY SCHOFIELD

Country: England
Born: Apr 1893 **Died:** 20 Jun 1968
Debut: 1 Oct 1921 v Preston North End
Position: Inside-forward
Appearances: 1 **Goals scored:** 0
Seasons: 1921/22
Clubs: Eccles Borough, Manchester United, Eccles United, Hurst

PAUL AARON SCHOLES

Country: England
Born: 16 Nov 1974
Debut: 21 Sep 1994 v Port Vale
Position: Midfield/Forward
Appearances: 577 (141) **Goals scored:** 155
Seasons: 1994/95 – 2012/13
Clubs: Manchester United

Paul Scholes was about as far removed from your stereotypical modern-day footballer as you can get, shunning the trappings that go hand in hand with the celebrity lifestyle and great wealth, content with the quiet family life away from the spotlight. On the pitch, he also appeared to have no ego, either, yet he was a player of immense ability and considered by his peers as the outstanding midfielder of his generation.

When he was first spotted by Brian Kidd, Scholes was very small, and in his teens he had a few asthma and fitness problems that meant he didn't develop as quickly as some of his contemporaries, such as David

Beckham and Nicky Butt, and so he didn't play in the FA Youth Cup side of 1992. But no one was deceived by the ginger-haired Salfordian's physical build, and soon the world was more than aware of the attributes that Scholes possessed. Indeed, ever since Alex Ferguson unleashed him in the Coca-Cola Cup against Port Vale in September 1994, scoring twice, with another goal on his league debut three days later, his name was filed away as a future star.

In his earlier years, he tended to play as a second striker, and was regularly on the scoresheet, forming a particularly prolific partnership with Ruud van Nistelrooy during the 2002/03 title-winning season, when he scored 20 goals in all competitions. Later on, he played in a deeper-lying role and acquired the nickname 'Sat Nav' as his passes seemingly always found their target. If Scholes had a fault, it was his tackling, or more to the point his seeming inability to tackle, earning him many bookings, his 97th coming in his final match with yet another mistimed tackle. Along with ten sendings-off, his bookings led to several suspensions, one of which forced him out of the 1999 Champions League final. He holds the record for the most yellow cards in both the Premier League and the Champions League.

His form for United earned him his first England cap against South Africa in 1997, amid the familiar surroundings of Old Trafford, and he went on to win 66 caps, scoring 14 goals, before announcing his retirement in the summer of 2004, stating that family reasons and his United career were greater priorities. With United he continued to impress, scoring 'goals galore', as his terrace chant proclaimed, but in true Scholes fashion, he decided at the end of season 2010/11 that he had had enough and was retiring from the game, deciding to concentrate on coaching and teaming up with the United reserve side.

Although enjoying his role as a coach, the pull of being involved in an actual game proved to be too much, and in January 2012 he was surprisingly named as substitute against Manchester City in the FA Cup and his career was back on track, with his 718 appearances pushing him into third place in the club's all-time chart. Injury curtailed his appearances during 2012/13, but he was still able to add an 11th Premier League medal to his collection, bowing out with a substitute appearance against West Bromwich Albion in the final game of the season – his 499th in the Premier League. He also won the FA Cup three times, the League Cup twice, and was arguably the first name on the teamsheet in the Champions League final of 2008 – a game he had done so much to help

United reach, with his stunning drive in the semi-final against Barcelona that won the tie.

No wonder Xavi described Scholes as 'the best central midfielder I have seen' or that Sir Bobby Charlton would say of him that he was 'a beautiful player to watch'. They are statements that few would disagree with.

JOHN 'JACKIE' SCOTT

Country: Northern Ireland
Born: 22 Dec 1933 **Died:** Jun 1978
Debut: 4 Oct 1952 v Wolverhampton Wanderers
Position: Forward
Appearances: 3 **Goals scored:** 0
Seasons: 1952/53 – 1955/56
Clubs: Boyland, Ormond Star, Manchester United, Grimsby Town, York City, Margate

JOHN M. M. SCOTT

Country: Scotland
Born: Unknown **Died:** Unknown
Debut: 27 Aug 1921 v Everton
Position: Half-back
Appearances: 24 **Goals scored:** 0
Seasons: 1921/22
Clubs: Hamilton Academical, Bradford Park Avenue, Manchester United, St Mirren

Born in Motherwell, John Scott began his career with Hamilton Academical, before moving to Bradford Park Avenue in October 1910. With Bradford, he was a member of their promotion-winning Division Two side of 1913/14. After the war, where he served with distinction, a fee of £750 took Scott across the Pennines to Old Trafford, where he began season 1921/22 at left-half, playing 17 games, before playing a further five games at full-back. He returned to the left-half berth on New Year's Eve against Newcastle United, but the 3-0 defeat not only marked the final game of that year, but also the final first-team match of Scott's United career.

He was to languish in the reserve side until the end of the season and during the close season returned to Scotland and joined St Mirren.

LESLIE JESSE 'LES' SEALEY

Country: England
Born: 29 Sep 1957 **Died:** 19 Aug 2001
Debut: 14 Apr 1990 v Queens Park Rangers
Position: Goalkeeper
Appearances: 55 (1) **Goals scored:** 0
Seasons: 1989/90 – 1990/91 & 1993/94
Clubs: Coventry City, Luton Town, Plymouth Argyle (loan), Manchester United, Aston Villa, Coventry City (loan), Birmingham City (loan), Manchester United, Blackpool, West Ham United, Leyton Orient, West Ham United, Bury (loan)

'A typical goalkeeper, brave and totally mad,' would sum up Les Sealey perfectly. By the time he reached Old Trafford, he was a well-travelled custodian, having made a name for himself at the likes of Coventry and Luton, and it was from the latter that he arrived at Old Trafford in December 1989, initially on loan, as cover for Jim Leighton.

However, when the unfortunate Scot was dropped for the 1990 FA Cup final replay, Sealey stepped in and helped the Reds to Alex Ferguson's first trophy at the club. He immediately offered his winner's medal to the ousted Leighton. Now on a permanent contract, the following season he appeared in both the League Cup and European Cup-Winners' Cup finals, with a gashed knee in the former almost putting paid to any hopes he had for appearing in the latter. Indeed, he refused to leave the Wembley pitch despite the severity of the injury and collapsed in the dressing room after the match. There was also some concern about his long-term health, but Sealey was made of sterner stuff and took his place in the European final, playing his part in the 2-1 win over Barcelona. Turning down a new 12-month contract with United, he left to join Aston Villa, followed by loan spells with Coventry and Birmingham City.

He returned to United in January 1993 as back-up for Peter Schmeichel, following injuries to United's second- and third-choice keepers Gary Walsh and Ian Wilkinson, and once again made a Wembley appearance in the 1994 League Cup final, ironically against Aston Villa. His last four appearances for United included three cup finals. Leaving for second time in May 1994, it was again a case of 'have gloves must travel', seeing action with a further handful of clubs.

MAURICE EDGAR SETTERS

Country: England
Born: 16 Dec 1936
Debut: 16 Jan 1960 v Birmingham City
Position: Half-back
Appearances: 194 Goals scored: 14
Seasons: 1959/60 – 1964/65
Clubs: Exeter City, West Bromwich Albion, Manchester United, Stoke City, Coventry City, Charlton Athletic

Maurice Setters was an outstanding, robust, hard-tackling half-back who signed for local club Exeter City after winning England Schools honours, making his league debut in 1954. Eleven games and two seasons later, he joined West Bromwich Albion for £3,000 in the summer of 1955 where he was to gain Army and England Under-23 honours. Although playing mainly at half-back, he could also play a more defensive role, turning in some good performances at full-back prior to joining United in January 1960 for a fee of £30,000.

Setters added a physical side to United's game, captaining the side from December 1960 to early 1963, leading by example with his no-frills, uncompromising play, as Matt Busby continued his rebuilding work following Munich. He was a member of the 1963 FA Cup-winning side, but in 1964, Setters lost his No.6 shirt to Nobby Stiles, and his days at Old Trafford were numbered. Still having much to offer, Stoke City paid United £30,000 for his services in November 1964, where he became an instant favourite. After retiring as a player, he spent almost a decade as Jack Charlton's assistant manager for the Republic of Ireland.

LEE STUART SHARPE

Country: England
Born: 25 May 1971
Debut: 24 Sep 1988 v West Ham United
Position: Left-winger/Full-back

Appearances: 213 (50) **Goals scored:** 36
Seasons: 1988/89 – 1995/96
Clubs: Torquay United, Manchester United, Leeds United, Sampdoria (loan), Bradford City, Portsmouth (loan), Exeter City, Grindavik, Garforth Town

Lee Sharpe was an associate schoolboy with Birmingham City before joining Torquay United as a trainee in July 1987, becoming the Plainmoor club's youngest ever-debutant at the age of 16, and within a month of signing professional forms, he was snatched by United in June 1988 for a fee of £185,000 following a clandestine visit to Torquay by Alex Ferguson. It was at full-back that he kicked off his United career, but was soon to be found jinking down the touchline in a more attacking role. Although he was more of a creator than a goalscorer, his outstanding performance came at Highbury in the 1990/91 League Cup campaign, when he scored a memorable hat-trick in a 6-2 win. It is worth noting that of the 36 goals that Sharpe scored for United, four were in semi-finals – showing his ability to rise to the big occasion.

A member of the 1991 European Cup-Winners' Cup side, he was subsequently named the PFA Young Player of the Year and brought into the England set-up. But it wasn't all a bed of roses for the youngest-ever player to win an England Under-21 cap, as he was soon to suffer a catalogue of injuries and illness, with groin and hernia problems being the least of his worries when he discovered that he was suffering from meningitis.

He recovered from the latter and regained his place in the United side that was to end a 26-year wait for the elusive league title and, with his own fan club, he was the golden boy of Old Trafford. But, with the emergence of Ryan Giggs and further competition in Andre Kanchelskis, Sharpe had a fight on his hands for regular place in United's starting line-up. By August 1996, having added two further Championship medals, an FA Cup winner's and League Cup winner's medals to his collection, he found a move to Leeds United appealing, with the Yorkshire side paying £4.5 million to secure his signature. His creative line on goal celebrations would grace Old Trafford no more.

WILLIAM H. SHARPE

Country: England
Born: Unknown **Died:** Unknown
Debut: 4 Oct 1890 v Higher Walton

Position: Outside-left
Appearances: 2 **Goals scored:** 0
Seasons: 1890/91 – 1891/92
Clubs: Newton Heath, Oldham County, Wigan County, Oldham Athletic

RYAN JAMES SHAWCROSS

Country: England
Born: 4 Oct 1987
Debut: 25 Oct 2006 v Crewe Alexandra
Position: Defender
Appearances: 0 (2) **Goals scored:** 0
Seasons: 2006/07
Clubs: Manchester United, Royal Antwerp (loan), Stoke City

Although he managed just two substitute appearances for United, he moved to Stoke City, initially on loan, before signing for the club for a fee that eventually rose to £2 million. He became club captain in 2010/11, and missed only five league games in his first three seasons since taking on the role and won his first England cap against Sweden in November 2012.

JOHN SHELDON

Country: England
Born: Jan 1887 **Died:** 19 Mar 1941
Debut: 27 Dec 1910 v Bradford City
Position: Outside-right
Appearances: 26 **Goals scored:** 1
Seasons: 1910/11 – 1912/13
Clubs: Nuneaton, Manchester United, Liverpool

One of the players involved in the 1915 Good Friday match-fixing encounter between United and Liverpool at Old Trafford, John Sheldon was by that time a Liverpool player, having joined the Merseysiders from United in November 1913. Having signed for United in November 1909, his appearances were always going to be limited due to the competition he faced from Billy Meredith and when the chance of a move to Liverpool materialised, he had no hesitation in accepting their offer.

Soon a first-team regular, he was a member of the Liverpool 1914 FA Cup final side, but in the infamous fixture at Old Trafford the following year, he was found by the investigations that followed to have been the ringleader of the plot, and he was suspended for life. The ban, however, was lifted at the end of the First World War and he returned to Liverpool for a further two seasons before retiring through injury.

EDWARD PAUL 'TEDDY' SHERINGHAM

Country: England
Born: 2 April 1966
Debut: 10 Aug 1997 v Tottenham Hotspur
Position: Centre-forward
Appearances: 101 (52) **Goals scored:** 46
Seasons: 1997/98 – 2000/01
Clubs: Millwall, Aldershot (loan), Djurgardens (loan), Nottingham Forest, Tottenham Hotspur, Manchester United, Tottenham Hotspur, Portsmouth, West Ham United, Colchester United

Teddy Sheringham was an outstanding individual with superb poise, natural flare and a goalscoring ability to match, and despite the daunting task of being signed as a replacement for Eric Cantona, he grasped the opportunity with both hands, winning over the Old Trafford crowd after a difficult first season and writing his name into Manchester United folklore.

A Londoner, Sheringham began his career with Millwall as a 16-year-old in 1982 and was their leading scorer for three consecutive seasons (1986/87 to 1988/89) and in 1990/91 scored 33 goals in 46 league appearances. A £2 million move to Nottingham Forest followed in July 1991, but after little more than a season he was back in London, signing for Tottenham Hotspur for £2.1 million. Hugely popular with the White Hart Lane supporters, he continued to score on a regular basis, but the only success that those goals were to bring were England international honours, as he earned his first cap at the age of 27 in 1993.

His £3.5 million transfer to United came as something of a surprise to many, but the 31-year-old was soon to prove that he was a more than capable replacement for the Frenchman. Silverware came thick and fast in the form of title medals in 1998/99, 1999/2000 and 2000/01, an FA Cup winner's medal in 1999 and, the pinnacle of them all, a Champions League medal, when he scored the all-important first goal in that Barcelona final of 1999. The previous Saturday, he had also scored in the FA Cup final victory over Newcastle United. He was also named PFA and FWA Footballer of the Year in 2001, and finished the campaign as United's top scorer, with 21 in all competitions.

As a free agent, he was offered a further one-year contract with United in 2001, but decided that his future lay elsewhere and returned to Tottenham Hotspur, later winding his distinguished career down at Portsmouth, West Ham (where, at the age of 40 years and 268 days, he became the oldest player to score a Premier League goal) and Colchester, but it will always be as a Manchester United player that he is remembered.

ARNOLD 'ARNIE' SIDEBOTTOM

Country: England
Born: 1 Apr 1954
Debut: 23 Apr 1973 v Sheffield United
Position: Centre-half
Appearances: 20 **Goals scored:** 0
Seasons: 1972/73 – 1974/75
Clubs: Manchester United, Huddersfield Town, Halifax Town

A very gifted cricketer, who made his debut for Yorkshire County Cricket Club on 20 June 1973, Arnie Sidebottom had by then also made his debut for United, against Sheffield United at the end of the 1972/73 season. Up until 1974/75, because of competition from Martin Buchan and Jim Holton, his appearances were restricted, but following an injury to Holton, he secured an extended run in the side, before he himself suffered an injury and lost his place and with it the opportunity to make a career at United.

Given a free transfer in 1975, he joined Huddersfield Town that December, but by 1979 he had decided to focus on cricket. It proved to be a good decision, as he played one Test, against Australia at Nottingham in the Ashes-winning summer of 1985. Sport continued in the family, as his son Ryan followed him into the England team.

JOHN 'JACK' SILCOCK

Country: England
Born: 15 Jan 1898 **Died:** 28 Jun 1966
Debut: 30 Aug 1919 v Derby County
Position: Full-back
Appearances: 449 **Goals scored:** 2
Seasons: 1919/20 – 1933/34
Clubs: Atherton, Manchester United, Oldham Athletic, Droylsden

Jack Silcock was a teenager working down the mines when he was signed by Jack Robson in April 1916, the United manager having originally gone to the Atherton v Eccles Borough match to watch another player. Eighteen seasons and 449 games later Jack Silcock was still at United, albeit at the end of his glorious career.

He was a no-nonsense full-back – 'fearless to a degree and fewer full-backs more difficult to beat' is how the United match programme of 1926 described him. Sadly for him, his reward for such lengthy service did not come in the form of medals and trophies, as his career coincided with United's least successful period. This was hardly the fault of the player himself, as he did win representative honours with England and at Football League level, earning three caps between 1921 and 1923. What he did display was a high level of consistency that showed throughout his long career, and by the time he retired he was second only to long-time team-mate Joe Spence as the player who had made the most appearances for the club.

His loyalty to the club could never be questioned and he once played with several stitches in his head following an accident at work, his game not suffering in any way. His performances earned the respect of team-mates, supporters and opponents alike and he is regarded as one of the best full-backs to play for United.

MIKAEL SAMY SILVESTRE

Country: France
Born: 9 Aug 1977
Debut: 11 Sep 1999 v Liverpool
Position: Defender
Appearances: 326 (35) **Goals scored:** 10

Seasons: 1999/2000 – 2007/08
Clubs: Rennes, Internazionale, Manchester United, Arsenal, Werder Bremen, Portland Timbers

French defender Mikael Silvestre began his career with Rennes before moving to Inter Milan in 1998. After only one season with the Italian club, where he came up against United in the Champions League, he was signed by Alex Ferguson, as the manager looked to build on the success of the Treble-winning season. He endeared himself to United fans before he had even kicked a ball for the club, turning down an approach by Liverpool in favour of a £4 million move to Old Trafford. Ironically, his United debut was against Liverpool at Anfield and he showed the locals what they had missed in a solid performance in United's 3-2 win.

He took a little time to settle in Manchester, but his ability to play as both a central defender and full-back was a bonus to Sir Alex Ferguson, and he soon established himself a first-team regular, with his forays down the left flank giving the team some additional options in attack. His performances for United earned him the first of his 40 French caps in February 2001. Having replaced Denis Irwin as United's regular left-back, he would soon become Rio Ferdinand's regular partner in the centre of defence, where his pace was a crucial asset. While at United he was to win five Premier League titles, as well as an FA Cup and a League Cup winner's medal.

Towards the end of his career at the club, a knee injury restricted his chances and he found it difficult to regain his first-team place, leaving to join Arsenal in the summer of 2008. By the end of the 2013 season, only Peter Schmeichel and Ole Gunnar Solskjaer, among United's foreign signings, had made more appearances for the club than the Frenchman.

DANIEL PETER 'DANNY' SIMPSON

Country: England
Born: 4 Jan 1987
Debut: 26 Sep 2007 v Coventry City
Position: Defender
Appearances: 4 (4) **Goals scored:** 0
Seasons: 2007/08

Clubs: Manchester United, Royal Antwerp (loan), Sunderland (loan), Ipswich Town (loan), Blackburn Rovers (loan), Newcastle United, Queens Park Rangers

The Eccles-born youngster was unable to establish himself at United, having come through the ranks at the club. Having been loaned out to various clubs, he eventually joined Newcastle United for an undisclosed fee, playing regularly for the Magpies before joining Queens Park Rangers in the summer of 2013.

JOHN SIVEBAEK

Country: Denmark
Born: 25 Oct 1961
Debut: 9 Feb 1986 v Liverpool
Position: Midfield/Full-back
Appearances: 32 (2) **Goals scored:** 1
Seasons: 1985/86 – 1986/87
Clubs: Vejle BK, Manchester United, Saint-Etienne, AS Monaco, Pescara, Vejle BK, AGF Aarhus

John Sivebaek had the distinction of scoring the first Manchester United goal of Alex Ferguson's reign, with his strike also giving the new man at the helm his first league victory, a 1-0 win over Queens Park Rangers at Old Trafford on 22 November 1986, as well as being the Dane's only goal of his United career.

Signed by Ron Atkinson in February 1986 for a reported fee of £285,000, he initially failed his medical, but a second opinion saw the transfer go through. However, it took the player some time to settle at the club, as he was not to appear in the first team again until April. A well-built, attacking defensive player, he was in the United side when Ferguson arrived at the club, but was soon to find his days numbered as the new manager shuffled his pack in order to find a winning formula. He was transferred to French side Saint-Etienne in August 1987.

J. F. SLATER

Country: Unknown
Born: Unknown **Died:** Unknown
Debut: 4 Oct 1890 v Higher Walton

Position: Goalkeeper
Appearances: 4 **Goals scored:** 0
Seasons: 1890/91 – 1891/92
Clubs: Newton Heath

THOMAS 'TOM' SLOAN

Country: Northern Ireland
Born: 10 Jul 1959
Debut: 18 Nov 1978 v Ipswich Town
Position: Midfield
Appearances: 4 (8) **Goals scored:** 0
Seasons: 1978/79 – 1980/81
Clubs: Ballymena United, Manchester United, Chester City, Linfield, Carrick Rangers, Coleraine, Larne

A slimly built Irishman, Tommy Sloan cost the club around £20,000 when signed from Ballymena United in August 1978 and although he made a dozen first-team appearances, only four were starts. Despite breaking into the Northern Ireland international side, it was obvious that he was never going to become a first-team regular at Old Trafford and he was released in the summer of 1982 and moved to Chester in the summer of 1982, more than 18 months after his last appearance for the club.

CHRISTOPHER LLOYD 'CHRIS' SMALLING

Country: England
Born: 22 Nov 1989
Debut: 8 Aug 2010 v Chelsea
Position: Defender
Appearances: 63 (23) **Goals scored:** 3
Seasons: 2010/11 – present
Clubs: Maidstone United, Middlesbrough, Fulham, Manchester United

Had it not been for homesickness following his summer 2008 move from Maidstone to Middlesbrough, Chris Smalling may never have become a Manchester United player. Returning south, Smalling's impressive performances at non-league level saw him snapped up by

Fulham and, a mere 18 months or so later, he was signing a pre-contract deal with United in January 2010, but remaining at Craven Cottage until the start of season 2010/11.

Winning a Premier League medal in his first season, his dramatic rise to fame was coupled with England recognition in September 2011, having previously won junior international honours. Injury unfortunately hampered his progress during the following two seasons, but he continued to show maturity and confidence whenever called upon by club and country, adding a second Premiership medal to his collection in 2013. Like Wes Brown before him, he seems equally comfortable in the centre of defence or at right-back. Alongside Jonny Evans and Phil Jones, he is expected to form the bedrock of United's defence for many years to come.

ALAN SMITH

Country: England
Born: 28 Oct 1980
Debut: 8 Aug 2004 v Arsenal
Position: Forward/midfield
Appearances: 61 (32) **Goals scored:** 12
Seasons: 2004/05 – 2006/07
Clubs: Leeds United, Manchester United, Newcastle United, Milton Keynes Dons

A Yorkshireman who made a name for himself at Leeds United, it was a big and certainly a brave step to make the move from Elland Road to Old Trafford in the close season of 2003/04 for a fee of £7 million. With his Leeds United side relegated from the Premier League at the end of that campaign, the club were in desperate need of the money and they were more than grateful to accept United's offer.

An energetic individual who would always give 100 per cent, whether playing in midfield or up front, Smith marked his United debut in the 2004 FA Charity Shield with a goal, but injury hampered his first season at the club and when he returned to fitness he found Wayne Rooney and Ruud van Nistelrooy in sparkling form. Despite sometimes being relegated to the bench, he was touted as a possible successor to Roy Keane, but in an FA Cup tie at Anfield in February 2006, he was to suffer a broken leg. When, a few days later, United won the Carling Cup against Wigan, his team-mates all wore t-shirts wishing him a speedy recovery – a sign of how well-liked he was in the squad.

Once again he fought back to fitness and showed he had lost none of his old zest, scoring his first goal for some 18 months in the emphatic 7-1 Old Trafford trouncing of Roma in the Champions League. His starting opportunities were limited and the injury seemed to have left him a touch slower, so in August 2007 a fee of around £6 million was agreed with Newcastle United and Smith moved to the north-east, but his bad luck was to continue and he was to struggle once again with injuries.

ALBERT C. SMITH

Country: Scotland
Born: 1905 **Died:** Unknown
Debut: 22 Jan 1927 v Leeds United
Position: Forward
Appearances: 5 **Goals scored:** 1
Seasons: 1926/27
Clubs: Petershill, Manchester United, Preston North End, Dolphin, Carlisle United, Ayr United

JOHN 'JACK' SMITH

Country: England
Born: 7 Feb 1915 **Died:** 21 Apr 1975
Debut: 2 Feb 1938 v Barnsley
Position: Forward
Appearances: 41 **Goals scored:** 15
Seasons: 1937/38 – 1945/46
Clubs: Huddersfield Town, Newcastle United, Manchester United, Port Vale, Macclesfield Town

Had it not been for the Second World War, then the name of Jack Smith may well have been entrenched in the Manchester United record books. Beginning his professional career with Huddersfield Town, he was to plunder 24 goals in 46 games before joining Newcastle United for £2,500 in September 1934. On Tyneside, he continued his emphatic goalscoring form, with 73 in 112 outings, their top scorer for three successive seasons, catching the attention of United, who had to pay £6,500 to lure him south in February 1938.

Scoring on his debut against Barnsley, the eight goals (in 17 starts) were to help United gain promotion to the First Division at the end of that first season. He was to miss a considerable part of the following campaign, but during the wartime regional leagues he was to come to the fore, scoring goals for fun, with 164 in 206 league and cup games, including a dozen hat-tricks. When football got back to normality after the war, Smith was still only 31, but Matt Busby, blessed with another goal-machine in Jack Rowley, allowed Smith to leave and join Port Vale.

LAWRENCE SMITH

Country: England
Born: Jul 1878 **Died:** Sep 1912
Debut: 22 Nov 1902 v Leicester Fosse
Position: Forward
Appearances: 10 **Goals scored:** 1
Seasons: 1902/03
Clubs: Manchester United, New Brompton

Local boy Lawrence Smith played in the first team for United for just one season, finding himself in and out of the side, and scoring his only goal for the club in a 5-1 victory over Leicester City on 21 March 1903.

RICHARD 'DICK' SMITH

Country: England
Born: Unknown **Died:** Unknown
Debut: 8 Sep 1894 v Burton Wanderers
Position: Forward
Appearances: 101 **Goals scored:** 37
Seasons: 1894/95 – 1897/98 & 1899/1900 – 1900/01
Clubs: Halliwell Rovers, Heywood Central, Newton Heath, Halliwell Rovers, Wigan County, Newton Heath, Bolton Wanderers, Wigan United

Dick Smith was the first player to score 20 goals in a season for Newton Heath, achieving that feat in his debut season, and on 3 November 1894 hit four goals in the local derby as the Heathens beat Manchester City 5-2 at Hyde Road. No other player in Newton Heath's history would emulate this achievement.

THOMAS GABLE 'TOM' SMITH

Country: England
Born: 18 Oct 1900 **Died:** 21 Feb 1934
Debut: 19 Jan 1924 v Fulham
Position: Inside-forward
Appearances: 90 **Goals scored:** 16
Seasons: 1923/24 – 1926/27
Clubs: Marsden Villa, Whitburn, South Shields, Leicester City, Manchester United, Northampton Town, Norwich City

A fee of £600 brought Tom Smith from Leicester City to United in January 1924, and he repaid them by scoring four goals in the final ten games of that season. An inside-forward who at times was considered a little overweight, he combined well with Joe Spence, but his performances were let down by his lack of goals, with only a dozen spread over his 83 league games. When things were not going right on the field, Smith was one of those to suffer from the terraces, and it was perhaps the voices of those supporters that the directors listened to when they decided to sell him to Northampton Town in June 1927 for a knockdown £250.

WILLIAM SMITH

Country: England
Born: Unknown **Died:** Unknown
Debut: 14 Sep 1901 v Middlesbrough
Position: Forward
Appearances: 17 **Goals scored:** 0
Seasons: 1901/02
Clubs: Stockport County, Manchester City, Stockport County, Newton Heath

William Smith played for Newton Heath in the club's final season under that name before it became Manchester United. The adaptable forward failed to score in any of his games for the Heathens, which may explain why he did not return when the club became United.

JOHN SNEDDON

Country: Unknown
Born: Unknown **Died:** Unknown
Debut: 3 Oct 1891 v Manchester City
Position: Forward
Appearances: 3 **Goals scored:** 1
Seasons: 1891/92
Clubs: Newton Heath

OLE GUNNAR SOLSKJAER

Country: Norway
Born: 26 Feb 1973
Debut: 25 Aug 1996 v Blackburn Rovers
Position: Forward
Appearances: 216 (150) **Goals scored:** 126
Seasons: 1996/97 – 2006/07
Clubs: Clausenengen, Molde, Manchester United

There will be no statue at Old Trafford for the 'baby-faced assassin', unless he returns to manage the club and surpasses the achievements of Messrs Busby and Ferguson, but if the supporters had their way, there would be a permanent monument for the player who gave so many of them the best night of their lives.

Signed as a complete unknown from Molde FK of Norway for a fee of £1.5 million in 1996, after United had failed to recruit Alan Shearer, he had first shown his prowess in front of goal with Norwegian Third Division outfit Clausenengen, where he scored 115 goals in 106 appearances. Such form was always going to attract attention and in 1994 he was transferred to Molde, where his two-year spell produced 31 strikes in 38 games.

Although some would have suggested that Alex Ferguson was taking a gamble, it was to prove one that would yield a priceless return. It took the new United No.20 only eight minutes of his debut to find the back of the net, and perhaps it was inevitable (given how his career developed) that he should do so having come off the bench. He became the first United substitute to score on his debut, and from then on he would terrorise defences while sending the terraces into raptures. He was the leading scorer in that first campaign, but his most prolific season would come in 2001/02 when he scored 25 goals.

In all, he would score 28 goals for United as a substitute, with Javier Hernandez (with 14) the closest to matching that tally. One of his finer moments came at the City Ground, Nottingham, in February 1999 when he came off the bench to score four in 12 minutes as United thrashed Forest 8-1, after having been sent on with instructions to keep it tight.

Solskjaer, however, might never have been anywhere near the City Ground that afternoon had a proposed transfer to Tottenham gone through the previous summer. United had, rather surprisingly, accepted the Londoners' bid, but with the decision down to the player, he decided to stay at United. Thankfully he did, as he was make the super-sub appearance to crown them all, coming on against Bayern Munich in the 1999 Champions League final in Barcelona with nine minutes remaining, and scored the dramatic 93rd-minute winner – the goal that clinched the Treble.

Later in his career he often found himself playing as a wide player, yet still managed to contribute regular goals from out there. In August 2004 he was forced to undergo surgery on a persistent knee injury and although he made a successful return, his playing days were now numbered and he announced his retirement in August 2007. Awarded a testimonial by United in August 2008, over 68,000 turned up to say thanks to the man who put the ball in the Germans' net.

But it was not a farewell to Old Trafford, as he took over the United reserve side, coaching them to a number of successes before returning to Molde as manager, guiding them to their first League Championship in their centenary year of 2011. Linked with a number of clubs who required a manager, he turned his back on them all, remaining at Molde and guiding them to a second title the following year, prompting numerous debates as to whether he might be the man to replace Sir Alex Ferguson at United.

JONATHAN MICHAEL PAUL SPECTOR

Country: USA
Born: 1 Mar 1986
Debut: 25 Aug 2004 v Dinamo Bucharesti
Position: Defender
Appearances: 4 (4) **Goals scored:** 0
Seasons: 2004/05
Clubs: Manchester United, Charlton Athletic (loan), West Ham United, Birmingham City

Having been spotted by a United scout while he was playing for the USA Under-17 side, Spector moved to Old Trafford, but after making eight appearances in 2004/05 was sold on to West Ham in June 2006 and played for them for five years before moving on to Birmingham City.

JOSEPH WATERS 'JOE' SPENCE

Country: England
Born: 15 Dec 1898 **Died:** 31 Dec 1966
Debut: 30 Aug 1919 v Derby County
Position: Forward
Appearances: 510 **Goals scored:** 168
Seasons: 1919/20 – 1932/33
Clubs: Scotswood, Manchester United, Bradford City, Chesterfield

'Give it to Joe' would echo around Old Trafford in the 1920s as, whenever a goal was required, you could almost guarantee that Joe Spence would either score, or conjure one up. Born in the north-east, he went down the mines at the age of 13 before joining the army three years later to serve in the First World War. On his demob, he returned to his roots but, before any of the local sides could react, United manager John Robson, having seen him score twice for amateur side Scotswood against Hartlepools United, invited him to Old Trafford.

In Manchester, he was to make an immediate impression, scoring four in his first unofficial appearance, against Bury on 29 March 1919, signing professional forms when normal football resumed soon afterwards. When regular league football began in August 1919, he was United's leading scorer in his first campaign. Capable of playing either centre-forward or outside-right with equal success, he went on to win England and Football League representative honours.

For much of that post-war decade or so, he was United's one true star performer. As well as being the leading scorer in 1919/20, he would achieve the same feat on five other occasions, with his best season coming in 1927/28 when his 22 goals saved the Reds from relegation – he hit a hat-trick against Liverpool on the last day of the season, as United finished a point above the drop zone. No wonder that a United programme 'Player Profile' from 1926/27 said that 'he would play anywhere in the interests of the club' and 'without Joe Spence, the United team would seem incomplete'. Frank Barson considered him 'one of the most dangerous leaders in the game'.

Scoring 168 goals in 510 appearances, it is unfortunate that he was never to win any honours with his club, but his place in the history of the club is guaranteed, as he gave so much to the United cause. He is the only pre-Second World War player to feature in United's all-time list of Top Ten goalscorers and appearance-makers, a mark of just how significant a figure he was outside of the Busby and Ferguson eras.

CHARLES WILLIAM 'CHARLIE' SPENCER

Country: England
Born: 4 Dec 1899 **Died:** 9 Feb 1953
Debut: 15 Sep 1928 v Liverpool
Position: Half-back
Appearances: 48 **Goals scored:** 0
Seasons: 1928/29 – 1929/30
Clubs: Newcastle United, Manchester United, Tunbridge Wells Rangers, Wigan Athletic

Having paid Newcastle United £3,250 for his signature, the United support might have expected more from Charlie Spencer than his 48 appearances. Signed to replace Frank Barson, having picked up an FA Cup winner's medal with the Tynesiders in 1924, plus a couple of England caps, he failed to offer the all-round play of the former No.5, being little more than a defensive player. Some thought he would regain his England place, but they were to be proved wrong, as, after a couple of years at Old Trafford, he dropped into non-league football.

WALTER SPRATT

Country: England
Born: Oct 1892 **Died:** Unknown
Debut: 6 Feb 1915 v Sunderland
Position: Full-back
Appearances: 13 **Goals scored:** 0
Seasons: 1914/15 – 1919/20
Clubs: Rotherham Town, Brentford, Manchester United, Brentford

Signed from Brentford for £175 in February 1915, following a month's trial, after the London club released all their players, Walter Spratt was to make all but one of his United appearances in season 1914/15. Things, however, could have been different had he not sustained an injury playing for Clapton Orient during the First World War. After one post-war appearance he rejoined Brentford.

GEORGE WILLIAM STACEY

Country: England
Born: Apr 1881 **Died:** 1972
Debut: 12 Oct 1907 v Newcastle United
Position: Full-back
Appearances: 270 **Goals scored:** 9
Seasons: 1906/07 – 1914/15
Clubs: Sheffield Wednesday, Thornhill United, Barnsley, Manchester United

Another of the many players who toiled in the mines before arriving at United, George Stacey moved to United from Barnsley in April 1907 for £400. Following his debut, a 6-1 victory over Newcastle United, Stacey went on to establish himself as a strong and capable full-back after claiming a regular first-team place in February 1908, as United strode to their initial First Division title. The following season, he was a member of the FA Cup-winning side, going on to claim a second Championship medal in 1911, when he made more appearances than anyone else in the squad.

Being in a successful United side and playing at a high and consistent level, he could perhaps consider himself unfortunate in that he never received any international recognition, other than playing in a trial match in 1912. He was still a first-team regular when the First World

War broke out; but he decided to hang up his boots and return to his home village of Thorpe Hesley, near Rotherham, where he ran a sweet shop and worked in the mines until he retired at the age of 65.

HAROLD 'HARRY' STAFFORD

Country: England
Born: 1869 **Died:** 1940
Debut: 3 Apr 1896 v Darwen
Position: Full-back
Appearances: 200 **Goals scored:** 1
Seasons: 1895/96 – 1901/02
Clubs: Southport Central, Crewe Alexandra, Newton Heath, Crewe Alexandra

Harry Stafford is a man to whom Manchester United owe so much, as it was the stocky full-back and Newton Heath captain who was unwittingly behind the influx of cash from John H. Davies that saved the club from going under. There are different versions of the story, but the more romantic one is that Stafford's St Bernard dog disappeared from the Heathens' fundraising bazaar and was found in one of Davies's pubs. With the brewery magnate's daughter wanting the animal for herself, a deal was done: the daughter got the dog, and Stafford got Davies to put some of his cash into the club. Soon after, with Davies now in charge, Newton Heath became Manchester United and everything began to change.

Before all that, Stafford was a full-back of distinction. He joined the Heathens from Crewe in March 1896, travelling there and back every day, never sure if he would have his expenses covered by the club. He also went on a door-to-door collection in order to find the train fares to take the team to Bristol for a fixture. While he may only have been captain during a period when the club was in the Second Division, there are few subsequent holders of that position who have had such an impact on the club's welfare. He was later to serve as a director.

JAKOB 'JAAP' STAM

Country: Netherlands
Born: 17 Jul 1972
Debut: 9 Aug 1998 v Arsenal

Position: Centre-back
Appearances: 125 (2) **Goals scored:** 1
Seasons: 1998/99 – 2001/02
Clubs: FC Zwolle, Cambuur Leeuwarden, Willem II, PSV Eindhoven, Manchester United, Lazio, AC Milan, Ajax

Having started his career with various smaller clubs in the Netherlands, Jaap Stam joined PSV in 1996 and spent two years with them, winning the league title in the first of them. By then already an established international, he joined United for a record fee of £10.75 million in the close season of 1998. He was given a torrid time on his debut against Arsenal in the Charity Shield. However, the tough-tackling, no-nonsense centre-back was quick to settle into the English game. He was a superb reader of the game and a huge obstacle in front of any forward, and was soon regarded as arguably the best defender in the country. Without doubt, Stam was the king-pin of the United defence as it strode to the Treble in 1998/99.

He continued to dominate United's defence in his second season, as they ended up runaway champions, and he was coveted by many. In his next season he picked up an Achilles injury, and while it didn't prevent him from picking up a third Premier League medal, the United manager decided he had lost a little bit and, given his age, decided to sell him to Lazio for £16.5 million in August 2001. He continued to play in Italy for five years, and eventually retired in 2007.

FRANCIS ANTHONY 'FRANK' STAPLETON

Country: Republic of Ireland
Born: 10 Jul 1956
Debut: 29 Aug 1981 v Coventry City
Position: Centre-forward
Appearances: 267 (21) **Goals scored:** 78
Seasons: 1981/82 – 1986/87
Clubs: Arsenal, Manchester United, Ajax, Anderlecht (loan), Derby County, Le Havre, Blackburn Rovers, Aldershot, Huddersfield Town, Bradford City, Brighton & Hove Albion

Frank Stapleton was the first player to score for two different teams in an FA Cup final – for Arsenal, ironically against United in 1979, and for United against Brighton in 1983. Invited to Old Trafford for trials as a

15-year-old Irish schoolboy but turned down by the club, he was to eventually cost United £900,000 when signed from Arsenal nine years later in August 1981.

Having joined the Highbury side in June 1972, Stapleton went on to score 109 goals in 300 games with the Londoners. Although not a prolific goalscorer, he had many admirers, one of them being the new United manager, Ron Atkinson, who, having lost Joe Jordan to Italian side AC Milan, sought a ready-made replacement. Although a vastly different player from Jordan, Stapleton was an experienced recruit and, with him being out of contract at Arsenal, this made the deal even more appealing to those who held the purse strings at Old Trafford.

He was soon to become a firm favourite with the United support, finishing top scorer in his first three seasons. He also turned in a couple of useful appearances in the centre of defence in the League Cup final of 1983 against Liverpool, following injury to Gordon McQueen, and in the 1985 FA Cup final following Kevin Moran's sending-off against Everton. Injury saw him lose his place in the starting line-up, with the signing of Brian McClair effectively ending his United career, and he was to join Ajax on a free transfer in August 1987.

R. STEPHENSON

Country: Unknown
Born: Unknown **Died:** Unknown
Debut: 11 Jan 1896 v Rotherham United
Position: Forward
Appearances: 1 **Goals scored:** 1
Seasons: 1895/96
Clubs: Talbot, Newton Heath, Northern Nomads

ALEXANDER CYRIL 'ALEX' STEPNEY

Country: England
Born: 18 Sep 1942
Debut: 17 Sep 1966 v Manchester City
Position: Goalkeeper
Appearances: 539 **Goals scored:** 2
Seasons: 1966/67 – 1977/78
Clubs: Tooting & Mitcham United, Millwall, Chelsea, Manchester United, Dallas Tornado, Altrincham

There is often talk about a player being 'the last piece of the jigsaw', and Alex Stepney was indeed the last piece of Matt Busby's jigsaw when he was signed in September 1966, as the United manager looked for the defensive stability to make a good team great.

Mitcham-born Stepney stepped into the senior ranks with Millwall in 1963, moving across London to Chelsea three years later in May 1966. One solitary appearance and four months later, he was on his way north to Manchester, joining United for a fee of £55,000, making Chelsea a £5,000 profit.

Keeping a clean sheet on his debut against Manchester City, he was still United's first-choice keeper 11 years later, seeing off challenges from the likes of Jimmy Rimmer and Paddy Roche. He also suffered the embarrassment of seeing a long punt from Tottenham keeper Pat Jennings bounce over his head and into the net during the 1967 FA Charity Shield match at Old Trafford. A few years later, however, Stepney would bring embarrassment to other keepers, as he was to score two penalties for United during season 1973/74, against Birmingham City and Leicester City. At one stage in that relegation campaign, he was United's joint leading scorer.

Awarded a testimonial by United in 1977 for his service to the club, few can have deserved one as much as he did. He had helped United to the league title in his first season, and followed it up the next year by making a crucial late save to prevent Eusebio from scoring what would surely have been the winner in the European Cup final, with the scores at 1-1. In the year of his testimonial, he won another medal, as United beat Liverpool 2-1 in the FA Cup final. It was an era of great English goalkeepers, with Gordon Banks, Ray Clemence and Peter Shilton preventing him from earning more than one cap. His 539 appearances for United is easily a club record for a goalkeeper.

ALFRED 'ALF' STEWARD

Country: England
Born: 18 Sep 1896 **Died:** Unknown
Debut: 23 Oct 1920 v Preston North End
Position: Goalkeeper
Appearances: 326 **Goals scored:** 0
Seasons: 1920/21 – 1931/32
Clubs: Manchester United, Manchester North End, Altrincham

Signed as an amateur in 1919, Steward was also a talented cricketer. Initially he couldn't break into the first team, so he ended up winning a Central League medal in 1920/21, but he did make his first-team debut that season. It wasn't until the early months of 1923/24 that he succeeded Jack Mew as the first-choice keeper.

He maintained a high level of consistency, missing few games over the course of the next three seasons, and his 25 clean sheets in 42 games, while conceding only 23 goals, played a major part in United gaining promotion from the Second Division in 1924/25. But a blip in form, when he let in 14 goals in three games during the early weeks of season 1927/28, cost him not just his United place, but a possible England cap. Happily, he bounced back with United, although international recognition passed him by. He remained a United player until June 1932 when he became player-manager of Manchester North End.

MICHAEL JAMES STEWART

Country: Scotland
Born: 26 Feb 1981
Debut: 31 Oct 2000 v Watford
Position: Midfield
Appearances: 7 (7) **Goals scored:** 0
Seasons: 2000/01 – 2002/03
Clubs: Manchester United, Royal Antwerp (loan), Nottingham Forest (loan), Heart of Midlothian (loan), Hibernian, Heart of Midlothian, Genclerbirligi, Charlton Athletic

A combative midfield player, his early club form, including a spell on loan at Royal Antwerp, promised so much, but Michael Stewart was never quite able to scale the heights. Born in Edinburgh, he began playing with local boys' club teams and Hutcheson Vale before being invited south by United as a 12-year-old for trials and training during the school holidays. He was subsequently snatched from under the nose of Rangers, with whom he trained regularly, signing for United as a trainee in June 1997.

Due to the competition for places in the United engine room, his appearances were limited, although he was to gain international recognition with Scotland. Loan spells at the likes of Nottingham Forest and Hearts brought him plenty of first-team experience, but he still couldn't break into United's first team on a regular basis. He was allowed to leave United in the summer of 2004, but it was not until the following year that he managed to obtain a permanent deal when he joined Hibs.

WILLIAM S. 'WILLIE' STEWART

Country: Scotland
Born: 11 Feb 1872 **Died:** Jun 1945
Debut: 4 Oct 1890 v Higher Walton
Position: Half-back
Appearances: 87 **Goals scored:** 5
Seasons: 1890/91 – 1894/95
Clubs: Dundee Our Boys, Warwickshire County, Newton Heath, Luton Town, Millwall Athletic, Luton Town, Thames Ironworks, Dundee

Born in Coupar Angus, Perthshire, in 1872, Stewart appeared in Newton Heath's initial match in the Football Alliance, scoring in the 4-1 victory over Sunderland Albion at North Road on 21 September 1889, ending the season as the club's leading scorer with ten goals. Later that season, on 7 April 1890, against Small Heath, he scored what was possibly the first hat-trick by a Newton Heath player in the 9-1 demolition of the club who were later to become Birmingham City, but none of these performances came in official games.

During the club's debut league season of 1892/93, he scored a hat-trick while playing at centre-half against Wolverhampton Wanderers in the 10-1 victory on 15 October – a match that still holds the record of the club's highest-scoring league win.

The week prior to that Wolves fixture, he was involved in a bizarre incident. In those days, hammer throwing was included in the training schedule and one of his attempts knocked Bob Donaldson unconscious. Fortunately, the striker made a quick and full recovery. Later that season, on 7 January 1893, he had to play in goal for the Heathens, but struggled as the Heathens lost 7-1.

Stewart was a more than capable player, but his reputation increased considerably following the switch to half-back. Opponents seldom outplayed him, and his footballing skills, something relatively rare in a defender's make-up at that time, enabled him to support his forwards time and time again. His association with Newton Heath came to an end in May 1895, when he moved south to join Luton Town.

WILLIAM TODD STEWART

Country: Scotland
Born: 29 Apr 1910 **Died:** Unknown
Debut: 19 Nov 1932 v Fulham
Position: Forward
Appearances: 49 **Goals scored:** 7
Seasons: 1932/33 – 1933/34
Clubs: Shettleston Juniors, Cowdenbeath, Manchester United, Motherwell

Glasgow-born Stewart was already familiar to United manager Scott Duncan through his performances for Cowdenbeath, a team he had joined at the start of 1931/32 season from Shettleston Juniors. The diminutive 5'5" outside-left soon became a favourite with the Cowdenbeath support, scoring 11 goals in 53 games. Duncan's return to his old club for his former player was to cost United £2,350, but despite this, he was to make only 49 appearances over two seasons, scoring a meagre seven goals. With United involved in a fight at the foot of the table in the latter half of 1933/34, money was urgently required to invest in players who could score goals, so Stewart and Charles McGillivray were sold to Motherwell. Back in Scotland, he helped his new club to the runners-up spot in the Scottish First Division.

NORBERT PETER 'NOBBY' STILES

Country: England
Born: 18 May 1942
Debut: 1 Oct 1960 v Bolton Wanderers
Position: Midfield/Defender
Appearances: 395 **Goals scored:** 19
Seasons: 1960/61 – 1970/71
Clubs: Manchester United, Middlesbrough, Preston North End

Nobby Stiles won five England Schoolboy caps before joining the Old Trafford groundstaff in September 1957. In his early days at the club, due to his tackles often being mistimed, Matt Busby sent him to an eye specialist, where it was found that an incident with a trolley bus some years previously had left him with impaired vision. Contact lenses immediately improved his game, although some might argue that his tackling was never to improve.

Having captained the youth team, the Collyhurst-born local lad made various first-team appearances in friendlies before his league debut at Bolton on 1 October 1960. With his competitive instinct and his tough, aggressive approach to the game, he made a big impact on the team, but he was to be severely disappointed at the end of 1962/63 when, despite having made 31 league appearances, he was omitted from United's FA Cup final line-up.

Regaining his place, he was soon knocking on the England international door, winning his first cap in April 1965, just before he earned a league title with United. A year later, he was dancing around Wembley holding aloft the World Cup, compensation indeed for missing out on United's visit in 1963. Further title honours (in 1967) and the ultimate club success of the European Cup in 1968 also came his way. The latter triumph meant that United were able to contest the Inter-Continental Cup against Estudiantes. Because of his tenacious performance against Argentina in the World Cup finals, he was greeted as a villain, and was provoked throughout the game in Buenos Aires, eventually retaliating when he was headbutted, and getting himself sent off for his pains.

To see him as just a destroyer would be to underplay his ability, for Stiles could play as well, setting the creative players ahead of him free to do what they did best. Furthermore, as a central defender, he was able to compensate for his lack of height through his reading of the game. Eventually, in the summer of 1971, he felt that the time was right to leave Old Trafford and he joined Middlesbrough for £20,000. He was later to return to United in a coaching capacity.

HERBERT HENRY STONE

Country: England
Born: Apr 1873 **Died:** Unknown
Debut: 26 Mar 1894 v Blackburn Rovers
Position: Half-back
Appearances: 7 **Goals scored:** 0
Seasons: 1893/94 – 1894/95
Clubs: Newton Heath, Ashton North End

IAN STOREY-MOORE

Country: England
Born: 17 Jan 1945
Debut: 11 Mar 1972 v Huddersfield Town
Position: Forward
Appearances: 43 **Goals scored:** 12
Seasons: 1971/72 – 1973/74
Clubs: Nottingham Forest, Manchester United, Burton Albion, Chicago Sting, Burton Albion, Shepshed Charterhouse, Burton Albion

Ian Storey-Moore was paraded at Derby's Baseball Ground in February 1972 as the Rams' new signing from Nottingham Forest, but it was a deal that had not been finalised and the goalscoring winger, who had notched up 117 goals in 271 appearances for Forest, was snatched by Frank O'Farrell the following month for £200,000. Scoring on his debut against Huddersfield Town, great things were expected from the England international, but his time at Old Trafford was blighted by injury and in December 1973 he was forced to retire on medical grounds at the age of only 28. He did make a brief return in lower league football, as well as playing briefly in the USA.

GORDON DAVID STRACHAN

Country: Scotland
Born: 9 Feb 1957
Debut: 25 Aug 1984 v Watford
Position: Midfield
Appearances: 196 (6) **Goals scored:** 38
Seasons: 1984/85 – 1988/89
Clubs: Dundee, Aberdeen, Manchester United, Leeds United, Coventry City

Born in Edinburgh, Gordon Strachan was a former Scottish Schoolboy international who joined Dundee in October 1971, straight from school. As a 14-year-old, he had been offered trials with Manchester United, but turned them down, as he had previously agreed to go to Dens Park. By the age of 19, he was team captain and over his two years there he was to make 87 appearances, scoring 15 goals. In November 1977, a cash-plus-player exchange saw him move to Aberdeen.

Under Alex Ferguson, Aberdeen became the top side in Scotland, pushing the 'Old Firm' of Rangers and Celtic into the background, winning the league in 1980 and 1984, the Scottish Cup in 1982, 1983 and 1984 and the European Cup-Winners' Cup in 1983. Strachan's performances won him the Scottish Player of the Year award in 1980, a year which also brought him his first Scotland cap. His effervescent play was soon attracting much attention beyond Scotland, with Ron Atkinson eventually winning a two-way battle for his signature, despite German side Cologne saying they had a pre-signed letter by Strachan, agreeing to sign for them. Eventually, Aberdeen agreed to pay the German club £100,000 in compensation and the player travelled south to join United, signing a four-year deal on 8 May 1984 for a fee of £600,000.

Strachan marked his United debut with a goal against Watford on the opening day of season 1984/85 and went on to score 15 in the league (one behind top scorer Mark Hughes), playing in all but one of the 42 fixtures. At the end of this season, he also added an FA Cup winner's medal to his already impressive hoard. An integral part of Ron Atkinson's attacking team, he became a firm favourite with the Old Trafford support, though he never replicated that first campaign's goalscoring success.

The arrival of Alex Ferguson meant he was relatively soon on his way to Leeds United in March 1989 for £300,000, where he was to have a late blossoming in his career, helping the Yorkshire side to the league title in 1992. After he retired, he managed various clubs, including Coventry City, Southampton, Celtic and Middlesbrough, before becoming Scotland boss in January 2013.

ERNEST STREET

Country: England
Born: 1878 **Died:** Unknown
Debut: 7 Feb 1903 v Liverpool
Position: Forward
Appearances: 3 **Goals scored:** 0
Seasons: 1902/03
Clubs: Sale Homefield, Manchester United

JOHN WILLIAM SUTCLIFFE

Country: England
Born: 14 Apr 1868 **Died:** 7 Jul 1947
Debut: 5 Sep 1903 v Bristol City
Position: Goalkeeper
Appearances: 28 **Goals scored:** 0
Seasons: 1903/04
Clubs: Bolton Wanderers, Millwall Athletic, Manchester United, Plymouth Argyle

When he signed for Manchester United in May 1903, John Sutcliffe was possibly the biggest name to have joined the club to that point. In February 1889, he had represented England against the New Zealand Maoris at rugby union, but with his Heckmondwike team suspended for alleged professionalism, he signed for Bolton Wanderers as a centre-forward, going on to win five England caps, thus becoming the last player to win international honours in both sports. He was also to win Football League honours and play in the 1894 FA Cup final. After spending 12 months in the Southern League with Millwall Athletic, he joined United at the age of 35, making 28 appearances before moving back down south to join Plymouth Argyle, where he continued to play until well into his 40s.

ERIC EDWIN SWEENEY

Country: England
Born: 3 Oct 1905 **Died:** Oct 1968
Debut: 13 Feb 1926 v Leeds United
Position: Forward
Appearances: 32 **Goals scored:** 7
Seasons: 1925/26 – 1929/30
Clubs: Flint Town, Manchester United, Charlton Athletic, Crewe Alexandra, Carlisle United

Sweeney made a perfect start at United, scoring on his debut in a 2-1 victory at Old Trafford. Despite that, he was to play only two more games in his first season at the club. The next campaign was his best, but after 13 games in the next three seasons he moved on to Charlton Athletic.

MASSIMO TAIBI

Country: Italy
Born: 18 Feb 1970
Debut: 11 Sep 1999 v Liverpool
Position: Goalkeeper
Appearances: 4 **Goals scored:** 0
Seasons: 1999/2000
Clubs: Licata, Trento, AC Milan, Como, Piacenza, AC Milan, Venezia, Manchester United, Reggina, Atalanta, Torino, Ascoli Calcio

NORMAN H. TAPKEN

Country: England
Born: 21 Feb 1913 **Died:** Jun 1996
Debut: 26 Dec 1938 v Leicester
Position: Goalkeeper
Appearances: 16 **Goals scored:** 0
Seasons: 1938/39
Clubs: Newcastle United, Manchester United, Darlington, Shelbourne

Signed from Newcastle in December 1938 for a fee of £850, Tapken got off to a reasonable start to his career in Manchester, but things went downhill quickly, when he conceded 16 goals in four games. Letting in five at Sunderland was the final nail in his United coffin, as he never played again. He joined Darlington in April 1947, after guesting for them, along with various others during the war years, while winning numerous honours in Ireland after joining Shelbourne in 1948/49.

CHRISTOPHER 'CHRIS' TAYLOR

Country: England
Born: 18 Oct 1899 **Died:** 16 Mar 1972
Debut: 17 Jan 1925 v Coventry City

Position: Forward
Appearances: 30 **Goals scored:** 7
Seasons: 1924/25 – 1931/32
Clubs: Evesham Town, Redditch United, Manchester United, Hyde United

A handful of games at inside-forward between January 1925 and April 1926 failed to elevate the £300 signing from Redditch into the First Division spotlight, after he had notched 20 goals in the United Central League side during 1924/25, but a switch to centre-forward in the fourth last game of 1925/26 saw Chris Taylor snatch a hat-trick, with another following ten days later. A cartilage operation put his out of action in 1927/28, while another injury the following season knocked a promising career completely off the rails. He did make something of a prolonged return during 1929/30, but as a centre-half, where he began to receive favourable attention, likening him to former United No.5s such as Frank Barson and Charlie Roberts. Sadly, injury struck once again and upon recovery he moved into non-league football.

ERNEST 'ERNIE' TAYLOR

Country: England
Born: 2 Sep 1925 **Died:** 9 Apr 1985
Debut: 19 Feb 1958 v Sheffield Wednesday
Position: Inside-forward
Appearances: 30 **Goals scored:** 4
Seasons: 1957/58 – 1958/59
Clubs: Hilton Colliery, Newcastle United, Blackpool, Manchester United, Sunderland, Altrincham, Derry City

With a build more suited to horse racing rather than football, Ernie Taylor made a name for himself as a play-making inside-forward with Newcastle, earning an FA Cup winner's medal in 1951, before joining Blackpool in a £27,000 move, where he formed an exciting partnership with Stanley Matthews, picking up a second FA Cup winner's medal in 1953. A few months later he won his only England cap in the notorious 6-3 Wembley defeat to Hungary.

Despite being 32 years of age, Jimmy Murphy considered him to be the ideal 'father figure' to guide his inexperienced players through the dark days following the Munich disaster, paying Blackpool £8,000. The diminutive and vastly experienced Taylor duly helped his young charges to Wembley, but was unable to win a third FA Cup with a third team. He returned to his native north-east, joining Sunderland in December 1958, for another 'life-saving' mission, with United recouping all but £1,000 of their initial outlay.

THOMAS 'TOMMY' TAYLOR

Country: England
Born: 29 Jan 1932 **Died:** 6 Feb 1958
Debut: 7 March 1953 v Preston North End
Position: Centre-forward
Appearances: 191 **Goals scored:** 131
Seasons: 1952/53 – 1957/58
Clubs: Barnsley, Manchester United

A new arrival at Old Trafford today comes accompanied by his agent and an entourage, all duly filmed by Sky TV, but back in March 1953, Tommy Taylor, United's new £29,999 signing from Barnsley, simply stepped off the train with his boots wrapped in a brown paper parcel to be met by assistant manager Jimmy Murphy and taken to Old Trafford and then to his new digs. Barnsley-born Taylor was in truth a record-breaking £30,000 signing, but not wanting to label his new acquisition with such a tag, Busby and the Barnsley directors gave the tea-lady a £1 tip.

Joining his local club from school, he made rapid progress from the groundstaff to the first team, and a hat-trick in only his second outing propelled him into the spotlight. Earmarked as a successor to Jack Rowley at Old Trafford, it was certainly a hard act to follow, but Rowley's 211 goals in 424 games was the target that Taylor began to aim for, marking his debut against Preston in March 1953 with a double, making it seven in 11 games by the end of that first season.

Within a matter of weeks of his United debut, he was pulling on the white shirt of England for the first time and soon the tall, well-built centre-forward with a strong shot, high work-rate and excellent heading ability was being recognised as one of the best in the country. Difficult to stop once he got into his stride, he was not, however, a greedy player in front of goal and was always prepared to support his fellow forwards. Championship medals in 1956 and 1957 were followed by an FA Cup runner-up medal in 1957, when he scored United's solitary effort in the 2-1 defeat by Aston Villa. In each of his four full seasons at Old Trafford he scored 20-plus goals, with a best of 34 in 1956/57. Further honours were certain to follow, while on the international front his 16 goals in 19 games suggested he would be a force to be reckoned with in the 1958 World Cup.

In February 1958, he was, at 26, approaching the peak of his career and with 131 goals in 191 United games, he was well on his way to surpassing Jack Rowley's record. The opportunity, however, was never to materialise as disaster struck at Munich. The boy who arrived with his boots in the paper parcel would score no more.

WALTER TAYLOR

Country: England
Born: 1901 **Died:** Unknown
Debut: 2 Jan 1922 v Sheffield United
Position: Forward
Appearances: 1 **Goals scored:** 0
Seasons: 1921/22
Clubs: New Mills, Manchester United

CARLOS ALBERTO TEVEZ

Country: Argentina
Born: 5 Feb 1984
Debut: 15 Aug 2007 v Portsmouth
Position: Centre-forward
Appearances: 73 (26) **Goals scored:** 34
Seasons: 2007/08 – 2008/09
Clubs: Boca Juniors, Corinthians, West Ham United, Manchester United, Manchester City, Juventus

From saint to sinner is the route that Carlos Tevez took, according to Reds fans, when he moved from United to City in the summer of 2009. The Argentinian had joined United from West Ham United on a two-year loan deal in August 2007, but negotiations over a permanent move were always going to prove difficult, because of the contractual arrangements he had. In May 2009, despite United stating that they would meet the required £25.5 million fee, the player was reported as saying that he no longer wanted to play for the club, allowing big-spending neighbours City the opportunity to step in and sign him.

He arrived in Britain to sign for West Ham in 2006, and became an immediate fans' favourite in London's East End, following a somewhat protracted, controversial move, having played for Boca Juniors in his native Argentina and Brazilian side Corinthians. Small, terrier-like and a handful for any defence, Tevez had the undoubted ability to both create and score chances, with Old Trafford a perfect stage for a player of potential world class. He played a key part in United's Champions League and Premier League-winning season of 2007/08, when the Reds boasted a forward line that also included Ronaldo, Rooney and Saha. Despite hinting before the end of season 2008/09 that his future lay elsewhere, the United support kept their fingers crossed that a deal could be sorted out, but it was not to be and he crossed Manchester where more controversy awaited.

HENRY 'HARRY' THOMAS

Country: Wales
Born: 28 Feb 1901 **Died:** Unknown
Debut: 22 Apr 1922 v Oldham Athletic
Position: Outside-left
Appearances: 135 **Goals scored:** 13
Seasons: 1921/22 – 1929/30
Clubs: Swansea Town, Porth, Manchester United, Merthyr Town, Abercam

Harry Thomas failed to make an impression with Swansea, but caught the attention of United manager John Chapman in the Welsh League with Porth, joining United in April 1922. It wasn't, however, until season 1925/26 that he gained a settled place in the first team, managing six goals in his 35 outings, having previously made only fleeting appearances. But it was a lack of goals that was to be his downfall as, despite making a further 70 first-team starts, he was to score a mere seven goals. He won his solitary Welsh cap in 1927 and in October 1930, having lost his first-team place, returned to his native Wales and joined Merthyr Town.

MICHAEL REGINALD 'MICKEY' THOMAS

Country: Wales
Born: 7 Jul 1954
Debut: 25 Nov 1978 v Chelsea
Position: Midfield
Appearances: 110 **Goals scored:** 15
Seasons: 1978/79 – 1980/81
Clubs: Wrexham, Manchester United, Everton, Brighton & Hove Albion, Stoke City, Chelsea, West Bromwich Albion, Derby County (loan), Wichita Wings, Shrewsbury Town, Leeds United, Stoke City, Wrexham

Mickey Thomas was a much-travelled individual, who by his own admission found the Old Trafford stage too big despite his undoubted talent. He began to hit the headlines with Wrexham, winning a Third Division Championship medal and 11 Welsh caps while at the Racecourse Ground before a £300,000 move took him to Old Trafford in November 1978. An all-action winger-cum-midfielder, his game improved under manager Dave Sexton. He helped United to the 1979 FA Cup final, but unfortunately not to success, as Arsenal grabbed a last-gasp winner. However, following Sexton's departure in 1981, he found himself surplus to new manager Ron Atkinson's requirements and was part of the transfer deal that brought full-back John Gidman from Goodison Park to Old Trafford, Thomas travelling in the opposite direction. Upon leaving United, he enjoyed a rollercoaster ride, once again hitting the heights with Wrexham.

JOHN ERNEST 'ERNIE' THOMPSON

Country: England
Born: 21 Jun 1909 **Died:** 28 Dec 1985
Debut: 21 Nov 1936 v Liverpool
Position: Forward
Appearances: 3 **Goals scored:** 1
Seasons: 1936/37 – 1937/38
Clubs: Newbiggin, Ashington, Stakeford United, Carlisle United, Bristol City, Bath City, Blackburn Rovers Manchester United, Gateshead, York City

WILLIAM THOMPSON

Country: Scotland
Born: Unknown **Died:** Unknown
Debut: 21 Oct 1893 v Burnley
Position: Forward
Appearances: 3 **Goals scored:** 0
Seasons: 1893/94
Clubs: Dumbarton, Aston Villa, Newton Heath

ARTHUR THOMSON

Country: England
Born: Jul 1903 **Died:** Unknown
Debut: 26 Jan 1929 v Bury
Position: Forward
Appearances: 5 **Goals scored:** 1
Seasons: 1928/29 – 1930/31
Clubs: West Stanley, Craghead United, West Stanley, Morecambe, Manchester United, Southend United, Coventry City, Tranmere Rovers

ERNEST THOMSON

Country: England
Born: 1884 **Died:** Unknown
Debut: 14 Sep 1907 v Middlesbrough
Position: Half-back
Appearances: 4 **Goals scored:** 0
Seasons: 1907/08 – 1908/09
Clubs: Darwen, Manchester United, Nelson, Cardiff City, Nelson

JAMES THOMSON

Country: Scotland
Born: Unknown **Died:** Unknown
Debut: 13 Dec 1913 v Bradford City
Position: Forward
Appearances: 6 **Goals scored:** 1
Seasons: 1913 /14
Clubs: Clydebank, Renton, Manchester United, Clyde, St Mirren

BENJAMIN LINDSAY 'BEN' THORNLEY

Country: England
Born: 21 Apr 1975
Debut: 26 Feb 1994 v West Ham United
Position: Winger
Appearances: 6 (8) **Goals scored:** 0
Seasons: 1993/94 – 1997/98
Clubs: Manchester United, Stockport County (loan), Huddersfield Town, Aberdeen, Blackpool, Bury, Halifax Town, Bacup Borough, Salford City, Wilmslow Albion, Witton Albion

A member of the famed 'Class of '92' youth team, Ben Thornley was a winger with a superb goal input and the potential to be one of the best of that multi-talented XI. He had already made his senior debut as a substitute against West Ham in February 1994, but when promotion to the first team looked more than a certainty, disaster struck. A crude tackle in a reserve-team fixture against Blackburn Rovers caused cruciate ligament damage to his knee, bringing a promising career to a premature halt. Thornley fought back, but despite occasional outings in the United starting line-up and from the bench, he could never quite recapture the form of his youth team days, becoming something of a journeyman footballer, plying his trade at a number of different clubs.

PAUL THOMAS TIERNEY

Country: Republic of Ireland
Born: 15 Sep 1982
Debut: 3 Dec 2003 v West Bromwich Albion
Position: Defender
Appearances: 1 **Goals scored:** 0
Seasons: 2003/04
Clubs: Manchester United, Crewe Alexandra (loan), Colchester United (loan), Bradford City (loan), Livingston, Blackpool, Stockport County (loan), Altrincham

MADS TIMM

Country: Denmark
Born: 31 Oct 1984
Debut: 29 Oct 2002 v Maccabi Haifa

Position: Forward
Appearances: 0 (1) **Goals scored:** 0
Seasons: 2002/03
Clubs: Manchester United, Viking (loan), Lyn (loan), Walsall (loan), Odense, Lyngby, Kerteminde

GRAEME MURDOCH TOMLINSON

Country: England
Born: 10 Dec 1975
Debut: 5 Oct 1994 v Port Vale
Position: Forward
Appearances: 0 (2) **Goals scored:** 0
Seasons: 1994/95
Clubs: Bradford City, Manchester United, Luton Town (loan), Bournemouth (loan), Millwall (loan), Macclesfield Town, Exeter City, Stevenage Borough, Kingstonian, Bedford Town, St Albans City, Billericay Town, Stotfold, Dunstable Town

WILLIAM EDWARD 'BILLY' TOMS

Country: Ireland
Born: 19 May 1895 **Died:** Unknown
Debut: 4 Oct 1919 v Middlesbrough
Position: Forward
Appearances: 14 **Goals scored:** 4
Seasons: 1919/20 – 1920/21
Clubs: Eccles Borough, Manchester United, Plymouth Argyle, Oldham Athletic, Coventry City, Stockport County, Wrexham, Crewe Alexandra, Great Harwood, Winsford United

Originally an outside-right, Toms was switched to centre-forward towards the end of season 1919/20 as relegation threatened and suddenly found his scoring touch with three goals in as many games. Three wins and three draws in the final seven games kept United in the First Division. Unfortunately, his contribution was to be ignored the following season, and he started only one fixture before being sold to Plymouth Argyle for £500 in September 1920.

HENRY TOPPING

Country: England
Born: 27 Oct 1908 **Died:** Jan 1977
Debut: 5 Apr 1933 v Bradford Park Avenue
Position: Full-back
Appearances: 12 **Goals scored:** 1
Seasons: 1932/33 – 1934/35
Clubs: Horwich RMI, Manchester United, Barnsley, Macclesfield

Although a full-back who managed only a dozen first-team appearances, Henry Topping deserves his place in United's history books, as had he not scored United's goal in the 1-1 draw with Swansea Town at Old Trafford in the penultimate game of season 1933/34, then relegation to the Third Division may well have been more than a possibility. He subsequently joined Barnsley in May 1935.

ZORAN TOSIC

Country: Serbia
Born: 28 Apr 1987
Debut: 24 Jan 2009 v Tottenham Hotspur
Position: Winger
Appearances: 0 (5) **Goals scored:** 0
Seasons: 2008/09 – 2009/10
Clubs: Budućnost Banatski Dvor, Banat Zrenjanin, Partizan, Manchester United, FC Cologne (loan), CSKA Moscow

Tosic never quite managed to establish himself at United, despite high hopes that he might be a winger for the future. Eventually he signed for CSKA Moscow in the summer of 2010 for an undisclosed fee. He has now won almost 50 caps for Serbia.

WILFRED 'WILF' TRANTER

Country: England
Born: 5 Mar 1945
Debut: 7 Mar 1964 v West Ham United
Position: Defender
Appearances: 1 **Goals scored:** 0

Seasons: 1963/64
Clubs: Manchester United, Brighton & Hove Albion, Baltimore Bays (loan), Fulham, St Louis Stars

JAMES EDWARD 'GEORGE' TRAVERS

Country: England
Born: 4 Nov 1888 **Died:** 31 Aug 1946
Debut: 7 Feb 1914 v Tottenham Hotspur
Position: Forward
Appearances: 21 **Goals scored:** 4
Seasons: 1913/14 – 1914/15
Clubs: Wolverhampton Wanderers, Birmingham, Aston Villa, Queens Park Rangers, Leicester Fosse, Barnsley, Manchester United, Swindon Town, Millwall Athletic, Norwich City, Gillingham, Nuneaton Town, Cradley St Luke's, Bilston United

Something of a footballing journeyman, George Travers put in a fair few miles during his lengthy career. He joined United in February 1914 from Barnsley, where he had gained an FA Cup winner's medal in the 1912 final. With United, he managed only 21 appearances, scoring four goals, before the First World War. After the war was over he moved to Swindon Town, before heading on to other clubs.

RYAN TUNNICLIFFE

Country: England
Born: 30 December 1992
Debut: 26 Sep 2012 v Newcastle United
Position: Midfield
Appearances: 0 (2) **Goals scored:** 0
Seasons: 2012/13 – present
Clubs: Manchester United, Peterborough United (loan), Barnsley (loan), Ipswich Town (loan)

Tunnicliffe has come up through the United academy, signing for the club on 1 July 2009, and helped the Reds to win the FA Youth Cup in 2011, winning the Jimmy Murphy Young Player of the Year award. An abrasive midfielder, fierce in the tackle, he has been loaned out to Ipswich Town for the first half of the 2013/14 season.

ALEXANDER 'SANDY' TURNBULL

Country: Scotland
Born: 30 Jul 1884 **Died:** 3 May 1917
Debut: 1 Jan 1907 v Aston Villa
Position: Forward
Appearances: 247 **Goals scored:** 101
Seasons: 1906/07 – 1914/15
Clubs: Hurlford, Manchester City, Manchester United

Sandy Turnbull was the scorer of the only goal in the 1909 FA Cup final and the following year he scored the first goal at United's new Old Trafford home. He was a product of Ayrshire and the Hurlford club, but United's scouts missed him and he was signed instead by Manchester City, who enticed him south in January 1902. Twelve goals in 22 games helped City to the Second Division Championship in 1903. Twelve months later he picked up an FA Cup winner's medal, scoring in every round up to the final.

But there was also another side to Turnbull, as he was occasionally caught up in disciplinary issues, once ending up in an onfield fist-fight during a game against Aston Villa.

There was more trouble, though not of his own doing, when he was one of several players caught up in an illegal payments scandal, and was suspended for the whole of 1906. United wasted little time in signing the player, unconcerned about any baggage that he carried, and he went straight into the United side, along with his City co-conspirators – Meredith, Burgess and Bannister – against Aston Villa on New Year's Day 1907. For Turnbull, it was a memorable afternoon on the muddied pitch, as he scored the only goal of the match from a Meredith cross in the 60th minute.

Season 1907/08 brought Manchester United their first major honour, in the form of the First Division Championship, with Sandy Turnbull the club's leading goalscorer with 25 goals from 30 league appearances. Injury interrupted his career in 1908/09, but for the next two season's he averaged a goal every two games, and so helped United to a second title in 1910/11. Turnbull continued to find the net on a fairly regular basis during the next three seasons, but his career was to come to an abrupt end in 1915, almost a year after having received a benefit match against City, when he was caught up in the match-fixing allegations centred on the 2 April game against Liverpool. He was suspended for life a result, along with Enoch West, Arthur Whalley and four Liverpool players.

By this time, however, he had joined the army and enlisted with the Middlesex Regiment. He always denied the allegations, and after he was killed at Arras, in France, on 3 May 1917, he was granted a posthumous pardon.

JAMES 'JIMMY' TURNBULL

Country: Scotland
Born: 23 May 1884 **Died:** Unknown
Debut: 28 Sep 1907 v Chelsea
Position: Forward
Appearances: 78 **Goals scored:** 45
Seasons: 1907/08 – 1909/10
Clubs: East Stirlingshire, Dundee, Falkirk, Rangers, Preston North End, Leyton, Manchester United, Bradford Park Avenue, Chelsea, Manchester United, Hurst

The summer of 1907 saw Jimmy Turnbull forsake the rigours of the Southern League to sign for Manchester United from Leyton. His debut at Chelsea on 28 September 1907 passed without note, but a week later he opened his scoring account, scoring a further five in the next four games. His United career was to be an eventful one, containing a mixture of highs and lows. On 29 August 1908 at Stamford Bridge, he scored a hat-trick against Southern League Champions Queens Park Rangers, which saw the name of Manchester United become the first to be engraved on the FA Charity Shield. The first match between the two sides, on 27 April 1908, had ended in a 1-1 draw, but Turnbull's hat-trick in a 4-0 replay win determined the first destination of the trophy.

Early in season 1909/10, he hit the headlines two weeks in a row, but for incidents that were to show a different side to Jimmy Turnbull. In the last four minutes of the match against Aston Villa at Clayton, on 16 October 1909, he was sent off, along with Villa's left-half Hunter. Seven days later, against Sheffield United away, he once again made an early exit, sent off in the second half for kicking an opponent.

In the summer of 1910, he caused a surprise by retiring from the game and returned home to Scotland. Rangers had offered £200 for his services, and Turnbull was keen to go, as he had intended going into business with his brother in the area. However, his retirement was short-lived as in September 1910 he joined Bradford Park Avenue, later moving to Chelsea in June 1912. In September 1914, Turnbull returned to Old Trafford in a reserve-team fixture, but Chelsea wanted a £300 transfer fee, which was beyond the cash-strapped United at that time.

TURNER

Country: Unknown
Born: Unknown **Died:** Unknown
Debut: 25 Oct 1890 v Bootle Reserves
Position: Forward
Appearances: 1 **Goals scored:** 0
Seasons: 1890/91
Clubs: Newton Heath

CHRISTOPHER ROBERT 'CHRIS' TURNER

Country: England
Born: 15 Sep 1958
Debut: 14 Dec 1985 v Aston Villa
Position: Goalkeeper
Appearances: 79 **Goals scored:** 0
Seasons: 1985/86 – 1987/88
Clubs: Sheffield Wednesday, Lincoln City (loan), Sunderland, Manchester United, Sheffield Wednesday, Leeds United (loan), Leyton Orient

Chris Turner was a £275,000 signing from Sunderland in August 1985, following a successful spell in the north-east where he made almost 200 appearances. Initially an understudy to Gary Bailey, he claimed the No.1 jersey for almost all of 1986, before losing his place to Gary Walsh. Despite reclaiming his first-team place in December 1987, his hopes of a long-term future as United's first-choice keeper were dashed when Alex Ferguson signed Jim Leighton and, realising that his opportunities were always going to be limited, he moved to Sheffield Wednesday in September 1988 for £175,000. He was to gain some revenge during 1990/91 when he was a member of the Wednesday side that beat United in the League Cup final. After retiring, he had various managerial roles and is currently chief executive of Chesterfield.

JOHN TURNER

Country: England
Born: Unknown **Died:** Unknown
Debut: 22 Oct 1898 v Loughborough Town
Position: Half-back
Appearances: 4 **Goals scored:** 0
Seasons: 1898/99
Clubs: Gravesend United, Newton Heath

ROBERT TURNER

Country: England
Born: 1877 **Died:** Unknown
Debut: 8 Oct 1898 v Port Vale
Position: Half-back
Appearances: 2 **Goals scored:** 0
Seasons: 1898/99
Clubs: Newton Heath, Brighton United, Fulham, Glentoran

MICHAEL JOHN TWISS

Country: England
Born: 26 Dec 1977
Debut: 25 Feb 1998 v Barnsley
Position: Midfield
Appearances: 1 (1) **Goals scored:** 0
Seasons: 1997/98 – 1999/2000
Clubs: Manchester United, Sheffield United (loan), Port Vale, Leigh RMI, Chester City, Morecambe, Stalybridge Celtic, Altrincham

SIDNEY TYLER

Country: England
Born: 7 Dec 1904 **Died:** 25 Jan 1951
Debut: 10 Nov 1923 v Leicester City
Position: Full-back
Appearances: 1 **Goals scored:** 0
Seasons: 1923/24
Clubs: Manchester United, Wolverhampton Wanderers, Gillingham, Millwall, Colwyn Bay United

U

JOHN FRANCOMBE 'IAN' URE

Country: Scotland
Born: 7 Dec 1939
Debut: 23 Aug 1969 v Wolverhampton Wanderers
Position: Centre-half
Appearances: 65 **Goals scored:** 1
Seasons: 1969/70 – 1970/71
Clubs: Dundee, Arsenal, Manchester United, St Mirren

For supporters of a certain age, Ian Ure's performances at Old Trafford conjure up only one image and that is in an Arsenal shirt, trading punches with Denis Law in the centre circle before both were sent off in October 1967. Ayrshire-born Ure made a name for himself with Dundee, where he was the cornerstone in the Dens Park club's Scottish First Division success in 1961/62. With a shock of blond hair and standing over six feet tall, he certainly stood out in more ways than one and was soon a target for numerous top sides. Arsenal won the chase in August 1963 when they paid £62,500 to take him south.

When Bill Foulkes called time on his United career, there was a need for a strong, commanding centre-half, with United paying out £80,000 to bring the Scottish international north, despite many feeling that his best days were behind him. Season 1970/71 was spent mainly in the reserves and at the end of 1971/72 he was given a free transfer, moving back to Scotland to join St Mirren. He was later to move into management with East Stirlingshire, taking over the reins from a certain Alex Ferguson.

LUIS ANTONIO VALENCIA MOSQUERA

Country: Ecuador
Born: 4 Aug 1985
Debut: 9 Aug 2009 v Chelsea
Position: Winger
Appearances: 113 (35) **Goals scored:** 17
Seasons: 2009/10 – present
Clubs: El Nacional, Villarreal CF, Recreativo (loan), Wigan Athletic, Manchester United

A horrific injury against Rangers in a Champions League fixture in September 2010 interrupted a promising start to Valencia's United career, following move from Wigan Athletic for an undisclosed fee in the summer of 2009. In his three-year spell at Wigan, originally on loan, he earned countless plaudits with his strong, direct wing play and his ability to provide great crosses for his strikers to feed off, and it soon became obvious that he was destined for bigger things.

Signed as a replacement for Cristiano Ronaldo, he focused on doing his job, rather than trying to replicate the Portuguese star. As such, his form continued to improve after moving to Old Trafford and he was one of the most regular names on the teamsheet, setting up Wayne Rooney's winner in the 2010 League Cup final. Returning from that broken ankle injury, his career took up where it had left off, and he ended the campaign with a Premier League medal. He was back to his best the next season, and it came as no surprise when he was named both fans' and players' Player of the Year, as well as scoring the Goal of the Season in 2011/12.

In 2012/13 he wore the legendary No.7 shirt, but had a relatively quiet start to the campaign, before gradually displaying his true form as United strode to yet another Premier League success. He has now won more than 60 caps for Ecuador.

ROBERT 'BOB' VALENTINE

Country: England
Born: Unknown **Died:** Unknown
Debut: 25 Mar 1905 v Blackpool
Position: Goalkeeper
Appearances: 10 **Goals scored:** 0
Seasons: 1904/05 – 1905/06
Clubs: Manchester United

Bob Valentine was perhaps one of United's oddest signings ever, coming from Swinton rugby league club. Due to his expertise with the oval ball, it is perhaps no surprise that he was to emerge as a goalkeeper, despite being signed as a full-back. He kept a clean sheet on his debut and was to concede only eight goals in his ten first-team outings. Upon being released by United at the end of the 1906/07 season, he returned to Swinton.

RAIMOND VAN DER GOUW

Country: Netherlands
Born: 24 Mar 1963
Debut: 21 Sep 1996 v Aston Villa
Position: Goalkeeper
Appearances: 48 (12) **Goals scored:** 0
Seasons: 1996/97 – 2001/02
Clubs: Go Ahead Eagles, Vitesse, Manchester United, West Ham United, RKC Waalwijk, AGOVV Apeldoorn

Raimond van der Gouw was signed by United in 1996 from Vitesse Arnhem for £500,000 as experienced cover for Peter Schmeichel, following a highly successful career in his native Netherlands. Although managing on average only ten games per season over his six years at Old Trafford, van der Gouw was a consistent and reliable goalkeeper and, despite being little more than a reserve, the popular custodian managed to claim Premier League, FA Cup and Champions League medals while at the club, but would obviously have enjoyed making a more telling contribution. When called upon he never let himself or the club down and had he been a couple of years younger might have claimed the No.1 jersey as United searched for a successor to Peter Schmeichel.

EDWIN VAN DER SAR

Country: Netherlands
Born: 29 Oct 1970
Debut: 9 Aug 2005 v Debreceni
Position: Goalkeeper
Appearances: 266 **Goals scored:** 0
Seasons: 2005/06 – 2010/11
Clubs: Ajax, Juventus, Fulham, Manchester United

Vying with Peter Schmeichel as United's greatest-ever goalkeeper, the Dutchman was seen by Sir Alex Ferguson as an ideal replacement for the big Dane, but the United manager missed out and van der Sar instead joined Juventus for a fee of about £5 million. At Ajax, he had won four Dutch league titles, the UEFA Cup in 1992, the Champions League in 1995 and countless international caps. His time in Italy was short-lived, and he moved to London after only two seasons to join Fulham for a fee of £7 million. Had he signed for United when interest was first shown, then who knows what the record books would show today, but what they do tell is that there have been few, if any, better goalkeepers in the history of the game.

Following four seasons at Craven Cottage, Ferguson finally got his man, saying: 'Edwin will bring the vital extra ingredients of personality and experience, someone who could encourage and talk to the defence and say the right things.' The Dutchman's arrival effectively signalled the end for Roy Carroll and Tim Howard at United. He settled quickly at Old Trafford, showing that he was every inch a world-class goalkeeper by the fact that he won 130 caps for the Netherlands, kept a clean sheet for a record-breaking 1,311 minutes and was voted UEFA's goalkeeper of the year in 2009.

There were, of course, occasional errors, but for United supporters around the globe, they will all have the same lasting memory of the 6'5" keeper: the moment when, on a rain-soaked night in Moscow, he flung himself to the right to save Nicolas Anelka's penalty, the last in the shoot-out against Chelsea in the 2008 Champions League final in Moscow. Thirteen years after he had last won a Champions League medal, he now had a second.

When he played his final game for United in the 2011 Champions League final, he became the oldest post-war player to represent the club, at 40 years and 211 days. Although there was no winner's medal that night, by then he had also won four Premier League titles, two League Cups and the Club World Cup while at United. It was a truly impressive haul from a truly impressive player.

RUTGERUS JOHANNES MARTINUS 'RUUD' VAN NISTELROOY

Country: Netherlands
Born: 1 Jul 1976
Debut: 12 Aug 2001 v Liverpool
Position: Centre-forward
Appearances: 200 (19) **Goals scored:** 150
Seasons: 2001/02 – 2005/06
Clubs: Den Bosch, Heerenveen, PSV Eindhoven, Manchester United, Real Madrid, Hamburg, Malaga

Ruud van Nistelrooy was due to join United in the summer of 2000 after scoring 29 goals in 23 league games for PSV, helping them to the Dutch title, but a cruciate knee ligament injury postponed the deal for a year. When he did eventually join, for a fee of about £19 million, he was coming in to a side that had won the league title in each of the previous three seasons.

It didn't take him long to show what he was all about, as he scored on his debut in the Community Shield against Liverpool. A week later, on his Old Trafford debut, he scored twice in the Reds' 3-2 victory over Fulham, and from then on there was little stopping him. He scored 36 goals in his first campaign, including a remarkable ten in the Champions League, and set a record by scoring in eight successive matches in the Premier League. Despite the fact United missed out on the title by ten points, he was the PFA Player of the Year.

He was even more prolific in 2002/03, scoring 44 goals, second only to Denis Law's record of 46 in season 1963/64. In the Premier League his 25 goals, including three hat-tricks, helped United to the title, while in the Champions League he scored 14 goals, including being on target in both legs of ties against Juventus and Real Madrid, showing that the bigger the foe the better he performed.

After scoring in the first two games of 2003/04, he had bettered his own record, scoring in ten successive Premier League games, but had to settle for the FA Cup at the end of the season, firing home twice in United's 3-0 victory over Millwall to ensure he ended the campaign with 30-plus goals for a third successive season. Injury interrupted his career in the next season, while his time at United was to end after 2005/06, as he was sold to Real Madrid, going on to win La Liga twice. By the time he left, he had reached a tally of 150 goals for United, almost all of them scored from inside the box, where he was at his predatory best. Only Tommy Taylor, at 68.59 goals per 100 games, beats his strike rate of 68.49, while in the Premier League he is easily top of the list.

ROBIN VAN PERSIE

Country: Netherlands
Born: 6 Aug 1983
Debut: 20 August 2012 v Everton
Position: Centre-forward
Appearances: 41 (8) **Goals scored:** 32
Seasons: 2012/13 – present
Clubs: Feyenoord, Arsenal, Manchester United

The magic of Manchester United was still in evidence with the signing of Robin van Persie from Arsenal in August 2012. Across the city, there was apparently the lure of a larger wage packet with the current Premier League champions, but the 'little boy' inside him said Manchester United, and Sir Alex Ferguson had his man, paying £24 million to land the 29-year-old.

Growing up in Rotterdam, the young van Persie's career had begun as a 14-year-old with SBV Excelsior's youth team in 1997, but a year later he moved to Feyenoord, breaking into the first-team set-up within two years, lifting the KNVB Best Young Talent award in 2001/02. He had also broken into the Dutch international scene, playing at Under-17, Under-19 and Under-21 levels. His senior debut came against Romania in 2005.

If his rise to the top had been swift, he was brought back down to earth with a bang when coach Bert van Marwijk sent him home prior to the 2002 Super Cup final against Real Madrid and banished him to the Feyenoord reserve side. He was also made available for transfer and, despite a commendable 22 goals in 78 games, there was little interest in him until Arsène Wenger decided that he was worth a gamble and took the 20-year-old to London for a modest £2.75 million fee.

With the Gunners, he was moved from his usual wide position into a more central role and he quickly showed that he had an eye for goal. Injuries often interrupted his progress, but he still managed to score some 96 goals in 194 Premier League appearances, eventually becoming Arsenal's captain. In 2011/12, he didn't miss a game, and his productivity immediately increased as he scored 30 times and was voted the Footballer of the Year by both the PFA and the FWA. However, his trophy haul with the Gunners was minimal, as he lifted only the FA Cup in 2005 and the FA Community Shield in 2004, and this lack of silverware was one of the major factors in his move away from the Emirates.

On his arrival at United, he scored on his home debut against Fulham and followed it up with a hat-trick in his next game. He kept on scoring, and finished his first season with United with 30 goals, helping the Reds secure the title with a stunning hat-trick against Aston Villa – the second of which (a brilliant volley from an inch-perfect Rooney pass) was voted the 'Goal of the Season' by the fans. It had been the lure of silverware that had helped persuade him come to United; his next aim was to win more.

JAMES VANCE

Country: Scotland
Born: 1877 **Died:** Unknown
Debut: 3 Feb 1896 v Leicester City
Position: Forward
Appearances: 11 **Goals scored:** 1
Seasons: 1895/96 – 1896/97
Clubs: Annbank, Newton Heath, Fairfield, Annbank

James Vance was one of a number of players signed from the Ayrshire side Annbank. The teenager stepped straight into the first team, making his debut on 3 February 1896, against Leicester City, at Clayton, in a 2-0 defeat. Five days later, he opened his scoring account with the Heathens, netting the only goal in the 4-1 defeat by Burton Swifts. Despite missing the next match, he returned to the side for the final eight games of the season, failing to score. Re-signed for season 1896/97, he played only one game by the end of October, and so just before the end of the year left for Fairfield, the Heathens' 'vulture' club – as the Manchester club always seemed happy to sign up any discarded individuals from their more illustrious neighbours.

MARNICK DANNY VERMIJL

Country: Belgium
Born: 13 January 1992
Debut: 26 Sep 2012 v Newcastle United
Position: Right-back
Appearances: 1 **Goals scored:** 0
Seasons: 2012/13 – present
Clubs: Standard Liège, Manchester United, NEC Nijmegen (loan)

A regular in United's Under-21 squad, playing mostly at right-back, he made his senior debut last season in the third round of the League Cup, helping the Reds to a 2-1 victory. Vermijl joined United from Standard Liège in 2010, and has won Under-21 honours for Belgium.

JUAN SEBASTIÁN VERÓN

Country: Argentina
Born: 9 Mar 1975
Debut: 19 Aug 2001 v Fulham
Position: Midfield
Appearances: 75 (7) **Goals scored:** 11
Seasons: 2001/02 – 2002/03
Clubs: Estudiantes, Boca Juniors, Sampdoria, Parma, Lazio, Manchester United, Chelsea, Internazionale (loan), Estudiantes, Brandsen, Estudiantes

Seba Verón followed in his father's footsteps by playing at Old Trafford, but as a United player, whereas his father had been a member of the Estudiantes side who snatched the Inter-Continental Cup from United's grasp in 1968. A hugely talented individual, who had begun his career with Estudiantes before moving to Boca Juniors, Sampdoria and Parma, he was signed from Lazio for a club record fee of £28.1 million.

Already an established international for Argentina, his performances on the Old Trafford stage didn't always live up to his hefty price tag, though injuries and a difficulty in settling down in Manchester did not help him. He was part of the 2002/03 title-winning side, but perhaps struggled to adapt to the frantic pace of the Premier League. He was signed to give the Reds European know-how, and many of his best performances came on European nights in the Champions League. The manager continued to stand by his man, but a £15 million bid by Chelsea persuaded United to cut their losses and allowed the 'Little Witch' to depart to Stamford Bridge.

NEMANJA VIDIĆ

Country: Serbia
Born: 21 Oct 1981
Debut: 25 Jan 2006 v Blackburn Rovers
Position: Centre-back
Appearances: 259 (8) **Goals scored:** 19
Seasons: 2005/6 – present
Clubs: Red Star Belgrade, Spartak Subotica (loan), Spartak Moscow, Manchester United

A rare mid-season signing by Sir Alex Ferguson, it did not take the relatively unknown Nemanja Vidić long to endear himself to the United faithful, following his £7.2 million move from Spartak Moscow in January 2006. He grew up during the Yugoslav civil war, before joining Red Star Belgrade where he soon had success, before joining Spartak in the summer of 2004. A tough, no-nonsense defender, whose physical approach to the game and bravery would cost him numerous appearances, he added the grit to his defensive partner Rio Ferdinand's more finessed approach, a combination that has served United well ever since.

He took a short while to adjust to the English game, but he soon adapted, although his progress was set back a little due to a broken collarbone in March 2007. He went on to become a fans' favourite, winning their Player of the Year award, and also the players' Player of the Year award in 2008/09. Succeeding Gary Neville as club captain, Vidić led by example, going on to win the Barclay's Player of the Season award in 2010/11.

His robust style of play occasionally brought him disciplinary problems, including seeing red in three successive games against Liverpool, and he spent considerable time on the sidelines following a cruciate knee ligament injury in 2011/12. Many commentators suggested that had he stayed fit, he would have made the difference in that year's title race.

Although he was to play less than a couple of dozen games during the 2012/13 title-winning season, he still maintains a massive influence within the club and plays an important part in the progress of the younger players around him. It was his fifth Premier League title at United, and he has also earned three League Cup winner's medals and the Champions League title in 2008.

ERNEST 'ERNIE' VINCENT

Country: England
Born: 28 Oct 1910 **Died:** 2 Jun 1978
Debut: 6 Feb 1932 v Chesterfield
Position: Half-back
Appearances: 65 **Goals scored:** 1
Seasons: 1931/32 – 1933/34
Clubs: Seaham Harbour, Southport, Manchester United, Queens Park Rangers, Doncaster Rovers

One thousand pounds for a player who had cost them nothing was considered good business by Southport when they sold Ernie Vincent to United in February 1932. He had represented Durham County as a schoolboy and worked down the mines before joining Seaham Harbour as a professional. A hard-tackling defensive player, he missed only two games out of 58 before finding himself out of the side at the start of 1933/34, a season that was to see the club struggle for Second Division survival. Despite long spells in the reserves, he remained at the club until the end of 1934/35, when he left to join Queens Park Rangers.

DENNIS SIDNEY VIOLLET

Country: England
Born: 20 Sep 1933 **Died:** 6 Mar 1999
Debut: 11 Apr 1953 v Newcastle United
Position: Forward
Appearances: 293 **Goals scored:** 179
Seasons: 1952/53 – 1961/62
Clubs: Manchster United, Stoke City, Baltimore Bays, Witton Albion, Linfield

Dennis Viollet could have made a name for himself in the light blue of Manchester City, not in the red of United. He was born in the shadow of their Maine Road ground, supported them as a boy and was due to have a trial with them, but this was when events took a different course. The captain of the Manchester, Lancashire and England Schools sides had been told by City goalkeeper Frank Swift to visit Maine Road in order to arrange a trial, but being kept waiting for an hour, he and his father returned home having seen no one. United, however, were on his case and despite the household's love for everything City, Busby persuaded the Viollets that Old Trafford was the place to be, with the Maine Road side's lack of courtesy swinging the decision in the direction of the Reds.

Viollet signed for United in September 1949 and made his league bow on 11 April 1953 at Newcastle, keeping his place and scoring the first of his many goals the following week against West Bromwich Albion at Old Trafford. Although slimly built, his ability more than made up for his lack of brawn and when he was handed the No.10 shirt against Huddersfield in October 1953, for what was his sixth first-team appearance, he grasped the opportunity with both hands and kept a tight grip on it for most of the next seven years.

With a regular place in the side, the goals began to flow and it was only the burly centre-forward Tommy Taylor that could surpass his total. But his game was not simply about scoring goals, as he was a hugely talented individual, capable of making darting forward runs, bringing his team-mates into the game with accurate, telling passes and creating positions for himself which would lead to those inevitable goals.

Munich put his career on hold, but having survived the crash he returned in the latter stages of 1957/58, playing in the FA Cup final for the second successive season, but failing to add a winner's medal to the league titles he'd won in the previous two campaigns. Neither did the disaster stem the flow of goals, with season 1959/60 producing a club record of 32 league goals in a season, his form earning him two England caps, a total that should have been more. He also won three Football League caps.

There was another side to Viollet, who was a jack-the-lad character, and it was perhaps this that brought his days at United to a premature close, with a £25,000 transfer to Stoke City in January 1962. At the Potteries, he helped his new club to the Second Division title the following season, with 23 goals in 37 games, with a League Cup runner-up medal coming 12 months later. After five years, he called time on his Stoke career and went to America to join Baltimore Bays, before returning to play for Witton Albion.

GEORGE VOSE

Country: England
Born: 4 Oct 1911 **Died:** 20 Jun 1981
Debut: 26 Aug 1933 v Plymouth Argyle
Position: Centre-half
Appearances: 209 **Goals scored:** 1
Seasons: 1933/34 – 1938/39
Clubs: Peasley Cross Athletic, Manchester United, Runcorn

'Vose now appears in the centre-half position with distinction' states the back of his 1939 cigarette card, going on to add that the St Helens-born, former Peasley Cross Athletic man was a talented natural ball-player, who was always eager to assist his attack with constructive play. The strong defender, who joined United in September 1932, perhaps deserved more than being part of an often struggling United side. He didn't make his debut until the first game the season after, and soon found himself in a relegation battle. He won a Division Two Championship medal in 1935/36, but was unable to prevent United from being relegated the next season. Fortunately, the Reds bounced straight back up and he played more games than anyone else in United's final pre-war season. He could perhaps have added further honours had it not been for the Second World War. During the hostilities, he guested for Chester, Manchester City, Stockport and Derby County, but retired when official football resumed in 1946.

COLIN WALDRON

Country: England
Born: 22 Jun 1948
Debut: 4 Oct 1976 v Sunderland
Position: Centre-half
Appearances: 4 **Goals scored:** 0
Seasons: 1976/77
Clubs: Bury, Chelsea, Burnley, Manchester United, Sunderland, Tulsa Roughnecks, Philadelphia Fury, Atlanta Chiefs, Rochdale

DENNIS ALAN WALKER

Country: England
Born: 26 Oct 1944 **Died:** 11 Aug 2003
Debut: 20 May 1963 v Nottingham Forest
Position: Midfield
Appearances: 1 **Goals scored:** 0
Seasons: 1962/63
Clubs: Manchester United, York City, Cambridge United

Former Cheshire Schoolboys captain Dennis Walker became the first black player to play for United when he was selected instead of Bobby Charlton for the last league game of the 1962/63 season, so that Charlton could be rested ahead of the FA Cup final. The former groundstaff boy did not make any more appearances for United, and in April 1964 he moved to York City, helping them to promotion the year after. Subsequently, he played for Cambridge United, and made 211 league appearances for his three clubs.

ROBERT WALKER

Country: Unknown
Born: Unknown **Died:** Unknown
Debut: 14 Jan 1899 v Glossop

Position: Defender
Appearances: 2 **Goals scored:** 0
Seasons: 1898/99
Clubs: Newton Heath

GEORGE WALL

Country: England
Born: 20 Feb 1885 **Died:** Apr 1962
Debut: 7 Apr 1906 v Leyton Orient
Position: Outside-left
Appearances: 319 **Goals scored:** 100
Seasons: 1905/06 – 1914/15
Clubs: Barnsley, Manchester United, Oldham Athletic, Hamilton Academical, Rochdale

Born in Boldon Colliery, near Sunderland, George Wall joined United from Barnsley for £175 on 31 March 1906, scoring the only goal of the game on his debut against Clapton Orient seven days later. He played an influential part in the last seven games of the season, ensuring that United clinched promotion to the First Division as runners-up to Bristol City.

A goalscoring outside-left with a sophisticated left foot, Wall was to become one of the outstanding wing men of the pre-First World War era, appearing in more first-team games for United than any other player, as well as being the club's most-capped England international until the 1950s. With United, he picked up two First Division, an FA Cup and an FA Charity Shield winner's medals. In addition to his seven England caps, he also won five at Football League level and represented the FA during the 1910 tour of South Africa. But it was his goals that really set him apart from other wide men of the time, and he was twice the club's leading scorer.

During the First World War, when he served as a sergeant in the Black Watch, Wall played only a few games for United, with his final outing in a friendly against Southport Vulcan in February 1919. He joined Oldham Athletic the following month, and later played for Hamilton and Rochdale.

DAVID LLOYD 'DANNY' WALLACE

Country: England
Born: 21 Jan 1964
Debut: 20 Sep 1989 v Portsmouth
Position: Left-winger
Appearances: 53 (18) **Goals scored:** 11
Seasons: 1989/90 – 1992/93
Clubs: Southampton, Manchester United, Millwall (loan), Birmingham City, Wycombe Wanderers

Danny Wallace made his name alongside his two brothers, Rod and Ray, at Southampton, where he made his league debut against United at Old Trafford at the age of 16 years 10 months in November 1980. Establishing himself as a first-team regular two seasons later, the diminutive winger was soon causing havoc in opposition defences, gaining England honours at Under-21 level and one full cap.

In 1989, with Alex Ferguson looking for a left-winger who could not only create but also score goals, he signed Wallace for a fee of £1.3 million. Settling quickly and becoming a terrace favourite, he won an FA Cup winner's medal in his first season, having scored on his debut against Saints' bitter rivals Portsmouth. He didn't perhaps manage to replicate his form at Southampton, and with the emergence of Messrs Sharpe, Kanchelskis and Giggs, his days were numbered. During 1992/93 he spent a loan spell at Millwall, but left Manchester for good the following season and joined Birmingham City for £400,000.

RONALD 'RONNIE' WALLWORK

Country: England
Born: 10 Sep 1977
Debut: 25 Oct 1997 v Barnsley
Position: Midfield
Appearances: 10 (18) **Goals scored:** 0
Seasons: 1997/98 – 2001/02
Clubs: Manchester United, Carlisle United (loan), Stockport County (loan), Royal Antwerp (loan), West Bromwich Albion, Bradford City (loan), Barnsley (loan), Huddersfield Town (loan), Sheffield Wednesday

A strong, well-built player, Ronnie Wallwork won the FA Youth Cup in 1995 and England Under-20 honours at Old Trafford, but failed to grasp a regular first-team place, despite being called 'a marvellous player' by Sir Alex Ferguson. Loan deals showed that he was a more than capable player and, after moving permanently to West Bromwich Albion, he was voted their Player of the Year in 2004/05.

GARY WALSH

Country: England
Born: 21 Mar 1968
Debut: 13 Dec 1986 v Aston Villa
Position: Goalkeeper
Appearances: 62 (1) **Goals scored:** 0
Seasons: 1986/87 – 1994/95
Clubs: Manchester United, Airdrieonians (loan), Oldham Athletic (loan), Middlesbrough, Bradford City, Middlesbrough (loan), Wigan Athletic

Had it not been for injury, then who knows how the United career of goalkeeper Gary Walsh would have panned out? Making his league debut as an 18-year-old in December 1986, he started the following campaign as first-choice keeper, but a head injury and then an ankle injury kept him out of the side for long periods, with the signings of Jim Leighton and then Peter Schmeichel also limiting his first-team opportunities. He won a number of honours as a non-playing substitute, but a £600,000 move to Middlesbrough (under Bryan Robson) in 1995/96 and then to Bradford City two seasons later showed that he was a more than capable goalkeeper. He is now a goalkeeping coach.

JOHN ANDREWS WALTON

Country: England
Born: 21 Mar 1928 **Died:** 17 Jul 1979
Debut: 29 Sep 1951 v Preston North End
Position: Forward
Appearances: 2 **Goals scored:** 0
Seasons: 1951/52
Clubs: Bury, Manchester United, Burnley, Coventry City, Chester, Kettering Town

JOSEPH W. 'JOE' WALTON

Country: England
Born: 5 Jun 1925 **Died:** 31 Dec 2006
Debut: 26 Jan 1946 v Preston North End
Position: Full-back
Appearances: 23 **Goals scored:** 0
Seasons: 1945/46 – 1947/48
Clubs: Manchester United, Preston North End, Accrington Stanley

Joe Walton was a former Manchester and Lancashire Schoolboy, who joined United in April 1940, but was loaned out to Goslings for a season in order to develop. The neat and accomplished full-back made his initial appearances in wartime football, representing England against Scotland in the 1946 Manchester Charity international. Following his official United debut in January 1946, against Preston in the FA Cup, he found his opportunities limited and moved to Preston in March 1948, playing for them for 13 years.

ARTHUR WARBURTON

Country: England
Born: 30 Oct 1903 **Died:** 21 Apr 1978
Debut: 8 Mar 1930 v Aston Villa
Position: Forward
Appearances: 39 **Goals scored:** 10
Seasons: 1929/30 – 1933/34
Clubs: Manchester United, Burnley, Nelson, Fulham, Queens Park Rangers

Signed as an amateur in February 1929, Arthur Warburton is one of the select band of players who scored on their United debut, with the *Guardian* reporter for that match writing: 'Warburton's display was quite promising and merited his place quite apart from his goal.' He retained his place the following week, but failed to appear again until the opening fixture of the following season, when he again scored, but a few games later missed several chances against Manchester City and was dropped. Playing for United at a time of turmoil did little to help his career and it wasn't until he joined Burnley in 1933 that he enjoyed a decent run of first-team football.

JAMES 'JIMMY' WARNER

Country: England
Born: 15 Apr 1865 **Died:** 7 Nov 1943
Debut: 3 Sep 1892 v Blackburn Rovers
Position: Goalkeeper
Appearances: 22 **Goals scored:** 0
Seasons: 1892/93 – 1893/94
Clubs: Milton, Aston Villa, Newton Heath, Walsall Town Swifts

Jimmy Warner had the honour of being Newton Heath's goalkeeper for their first game in the Football League, having joined the club from Aston Villa (where he had won the FA Cup in 1887) during the previous summer. He left the Midlands club under something of a cloud, after a poor performance in the 1892 FA Cup final was put down to match-fixing to pay off some gambling debts. It didn't get much better for the Heathens, as he conceded four goals in that initial league game. Having played in the club's first 20 games that season, he failed to turn up for a game against Stoke, and that was almost the end of his career in Manchester.

JOHN 'JACK' WARNER

Country: Wales
Born: 21 Sep 1911 **Died:** 4 Oct 1980
Debut: 5 Nov 1938 v Aston Villa
Position: Half-back
Appearances: 116 **Goals scored:** 2
Seasons: 1938/39 – 1949/50
Clubs: Swansea Town, Manchester United, Oldham Athletic, Rochdale

Trealaw-born Jack Warner learned his football in south Wales before joining Swansea in January 1934, winning Welsh international honours two years later. Joining United in the summer of 1938, he made his debut that November and his quick, constructive style of play kept him in the side for the remainder of the season. During the war years, he helped coach the United youngsters, captaining the reserve side in the late 1940s and was the travelling 12th man for the 1948 FA Cup final. Although never really a regular, he always made a telling contribution, but at the end of season 1950/51 he was given a free transfer and joined Oldham Athletic.

JOHN VICTOR 'JACKIE' WASSALL

Country: England
Born: 11 Feb 1917 **Died:** Apr 1994
Debut: 9 Nov 1935 v Swansea Town
Position: Inside-forward
Appearances: 47 **Goals scored:** 6
Seasons: 1935/36 – 1938/39
Clubs: Wellington Town, Manchester United, Stockport County

Shrewsbury-born Jackie Wassall was signed from Birmingham League side Wellington Town in February 1935, but it was not until season 1938/39 that he managed to establish himself in the United first team, as he struggled to come to terms with the higher level of football. Playing 27 games in that final pre-war season of 1938/39, it looked as though he had a bright future in front of him, but his career was to be disrupted by the war and he was only to manage a few games with Stockport County on the resumption of league football in 1946.

WILLIAM 'WILLIE' WATSON

Country: Scotland
Born: 4 Dec 1949
Debut: 26 Sep 1970 v Blackpool
Position: Full-back
Appearances: 14 **Goals scored:** 0
Seasons: 1970/71 – 1972/73
Clubs: Manchester United, Miami Toros (loan), Motherwell, Dundee

Willie Watson's career came during a period of managerial turmoil at Old Trafford, but when Tommy Docherty arrived, the young Scot was soon on his way back to his home country in the summer of 1973, playing for Motherwell for five years.

JEFFREY ANDREW 'JEFF' WEALANDS

Country: England
Born: 26 Aug 1951
Debut: 2 Apr 1983 v Coventry City
Position: Goalkeeper

Appearances: 8 **Goals scored:** 0
Seasons: 1982/83 – 1983/84
Clubs: Wolverhampton Wanderers, Northampton Town (loan), Darlington, Hull City, Birmingham City, Manchester United, Oldham Athletic (loan), Preston North End (loan), Altrincham, Barrow, Altrincham

NEIL JOHN WEBB

Country: England
Born: 30 Jul 1963
Debut: 19 Aug 1989 v Arsenal
Position: Midfield
Appearances: 105 (5) **Goals scored:** 11
Seasons: 1989/90 – 1992/93
Clubs: Reading, Portsmouth, Nottingham Forest, Manchester United, Nottingham Forest, Swindon Town (loan), Grimsby Town, Aldershot Town

With a father who had played the game at professional level, scoring 81 goals in 179 games for Reading, there was always a chance that Neil Webb would follow in his footsteps. Signing schoolboy forms with Reading in September 1978, he was soon attracting the attention of bigger clubs, joining Portsmouth for £87,500 in the summer of 1982. At Fratton Park, the attacking midfielder with a superb touch and passing ability also became a regular goal-getter and was to win a Third Division Championship medal in his first season.

Brian Clough liked what he saw and paid Portsmouth £250,000 in 1985 to take him to Nottingham Forest, where he continued to display some outstanding form, scoring 47 goals in 146 league games, winning a League Cup medal in 1989 to go with his full, Under-21 and England Youth caps. With Alex Ferguson installed as manager at Old Trafford and his team-building underway, he tempted Webb away from the City Ground, the £1.5 million fee settled by tribunal. By that stage, Webb and Bryan Robson were England's regular central midfield pairing.

Unfortunately, his career with United did not exactly continue on the up and up, as after only four games he ruptured his Achilles tendon while playing for England. He managed to return to the side later in the season, picking up an FA Cup winner's medal, with his pass setting up Lee Martin to score the only goal of the replay against Crystal Palace.

But in April and May 1991, he failed to make the starting XI for both the League Cup and the Cup-Winners' Cup finals, with Paul Ince usually preferred alongside Robson. Despite this, he did score for United on his debut in four different competitions – the Football League, FA Cup, League Cup and European Cup-Winners' Cup.

In November 1992, Alex Ferguson decided to transfer Webb back to Nottingham Forest, recouping £800,000 of the fee he had paid just over three years previously. The 1,000th player to be capped for England failed to recapture his old form and he saw out his career with a handful of games with Swindon and Grimsby, before moving to non-league Aldershot.

DANIEL VAUGHN 'DANNY' WEBBER

Country: England
Born: 28 Dec 1981
Debut: 28 Nov 2000 v Sunderland
Position: Forward
Appearances: 1 (2) **Goals scored:** 0
Seasons: 2000/01 – 2002/03
Clubs: Manchester United, Port Vale (loan), Watford, Sheffield United, Portsmouth, Leeds United, Doncaster Rovers, Accrington Stanley

COLIN WEBSTER

Country: Wales
Born: 17 Jul 1932 **Died:** 1 Mar 2001
Debut: 28 Nov 1953 v Portsmouth
Position: Forward
Appearances: 79 **Goals scored:** 31
Seasons: 1953/54 – 1958/59
Clubs: Cardiff City, Manchester United, Swansea Town, Newport County

Colin Webster began his senior career as a junior on Cardiff City's books, but was soon called up for National Service and upon completing this was given a free transfer by the Welsh club. One of his army footballing team-mates was Dennis Viollet, who recommended him to United and, following a trial, he signed professional forms in May 1952. He made his debut in November 1953 at Portsmouth, but it wasn't until the following season that he managed an extended run in the team, going on to win his first Welsh cap in 1957.

A bout of influenza prevented the versatile, but sometimes tempestuous, forward from travelling on the ill-fated trip to Belgrade, but he was to play a major part in the months that followed the disaster, scoring the only goal against West Bromwich Albion that put United into the semi-final of the FA Cup, and winning a runner-up medal in the final against Bolton. That summer, he stood in for John Charles in the World Cup quarter-final when Wales lost to Brazil. His United career came to an end in October 1958 when he returned to Wales to join Swansea. One unwanted accolade that came the Welshman's way was that he was the first post-war player to be sent off four times!

FRANCIS EDGAR 'FRANK' WEDGE

Country: England
Born: 28 Jul 1876 **Died:** Unknown
Debut: 20 Nov 1897 v Leicester City
Position: Forward
Appearances: 2 **Goals scored:** 2
Seasons: 1897/98
Clubs: Manchester Talbot, Newton Heath, Chorlton-cum-Hardy

DANIEL NII TACKIE MENSAH 'DANNY' WELBECK

Country: England
Born: 26 Nov 1990
Debut: 23 Sep 2008 v Middlesbrough
Position: Forward
Appearances: 69 (38) **Goals scored:** 19
Seasons: 2008/09 – present
Clubs: Manchester United, Preston North End (loan), Sunderland (loan)

Danny Welbeck is perhaps the typical 'local boy makes good'. The Longsight-born youngster first caught United's eye as a six-year-old before joining the club as a trainee in 2005/06, signing professional forms two years later. His performances in the youth and reserve teams soon had him earmarked as a potential first-team player, stepping up to this level for the first time in January 2008 during a friendly match in

Saudi Arabia. He had, however, to wait until September that year before making his competitive debut. But, with regular opportunities always likely to be few and far between (because of competition from Berbatov, Ronaldo, Rooney and Tevez), he found himself sent out on loan to both Preston and Sunderland. It was while he was with the Black Cats in 2010/11, under Steve Bruce, that he really came to the fore, earning his first England cap in March that season.

Returning to United, he claimed a place in the starting line-up at the beginning of 2011/12, and was a regular feature for the Reds that campaign, making 39 appearances in all and scoring 12 goals. In 2012/13, he continued to develop, though he found goals harder to come by. It was a mark of his growing importance in the squad that he was picked for the crucial Old Trafford Champions League fixture against Real Madrid, having scored in the first leg in Spain. With 16 England caps already, the future looks bright for the talented, hard-working forward.

RICHARD PAUL 'RICHIE' WELLENS

Country: England
Born: 26 Mar 1980
Debut: 13 Oct 1999 v Aston Villa
Position: Midfield
Appearances: 0 (1) **Goals scored:** 0
Seasons: 1999/2000
Clubs: Manchester United, Blackpool, Oldham Athletic, Doncaster Rovers, Leicester City, Ipswich Town (loan), Doncaster Rovers

ENOCH JAMES 'KNOCKER' WEST

Country: England
Born: 31 Mar 1886 **Died:** Sep 1965
Debut: 1 Sep 1910 v Arsenal
Position: Forward
Appearances: 181 **Goals scored:** 80
Seasons: 1910/11 – 1914/15
Clubs: Sheffield United, Nottingham Forest, Manchester United

The majority of supporters making their way along Railway Road to Old Trafford on a match day are unaware that they are pass the home of a former player who features prominently in the history of Manchester United. 'Knocker' West, as he was commonly known, was a strong, robust centre-forward of the old school and had signed for Sheffield United in November 1903, but it wasn't until he returned to his home county and joined Nottingham Forest that he came to the fore, scoring 93 goals in 168 appearances, helping them to the Second Division title in 1907.

June 1910 saw the prolific forward sign for United, scoring on his debut against Woolwich Arsenal and forging an excellent partnership with Sandy Turnbull, scoring 19 league goals to the Scot's 18 in that title-winning first season. But his goals, while bringing additional Football League representative honours, did not bring continued success at club level, and his playing career came to an abrupt end in 1914/15, after he was caught up in the match-fixing scandal. Following the war, all the players, except for West, had their bans lifted and it was not until some 30 years later that the man from Railway Road was given a belated reprieve.

JOSEPH 'JOE' WETHERELL

Country: England
Born: 1880 **Died:** Unknown
Debut: 21 Sep 1896 v Walsall
Position: Goalkeeper
Appearances: 2 **Goals scored:** 0
Seasons: 1896/97
Clubs: Newton Heath

ARTHUR WHALLEY

Country: England
Born: 17 Feb 1886 **Died:** 23 Nov 1952
Debut: 27 Dec 1909 v Sheffield Wednesday
Position: Half-back
Appearances: 106 **Goals scored:** 6
Seasons: 1909/10 – 1919/20
Clubs: Wigan Town, Blackpool, Manchester United, Southend United, Charlton Athletic, Millwall

Six games were all Arthur Whalley managed with Blackpool between March 1908 and June 1909 before he moved to United for £50. He was to win a League Championship medal, playing across the half-back line during 1910/11, but with international recognition beckoning, a knee injury disrupted his progress, although he was later to represent the Football League. Although involved in the match-fixing scandal of 1915, his ban was lifted following the First World War because of his war service – he had been wounded at Passchendaele. He made a complete recovery, but a dispute with the United directors over a benefit match saw him leave the club, with Southend paying United £1,000. He later played for Charlton and Millwall, before taking up the post of trainer/coach with Barrow.

HERBERT 'BERT' WHALLEY

Country: England
Born: 6 Aug 1912 **Died:** 6 Feb 1958
Debut: 30 Nov 1935 v Doncaster Rovers
Position: Centre-half
Appearances: 38 **Goals scored:** 0
Seasons: 1935/36 – 1946/47
Clubs: Stalybridge Celtic, Manchester United

Bert Whalley's playing career at Manchester United was a modest one, with much of it lost to the war. But his 38 appearances were only the start of the story of his crucial impact at the club. After the war, an eye injury brought his career to an end, but Busby had already used him as the captain of the reserve team, and clearly saw something in him and appointed him first team coach. Alongside Jimmy Murphy, Whalley provided Busby with loyal support, with the two men presenting contrasting characters – Murphy was the disciplinarian, while Whalley was a Methodist lay preacher. The pair were also responsible for making the night-time trip to Dudley to sign Duncan Edwards. With Murphy taking charge of Wales, Whalley was on the fateful trip to Belgrade, and lost his life on the runway at Munich.

ANTHONY GERARD WHELAN

Country: Republic of Ireland
Born: 23 Nov 1959
Debut: 29 Nov 1980 v Southampton
Position: Defender
Appearances: 0 (1) **Goals scored:** 0
Seasons: 1980/81
Clubs: Bohemians, Manchester United, Shamrock Rovers, Cork City, Bray Wanderers, Shelbourne, Dundalk, Drogheda United, Bray Wanderers

WILLIAM AUGUSTINE 'LIAM' WHELAN

Country: Republic of Ireland
Born: 1 Apr 1935 **Died:** 6 Feb 1958
Debut: 26 Mar 1955 v Preston North End
Position: Inside-forward
Appearances: 98 **Goals scored:** 52
Seasons: 1954/55 – 1957/58
Clubs: Manchester United

Known as 'Liam' or 'Billy', the 18-year-old former Republic of Ireland Schoolboy international joined United as an amateur from Home Farm in May 1953, but within a fortnight of his arrival he had signed professional forms and also starred in the FA Youth Cup final, scoring in both legs against Wolves. The following May, his talents were reaching a much wider audience, as United's youth team travelled to Switzerland for the prestige Zurich Blue Stars Tournament. A couple of friendly fixtures were also squeezed into the itinerary, and in one of these, against a Swiss Youth Select which was played prior to a full international match, Liam and his United team-mates outshone the main act.

With the World Cup imminent, the match was watched by the Brazilian national side, who were in Switzerland at the time and Liam's performance produced more than a few admiring glances and also enquiries to his availability. Despite this, he still had to wait until March 1955 to make his league debut, but it wasn't long before his deceiving body swerve was causing defenders problems, as he created scoring opportunities for both himself and team-mates.

He played only 13 games in the title-winning season of 1955/56, but the next season was a regular and he finished as the leading scorer in the league with a remarkable 26 goals as United retained their title. Established in both the United and Republic of Ireland side, he would have gone on to become undoubtedly one of the top players in the game, with a host more honours surely due to come his way before that fateful afternoon in Munich.

JEFFREY 'JEFF' WHITEFOOT

Country: England
Born: 31 Dec 1933
Debut: 15 Apr 1950 v Portsmouth
Position: Half-back
Appearances: 95 **Goals scored:** 0
Seasons: 1949/50 – 1955/56
Clubs: Manchester United, Grimsby Town, Nottingham Forest

A graduate of the Stockport and England Schools sides, Whitefoot had the opportunity to join numerous clubs but decided upon United, signing in August 1949 as an amateur, while at the same time taking on the post of office boy. Following rapid progress through the junior teams, he became the youngest player ever to start in United's league side at the age of 16 years and 105 days when he made his debut at Old Trafford on 15 April 1950.

Although a little on the small side, he was a more than capable wing-half and continued to make progress, going on to win England Under-23 honours and a league title medal in 1956, but lost his place to Eddie Colman in November 1956. Following a year in the reserves side, he asked for a transfer, which was granted and he left United to join Grimsby Town, but eight months later signed for Nottingham Forest, winning an FA Cup winner's medal in 1959.

JAMES LEWINGTON' 'JIMMY' WHITEHOUSE

Country: England
Born: Apr 1873 **Died:** 7 Feb 1934
Debut: 15 Sep 1900 v Burnley
Position: Goalkeeper

Appearances: 64 **Goals scored:** 0
Seasons: 1900/01 – 1902/03
Clubs: Albion Swifts, Birmingham St George's, Grimsby Town, Aston Villa, Bedminster, Grimsby Town, Newton Heath/Manchester United, Manchester City, Third Lanark, Hull City, Southend United

Signed from Grimsby Town in September 1900, following his second spell with the Mariners, goalkeeper Jimmy Whitehouse had already tasted success as a League and FA Cup Double winner with Aston Villa in 1896/97. A reliable and dependable custodian, his 64 appearances do not tell the complete story of his three years with Newton Heath/Manchester United, as a look through the record books show the net minder became an inside-forward for the afternoon of 25 February 1901 at Walsall, as United grabbed a point in the 1-1 draw. Upon leaving United, he crossed Manchester and joined City, but his stay there lasted only seven months before he joined Third Lanark. A year later he was at Hull City, seeing out his career with Southend United.

WALTER WHITEHURST

Country: England
Born: 7 Jun 1934 **Died:** 20 Jan 2012
Debut: 14 Sep 1955 v Everton
Position: Half-back
Appearances: 1 **Goals scored:** 0
Seasons: 1955/56
Clubs: Manchester United, Chesterfield, Crewe Alexandra, Macclesfield Town

KERR D. WHITESIDE

Country: Scotland
Born: 1887 **Died:** Unknown
Debut: 18 Jan 1908 v Sheffield United
Position: Half-back
Appearances: 1 **Goals scored:** 0
Seasons: 1907/08
Clubs: Irvine Victoria, Manchester United, Hurst

NORMAN JOHN WHITESIDE

Country: Northern Ireland
Born: 7 May 1965
Debut: 24 Apr 1982 v Brighton & Hove Albion
Position: Midfield/Forward
Appearances: 256 (18) **Goals scored:** 67
Seasons: 1981/82 – 1988/89
Clubs: Manchester United, Everton

Discovered by Bob Bishop as a schoolboy footballer, Norman Whiteside had come to the attention of the eagle-eyed scout while playing with Cairnmartin Secondary School in his native Belfast, and was described by his coach as 'very much his own man, in a pleasant way'. But, despite being captain of his school side, he shunned the limelight, hiding in the back row when team pictures were being taken. However, the boy from Shankill Road began visiting Manchester shortly after his 13th birthday and would be flown over to play for the junior sides on Saturday mornings.

Progress, as expected, was rapid and the new arrival was soon attracting attention beyond the confines of the Cliff training ground, as the junior and FA Youth Cup games saw the development of a player with numerous attributes. United manager Ron Atkinson knew that he had a special player on his hands and had no hesitation in picking him as a substitute to face Brighton at the Goldstone ground on 24 April 1982. And he wasn't simply taken along for the ride, he came on as a second-half replacement for Mike Duxbury, fitting into the game like a seasoned professional.

Having made the breakthrough, his full United league debut, a belated 17th birthday present, came at home to Stoke City on the last day of the season, and the young striker scored United's second goal in a 2-0 win. Surprisingly, he was then named in the Northern Ireland squad to take part in that summer's World Cup in Spain and featured in all five of the Northern Ireland games. The following season, he played in all but three of United's league fixtures, scoring eight goals, and became the youngest player to score in both the Football League Cup final (v Liverpool) and the FA Cup final (in the replay v Brighton). This was the first time a player had scored in two finals in the same season.

Two years later he was back at Wembley, scoring ten-man United's dramatic extra-time winner against Everton. Whiteside had filled out physically and was increasingly used in more of a midfield role, having started his career as a striker, where a lack of pace was arguably his one shortcoming as an all-round talent. His natural ability was sometimes overshadowed by his robust tactics, which brought unnecessary publicity and closer attention from referees. He was also beginning to attract some of the Continent's big clubs, with AC Milan testing United with an offer of £1.5 million prior ahead of 1983/84.

His off-the-field activities began to cause concern, especially with the arrival of new manager Alex Ferguson, and chronic knee problems didn't help matters. Beginning Ferguson's first full season in charge with two goals in the opening-day fixture at Southampton, he then lost some of his form, and asked for a transfer. More injury problems followed, and after only six appearances in season 1988/89, he left his United to join Everton in July 1989 for a £750,000 fee. Within two years, his career was over as his knee problems were so severe. It was these, rather than any other shortcomings, that arguably prevented him from becoming the true great he might have been. As it was, he was still one of the club's biggest stars of the 1980s.

JOHN WHITNEY

Country: England
Born: 1874 **Died:** Unknown
Debut: 29 Feb 1896 v Burton Wanderers
Position: Half-back
Appearances: 3 **Goals scored:** 0
Seasons: 1895/96 & 1900/01
Clubs: Newton Heath
Walter Whittaker

WALTER WHITTAKER

Country: England
Born: 20 Sep 1878 **Died:** 2 Jun 1917
Debut: 14 Mar 1896 v Grimsby Town
Position: Goalkeeper
Appearances: 3 **Goals scored:** 0
Seasons: 1895/96
Clubs: Newton Heath, Grimsby Town, Reading, Blackburn Rovers, Derby County, Exeter City, Swansea Town

JOHN T. WHITTLE

Country: England
Born: 29 Jun 1910 **Died:** 31 Jul 1987
Debut: 16 Jan 1932 v Swansea Town
Position: Outside-left
Appearances: 1 **Goals scored:** 0
Seasons: 1931/32
Clubs: Manchester United, Rossendale United, Fleetwood

NEIL ANTHONY WHITWORTH

Country: England
Born: 12 Apr 1972
Debut: 13 Mar 1991 v Southampton
Position: Full-back
Appearances: 1 **Goals scored:** 0
Seasons: 1990/91
Clubs: Wigan Athletic, Manchester United, Preston North End (loan), Barnsley (loan), Rotherham United (loan), Blackpool (loan), Kilmarnock, Wigan Athletic (loan), Hull City, Exeter City, Southport, Radcliffe Borough (loan)

THOMAS WALTER J. 'TOM' WILCOX

Country: England
Born: 1879 **Died:** 10 Sep 1963
Debut: 24 Oct 1908 v Nottingham Forest
Position: Goalkeeper
Appearances: 2 **Goals scored:** 0
Seasons: 1908/09
Clubs: Norwich City, Blackpool, Manchester United, Carlisle United, Huddersfield Town, Goole Town

RAYMOND COLIN 'RAY' WILKINS

Country: England
Born: 14 Sep 1956
Debut: 18 Aug 1979 v Southampton
Position: Midfield

Appearances: 191 (3) **Goals scored:** 10
Seasons: 1979/80 – 1983/84
Clubs: Chelsea, Manchester United, AC Milan, Paris Saint-Germain, Rangers, Queens Park Rangers, Crystal Palace, Queens Park Rangers, Wycombe Wanderers, Hibernian, Millwall, Leyton Orient

An England Schoolboy and Under-21 international, Ray Wilkins became Chelsea's youngest captain at the age of 18, having joined them as an apprentice in 1971. A truly gifted individual, his ability as a playmaker was soon attracting much attention and it was United manager Dave Sexton who won the race for his signature, paying the Stamford Bridge club £825,000 to bring him north in August 1979 after Chelsea were relegated.

By then, he was already an established international, having won his first cap in May 1976. He was seen as an excellent acquisition, but, for many, never fulfilled his true potential on the Old Trafford stage. If anything let him down, it was his distinct lack of goals, but many will recall his outstanding strike in the 1983 FA Cup final against Brighton, a season in which he missed numerous games due to injury. Having been appointed club captain, as well as England captain, he went on to win 64 caps for his country, but a broken cheekbone forced him out of both squads, and team-mate Bryan Robson took over both captaincies.

His form upon his return dipped briefly, but he showed outstanding qualities by turning it around, and he did not miss a league game in 1983/84. His displays brought in an offer of £1.5 million from AC Milan, which United accepted. Spells in France and Scotland followed, before he returned to London to join Queens Park Rangers, and he played on beyond his 40th birthday. In June 1993, he was awarded the MBE for his services to the game, which more than made up for the lack of honours to come his way on the pitch. He had various managerial roles, most recently being assistant manager at Chelsea, and now works in the media.

HENRY 'HARRY' WILKINSON

Country: England
Born: 1883 **Died:** Unknown
Debut: 26 Dec 1903 v Burton United

Position: Outside-left
Appearances: 9 **Goals scored:** 0
Seasons: 1903/04
Clubs: Newton Heath Athletic, Hull City, West Ham United, Manchester United, Haslingden

IAN MATTHEW WILKINSON

Country: England
Born: 2 Jul 1973
Debut: 9 Oct 1991 v Cambridge United
Position: Goalkeeper
Appearances: 1 **Goals scored:** 0
Seasons: 1991/92
Clubs: Manchester United, Stockport County, Crewe Alexandra

DAVID REES WILLIAMS

Country: Wales
Born: Jan 1900 **Died:** 30 Dec 1963
Debut: 8 Oct 1927 v Everton
Position: Outside-right
Appearances: 35 **Goals scored:** 2
Seasons: 1927/28 – 1928/29
Clubs: Merthyr Tydfil, Sheffield Wednesday, Manchester United, Thames Association

Rees Williams replaced Billy Meredith in the Welsh international side in 1921, but replacing the legendary winger in the United side was nigh on impossible. Having played 13 league games in his debut season of 1927/28, he started 15 of the opening 17 games the next campaign, but despite hopes that he could establish himself, he was to play only three league outings before leaving the club for Thames Association in August 1929. Sadly, he was to take his own life in December 1963, following personal concerns regarding his health.

FRANK H. WILLIAMS

Country: England
Born: 1908 **Died:** Unknown
Debut: 13 Sep 1930 v Newcastle United
Position: Half-back
Appearances: 3 **Goals scored:** 0
Seasons: 1930/31
Clubs: Stalybridge Celtic, Manchester United, Altrincham

FREDERICK 'FRED' WILLIAMS

Country: England
Born: 1873 **Died:** Unknown
Debut: 6 Sep 1902 v Gainsborough Trinity
Position: Forward
Appearances: 10 **Goals scored:** 4
Seasons: 1902/03
Clubs: Hanley Swifts, South Shore, Manchester City, Manchester United

Thirty-eight goals in 125 games with Manchester City, including 11 in 25 outings during their Second Division title-winning season of 1898/99, was enough to convince United to sign Fred Williams in the summer of 1902. It was, however, a gamble that was not to pay off, as he lasted only one season at United, although an FA Cup hat-trick against Accrington Stanley in the 7-0 third qualifying round victory on 1 November 1902 prompted hopes of a career lift-off – but it was not to be.

HARRY WILLIAMS

Country: England
Born: 1899 **Died:** Unknown
Debut: 28 Aug 1922 v Sheffield Wednesday
Position: Forward
Appearances: 5 **Goals scored:** 2
Seasons: 1922/23
Clubs: Chesterfield, Manchester United, Brentford

HENRY 'HARRY' WILLIAMS

Country: England
Born: 1883 **Died:** Unknown
Debut: 10 Sep 1904 v Bristol City
Position: Forward
Appearances: 37 **Goals scored:** 8
Seasons: 1904/05 – 1907/08
Clubs: Bolton Wanderers, Burnley, Manchester United, Leeds City

Harry Williams scored on his United debut at Bank Street in a 4-1 win, and kept his place for much of the 1904/05 season, until he lost his place to Dick Wombwell in March. When United won promotion to the First Division, he spent much of his time in the reserves before moving on.

JOSEPH 'JOE' WILLIAMS

Country: England
Born: 1873 **Died:** Unknown
Debut: 25 Mar 1907 v Sunderland
Position: Forward
Appearances: 3 **Goals scored:** 1
Seasons: 1906/07
Clubs: Macclesfield Town, Manchester United

WILLIAM 'BILL' WILLIAMS

Country: England
Born: Unknown **Died:** Unknown
Debut: 7 Sep 1901 v Gainsborough Trinity
Position: Forward
Appearances: 4 **Goals scored:** 0
Seasons: 1901/02
Clubs: Everton, Blackburn Rovers, Bristol City, Newton Heath

JOHN WILLIAMSON

Country: England
Born: 1893 **Died:** Unknown
Debut: 17 Apr 1920 v Blackburn Rovers

Position: Half-back
Appearances: 2 **Goals scored:** 0
Seasons: 1919/20
Clubs: Manchester United, Bury, Crewe Alexandra

DAVID GRAHAM WILSON

Country: England
Born: 20 Mar 1969
Debut: 23 Nov 1988 v Sheffield Wednesday
Position: Midfield
Appearances: 0 (6) **Goals scored:** 0
Seasons: 1988/89
Clubs: Manchester United, Lincoln City (loan), Charlton Athletic (loan), Bristol Rovers, RoPS, Ljungskile, Haka, HJK Helsinki, Ljungskile, Rosseröd

EDGAR WILSON

Country: Unknown
Born: Unknown **Died:** Unknown
Debut: 18 Jan 1890 v Preston North End
Position: Forward
Appearances: 1 **Goals scored:** 0
Seasons: 1889/90
Clubs: Newton Heath

JOHN THOMAS 'JACK' WILSON

Country: England
Born: 8 Mar 1897 **Died:** Unknown
Debut: 4 Sep 1926 v Leeds United
Position: Half-back
Appearances: 140 **Goals scored:** 3
Seasons: 1926/27 – 1931/32
Clubs: Leadgate United, Newcastle United, Durham City, Stockport County, Manchester United, Bristol City

Jack Wilson was tipped for England honours while with Newcastle, but injuries, including two broken legs, set him back and he was given a free transfer. Moving back into non-league football, he made a return to the senior game with Durham City before joining Stockport County in June 1922. A contract dispute at Edgeley Park in the summer of 1926 saw United paying £500 for a player who was to mature into one of the best wing-halves that the club had employed. Outstanding as he was, he also had a darker side, as he was sent off in a reserve match and suspended for two months, and involved in a near-riot at Blackburn Rovers which saw some 5,000 locals invade the pitch and assault the United players. A hard worker, Wilson rarely had a bad game, although injuries and illness took their toll. So, at the end of season 1931/32, having played in only nine of the 43 fixtures, he was released and joined Bristol City.

MARK ANTONY WILSON

Country: England
Born: 9 Feb 1979
Debut: 21 Oct 1998 v Brondby IF
Position: Midfield
Appearances: 6 (4) **Goals scored:** 0
Seasons: 1998/99 – 1999/2000
Clubs: Manchester United, Wrexham (loan), Middlesbrough, Stoke City (loan), Swansea City (loan), Sheffield Wednesday (loan), Doncaster Rovers (loan), Livingston (loan), FC Dallas, Doncaster Rovers, Tranmere Rovers (loan), Walsall (loan), Oxford United, Gainsborough Trinity, Doncaster Rovers

Having joined United as a trainee, Mark Wilson was unable to make the breakthrough during the Treble season and was eventually sold to Middlesbrough for £1.5 million, but it has been at Doncaster Rovers where he has seen the most consistent first-team action, and he returned to the club during 2012/13.

THOMAS CARTER 'TOMMY' WILSON

Country: England
Born: 20 Oct 1877 **Died:** 30 Aug 1940
Debut: 15 Feb 1908 v Blackburn Rovers
Position: Winger
Appearances: 1 **Goals scored:** 0
Seasons: 1907/08
Clubs: Ashton-in-Makerfield, West Manchester, Ashton Town, Ashton North

End, Oldham County, Swindon Town, Blackburn Rovers, Swindon Town, Millwall Athletic, Aston Villa, Queens Park Rangers. Bolton Wanderers, Leeds City, Manchester United

WALTER WINTERBOTTOM

Country: England
Born: 31 Jan 1913 **Died:** 16 Feb 2002
Debut: 28 Nov 1936 v Leeds United
Position: Half-back
Appearances: 27 **Goals scored:** 0
Seasons: 1936/37 – 1937/38
Clubs: Mossley, Manchester United

Much better known as the England manager between 1946 through to 1962, Walter Winterbottom enjoyed a couple of seasons at Old Trafford as a cultured centre-half. Signed from Mossley in May 1936, he was regarded as promising individual with a good future in the game, but it was to be a career cut short by a back injury and the outbreak of war, which forced him to retire and concentrate on the coaching side of the game.

During the war he trained PE instructors and ran coaching courses for the FA. Sir Stanley Rous, the secretary of the FA, then recruited him to be the FA's director of coaching. Almost as an afterthought, he added the role of England manager to his job spec, and Winterbottom would remain in charge until 1962. It was a change of approach for the FA, as previously the England side had been selected by a committee, and Winterbottom brought a new professionalism to the way the England team was organised. Along with Matt Busby, Bobby Charlton and Alex Ferguson, he is one of four United figures to have been knighted.

RICHARD 'DICK' WOMBWELL

Country: England
Born: Jul 1877 **Died:** Jul 1943
Debut: 18 Mar 1905 v Grimsby Town
Position: Forward

Appearances: 51 **Goals scored:** 3
Seasons: 1904/05 – 1906/07
Clubs: Derby County, Bristol City, Manchester United, Heart of Midlothian, Brighton & Hove Albion, Blackburn Rovers

Originally an outside-left, Dick Wombwell later moved to a more central role for the club. He joined United from Bristol City, having previously played with Derby County, and in his second season with United, he played a part in securing promotion to the First Division as runners-up. Having been an automatic first choice with both of his previous clubs, he found life at United completely different and could never command a regular starting place and in January 1907 was transferred to Hearts.

JOHN WOOD

Country: Scotland
Born: 17 Sep 1894 **Died:** 9 Sep 1971
Debut: 26 Aug 1922 v Crystal Palace
Position: Outside-right
Appearances: 16 **Goals scored:** 1
Seasons: 1922/23
Clubs: Hibernian, Dunfermline Athletic, Lochgelly United, Dumbarton, Manchester United, Lochgelly United, St Mirren, East Stirlingshire

John Wood made a name for himself north of the border with Hibs, Dunfermline and Dumbarton, arriving in Manchester in May 1922, for a fee of £1,750, on the back of scoring 25 goals in 36 games for the Boghead club. A tricky, hardworking individual, he was seen as an excellent acquisition, and it was hoped he would provide plenty of chances for his forwards, as well as scoring plenty himself, after United's lack of goals the previous season had seen them relegated.

He scored on his debut against Crystal Palace on the opening day of season 1922/23, but failed to score again in his 15 outings scattered through the first half of the season. Following the 1-1 FA Cup first round draw at Bradford City, he was promptly dropped for the replay and was not to be seen in the first-team line-up again.

NICHOLAS ANTHONY 'NICKY' WOOD

Country: England
Born: 6 Jan 1966
Debut: 26 Dec 1985 v Everton
Position: Winger
Appearances: 2 (2) **Goals scored:** 0
Seasons: 1985/86 – 1986/87
Clubs: Manchester United

RAYMOND ERNEST 'RAY' WOOD

Country: England
Born: 11 Jun 1931 **Died:** 7 Jul 2002
Debut: 3 Dec 1949 v Newcastle United
Position: Goalkeeper
Appearances: 208 **Goals scored:** 0
Seasons: 1949/50 – 1958/59
Clubs: Darlington, Manchester United, Huddersfield Town, Bradford City, Barnsley

Born in Hebburn, the ex-Durham County Schools player was on Newcastle's books as an amateur before joining Darlington in September 1949. Signed by United two months later, for a fee of £5,000, following an excellent game in an FA Cup tie against Crewe, he presented a challenge for Jack Crompton's first-team place, but he was knocked down the pecking order by the arrival of Reg Allen the following year and briefly ended up playing centre-forward in the juniors, scoring six goals.

Having previously made his debut, ironically against Newcastle United in December 1949, he had to wait until 1952/53 before he made his second appearance, claiming the No.1 spot for himself the following season. In autumn 1954, the steady, reliable keeper added to his England Under-23 and Football League caps with full international honours. Things got even better in 1955/56 and 1956/57 when he missed just four league games as United won back-to-back titles. The opportunity to claim an FA Cup winner's medal was to be denied him in May 1957, when he suffered a broken cheekbone following a collision with Aston Villa's Peter McParland after only six minutes of the Wembley final. Following treatment, he was forced to play on the wing, but when

United pulled a goal back with around five minutes remaining, Wood returned between the sticks as United fought for an equaliser.

He found his place under threat upon the arrival of Harry Gregg and following Munich he lost some confidence, and was transferred to Huddersfield Town for £1,500 in December 1958. Later, he was to join Bradford and Barnsley before concentrating on coaching in various parts of the world.

WILFRED 'WILF' WOODCOCK

Country: England
Born: 15 Feb 1892 **Died:** Oct 1966
Debut: 1 Nov 1913 v Liverpool
Position: Forward
Appearances: 61 **Goals scored:** 21
Seasons: 1913/14 – 1919/20
Clubs: Stalybridge Celtic, Manchester United, Manchester City, Stockport County, Wigan Borough

Wilf Woodcock was regularly United's leading scorer in the wartime seasons between 1915/16 and 1918/19, but was unable to transfer such statistics into the Football League records, though he was the second highest scorer for United in 1919/20. An extremely skilful individual, although perhaps lacking a little in his physical build, illness and injury did not help his appearance record, but he was selected to go on the FA tour of South Africa in 1920. However, he went as a Manchester City player, falling out with the United directors over a benefit match, and subsequently transfer listed at £1,000. He was eventually sold for £500, with Woodcock receiving £250.

SCOTT JAMES WOOTTON

Country: England
Born: 12 Sep 1991
Debut: 26 Sep 2012 v Newcastle United
Position: Defender
Appearances: 3 (1) **Goals scored:** 0
Seasons: 2012/13 – 2013/14
Clubs: Manchester United, Tranmere Rovers (loan), Peterborough United (loan), Nottingham Forest (loan), Peterborough United (loan), Leeds United

Scott Wootton was offered a chance to join Liverpool, but instead decided to come to United in 2007. He made his first-team debut in Gary Neville's testimonial in May 2011, but after getting loan experience at various other clubs eventually made his official United debut in the League Cup, helping United to a 2-1 victory over Newcastle United.

HAROLD 'HARRY' WORRALL

Country: England
Born: 19 Nov 1918 **Died:** 5 Dec 1979
Debut: 30 Nov 1946 v Wolverhampton Wanderers
Position: Full-back
Appearances: 6 **Goals scored:** 0
Seasons: 1946/47 – 1947/48
Clubs: Manchester United, Swindon Town

PAUL WRATTEN

Country: England
Born: 29 Nov 1970
Debut: 2 Apr 1991 v Wimbledon
Position: Midfield
Appearances: 0 (2) **Goals scored:** 0
Seasons: 1990/91
Clubs: Manchester United, Hartlepool, York City, Bishop Auckland

WILLIAM HERBERT 'BILLY' WRIGGLESWORTH

Country: England
Born: 12 Nov 1912 **Died:** 8 Aug 1980
Debut: 23 Jan 1937 v Sheffield Wednesday
Position: Outside-left
Appearances: 34 **Goals scored:** 9
Seasons: 1936/37 – 1946/47
Clubs: Chesterfield, Wolverhampton Wanderers, Manchester United, Bolton Wanderers, Southampton, Reading, Burton Albion, Scarborough

A mere 5'4" and weighing just over nine stone, Billy Wriggesworth was an excellent winger, fleet of foot, with a body swerve that easily deceived defenders and a great crowd-pleaser. He was quite a prolific goalscorer for a winger, with 22 in 52 games for Wolves over three seasons, which went a long way in persuading United to pay out £3,750 for his signature in January 1937. His highly promising career at Old Trafford, however, was interrupted by the Second World War, as by the start of 1946/47 he was almost 34, with his best years behind him. He joined Bolton in January 1947, retiring at the end of 1947/48 following spells with Southampton and Reading.

WILLIAM YATES

Country: England
Born: 1883 **Died:** Unknown
Debut: 15 Sep 1906 v Sheffield United
Position: Forward
Appearances: 3 **Goals scored:** 0
Seasons: 1906/07
Clubs: Aston Villa, Brighton & Hove Albion, Manchester United, Heart of Midlothian, Portsmouth, Coventry City

DWIGHT EVERSLEY YORKE

Country: Trinidad & Tobago
Born: 3 Nov 1971
Debut: 22 Aug 1998 v West Ham United
Position: Centre-forward
Appearances: 120 (32) **Goals scored:** 66
Seasons: 1998/99 – 2001/02
Clubs: Aston Villa, Manchester United, Blackburn Rovers, Birmingham City, Sydney FC, Sunderland

A smile was never far from Dwight Yorke's face, nor a goal from his boots, with the Yorke–Cole partnership being one of the deadliest in the club's history. Their 53 goals in 1998/99 were a crucial factor in helping United towards that memorable Treble. Born in Tobago, Yorke caught the attention of Aston Villa's Graham Taylor during a 1989 pre-season tour and was offered a trial and then a contract at Villa Park. With 73 goals in 231 league games over nine years, Yorke was hot property and when Alex Ferguson turned to the Villa man it took £12.6 million to persuade the Midlands club to sell in August 1998.

Almost immediately Yorke hit it off with Andy Cole, going on to make goalscoring fun with a wide array of strikes as United secured the Premier League, FA Cup and the Champions League. He finished that campaign with 29 goals, including a hat-trick in the 6-2 romp against Leicester City in January. The following season, he was almost as lethal, hitting the target 22 times. But his productivity slowly slipped and his lack of first-team starts in 2000/01 and 2001/02 meant his strike-rate faded. In the summer of 2002, he was sold to Blackburn Rovers for £2 million. He was later to serve Birmingham City and Sunderland, but he was never to reach the heights of his first two seasons at Old Trafford.

ANTHONY TERENCE 'TONY' YOUNG

Country: England
Born: 24 Dec 1952
Debut: 29 Aug 1970 v West Ham United
Position: Full-back/Midfield
Appearances: 79 (18) **Goals scored:** 1
Seasons: 1970/71 – 1975/76
Clubs: Manchester United, Charlton Athletic, York City, Bangor

Signed in July 1968 after featuring with Manchester and Lancashire Schools, Tony Young signed professional a year later. He was included in the first-team tour of America, making his debut against Bermuda and scoring in a 6-1 win. He made his full league debut in August 1970 as a substitute at home to West Ham, but had to wait until 3 April 1972 before his next outing, again as substitute. The following day he made his full debut against Sheffield United, as the Reds played three games in four days. He began as an inside-forward, but was also to feature as both a full-back and a midfielder, his adaptability making him an ideal player to fill the substitute role in the days when only one player could be named on the bench. At the end of season 1974/75 he refused to go on the tour of Australia and was fined and put up for sale, joining Charlton Athletic.

ARTHUR YOUNG

Country: Scotland
Born: Unknown **Died:** Unknown
Debut: 27 Oct 1906 v Birmingham
Position: Outside-right
Appearances: 2 **Goals scored:** 0
Seasons: 1906/07
Clubs: Hurlford Thistle, Manchester United

ASHLEY SIMON YOUNG

Country: England
Born: 9 Jul 1985
Debut: 7 Aug 2011 v Manchester City
Position: Forward
Appearances: 45 (11) **Goals scored:** 8
Seasons: 2011/12 – present
Clubs: Watford, Aston Villa, Manchester United

The England international and winner of the 2009 PFA Young Player of the Year Award joined United from Aston Villa in the summer of 2011 for an undisclosed fee. The Stevenage-born player began his professional career with Watford in 2003, where he made 98 appearances before joining Aston Villa for £8 million in January 2007. A further 157 games and 30 goals later, with his contract running out, United made their move and brought him north to Manchester. By then, he was already an established England international, scoring goals in four successive matches before Euro 2012.

His first goals for United came in the famous 8-2 thrashing of Arsenal on 28 August, as Sir Alex Ferguson's youthful side started the campaign in flying form. Just as he was beginning to settle down into life at Old Trafford, injury interrupted his progress. During 2012/13, he was again to suffer injuries, but he did pick up his first league title medal. Usually played out wide on the left, Young can also operate more centrally.

DAZET WILFRIED ARMEL ZAHA

Country: England
Born: 10 Nov 1992
Debut: 11 Aug 2013 v Wigan Athletic
Position: Winger
Appearances: 1 **Goals scored:** 0
Seasons: 2012/13 – present
Clubs: Crystal Palace, Manchester United, Crystal Palace (loan)

Ivory Coast-born Wilfried Zaha moved to Croydon as a four-year-old. He signed his first professional contract for local club Crystal Palace in 2010. His performance against United in the Carling Cup quarter-final on 30 November 2011, when the Eagles won 2-1 at Old Trafford, impressed and just over a year later he was a United player. The winger has great pace and is always willing to attack the opposition defence. Having been signed for an undisclosed fee, Sir Alex Ferguson's final signing was immediately loaned back to Palace, where he helped them win promotion to the Premier League, via the play-offs. By then he was also a full England international. He made his debut for United in a friendly against a Thai All-Star XI in Bangkok on 13 July 2013.